Praise

¡POPULISTA!

'An astute account of how the strongmen of the left gained and then lost power in Latin America... Grant is an excellent reporter and astute enough to understand why Latin Americans turned to pink-tide leaders.'

The Times

'Detailed and enlightening. Grant puts the leaders and their reigns in their historical context while asking why the movements they fronted worked... There is plenty in this book to shock. There's also plenty there that should serve as a warning.'

Spectator

'An excellent look at the group of strongmen who came from left field... ¡Populista! is action-packed with a large cast of characters, but Grant's lively style never sags under the weight of the detail he manages to pack into the book.'

Guardian

'Grant expertly traces how the actions and views of his subjects played out on ordinary lives, for better or worse.'

Art Review

'Only a first-class writer with a deep, hands-on experience of their subject matter would even attempt something as ambitious as looking at Latin American "strongmen". Will Grant is just such a writer... This is a superb book that deserves a wide audience.'

Sorted

'With a reporter's eye and writer's skill, Will Grant brings to life the colorful, flawed, and hugely consequential leaders who shaped the politics of Latin America in the early 21st century. *¡Populista!* is an ambitious, riveting and essential book that has much to teach us about the recent history of this region, and about the human impulse towards populism that continues to shape the world.'

Ben Rhodes, author of *The World As It Is*

'Grant is one of the shrewdest and best informed journalists working in Latin America today. He has spent more than a decade roving its barrios, farms, factories, chanceries and palaces, giving him a kaleidoscopic view of the region. It is on full display in *¡Populista!* A tour-de-force of reportage and analysis that makes sense of historic, complex forces that shook Latin America – and in many ways foreshadowed what we are now seeing in the US, Europe and elsewhere. Grant has produced a lucid, important book.'

Rory Carroll, author of *Comandante*

'Will Grant is one of the BBC's great scholar-correspondents, and without peer when it comes to explaining Latin America. In *¡Populista!*, he marries the depth of knowledge of a fine historian, with the elegant storytelling of a gifted journalist.'

Nick Bryant, author of *When America Stopped Being Great*

'Will Grant's spirited, vivid and even-handed portrait of modern Latin American populist leaders – the gaping social needs and popular frustrations that helped bring the likes of Hugo Chávez and Luiz Inácio Lula da Silva to power; and the broken dreams and economic ruin that they left behind – is a valuable and timely guide. From the region that practically invented the term "populism", it is also a sombre warning to those in more developed countries who once vainly imagined that the same could never possibly happen there. Grant's *¡Populista!* describes how the playbook of charismatic autocrats and chronic cronyism can unfold anywhere.'

John Paul Rathbone, author of *The Sugar King of Havana*

Will Grant is one of the UK's leading broadcast journalists on Latin American affairs. He has been a BBC correspondent in Latin America since 2007 with successive deployments to Venezuela, Mexico and Cuba. Across his career, he has been responsible for covering the region from Patagonia to the Rio Grande and has travelled to every part of the continent in that time. He is currently based in Havana and Mexico City.

★ WILL GRANT ★
¡POPULISTA!

THE RISE OF LATIN AMERICA'S
21ST CENTURY STRONGMAN

HEAD
ZEUS

An Apollo Book

An Apollo book
First published in the UK in 2021 by Head of Zeus Ltd
This paperback edition first published in 2021 by Head of Zeus Ltd

9 7 5 3 1 2 4 6 8

A catalogue record for this book is available from
the British Library.

ISBN (PB): 9781789543971
ISBN (E): 9781789543988

Typeset by Adrian McLaughlin

Printed and bound in the UK by
CPI Group (UK) Ltd, Croydon CRO 4YY

Head of Zeus Ltd
First Floor East
5–8 Hardwick Street
London EC1R 4RG
WWW.HEADOFZEUS.COM

For Julia and Isla

Contents

Introduction

'Populism is ultimately always sustained by the frustrated
exasperation of ordinary people, by the cry "I don't know
what's going on, but I've just had enough of it!
It cannot go on! It must stop!"'

SLAVOJ ŽIŽEK

opulism is the defining political issue of the twenty-first
century. Electorates from London to Lahore, Moscow to Manila
are struggling to distinguish between the half-truths and outright falsehoods being peddled by populist leaders of every political
hue. In Europe, anti-democratic figures have risen to prominence
in several nations, riding waves of xenophobic popular support not
seen since the 1930s. In Turkey, Hungary, the Philippines and Russia,
strongmen have taken hold of the apparatus of the state and show
few signs of letting go. The United Kingdom is coping with a new
and destabilizing current of populist discourse while the United
States is being led by the most polarizing and capricious president
it has ever known.

The populist leader can change a nation to its very fundament,
leaving a mark so deep it takes decades to fade. But amid the hand-
wringing and gnashing of teeth taking place in European capitals and
on US campuses, an important precedent has often been overlooked:
the personality-driven politics in Latin America over the past two

decades. On 2 February 1999, Hugo Chávez received the presidential sash in oil-rich Venezuela following a landslide win at the polls. On 25 November 2016, his mentor and political father, Fidel Castro, died in Havana at the age of ninety. For me, those two dates bookended the so-called 'Pink Tide', the name given to a swing to the left across the Americas at the turn of the century.

For a decade and a half, populist left-wing presidents were in power from the Amazon to the Andes. The leaders of the Pink Tide were democratically elected and radical in their socialist reforms, though not sufficiently communist to be deemed 'red'. Parties became secondary to individualism in Venezuela and Brazil, Central America and the Caribbean. It was a period of outsized, exuberant personalities, figures who shook up the natural order of politics in their countries and shifted the continental balance of power. Their stories are the stuff of political thrillers, from the torture victim who became Chile's first woman president to the rebirth of a Peronist presidential couple in Argentina. But six individuals from that period fascinate me the most. In order of their ascension, they are Hugo Chávez in Venezuela, Luiz Inácio 'Lula' da Silva in Brazil, the Bolivian president Evo Morales, the Ecuadorean leader Rafael Correa, and Daniel Ortega in Nicaragua. Plus the man who first cleared a path for their rise, father of the Cuban Revolution, Fidel Castro.

All too often painted as a monolithic or homogenous group of 'radical leftists', in reality the six differ greatly as leaders and as men. A military cadet, a steelworker, a coca farmer, a boy scout, a guerrilla and a lawyer, they came from starkly different socio-economic backgrounds and geographical locations. At least two were barefoot poor while one was from the landed gentry, and their upbringings and political formation in distant corners of the continent varied considerably. If nothing else, I hope the extent of those differences becomes clearer over the following pages.

As much as the men differed, so, too, did their political movements. Each arose from its own specific nationalist context and was created to a large degree in its leader's image. Of Hugo Chávez came '*Chavismo*', Lula was the father of '*Lulismo*' in Brazil, the Sandinistas in Nicaragua became '*Orteguistas*' for their undying loyalty to Daniel Ortega and the power structure in Cuba was always better defined as Castroite than Marxist. Yet in the first decade of the twenty-first century they coalesced in a unique moment of Latin American political history.

Fuelled by sky-high commodities prices, they achieved huge reductions in extreme poverty and inequality. They funnelled their resource-based riches into new social programmes and expensive infrastructure from oil refineries to cable-car systems above the shanty towns. Their largesse with the oil and gas money knew no bounds at home and around the region.

And they were untouchable at the polls. Their fervently committed followers were elated to at last have 'one of their own' inside the presidential palace. Within just seven years, they had fundamentally redrawn the political landscape in the Americas. Cuba, for decades a communist pariah and an outcast, was brought back into the fold and its waning revolution was propped up by Venezuelan oil. Latin America had changed before its voters' eyes and the rest of the world was forced to sit up and take notice. It was, quite simply, the most important political movement in the Western Hemisphere of the modern era.

Yet within a decade and a half, the party was over. Hugo Chávez was dead. Lula was in jail. Rafael Correa was in exile facing corruption and kidnapping charges. By late 2019, Evo Morales resigned at the behest of the military and went into exile, too. As the price of oil fell, so did the era of unconstrained generosity and benevolence. In Venezuela, the front runner and the most radical of the Pink Tide nations, the economy collapsed completely. More than four million people fled the country in barely three years. A movement that had once promised so much was either floundering or had crumbled entirely. In its place, several governments morphed into pseudo-left-wing kleptocracies run by repressive authoritarians. In some cases, the constitutions had been changed to allow indefinite presidential re-election and concentrate power in the hands of the executive. The leaders in Venezuela and Nicaragua clung on to power in the face of massive student-led uprisings and, rather than engaging in dialogue, they unleashed lethal military force against the demonstrators. Hundreds were killed on the streets.

Elsewhere in the region, the leftists were forced out by their polar opposites. Lula in Brazil, for example, was a genuinely democratic socialist with a clear sense of the value of participatory democracy, of negotiation and diplomacy. The man who eventually took his place in the presidential palace, the far-right former army captain Jair Bolsonaro, has reverted to the ugliest strongman tactics of Latin America's past. He has brutalized his opponents, debased political discourse in Brazil and divided the nation more starkly than at any time since the military dictatorships of the 1960s and 1970s. In Bolivia a staunchly conservative and evangelical group of politicians was instrumental in ejecting the indigenous left-wing president, Evo Morales, from power and then banishing him from the country. In both cases, the right-wing dug in its heels having employed many of the populist tactics and rhetoric of the very leftists they replaced.

The question many now ask is whether the Pink Tide in Latin America was a passing political current or a genuine sea change. Millions of the poorest in the region were left marooned or drowning. Others fared better by the hard turn to port and remain faithful to the populist leaders who navigated its waters. Certainly, though, the *caudillismo* exhibited by its protagonists is as old as Latin America itself. In the early nineteenth century, referred to in Latin American history as 'the Age of Caudillos', the first popular strongmen – independence heroes like Simón Bolívar, Francisco de Miranda, Antonio José de Sucre and Francisco de Paula Santander – drove the Spanish out of La Gran Colombia, what is today Venezuela, Ecuador and Colombia. Yet the *caudillo* is not only a historical figure in Napoleonic garb who liberated the continent from colonial rule. He is also a contemporary leader whose face and story we know, from General Manuel Noriega in Panama to Juan Perón, the father of Peronism.

Defining modern Latin American populism is a fraught exercise. A phenomenon which transcends the categories of left and right, it has become lazy shorthand in Western journalism for 'radical', 'extreme' or 'firebrand'. Frequently dismissed as being engaged in mere clientelism, the twenty-first-century popular leftist leaders in the Americas deserve credit for opening new political spaces for the region's unheard and often ignored voices. They placed the poor at the top of the political agenda and tackled the stigma of poverty and indigenous identity.

As the Pink Tide was rising, Argentine philosopher Ernesto Laclau wrote: 'Populism presents itself both as subversive of the existing state of things and as the starting point for a more or less radical reconstruction of a new world order wherever the previous one has been shaken.'[1] The American populist's appeal, he suggests, comes from identifying and vocalizing the problems facing the continent's poor while simultaneously presenting their leadership as the only viable solution. One of the leading academics on populism and authoritarianism, Carlos de la Torre, distilled the idea further when discussing Ecuador's twentieth-century strongman, José María Velasco Ibarra: 'Populist leaders are also innovators, but the success of their discourse is contingent on articulating and giving form to existing grievances and aspirations.'[2]

Anyone who lived in Venezuela under Hugo Chávez will recognize that description. He used his television programme, *Aló Presidente*, as a novel way to cast himself as the people's president and would verbalize the audience's 'grievances and aspirations' for hours in endless, rambling live broadcasts called *cadenas*. De la Torre's description also neatly captures the theatrics of Rafael Correa in Ecuador and the singlemindedness of Lula, the moral indignation of Evo Morales and the born-again religious conversion of Daniel Ortega. In each case, the leaders personalized politics. It was about them and, by extension, about *el pueblo* – the people. In essence, the political movements of the Pink Tide echoed the well-worn populist trope that the leader is the people and the people are the leader.

I was in the crowd in Caracas on 23 January 2010 when Hugo Chávez famously declared exactly that. He 'demanded absolute loyalty' to his leadership because – as he paraphrased the murdered Colombian Liberal leader Jorge Eliécer Gaitán – '*Yo no soy yo, ¡yo soy un pueblo, carajo!*', 'I am not me, I'm the people, goddammit!'

★

Although the six differed in many aspects, the leaders in this book naturally also shared much in common. A central theme which echoed throughout their reigns was the concept of '*el pueblo contra la oligarquía*' – 'the people against the oligarchy'. The class war was a potent tool in their campaigning and in government, understandably given the long and unfettered rule of a white, privileged elite craven to Washington. Whether it was the Somoza dynasty in Nicaragua or the Bolivian dictator Hugo Banzer, the Pink Tide generation had ample examples of past abuse to draw on when encouraging the electorate to think – and vote – differently in the early years of the twenty-first century.

Religion is also a common thread, or, rather, pseudo-religion. The populist strongman is often associated with Christ and practically deified by his followers, an undiluted devotion that was liberally bestowed on some very fallible human beings. The Ecuadorean sociologist Agustín Cueva recalled President Velasco Ibarra's appearance at a rally in May 1944 writing: 'the caudillo lifted his arms as if trying to reach the height of the bells extolling him. At the climax of the ceremony, his face, his eyes, even his voice, were pointed towards heaven. His bodily tension had something of crucifixion, and the whole rite evoked a passion in which both the words and the *mise en scène* pointed to a dramatic if not tragic sense of existence.'[3] The scene is reminiscent of Hugo Chávez's last stand in Caracas, soaked to the skin in the pouring rain, his hands clasped before him in the final rally of his campaign, and of his life, just weeks before he succumbed to cancer. After he died the United Socialist Party of Venezuela even wrote a form of the Lord's Prayer to him, in which the words were changed to 'Our Chávez, who art in heaven, on earth, in the sea and in us, hallowed be thy name...'

Several of the leaders came from no great material wealth and some experienced many years in extreme poverty. As they launched their political or military careers, it would be churlish to suggest they weren't first driven by a desire to improve the lives of the poorest, of their families and the communities they had grown up in. For the most part, their initial reasons for fomenting revolution or joining socialist organizations were genuine, a product of the relentless poverty and the repressive dictatorships which surrounded them. Yet over time, they became so enchanted by power and its trappings that they struggled to let it go. Some never did. Especially towards the end of their political moment, their motivations had often become vainglorious and selfish, driven primarily by the desire to retain control. In a 2016 referendum in Bolivia, Evo Morales was denied the right to stand for a third re-election by the very people he claimed to represent. He went on to stand anyway, with the backing of a highly questionable decision from the constitutional court. If one were feeling generous, it could be suggested that their thirst for power sprang from a concern that their socialist reforms would be overturned by their successors and an unyielding belief that they – and they alone – understood how to 'fix' the country. In a less forgiving analysis, however, they could reasonably be accused of a deep-seated egotism and the worst kind of addiction in public life: to privilege, power, money, influence and personal status.

For all the clumsiness of its English translation to 'strongman', the word *caudillo* is one of the most relevant to a true understanding of Latin America. The region's history is littered with military men who openly boasted that they held all the strings of their nations, the supreme being through whom all decisions must pass. 'Not a leaf moves in Chile without my knowledge,' General Augusto Pinochet infamously said. Naturally, the socialist leaders of the modern era were far removed from the murderous Cold War dictatorships – indeed were largely born in reaction to them and their conservative civilian successors. Clearly, the leaders of the Pink Tide never engaged in the wholesale torture and disappearance of thousands of their citizens as had the likes of Pinochet or Paraguay's General Alfredo Stroessner, or '*el Jefe*', Rafael Trujillo, in the Dominican Republic. Yet they do share one thing in common with those brutes. For all their claims to lead 'bottom-up' revolutions, the leftist political movements were always built around one man, whether he was Chávez, Evo, Lula, Correa,

Ortega or, of course, Fidel. The result, particularly in Venezuela and Nicaragua, was a fundamental weakening of the institutions of the state, leading to their eventual dominance by the governing parties.

Perhaps the most relevant question to be asked of these leaders, indeed of any populist movement around the world, is why did they work? Why was their appeal so broad? In the case of Venezuela, why did so many millions fall for a former soldier who had attempted a coup and claimed to be nothing less than the modern incarnation of Simón Bolívar? Why did impoverished Brazilians finally throw their lot in with Lula, a strike organizer and a rough northeasterner from the metalworkers' unions, on his third time of asking? Why did Ecuadoreans choose an outspoken economist with just 106 days of ministerial experience or the Bolivians a coca growers' union leader? How did Daniel Ortega manage to make a political comeback seventeen years after the end of the Cold War?

The answers lie in the rulers who preceded them, in the military dictatorships of the Cold War and the Washington-compliant conservatives of the 1990s. Beholden to the International Monetary Fund and the World Bank, Latin American governments slavishly followed the much-vaunted economic policies of the 'Washington Consensus' which left their populations as poor and destitute as they could remember. They implemented harsh austerity reforms to service the foreign debt, sparking angry outpourings of social unrest on the streets which tore up the existing contract between the voters and the ruling political class. The conditions were ripe for change. Quite simply, the past hadn't worked for most Latin Americans and they yearned for a new kind of politics.

In 1999, they got it. When a young, forthright former coup leader came out of Yare prison in Venezuela and onto their televisions, he certainly began to 'articulate and give form to their grievances' and present himself as 'the starting point for a new world order'. *El pueblo venezolano* wanted a leader – wanted a strongman, in fact – who would listen to and prioritize them. Hugo Chávez had tried to storm the presidential palace of Miraflores with a tank and then told the people he'd done it because they deserved better, that they were entitled to expect more from their leaders than the unbridled corruption and impunity they had endured for decades. The electorate's love affair with him was immediate, mutual and lasting.

I was fortunate enough to speak to many of the protagonists of this unique political moment. I lived in Venezuela under Hugo Chávez and attended scores of his hours-long press conferences. I followed his travelling circus around the country, asked him questions live on state television and was subjected to one of his infamous broadsides at the media. I also spent six years in Cuba coinciding with the announcement of a diplomatic thaw with the United States and the death of Fidel Castro. After they left power, I had the opportunity to speak at length with Lula languishing inside prison in the Brazilian town of Curitiba and Ecuador's Rafael Correa in his self-imposed exile in Belgium. I caught up with Evo Morales in Mexico, just days after he was forced to flee Bolivia, still bruised and grieving the abrupt end to his rule.

More importantly, I have spent time with countless supporters and opponents of these men in every corner of the continent. From noisy *Chavista* rallies to opposition student protests, from terrorism trials to heart-wrenching funerals of teenagers, from cups of watery coffee in dirt-floor shacks to lavish cocktail receptions in ambassadorial residences, I have had the opportunity to hear a great many views on the politics of Latin America over the past twenty years. Many people have opened their homes and shared their lives with me, a stranger clutching a microphone, to explain how the political winds have buffeted them or carried them to calmer seas. I will be eternally grateful to them for their time and this book is entirely thanks to their generosity.

In terms of the Pink Tide's legacy, I can't help but think of the often-misquoted line about the significance of the French Revolution by the late Chinese premier Zhou Enlai, that 'it's too early to tell'.[4] Replace the French Revolution with the Cuban one or Venezuela's nebulous 'Bolivarian Revolution' and the quip works well. Two decades may have passed since Chávez's first boisterous inauguration ceremony, but it is still too early to make any definitive conclusion on the pancontinental political movement that followed him. Especially because in some places the remnants of the Pink Tide still hold a grip on power.

The six leaders profiled here always insisted they brought about meaningful change in their nations and tangible improvements to the lives of the poor. Their opponents claim those improvements collapsed with the commodities prices and that the leaders themselves were 'revolutionary' in nothing more than name. When we tune out the noise and shrill rhetoric from both sides a moment, much has already become apparent. From the rampant corruption, illegality and economic ruin which reigns in Venezuela to the unabated demagoguery in Nicaragua, it's clear that millions in those two nations, at least, are worse off today than when they began. Elsewhere, the argument over the costs and benefits of the past twenty years of populism continues to rage before every election.

Now that the moment of high tide has passed we can examine a little better the flotsam and jetsam left behind, see more clearly the horizons between the elegant and the ugly, the laudable and the downright despicable.

VENEZUELA /
HUGO CHÁVEZ

*'Damned be the soldier who turns his
weapons against his people'*

SIMÓN BOLÍVAR

Olga Villalba began the day uneasy. A nurse at the San Roman urological hospital, she was leaving her small but neat breeze-block home at the edge of a sprawling slum in Santa Fe Sur when a neighbour shouted that a curfew had been put in place.

'Soldiers are on the streets, it's chaos,' she yelled.

Olga, though, needed to get to work. She gingerly ventured out wearing her nurse's uniform hoping it might help the soldiers distinguish her from the people sacking and looting Caracas.

Just two weeks after taking office in early February 1989, President Carlos Andrés Pérez announced a package of structural reforms recommended by the International Monetary Fund. Despite having campaigned on an anti-neoliberal platform and criticized the IMF, he quickly called on the financial institution once in power. The move was known as '*el Gran Viraje*' meaning 'the Great Turn'.

To receive a $4.5 billion loan and service the external debt, Pérez's '*paquetazo*' of measures was straight out of the Washington Consensus playbook. It included privatizing state utility companies, floating the currency exchange, price hikes on water, electricity, domestic gas and petrol, which was particularly galling for citizens of a major oil producer. Costs of other basics like bread and maize flour began to shoot up, too, prompting scarcity and hoarding.

Late on 26 February 1989, the measure was imposed on public transport, and transit companies increased their prices by 100 per cent overnight. In the early hours of the following morning, when factory workers and labourers in the suburb of Guarenas set off for work in Caracas they were greeted by bus drivers demanding the new price of a ticket – a threefold increase on some routes from six bolívars to eighteen.

It was the moment that popular discontent at the Great Turn turned ugly. Already furious at their worsening economic situation, people were now incensed. In Guarenas they started to set fire to the buses, smash shop windows and throw stones at the police. The rioting quickly spread to Caracas as many months of pent-up frustration were vented in an explosion of mob rule. People streamed down from the *barrios*, the low-income neighbourhoods and shanty towns that ring Caracas, leaving 1950s social housing blocks and tin-roofed shacks and looting stores through a combination of necessity and opportunity.

The police attempted to control the crowds with tear gas and rubber bullets, but people made off with everything from urgently needed basics like flour and water to luxury goods like household appliances and Scotch whisky.

The National Police were on partial strike and were slow to react. As the fires and ransacking spread, President Pérez ordered in the military. He took to national television to tell people what was coming. A bald man with close-set features and a thick curtain of hair that framed the sides of his head, he spoke in an outraged tone, apparently scandalized that people would have the audacity to rise up against his economic decision-making.

'We have been in government for just twenty days,' he reminded them, pointing a finger in the air in indignation. 'But the situation we're in is one of impatience, the restraints of all Venezuelans have burst. Well, fine. Now the possibility has been opened of taking the rest of the measures [available to us],' he warned them.

By the following morning, as Olga was heading off to work amid the mayhem, barely trained soldiers from the interior of the country were prowling the streets of the capital in AMX-13 armoured vehicles, carrying 7.62mm assault weapons.[1] The repression from Carlos Andrés Pérez was brutal and utterly uncompromising. People were killed first in their dozens, then in their hundreds. Some estimates even reached the thousands as scores of corpses were dumped in mass graves at La Peste on the state's orders, blurring the exact number of dead.

The two days of looting and repression would become known as the *Caracazo*, an event forever burnished into the Venezuelan psyche. It still haunts generations of Venezuelans who lived through it and has become a historical reference point for those who didn't, the Venezuelan watchword for state brutality against the people.

A previously secret military plan was enacted, Plan Ávila, which allowed the military to crush civil disobedience swiftly and with impunity. A raft of constitutional freedoms were suspended including the right to immunity of domicile (Article 62), the freedom of movement (Article 64), the freedom of expression (Article 66), the right of assembly (Article 71) and the right to take part in peaceful manifestations (Article 115).[2]

For many of the troops who opened fire on the people, it was the worst day of their young lives. Many hailed from the *barrios* and had struggled with the order to quell the uprising with force. One soldier who avoided that internal conflict, however, was Hugo Rafael Chávez Frías. Lying in bed with chickenpox in the city of Maracay, the thirty-four-year-old paratrooper didn't participate in the crackdown but would use the *Caracazo* for his own political ends in the years to come.

Olga reached the hospital to find it overflowing with casualties. Bodies were stacked up in every available space as people had simply driven the injured and dying to the nearest place with doctors and nurses inside, even a urological clinic. Word reached them that the clinic's security guard who'd had the day off had been shot in the head. A senior consultant drove to the Miguel Pérez Carreño hospital and found the guard dumped on the floor, left for dead among the corpses. An operation by the surgeons saved his life but left him permanently brain damaged.

'There were so many stories like his,' Olga told me, her salt-and-pepper afro pulled back with a yellow hairband. 'So, so many.'

As we spoke, Olga was clearing away the blood-matted dressings of another looting victim, thirty years after the *Caracazo*, almost to the day. In early March 2019, a nationwide blackout affected the vast majority of Venezuela. When the power cut entered its fourth consecutive day, people in Olga's neighbourhood snapped, echoing the popular discontent of three decades earlier.

Emboldened by reports of looting elsewhere in the city and desperate for food and potable water, dozens of people smashed the windows of the local supermarket directly opposite Olga's house and grabbed whatever they could. Nearby, a cashier defending the shop she worked in sliced her leg on broken glass and needed fifty stitches.

As the neighbourhood's resident black-market nurse, Olga stitched the girl up and changed the dressing the next morning.

'The price rises in 1989 were tiny. They were like this,' Olga said, holding up her pinky fingernail as an illustration, 'compared to what we're living through now.'

Her inference was clear. Another *Caracazo* was long overdue.

The soldier who was saved by the chickenpox, Hugo Chávez, was largely brought up by his paternal grandmother. Rosa Inés Chávez, or 'Mamá Rosa' as he affectionately called her, left more of a mark on the young boy than his own parents. The story of Chávez's rural roots is now socialist party folklore in Venezuela. Some of it is undoubtedly embellished to underscore his credentials as a legitimate member of the poor. Yet much of it is true and his simple upbringing certainly influenced how he saw the world – first as a young cadet, later as a coup conspirator and finally as president.

Chávez was born in Sabaneta, a dusty little town in the heart of the Venezuelan plains known as *Los Llanos*. It is flat, verdant, cattle-rearing country in the state of Barinas dotted with sugarcane fields and maize plantations, the town itself nestled among royal palms and mango trees. The town is typical of the tiny villages in the Venezuelan countryside, little more than a modest collection of streets around a neatly manicured central square, the Plaza de Bolívar. Despite the overwhelming sensation that the hamlet hasn't changed as much as a streetlight in a century, Hugo Chávez was raised in a very different Venezuela to the one he would eventually rule.

Chávez grew up under the military dictatorship of General Marcos Evangelista Pérez Jiménez. Always dressed in a pristine uniform, thick horn-rimmed glasses on his chubby, childlike face, Pérez Jiménez was a repressive *caudillo* from the Andean state of Tachira. Initially the power behind the scenes in a military junta, he took sole control in 1953 coinciding with a sharp rise in the oil price. General Pérez Jiménez launched what he called the New National Ideal for Venezuela, underpinned by the 'Doctrine for the National Good', a sort of pseudo-political philosophy based on major public works, an influx of immigrants and foreign capital, and the ruthless crushing of dissent.

Pérez Jiménez spent the new oil wealth on a social development programme aimed at improving the lives, and securing the votes, of communities in the vast slums that encircle the valley around Caracas. It was a strategy that Hugo Chávez would also employ to devastating effect five decades later. Flush with petrodollars, throughout the mid-1950s Marcos Pérez Jiménez modernized the oil-rich nation. He ordered large infrastructural projects from motorways, bridges and lavish plazas to an expansive university complex and a cable car that ran the entire height of the Ávila mountain, the natural barrier separating the capital city from the coast.

He even changed the name of the country, from the United States of Venezuela to the Republic of Venezuela. Again, Chávez did something similar when he was in power and later became a key voice in the modern revisionism of Pérez Jiménez's rule.[3] By the late 1950s, however, Pérez Jiménez's populist moves were wearing thin. The public had grown weary of his dictatorial regime and of constitutional changes designed to concentrate power into his hands.

The situation came to a head in the Christmas of 1957. That December, a referendum was held to extend the military strongman's rule for a further five-year term. The government claimed victory but the widely rigged election was not recognized by any opposition party. As would be the case in Cuba a year later, New Year's Day proved the crucial turning point. The first uprising within the military, mainly involving figures from the air force, was quickly put down but it sent shockwaves through the regime. Aware that an insurrection was growing, Pérez Jiménez cracked down, arresting more civilian dissidents and turncoat members of the military.

He was clutching at straws. Within three weeks, the military government unravelled completely. A general strike on 21 January laid the groundwork for the final putsch. In the early hours of 23 January, the marine corps and the Caracas garrison announced they were withdrawing their support for the president and Marco Pérez Jiménez was faced with no choice but to flee to the Dominican Republic. There *el Jefe*, Generalissimo Rafael Trujillo, was waiting to receive him.

In the rich Barinas countryside, Elena Frías de Chávez was a teenager as Pérez Jiménez was coming to power. In 1952, at just seventeen years old, she married the village schoolteacher, Hugo de los Reyes Chávez, and a year later, she had her first son, Adán. Six more children would follow, all boys, although the penultimate, Enzo, died at six months old. Hugo Rafael was the second, born in the family's dirt-floor and palm-roofed adobe shack on 28 July 1954.

The economic situation in the burgeoning household was so precarious it was decided that the two oldest boys, Adán and Hugo, would live with their *abuela*, Rosa Inés, a common solution to family poverty in those parts. Elena Frías had also been raised by her grandmother for the same reason. By all accounts, Rosa Inés was firm and patient with the young 'Huguito'. She taught him to read and gave him far more love and attention than he might have expected living with his brothers at his parents' home. Some biographers suggest that Hugo retained a residual resentment towards his mother for passing him over, a theory backed up by disparaging comments Chávez once made about Elena to his lover, a university professor called Herma Marksman.[4] Adán and Hugo remained with Rosa Inés until they left for university and the military academy respectively, and both were profoundly affected by her death in 1982.

I visited the sleepy town of Sabaneta in early 2009, around the tenth anniversary of Chávez's rise to power. At the height of the midday sun, barely a stray dog ventured out in the soporific Barinas heat. But in the mornings and the relative cool of the evenings, there was a pleasant village bustle around the Plaza Bolívar. Mamá Rosa's house had long since been converted into the headquarters of the United Socialist Party of Venezuela (PSUV). After Chávez's death, it was designated part of the cultural patrimony of the nation, putting it on a par with the homes of nineteenth-century independence leaders like Bolívar and Sucre.

I knocked at Elena's house, which sits next door. Despite the fact that she was Bolivarian royalty – her son was president and her husband the state governor – and despite the extensive land the Chávez clan had acquired in Barinas, she still occasionally visited the tight-knit town. After a long pause, a voice from inside asked who I was and then instructed me to go to a house down the road to find Joaquina Frías, Elena's sister and Hugo's aunt.

'We couldn't believe it when he won,' the diminutive aunt told me. 'That little boy who used to run about and play with his friends, and sold the mango and papaya sweets his grandmother made on the streets.' Joaquina was in her eighties and mentally alert but physically quite frail. '*Era muy noble, muy noble*,' she repeated over and over, like a marketing slogan for her nephew, 'he was very noble, very decent'. She had lived in the same home for forty years, chickens pecking around in the backyard and only a curtain to separate lavatory from living room. Joaquina didn't complain, though, especially not to a visiting foreign journalist. '*Era muy noble.*' Off camera, her daughter and son-in-law were more forthright in voicing their frustrations that the Chávez family's benevolence hadn't reached his mother's older sister.

Still, no one in Sabaneta had a bad word to say about the town's famous son, at least not in public or on camera. A few years after his death, though, with Venezuela spiralling towards economic collapse, a group of protesters set fire to a statue of Hugo Chávez in Sabaneta that Vladimir Putin had donated to the town. The photographs show a charred-looking Chávez, a hitherto unthinkable statement of rejection in his birthplace, and reminded me of perhaps why Fidel Castro famously never wanted busts or statues of him erected or streets named after him.

A left-handed pitcher with a vicious spin, young Huguito dreamed only of baseball and of making it to the US Major Leagues. He idolized a player with the same surname, Nestor Isais '*el Latigo*' Chávez, meaning 'the Whip', and the precocious boy from the savannah plains wanted nothing more than to follow his hero's path in life. Hugo had his own nickname: '*Tribilín*', the Spanish name for the Disney character Goofy, supposedly because of his tall stature and long feet. Politics could hardly have been further from *Tribilín*'s mind.

In Sabaneta I was introduced to an old schoolfriend of Hugo's, Hely Rafael Lucena, who made a living breeding roosters for cockfighting and had remained in the town his entire life. We walked together to Sabaneta's baseball field, a small diamond of scorched grass at the far end of the town, Hely pointing out important Chávez landmarks on the way. 'That's the Escuela Julián Pino, where we went to primary school. This is where people sign up to join the party. *El comandante* visited us just last week with Oliver Stone', and so on. Upbeat salsa songs with pro-Chávez lyrics blared out from a loudspeaker as party activists sitting under a red gazebo encouraged passers-by to register as members ahead of the next vote. 'There's no *escuálidos* [opposition supporters] in Sabaneta,' laughed Hely. 'Well, maybe one or two but virtually none.'

Despite the watchful eye of the PSUV over our little tour, Hely was honest enough to admit that when they were young, there was little to suggest Huguito Chávez would stand out as remarkable in any environment other than baseball. Certainly nothing to indicate he was destined to become Venezuela's strongman and the most significant Latin American leader of his generation. As we sat in Hely's dirt backyard, drinking ice-cold Polar beer around a cement cockfighting ring, the birds scrabbling around in their cages behind us, he said that although he could never have predicted Chávez's astronomical rise, his friend's meticulous character had always shone through.

'Hugo was a very serious boy, very bright and he always wanted things to be just so. He was quite particular about planning. Everything had to be done properly or not at all,' Lucena recalled.

It was baseball that led Chávez to the military rather than any burning desire to be a soldier. The military academy was a route to the capital, Caracas, and he figured that once there he could abandon the army for the national baseball league. Ideally, Hugo was looking for the fastest track to a professional contract in the United States. Quickly, though, the rigour and discipline and camaraderie of military life took hold of the cadet from Barinas and there would be no return to baseball except as a pastime.

★

Quietly, seamlessly, Hugo Chávez had been leading very different lives. Since 1983 he adopted at least three identities for different circumstances and audiences.[5]

The first was that of dutiful soldier. Before his superiors, Chávez strived to give the impression of a model paratrooper. He was loyal, dedicated, a little eccentric perhaps, with an old-fashioned manner and turn of phrase. But as far as most of them could see, Lieutenant Chávez was a man primarily concerned with military matters and possessed of a keen sense of hierarchy, formality and propriety.

The second was that of an apolitical family man. In front of his wife, a primary school teacher called Nancy Colmenares whom he married at just twenty-three, and his three children, he reined in his more radical opinions and pretensions of power. Nancy was from a simple family in Barinas and was not an especially political woman. Although his father had once been a militant for the Christian Democrats, his mother was openly opposed to discussing politics at home. Around them Hugo stayed guarded and silent, and shared few of his thoughts about the direction the country was heading. Much less his plans.

The third was conspirator and coup plotter. Here, among a cabal of like-minded thinkers and strategists, he could flex his intellectual muscle and exercise his genuine identity. As a teenager in the rural state of Barinas, Hugo had been taught by a former leftist guerrilla and Communist Party militant called José Esteban Ruiz-Guevara. A writer and academic who was imprisoned during the military dictatorship, Ruiz-Guevara introduced the impressionable boy to the works of Victor Hugo, Machiavelli and Marx, to the romantic heroism of Che Guevara and to Simón Bolívar's vision of regional unity. Years later, when Chávez was a cadet on leave from Caracas, the Ruiz-Guevara home would be his second port of call after seeing his beloved grandmother, Rosa Inés, and his parents. He would drink copious cups of black coffee, smoke Belmont cigarettes and debate vigorously with José Esteban and his sons, named Vladimir and

Federico after Lenin and Engels. They would sit up until the small hours arguing over the right conditions for revolution or the ideals of the country's nineteenth-century federalist leader Ezequiel Zamora – another of Chávez's personal heroes.

He began to formulate ideas of what could perhaps best be called 'Llanero Socialism' – a broad, open-ended socialist philosophy based on his life experiences in the poverty of the Venezuelan savannah. In 1974, Chávez was selected for a trip to Peru which left a profound effect on him. With nine other soldiers from the military academy, he travelled to Lima for the 150th anniversary of the Battle of Ayacucho. During the visit, the Venezuelan cadets met the president, General Juan Velasco Alvarado, a left-wing military strongman.

At just twenty-one, Hugo Chávez thought his chest would burst with pride at being part of the select group to travel to Peru, to represent the Venezuelan flag. By his own account, he didn't stop asking questions of everyone he met on the trip and the visit 'accelerated [his] own internal process, forged [his] political direction'.[6] Meeting Velasco touched him on a personal level, too, and he kept the two books given to the visiting cadets by the progressive soldier: *The Peruvian National Revolution* and *The Manifesto of the Revolutionary Government of the Armed Forces of Peru*. Chávez said he learned great chunks of them off by heart and that his copies were only taken from him when he was arrested on 4 February 1992. In government, Velasco's civic-military partnership in Peru was a nationalist model that would inform Chávez's thinking for Venezuela until his death.

For those on the political left at that time, the radical party of the day was MIR, *Movimiento de Izquierda Revolucionaria*, or the Revolutionary Left Movement. The group emerged following Fidel Castro's visit to Venezuela a year after the overthrow of Marcos Pérez Jiménez and in the first flush of his own victory in Havana in 1959. With an eye on turning a country of such vast oil wealth to his side, the leader of the Cuban Revolution actively supported the group's armed struggle in the 1960s and sent some of his most trusted men to help organize their guerrilla movement.

Other leftist groups included *La Causa R* – the Radical Cause – and Movement to Socialism (MAS), which merged with MIR in the 1980s. Yet despite their appeal among labour unions and factory workers, none of them could challenge the dominance of two established parties: Acción Democrática and COPEI.

After Pérez Jiménez was ousted in 1958, Venezuela was initially in the hands of more military men until a presidential election could be held. Ahead of that vote, the three main parties of the day – the social democratic party Acción Democrática, the Christian democrats COPEI, and a smaller party, URD – reached an agreement to mutually respect the result to preserve Venezuela's fledgling democracy. The deal was signed between their respective leaders, Rómulo Betancourt, Rafael Caldera and Jóvito Villalba at Caldera's home, Quinta Punto Fijo in Caracas. It became known as the Pact of Punto Fijo. Eventually, the URD dropped out and, rather than being the guarantor of democracy and a bulwark of stability in Venezuela, the pact came to be seen by many as a shady gentlemen's agreement, a grubby backroom deal made behind closed doors to maintain the two main parties' grip over the country to the exclusion of everyone else. Acción Democrática and COPEI dominated Venezuela's politics and government for decades. First us, then you, ad infinitum.

The relationship with the United States at that time was predictably close. Throughout the Cold War, Washington had a reliable and oil-rich hemispheric partner in Venezuela, a mutual understanding which barely deviated in forty years. There were a few bumps along the way, naturally. Venezuela's immense oil wealth ensured it an outsized role in regional politics and there was real distance between Caracas and Washington over US support for right-wing dictatorships in the Southern Cone. There was also some nervousness in Washington after the Venezuelan oil industry was nationalized in the mid-1970s.

But at no stage did Venezuela renege on its energy commitments to the Americans or fail to send a single oil shipment to US ports on time. Indeed, the energy relationship was untouchable even at the height of Chávez's anti-American rhetoric with not a single drop of Venezuelan crude failing to reach its destination in the north.

All in all, post-war Venezuelan politics amounted to a domestic pact and an international understanding. At home, the two parties passed control back and forth, neither one ever jeopardizing the country's most important bilateral bond. Furthermore, American culture filtered into Venezuela from its baseball and fast food to the modern highways and skyscrapers which made Caracas resemble US oil-rich cities like Houston or Dallas. Leftists said Venezuela was becoming a pale impersonation of American capitalism led by a group of self-interested sycophants.

Chávez certainly saw it that way. So, he plotted. In 1983, he formed a secret group with three other low-ranking officers to begin working on a plan to seize control of Venezuela when the moment was right. They called themselves the EBR-200, *Ejército Bolivariano Revolucionario* (the Revolutionary Bolivarian Army), the '200' denoting the bicentennial year of Bolívar's birth.

Their formal inception came on the anniversary of the independence hero's death, 17 December. After addressing his fellow troops on the memory of Bolívar in one of his earliest ad-libbed public speeches, Hugo Chávez gathered with three trusted comrades in Maracay: Jesús Urdaneta, Felipe Acosta and Raúl Baduel. With the afternoon off, the four men went on a run to the Samán de Güere, a gigantic, imposing saman tree on the outskirts of the city which once captured the imagination of Alexander von Humboldt for its uncommonly thick trunk and which was declared a national monument in the 1930s. There, entertaining their shared penchant for ceremony and spiritualism, they each picked a leaf from the broad branches and took an oath. In essence, it was a pact of insurrection as they vowed to rise up one day over the country's political direction. The ritual extended to repeating an oath Simón Bolívar had taken in 1805, the Oath of Monte Sacro, swearing his life to the struggle for an independent Latin America. In unison, the four men recited: 'I swear before you, before the God of my forefathers, I swear before them, I swear by my honour and my fatherland that I will give no rest to my arm nor my soul until the chains that oppress us are broken by the will of the Spanish power.'

It was a moment heavy in symbolism and theatre as they substituted the words 'Spanish power' for a more contemporary term 'the powerful'. Once in office, Chávez was reportedly prone to summoning the spirit of Simón Bolívar with such dramatic flourishes. Courtiers told of how he would leave a seat empty for Bolívar at the table in the presidential palace, Miraflores. He even later exhumed the Founding Father's remains in a vain attempt to show he'd been poisoned. When Chávez later fell ill with cancer, more than a few superstitious Venezuelans and followers of the Yoruba religion, *Santería*, muttered it was comeuppance for having disturbed the dead.

It was often said that Chávez was trying to emulate Bolívar and in many ways that is true. Especially in the attempt to unite all of Latin America under one vision, an endeavour so fraught with difficulty that Bolívar eventually likened it to 'ploughing the sea'. In fact, rather than considering himself the reincarnation of the nineteenth-century hero of independence, Chávez reportedly thought of himself as the modern-day *'Maisanta'* – a Venezuelan revolutionary called Pedro Pérez Delgado who the Chávez clan often claimed was Hugo's great-great-grandfather.

Beyond the symbolism, though, that oath under the saman tree would have lasting consequences for the military and the country. When the original four soldiers were later promoted to higher ranks, including inside the military academy in charge of troops and cadets, they could pick and choose the right minds to bring on board their clandestine movement. More young men soon took the same oath, signing up for an undefined plan of insurrection on a date to be determined in defence of an unspecified cause for which many ended up dying.

As Carlos Andrés Pérez's plane swooped down from the night sky and into Maiquetía airport, there was a reception waiting for him inside. It was led by Defence Minister Fernándo Ochoa Antich, whose brow had been constantly furrowed over the past few hours.

Rumours had been circulating of an imminent coup by unknown plotters within the military. The president had been at the World Economic Forum in Davos, Switzerland, and word was that he would be kidnapped on his return. The plane arrived at 10 p.m. and President Pérez emerged looking exhausted. Any hope he might have had for rest was about to evaporate.

'What are you doing here?' he asked his defence minister.

'President, a rumour has been going around all afternoon of a possible insurrection against you by a group of junior officers,' the bespectacled general replied.

'Rumours, nothing but rumours!' Pérez snapped. 'Such tales are what hurt this government.'[7] The very idea was preposterous, he said. Nobody had attempted a coup in Venezuela since 1962. The president ordered a meeting for early the next morning and the two men travelled back to Caracas in uncomfortable silence. Carlos Andrés Pérez was taken to the presidential residence, La Casona, and Ochoa Antich drove to his ministerial home at the Fuerte Tiuna military base.

It was midnight, 4 February 1992. Around sixty miles away in Maracay, the coup plotters had taken their first decisive action of the night. The army barracks, Cuartel Paez, was already in their hands, the commanding officers locked in the cells. As well as Maracay, an uprising was simultaneously unfolding in three more strategic points around the country: Valencia, Maracaibo and, of course, Caracas.

The MBR-200 was making its strike. They called it Operation Zamora. Even the date they chose for the attack had nineteenth-century symbolism, 4 February being the birthday of Antonio José de Sucre, the second-in-command to Simón Bolívar.

The assault on the capital was being led by Lt-Col. Hugo Chávez. He was holed up in the Military Museum in Caracas, a few blocks from the presidential palace, Miraflores, chain-smoking and frantically issuing orders to his units on the ground. Years later, renamed the Mountain Barracks with the symbols '4F' placed on the roof to mark the date of the putsch, the Military Museum became Hugo Chávez's final resting place.

Not that night, though. While he could easily have died in the ill-fated insurrection, not for the only time in his life he was destined to make it out of an attempted coup alive.

By 1 a.m., the rebels appeared to be gaining the upper hand. In Maracaibo, a company of troops under the command of Lt-Col. Francisco Arias Cárdenas had detained the governor of the state of Zulia, Oswaldo Álvarez Paz. From Valencia, reports came in on crackly phone lines of a breakaway parachute regiment, tanks surrounding the barracks and gunfire. Venezuela's troops had pitted themselves against one another. It would later become apparent that more than 2,500 troops, representing around ten battalions, or 10 per cent of the armed forces, had turned and were being directed by the coup leaders.[8]

In Caracas, Chávez had several main targets to secure, including the Defence Ministry, La Carlota military airport and, most importantly, Miraflores itself. Instead of staying inside the residence with his family, Carlos Andrés Pérez drove to Miraflores, slipping unnoticed past the rebels' military vehicles. After a hapless hour or so, he phoned his defence minister for an update and Fernándo Ochoa Antich told him to get out of Miraflores and get on to television. By now, Chávez's men had secured the headquarters of the state-owned TV channel, Venezolana de Televisión (VTV), but hadn't been able to play their recorded message to the nation after a quick-thinking technician told them their VHS tape was the wrong format for broadcasting. If President Pérez could get onto one of the privately owned TV channels, he could get the word out to loyalist troops and quell fears that his presidency was about to fall.

'I'm completely surrounded,' wailed the president, the unmistakable crack of gunfire echoing behind him. 'They'll capture or kill me.' It was a fair assessment.

'The tunnels, sir. Use one of the tunnels,' answered Ochoa Antich. Venezuela's presidential palace has a series of underground exits and, if the rebels hadn't yet posted soldiers to every gate, the president might make it out in one piece.

Driving a nondescript grey Ford LTD with the headlights switched off, Pérez escaped with minutes to spare. No sooner had he fled than an armoured vehicle began to force its way into the compound. Scores of rebel and loyalist soldiers were killed or wounded. At home, Venezuelans watched the live footage in disbelief as a tank drove up the steps and busted down the doors of Miraflores. Troops took up positions around the building, bathed in the red glow of the street lights, signalling to each other between volleys of gunfire to close in further on the palace. In the rural backwater of Sabaneta, Elena Frías de Chávez was inconsolable, unable to reach Hugo on the telephone and convinced her headstrong, rebellious son was somehow involved.

Within minutes of arriving at Venevisión, a TV station owned by the Cisneros family, the richest family in Venezuela, President Pérez appeared on air to deliver his address. Standing in front of a black background and next to a Venezuelan flag, his speech had all the sophistication of a hostage video. Which, in a sense, it was.

Angry and visibly shaken, Pérez occasionally stumbled as he delivered a fuming defence of his legitimacy as president. He began by listing the heads of state who had called him to offer their backing, from President Mitterrand of France to Colombian president César Gaviria. Even President George Bush had 'come out of his room at 2 a.m.' to lend words of support, he said.

This putsch was 'infamy', he told the Venezuelan people, 'a criminal attempt to knock out democracy by a group of ambitious careerists' whose sole aim was to install a military dictatorship. 'Just when we thought we'd never see another in Latin America,' he spat. 'I'll soon be back in Miraflores,' Pérez insisted, saying the coup plotters were already giving themselves up.

Then he delivered his key point to the armed forces:

Officials and soldiers, your Commander-in-Chief is speaking to you: your obedience is with me, he who has the mandate of the people, he who swore on the constitution. Any other official or hierarchy who tries to get you to recognise their mandate should be ignored.

Stirring it wasn't. But it was direct and it was effective.

Within hours, the game was up. Hugo Chávez had gambled and lost. Estimates vary but around eighteen soldiers and perhaps as many as fifty civilians were killed in the events of 4 February 1992. Dozens more were injured.

Chávez's side had done their part in the provinces but in Caracas he had made simple mistakes from which they could never recover. Orders went ignored or unfulfilled. Meanwhile, reinforcements arrived to claw back Miraflores for the government. Cornered in the Military Museum with a handful of his troops, the net was tightening around Chávez. The other three conspirators had made important gains in their designated areas of the country but as the hours passed it was increasingly clear that Caracas was not about to fall. Nor was Pérez's government. At nine-thirty in the morning, Chávez agreed to hand himself in but with one caveat. He insisted on making a live television address to tell his forces to stand down himself. As their commander, he argued, the soldiers needed to hear it from him that their coup had failed or they wouldn't lay down their weapons.

President Pérez had ordered that any message be pre-recorded and wanted Chávez to appear in handcuffs. However, voices on all sides insisted that time was of the essence. A breakaway tank regiment still held the military airstrip in Maracay, La Carlota remained in rebel hands and there were coup operations in Valencia and Maracaibo that could only be called off by Chávez himself.

Defence Minister Ochoa Antich relented and let Chávez go live on TV. 'I made a mistake,' the retired minister acknowledged when I met him in his home in Caracas, now aged and grey. As I walked into his apartment in a well-heeled, gated community, the lights went out at the start of what was a four-day-long nationwide blackout. Dressed in a smart dark suit and tie for our meeting, Ochoa Antich was a throwback to a more gentlemanly if thoroughly corrupt era of Venezuelan politics. Even when he offered me a drink despite the early hour, it was done with a certain lament for how times had changed: 'I'm afraid I've used up all the good rum and whisky but there's still some liqueur left,' he said. Over glasses of warm amaretto and with no air-conditioning or lights, the general told me his story of 4 February 1992. Peppered with minutiae, tangents and reminiscences of long-dead contemporaries, it was clear he's still more than a little haunted by the brief moment he granted Hugo Chávez in the national spotlight.

'People never let me forget it,' he said, twenty-five years on. 'This one woman stopped me in the supermarket to say "It's all your fault! You should have killed him while you had the chance!" I said, "I'm sorry madam, but it just wasn't that simple".'

He's right, it wasn't. No one could have known it then – neither Ochoa Antich nor Chávez – but the decision to let the rebel soldier speak live on air would fundamentally alter the course of Venezuela. Like Hugo Chávez, Fernándo Ochoa Antich's life reached a crucial crossroads on the night of 4 February 1992, both personally and for his nation. By his own admission, he got it wrong at the most critical point.

Chávez didn't waste the opportunity afforded to him. In total, he delivered a seventy-two-second speech. The words transcended a simple address to his co-conspirators and became a call to arms to all Venezuelans. Subsequently, and helped in no small part by his government's public relations machinery, they took on a sort of strange immortality in Venezuela. Likened to Fidel Castro's 'History Will Absolve Me' defence of his own failed coup in 1953, some see Chávez's televised speech as the opening salvo of a process of change. Others consider it the moment the country began its gradual descent into chaos. Either way, his words have echoed through Venezuelan politics ever since:

'Comrades, unfortunately, for now, the objectives we had set for ourselves have not been achieved in the capital,' Chávez said. He thanked them for doing their part and said it was time for the country 'to move forward to a better future'.

Furthermore, he 'assumed the responsibility' for the actions of the breakaway Bolivarian Military Movement. It is difficult to over-state now how revolutionary that was at the time. In a profoundly corrupt and dysfunctional country, in which no politician had taken responsibility for anything in recent memory, including the hundreds of dead during the *Caracazo*, Venezuelans applauded Chávez for his unvarnished honesty.

Two words stuck out: 'for now'. They seemed to hint at an unfinished story and carry the promise of further action to come against the Pérez government. In fact, another coup attempt, a far bloodier one carried out by disaffected members of the air force and the navy, would take place in November of that same year.

Whether that 'for now' really was the cleft with the past the *Chavista* government would have people believe is debateable. Certainly, though, as Fernándo Ochoa Antich reflected, Chávez used the address to 'turn a military failure into a political success'. Hugo Chávez would come to understand something crucial from that moment: that unembellished, direct speech to the Venezuelan public was a uniquely powerful tool. That night it was the difference between success and failure. If television could save a presidency, Chávez reasoned, it was surely powerful enough to win him one, too.

It would be something he would have time to reflect on during the next two years in jail.

As Hugo Chávez sat in a bare cell in Yare prison, he thought of Mamá Rosa.

'She didn't like it one bit that I joined the military,' he recalled of his grandmother in 1998.[9] If Rosa Inés didn't approve that he was in the army, one can only imagine what she would have thought of him attempting a coup and ending up in Yare.

Yare prison is foul. Comprised of three buildings of dank, heavily overcrowded cells, it's a crumbling and inadequate institution which is essentially run by the inmates. Before being transferred there, the coup leaders spent a grim sixteen days in solitary confinement in the cells of the Directorate of Military Intelligence (DIM). Once in Yare, things eased a little with the conspirators given more space and food and allowed to receive visitors for long conversations about Venezuela's future. Chávez even conducted high-profile interviews from his cell within weeks of the insurrection. Years later, some compared the relative comfort of Hugo Chávez's jail conditions to those he granted his own political prisoners, in particular to his one-time defence minister and founding member of the MBR-200, Raúl Baduel, or the opposition leader, Leopoldo López. Both men were imprisoned on charges (drug trafficking and incitement to violence respectively) their families and supporters say were spurious, spent long spells in solitary confinement and were repeatedly denied basic prisoner rights.

Chávez perhaps learned something about keeping serious opponents behind bars from his own release. Like Fidel Castro in Cuba in 1953, his period of incarceration for attempting a coup was mercifully short, lasting just two years before clemency and early release – a critical error of underestimation that allowed both men to rise to prominence. How their opponents must wish they'd been forced to spend the rest of their days in jail! Certainly, they weren't going to make the same mistake themselves with any potential threat, large or small, condemning key critics to long prison sentences and either forcing them into exile or making them serve every single day in harsh conditions.

As for Chávez's stint in prison, he busied himself with writing a paper about his vision for the country's future. It was called 'How to Leave the Maze'.

When he finally left the maze that was Yare, Hugo Chávez was greeted by his supporters like a returning hero. Dressed in a beige suit with a Chairman Mao collar known as a *liqui liqui*, he stood in sharp contrast to the soldier who'd delivered the infamous '*por ahora*' speech just two years and two months earlier. Slim, dashing, smiling and confident, it was Chávez the civilian who emerged from jail, supposedly now ready to take the democratic path to the presidency; to use the ballot, not the bullet.

In reality, he still wasn't entirely convinced that democracy could deliver him the keys to Miraflores and it would take some time and no little internal argument in his movement before he agreed to abandon further plans of armed uprising. Eventually, though, calmer heads in his inner circle prevailed and Chávez signed up as a candidate in the 1998 presidential election campaign. Notably, one of those most committed to staying the course with an armed revolution was a moustached former bus drivers' unionist, Nicolás Maduro.[10]

His spell in prison marked the start of both his popularity and his populism. He'd had time to write out his thoughts, to hone his media persona, to deliver interviews on radio, television and for the newspapers. Only two years had passed since the bungled coup. If his next attempt to take the presidency was not to end in similar ignominy, Chávez would need to present another face to the Venezuelan public than the coup-monger who drove a tank through the front door of Miraflores.

That's not to say that being a *caudillo* was necessarily a disadvantage in Venezuela. Far from it. The collective political memory is often short in Latin America and the romanticism of General Pérez Jiménez's time as a kind of golden era was already underway. However, Chávez wanted to take a wrecking ball to Venezuelan politics. He intended to destroy the entrenched and corrupt two-party system and grind the Pact of Punto Fijo into the dust. He'd made that abundantly clear in February 1992 and had reiterated it in every interview he'd given subsequently.

In order to achieve it, he would need to reach those parts of the electorate who had grave doubts about him. Revisiting his post-Yare media interviews today is fascinating. Sufficient time has passed – as indeed has Hugo Chávez – to give a proper perspective on what he said compared to where he ended up as a leader.

In them, he was quick to laud the then British prime minister Tony Blair and his centrist policies of the 'Third Way'. He likened himself to Blair as part of a 'young new leadership... that is rising up in the world' and spoke of the 'mutual respect' he had for President Bill Clinton (although baulked at using the word 'admire').[11] He held forth on Cuba and while reticent about openly attacking Fidel Castro, saying that Cuba's future was solely for the Cuban people to decide, he did say that he thought the island 'should march to a different tune, one of real democracy and equality'.[12] In a clip that opponents later tried to wield against him as evidence of his hypocrisy, Chávez even described Cuba as a 'dictatorship'.[13] If anything, though, it was simply part of his attempt to say whatever he thought the audience needed to hear to get elected.

The changes weren't just in toning down his message and making it more palatable to the middle classes. They extended to his personal life and public persona, too. His marriage of almost two decades with Nancy Colmenares ended abruptly, as did his extra-marital relationship with Herma Marksman. In their place stepped Marisabel Rodríguez Oropeza. A radio personality and journalist, the second wife was everything Chávez was not. Telegenic, blonde and blue-eyed, she had the effect of *suavizando* – smoothing out – the harder edges of his image. A westernized First Lady-in-waiting next to this dark-skinned, black-haired mestizo ex-soldier.

The evolution of Hugo Chávez could also be seen in the details. In those same interviews, campaigning on measured reforms and European-style Third Way Blairism, he wore shiny, tailored suits, crisp shirts and gaudy silk ties. He slipped out of military dress and comfortably into the uniform of a Latin American politician, asking to be entrusted with the country's coffers. 'A greeting to everyone in Miami,' he began one interview with a US-based channel in 1998, perhaps the last time he referred to the Venezuelan diaspora in Florida with anything but revulsion.

He travelled, too. As part of an international publicity campaign, he visited Europe and the UK but was denied a visa to the US. In Britain, he was hosted by Oxford University's Student Union and met well-placed members of Blair's government. Colleagues at the BBC World Service remember that he came by Bush House in search of radio airtime. In those days, Hugo Chávez was just a failed coup plotter and an outsider in the next Venezuelan presidential election. Hardly the burning interview of the day. But he was being touted as the dark horse in the race and he was keen to spread the word on the international media. As the leftist candidate arrived at the Spanish

American Service's newsroom that morning, he was at his charming best, Chávez the persuader rather than the pugilist. His low-key trip to the BBC radio studios in Aldwych was in stark contrast to the great lengths to which celebrity journalists would go to a few years later to secure a coveted one-to-one with him.

Gradually, though, his campaign was working. COPEI and Acción Democrática were rapidly losing ground. From languishing at around 7 per cent popularity when he started, Chávez was clearly the leading candidate heading into the final days of the campaign, well ahead of a Yale-educated economist, Henrique Salas Römer, and a former beauty queen, Irene Sáez.

He was being listened to by millions of voters who weren't prepared to reward either of the two main parties with another stint at the presidency. Chávez had an innate gift for describing exactly the kind of corruption and abuse that the large parts of the electorate were exhausted with. Venezuela was experiencing 'a process of political and moral degeneration,' he told viewers of a televised debate on Venevisión, and the time had come to bring it to an end.[14] 'This [vote] isn't just about the presidency or a change of government,' he insisted. 'The life of the nation is at play, the future of generations still to rise up.'

He tried to allay fears about his military past by quoting from a book with which he was fascinated at the time called *Path of the Warrior* by an Argentinean writer, Lucas Estrella Schultz: 'Warrior, after victory, sheath your sword because tomorrow there will be further battles to come.' To warm applause from the studio audience, he ended by avowing that 1999 would mark, 'my God help us, the first year of the new Venezuela, the first year of the Fifth Republic'. It was the kind of messianic message Venezuelans would later get used to. He'd managed to elevate the grubby and unsavoury task of voting in a Venezuelan presidential election to something akin to going to church. A kind of evangelical church with him as its pastor, Venezuela's televangelist-in-chief.

The election was held five days later. Chávez won by a landslide.

★

From the very start it was clear this wasn't going to be an ordinary presidency. His left hand on the 1961 constitution, his right hand raised, Chávez answered the president of the Congress in a crisp, baritone timbre. But he had a surprise for the gathered congressmen, visiting dignitaries and the audience at home.

'Do you swear before God and the Fatherland to loyally carry out the duties and responsibilities of the constitutional president of the Republic, and to fulfil the laws of the constitution and the Republic?' he was asked. Instead of simply answering 'I swear' as every president before him had, Chávez added his own twist.

'I swear before God, I swear before the Fatherland, I swear before my people, that on this moribund constitution...'

There was a sharp intake of breath and a loud ripple of disapproval from the deputies in the chamber. Moribund? Who did he think he was? But there was more.

'... I will complete and promote the necessary democratic transformations so that the new Republic has an adequate Magna Carta for these new times. I swear.'

The outgoing president and eighty-three-year-old architect of the Pact of Punto Fijo, Rafael Caldera, couldn't contain his disgust.[15] If they were abandoning protocol, then so would he. Rather than bestow the presidential sash on Chávez himself, as was tradition, he passed it to Luis Alfonso Dávila, head of the Congress, to do so instead.

Hugo Chávez stood impassively for his first national anthem as the country's leader, the *cañonazos* of a twenty-one-gun salute echoing outside. It had taken him seven years almost to the day to go from an unknown soldier with radical pretensions of power to wearing the presidential sash. It was already a rise of extraordinary speed, but, as he settled into his first speech as president, he was about to consolidate his remarkable ascent even further.

The next two hours were spent giving the deputies a flavour of Chávez's penchant for epic Castro-esque speeches. By his later standards, it was a quick run-through of his initial thoughts. Yet it still lasted two hours and quoted everyone from Walt Whitman to Pablo Neruda to Carl von Clausewitz.

In it, he unveiled his next surprise. He called for an extraordinary executive privilege known as the 'Habilitating Law' so that he could push ahead with a new Constituent Assembly to replace the current legislature which would then draft a new constitution. He hadn't been in the seat of power for an hour and already he wanted to bypass Congress and have the people vote for its removal.

'As I am committed to the people, I have decided to bring forward the signing of the decree to convoke a referendum. I'm not going to wait until 15 February as I'd said. No. This is a clamour that runs through the streets, a clamour of the people. So, within a few minutes in Miraflores, I will swear in the new Cabinet and immediately convoke the first Extraordinary Council of Ministers. And today, I will sign the presidential decree calling the Venezuelan people to a referendum.'

When the speech was over, he did exactly that. He left the ostentatious parliament building and returned to Miraflores on foot, striding several blocks thronged with thousands of his delirious supporters. At certain points the crowd formed such a bottleneck that Chávez could barely be distinguished within the mass of bodies and outstretched arms, his faithful hoping for a high five or, at the very least, to touch the hem of his garment. It must have been a nightmare for the new president's security detail, a momentary insight of what was to come. In a sense, that quick trot to the palace was an apt metaphor: this would be an accelerated, improvised and popular presidency in which Chávez would throw off the long-established norms and enact decrees of great consequence for Venezuela from inside Miraflores.

The first twelve months passed in an electoral blur.

On 25 April 1999, there was a referendum on convening a Constituent National Assembly. The 'Yes' vote won by a huge margin, over 80 per cent. Turnout was low with more than 60 per cent of the electorate abstaining. But it was another big victory for the Chávez agenda ensuring the two houses of Congress and Senate would be merged into a more malleable, single-chamber assembly.

On 25 July 1999, an election was held for the members of the new National Assembly. This was perhaps the biggest election win of Chávez's career. Of a total of 131 seats, all but six went to Chávez's Polo Patriótico party or its allies. There were angry complaints from his opponents about the methodology used to draw up the electoral map, known as El Kino, which was said to be unfairly weighted in Chávez's favour. None of those objections made the slightest difference. Even in the newspapers owned by Chávez's critics, all the headlines spoke of knockouts, home runs and other victorious sporting metaphors. Within just six months of coming to power, Chávez had laid waste to the opposition. They would take a decade to recover. Even the First Lady was now a member of parliament.

With the *Chavistas* now controlling parliament, they wrote up a new constitution. On 15 December, the final vote of the year was to replace the 1961 charter with a statute for the Chávez era. Among other things, it extended the presidential term from five years to six and centralized the power of the executive. Opponents insisted it was a power grab, but the socialist juggernaut had gathered such pace that few voters cared to listen to anyone on the sidelines calling for it to slow down.

Chávez won the referendum, naturally. Yet neither the result nor the new constitution mattered much that night. More than half the electorate never left their homes. A tropical downpour had begun earlier in the week and lasted for several days. The equivalent of the annual rainfall was dumped in a matter of hours especially in the coastal state of Vargas. The rainstorms in Venezuela have an almost biblical quality to them and feel potentially far more destructive than those in other countries. Even with a normal cloudburst, the water thunders down the hillsides in Caracas in great torrents, blocking storm drains and bringing the city's choking traffic to a standstill.

The 15 December 1999 wasn't a normal thunderstorm at all. In fact, it would become known as 'the day the mountain moved towards the sea'. The subsoil slickened by the days of torrential rain, a huge section of the ocean-facing side of the Ávila sheared off in a vast landslide of mud, boulders and tree trunks which tore its way down the mountainside and engulfed the communities below. Built in precarious conditions on alluvial fans, entire neighbourhoods vanished in an instant, their residents lost beneath the mud. The state of Vargas was devastated. The final number of dead was never fully established. The early estimates, including from the Red Cross, were between ten and thirty thousand. Years later, a more sober analysis put the death toll in the high hundreds or low thousands.[16] Undisputedly though, tens of thousands were left homeless.

It was Chávez's first real test as leader. Initially he froze, unable to calm the nation once the full scale of the tragedy was known. To begin with, he had to recover from a thoroughly misjudged decision to quote Simón Bolívar as the rain was still lashing down on Venezuela: 'If nature is against us, we will fight her and make her obey us.' Nineteenth-century concepts of dominating the natural world were no comfort to the families facing total ruin. Quickly, though, he stepped up to confront the chaos, and even thrived on co-ordinating the relief effort on the screens and behind the scenes. Coming so early in his mandate, the Vargas disaster would bring him to a decision that in some ways would define his presidency. Venezuela's armed forces and emergency services were ill-equipped for the scale of the disaster and, as they struggled to cope, the Pentagon offered aid in the form of helicopters and around 150 troops. Venezuela accepted, as part of the wider international relief effort.

Within days, questions began to turn to the destroyed port and rebuilding communication links in the state. It was clear it would take months and require billions of dollars in aid. The USS *Tortuga* was on route, bringing urgently needed earth-moving equipment, supplies and expertise from Norfolk, Virginia. Hugo Chávez had approved the plan and seemingly welcomed the assistance from the Clinton administration.

On 2 January, however, he abruptly changed his mind. Fidel had got to him.

In retrospect, it marked a crucial turning point for Chávez. When faced with the stark choice – Washington or Havana, Clinton or Castro – he chose Havana, obeyed Fidel. No matter that lives were in the balance, livelihoods had been lost and tens of thousands were in desperate need of emergency relief whatever its providence. Chávez had decided against letting US troops disembark onto Venezuelan soil. Fidel had convinced him it was a dry run for beach landings in Latin America and advised him to send them back.

This signalled where the Bolivarian Revolution's allegiance would thereon lie. Much to the fury of his defence minister and the Pentagon, the president's order was given, and the ship turned around. It wouldn't be the only time Fidel Castro would shape the course of Venezuela with a furtive late-night phone call.

Neither palace intrigue nor frayed international relations mattered to Olga Hedler, though. In her late teens, her family home in the district of Los Corales was swept away with several relatives still inside. She was one of the thousands from Vargas who took refuge anywhere they could in Caracas. President Chávez promised that everyone still homeless would be given a home by Christmas of the year 2000, that Vargas would rise from the mud. The majority of the homeless, Olga included, had resisted government efforts to relocate them in the interior of Venezuela, preferring instead to stay put and await some kind of reconstruction in Vargas. Around 13,000 new homes were delivered in the first year, not as gifts but at a cost of between $3,000 and $10,000 with preferential repayment rates. It was a decent start, but no way near enough to meet demand.[17]

Olga and her family missed out. Instead, they returned to Los Corales and began living in a mud-caked shell of what had once been someone's holiday villa. The supporting columns were cracked and the building was structurally unsound. There was no electricity or running water. It was a roof over their heads but little more.

By early 2005, thousands of Vargas victims still hadn't been rehoused. In his weekly TV show, *Aló Presidente*, Chávez acknowledged the extent of the problem and called on the gathered ministers to quicken the pace.

'Emergency is emergency,' he said. 'This must be fast. There can be no Saturdays or Sundays.' Three months later, Jesse Chacón, the then interior minister, unveiled Plan Vargas 2005, a multimillion-dollar investment programme to build ninety-four different housing and infrastructural projects over two years. They included the creation of self-contained satellite towns around the capital to house the homeless and simultaneously ease the pressure on Caracas. 12,700 homes were supposed to be completed with all of the amenities and services that the affected families would need to rebuild their lives.

The reality was despairingly, grindingly inevitable. By one local NGO's estimate, just 240 of those houses were finished by late 2016.[18] Billions of dollars in aid money and investment were siphoned off by ministries, managers and middlemen long before it reached the ravaged state of Vargas.

Throughout my time in Venezuela, I periodically met survivors of the disaster residing in abandoned buildings in Caracas. In December 2010, there was another period of heavy rain and flooding in the country and the government housed the evacuated families in a shopping mall, the Centro Comercial Sambil La Candelaria, that Chávez had expropriated. I sneaked past the military through a side entrance to interview the victims and, incredibly, found among them people who had never properly been rehoused after 1999.

In the pressure for living space in Caracas, hundreds of families set up home in a bizarre abandoned bank tower in the capital's business district. In late 2010, the community's nominal leader, Alexander 'el Niño' Daza, a former gang leader-turned-evangelical pastor, let me take a tour of the vertical shanty town they'd created. Known as the Tower of David, it was one of the riskiest and most makeshift spaces in which to improvise a home I have ever seen in Latin America. Sewerage water dripped directly into many of the brick shacks and residents walked up to the twenty-eighth floor with no railings. Mothers of small children lived in constant fear of their kids slipping through the gaping holes in the half-finished skyscraper and there were regular reports of people having fallen to their deaths. The Tower of David later gained international notoriety after it appeared as a set in an episode of the Showtime series *Homeland*. And even here, a trace of the Vargas mudslide lingered as several families in the abysmal and dangerous conditions hailed from the state and had lost everything in 1999.

By the time I met Olga Hedler she was a twenty-eight-year-old mother of four, her kids tramping barefoot and naked through puddles of fetid water in the cracked and broken skeleton of the abandoned villa in Los Corales, surrounded by clouds of mosquitos. She and her children shared the space with two other families. 'These pillars won't last much longer,' she said, all too aware that a downpour even half as bad as they had seen in December 1999 could condemn them to join her lost aunts and uncles under the mud.

Worse still, the environmental protections stipulated under Plan Vargas 2005 to provide a causeway for the excess river water and rain run-off, to help prevent a repeat of the tragedy, weren't carried out. Some communities just resorted to building further up the sides of the Ávila, a higgledy-piggledy collection of brick shacks creeping up the mountain and denuding the forest cover, the very act which contributed to the mudslide becoming so ferocious in the first place.

'It could happen again at any time,' Olga told me, glancing up at the Ávila.

There was a word Chávez used in his inaugural speech which shook his adversaries: revolution. Few had much of a concept of what kind of revolution it would be. Nor, it seemed, did Chávez. Nationalist, certainly, and left-wing. The term used most often by its leader was 'Bolivarian', whatever that meant.

Yet as he grew into his first term, Chávez began to show that he intended it to be genuinely revolutionary and not just business as usual by a group of people in government suddenly addressing each other as 'comrade'. As a candidate, he had paid a visit to Cuba to give a speech at the Casa de las Americas and was surprised to be received at the airport by Fidel Castro. For the ageing leader of the Cuban Revolution, there were few risks in extending a warm embrace to a recently released coup plotter. First, he had a profound dislike of the then Venezuelan president, Rafael Caldera. Anything to needle him in his last months in office was welcome as far as Fidel was concerned.

More importantly, however, on the off chance that this maverick former soldier might actually make it to Miraflores, he could be the answer to many of Cuba's headaches. The island was languishing economically under what became euphemistically known as the 'Special Period', a decade of deep austerity characterized by shortages, rationing and blackouts following the collapse of the Soviet Bloc.

The past ten years had been grim for Cubans. The tales of desperation are legion with the island experiencing a drop in around a third of its GDP and as much as 80 per cent of its exports. Life for families grew increasingly tough, with people eating whatever they could get their hands on – reportedly even stray cats and dogs. With no Soviet Union to supply Cuba's energy needs, after the fall of the Berlin Wall oil imports plummeted. Cars were abandoned in favour of bikes, scarce public transport or walking. Often the lights in Havana were out for longer than they were on. In the provinces, it was even worse.

Enter Hugo Chávez (stage left). Fidel had had designs on Venezuela for decades. The idea of a genuine left-wing ally in an oil-rich Latin American neighbour was beyond appealing, it was urgent. He reasoned that if Chávez did somehow win, the best idea would be to begin grooming him early. The charm offensive started on the airport's tarmac.

It worked. Hugo Chávez was smitten by the communist icon whose tales of heroism he had first heard sitting at the feet of the former guerrilla José Esteban Ruiz-Guevara in Barinas. It was the beginning of a personal bond which would only be broken by death and the thoroughly unlikely prospect that the then septuagenarian Fidel would outlive his youthful disciple.

Fidel was present at Hugo Chávez's unconventional inauguration, another moment which added to the nervousness of the outgoing administration. However, it was his return in October 2000 which cemented the relationship. Fidel Castro spent five days in Venezuela, never leaving Chávez's side. The two men visited Sabaneta, went to the world's highest waterfall, Angel Falls, spoke to peasant farmers, took part in a Cuba–Venezuela exhibition baseball match. Everywhere crowds appeared chanting for Castro and Chávez, the first comrades of a new leftist brotherhood they insisted was coming in Latin America.

'I'm convinced that a true democracy can happen, true freedoms,' Fidel told throngs of adoring supporters in Chávez's hometown. He vouched for and blessed Chávez at every opportunity, and bestowed on him the legitimacy of his decades at the helm of a leftist revolutionary movement. Chávez responded by promising to 'give oxygen to Cuba'.

It was the words spoken away from the cameras that mattered most, however. The leaders reached an agreement for Venezuela to send 100,000 barrels of oil a day to Cuba in exchange for goods and services. In effect, that meant the communist-run island would pay for the much-needed oil with tens of thousands of healthcare professionals, agricultural workers and teachers. Oil-for-doctors, as it became known, was the backbone of Chávez's healthcare reforms, his education programmes and his social 'missions' in the poorest neighbourhoods.

The medical missions saw Cuban doctors thrust into the shanty towns where they set up small clinics to deal with the day-to-day healthcare issues of the community for free. Millions benefited from the primary attention and there were plans to extend the Cuban programmes to offer more complex procedures and treatments in the future. The Venezuelan Medical Federation was up in arms about the arrangement, but Chávez couldn't care less. He was giving free medical treatment to the poorest who were in dire need of it and hugely grateful.

For Cuba, it was a lifesaver. Chávez emerged when the island most needed the help. Unlike in the rest of the region over the past four decades, he was a leader who didn't think twice about tightening the ties with the brother nation of Cuba, even in the face of outcry at home and in Washington. In fact, probably *because* of it. Alongside the doctors and nurses came thousands of Cuban intelligence agents and military advisers. It was always the murkiest part of the arrangement, left deliberately unclear as to how many arrived in Venezuela or what their exact roles were behind the scenes at the ministries and in the barracks. In time, though, it would become evident that they were ultimately more important than the healthcare workers, a linchpin in maintaining Chávez and his hand-picked successor in power and, by extension, keeping the oil flowing to the last bastion of communism in the Western Hemisphere.

Venezuela and Cuba were swimming together 'in the same sea of happiness', Chávez said.

It was the first time I'd been late for work in the new job. The phones were already ringing incessantly following a chaotic twenty-four hours in Caracas.

'Sorry I'm late,' I mumbled, taking off my jacket. 'Delays on the underground.'

'You haven't missed much,' a producer answered sarcastically, barely looking up from the reel-to-reel tape machine. 'Chávez has just resigned is all.'

On 11 April 2002 I'd been working at the BBC World Service for about six months. After completing a master's degree in London, I'd managed to land a job making radio in Spanish for Latin American audiences, ideal for someone with hopes of one day becoming a foreign correspondent. It was my first real job in journalism and I was thrilled – especially as everyone had told me to expect to spend years working my way up from a local newspaper or radio station before getting the chance to walk the hallowed halls of Bush House, the glorious 1930s home of the BBC's international radio output.

Exactly what happened that day in April 2002 – how a demonstration turned into a coup, how people were killed in the streets and how the controversial, charismatic figure of Chávez was escorted out of the presidential palace in military custody – have been pored over in painstaking detail ever since.[19] Still, with no Chávez in *Chavismo* any longer, it's worth revisiting the pivotal moment for him and his revolution, and the impact of those few hours he wasn't at the helm in Venezuela.

Whether one thinks it was a carefully prepared operation devised in Washington or a moment of spontaneity which escalated into an opportunistic putsch – or perhaps some combination of the two – matters little now. It has passed into Latin American folklore as another bloodstained episode in Venezuela's seemingly eternal struggle for the throne.

One thing is for sure, though: it was the moment Chávez's anti-Americanism became etched in stone. And it made him more determined than ever to crush his opponents who owned the country's private media.

It might have come as a surprise to many international audiences when Chávez was suddenly removed from office amid pitched street battles. Perhaps all they had heard of him up to that point was that he was 'using the country's oil wealth to tackle poverty', as the lazy shorthand version of his first few years in office often went in the more sympathetic sections of the foreign media. But the tensions leading up to that day had been building for some time. There are reports that Venezuela's opposition had been openly talking of a coup, even plotting one in meetings in Caracas and Washington, in late 2001. The events of September 11 2001 had drastically changed the outlook for the Bush administration towards both its allies and its opponents in the region. A zero-sum question of 'with us or against us?' was being pronounced by Washington in the wake of the 9/11 terrorist attacks and President George W. Bush and the State Department weren't much in the mood for any nuance or tolerance. Opposition to US strategic interests in Latin America, such as Chávez had already repeatedly displayed, would not be given a chance to prosper. One only need look at the names advising President Bush at the time to see the hawkish nature of his foreign policy team.

These included John Negroponte, a former ambassador in Central America during the Reagan administration, promoted to US ambassador to the United Nations. Meanwhile, the State Department's top job on Latin America – Assistant Secretary of State for Western Hemispheric Affairs – went to Otto Reich. Born in Havana, Reich was a staunchly anti-Castro voice in the State Department. He'd risen through the diplomatic corps to become the US ambassador to Venezuela under Bush's father, having first made his name under

Ronald Reagan directing the Office for Public Diplomacy's propaganda campaign against left-wing guerrillas in Nicaragua. He was named on the fringes of the Iran-Contra affair albeit with no charges ultimately brought against him.

Lastly, there was Elliott Abrams. Controversial doesn't begin to describe Abrams' career. If Otto Reich was at the outer edges of the Iran-Contra investigation, Abrams was near its heart. His repeated denials to Congress of US involvement in arming right-wing Nicaraguan paramilitaries – despite having direct knowledge of the programme – led to him being found guilty on two misdemeanour charges of withholding information. He was later pardoned by George H. W. Bush. Recently, in an extraordinary twist in the career of a much-reviled figure, Abrams was put in charge of Venezuela policy by President Trump to direct efforts to squeeze Nicolás Maduro from power and help install opposition leader Juan Guaidó in Miraflores.

With that kind of line-up, the chances are that if certain people in Washington had known about a planned coup against Chávez, at the very least they would have done little to discourage it. Yet despite the desire among *Chavistas* to find the smoking gun of prior knowledge in the United States, the extraordinary events of April 2002 were primarily Venezuelan in their conception and execution. It was a homemade mess.

By the end of March, emotions about Chávez were bubbling over. There had already been a national strike in December and battle lines were being drawn over everything from the 'Cubanization' of children's textbooks to the names on the board at the state-owned energy company Petróleos de Venezuela SA, or PDVSA. Under the 'Enabling Law' that Chávez had been granted by the National Assembly, he passed a series of laws by presidential decree. Among them was the right to change the makeup of public ministries and the oil industry at will, without any recourse to parliament.

On 7 April, Chávez presented his regular Sunday edition of *Aló Presidente* from Miraflores. Gradually, he whipped himself and the cheering crowd into a frenzy. It was a lie that PDVSA was a meritocracy, he told them. Rather it was a 'myth-ocracy', built on the myths and lies spun by the oil industry's leadership that they alone should control the energy sector. Well, he was about to change all that.

'Those elites have crossed the line,' he said, stabbing a line in the air with his finger. 'They have turned into saboteurs of a company which belongs to all the Venezuelan people. What do they say in football? They're "offside",' pronouncing the word in heavily accented English.

'Can someone find me a whistle?' One was conjured up. Peeeep! he tooted. 'Offside!'

'So, I announce I'm firing the following people. Enough is enough! Eddy Ramírez, Director General until today of Palmaven [a PDVSA filial company]. Out! Eddy Ramírez, thank you very much for your service, you're fired, sir.'

The crowd loved it! Live firings of anti-revolutionaries. They finally had them against the wall. The original 'You're fired' catchphrase, long before Donald Trump ever uttered it. Hugo Chávez continued.

Peeeeep! 'Also fired, and many thanks for your service, Mr Juan Fernández. You're fired from PDVSA. You were the Manager of Planning and Finance Control. Until today.'

The whistleblowing cull went on until seven top executives had been fired from PDVSA and another twelve forced into retirement. For some in the military watching on, the one who was 'offside' was Chávez. Already furious about the growing influence of the Cuban military and Fidel Castro over their work, several career soldiers had lost faith with their commander-in-chief over the promotion of former guerrillas into positions of power and an increasing closeness to the Colombian left-wing rebel group, the FARC.

This latest humiliation on television of established oil industry leaders being replaced with Chávez stooges was a step too far for some generals and commanders. Crucially, however, plenty of others in uniform, including many rank-and-file troops, remained loyal to Chávez.

By the time the morning of 11 April came around, the sporadic protests and trade union strikes that had been held for weeks coalesced into a single moment, a vast anti-Chávez march in Caracas. The opposition said they had mobilized a million people. Starting outside a park in the east of Caracas, hundreds of thousands headed towards the offices of PDVSA.

This is where things get hazy. Once at the PDVSA headquarters, a decision was taken to push on to Miraflores to demand that Chávez step down. Some claim it was a spontaneous and organic response springing from the febrile mood on the streets. Others argue that was always the intention and, at least when it comes to the protest leaders, they may well be right. It does seem clear that there was some kind of plan in place, from at least the night before, to reroute the march to Miraflores as the opposition engaged in a dangerous game of brinkmanship with Chávez.

Similarly, though, the intelligence services probably knew of the plan and did nothing to stop it. There was no effort to prevent the detour or stop the demonstration from reaching Baralt Avenue, about a block from Miraflores. In such an atmosphere, confrontation was inevitable and was being stoked by actors on both sides.

When it came, it was brutal. In Baralt Avenue, the protesters edged closer and closer to the presidential palace, led by a line of Metropolitan Police under orders from the opposition Mayor of Caracas. On the other side were the National Guard and pro-Chávez radicals – the Bolivarian Circles – who had mobilized to defend the palace. Tear gas canisters were fired by the National Guard to turn the marchers back. Before long, though, much more than tear gas was being fired. TV crews filmed pictures which showed armed *Chavistas*, including at least one elected official, on the Llaguno Overpass which ran above Baralt Avenue, firing handguns down onto the street below.

Again, the details at this point are hazy and the moment is open to interpretation depending on one's politics.[20] What's clear is that over the course of the tumultuous day at least nineteen people died and close to 150 were wounded. There were casualties on both sides, though the majority were opposition marchers with several apparently hit by sniper fire coming from the surrounding rooftops and balconies. Among them was photojournalist Jorge Tortoza, who can be seen in television footage crumpling to a heap on the ground as a direct headshot from a high-powered rifle pierced his skull. National

Guardsmen and Chávez supporters were also killed and injured and were rushed to a field hospital set up outside Miraflores.

In Miraflores itself, Chávez was torn about how to react. The decision he ultimately reached showed beyond any doubt that he possessed a ruthless, authoritarian streak of which Fidel Castro would have been proud. Echoes of Marcos Pérez Jiménez himself, even. He ordered Plan Ávila.

Plan Ávila had only been implemented once before, with terrible consequences: the *Caracazo*. An emergency power in times of civil disturbance, it authorized the use of deadly military force to restore public order, and rode roughshod over the human rights of anyone in its path. As 1989 had proved, it was a licence to shoot first, and never be asked questions later. A licence to a bloodbath. So much so that it had been expressly banned under the 1999 constitution. Yet Chávez ordered it anyway. What then, of Bolívar's line 'Damned is the soldier' that he was so fond of quoting? Or of the *Caracazo* as the entire moral basis for his own coup attempt in 1992 and subsequent political movement? When it came down to it, Hugo Chávez was just as prepared as Carlos Andrés Pérez to issue the fateful order.

Conscious of being stained with the blood of unarmed political demonstrators, and of perhaps having to answer for it some day in an international criminal court, the general responsible for carrying it out, Major General Manuel Rosendo, baulked. In fact, he flatly refused.

That act of sedition was the start of Chávez's downfall. Once he'd lost the military, he lost the presidency. It would be the key lesson he took from 11 April 2002. His eventual successor, Nicolás Maduro, who'd been present throughout the day's violent proceedings, learned it, too.

Denied the strong arm of the army, Chávez turned to his other saviour in times of crisis: television. He ordered a *cadena*, literally translated as a 'chain', under which the president could interrupt programming on all domestic channels to make a national address. In previous governments, it was a device reserved for major emergencies. Chávez had started using them at every available opportunity from unveiling bridges to visiting dairy farms. In the middle of watching a movie or a baseball game, suddenly the unmistakable logo of a galloping horse would appear, announcing that the airwaves had been yet again sequestered by Chávez. Depending on one's allegiance, viewers at home would either applaud with glee and turn the volume up or curse at the TV and find something else to do for the next three hours.

This time, though, it actually *was* a national emergency.

'We're here in the Palace of Miraflores. It is, by my watch, 3.45 in the afternoon,' he began, looking distinctly shaken. He insisted that there was 'normality in almost all of the national territory' and that just 'a minority who don't want to accept reality' were on the streets of Caracas. He urged people to remain calm.

However, as the clashes continued to escalate, several private television channels took a decision which set them on a course of bitter conflict with Chávez for years to come. They split their screens in two to show his address in one window and the street violence in the other. It had the effect of making the president look completely out of touch with the reality taking place around him. Outside the palace, plumes of tear gas and protesters scattering from an authoritarian crackdown. Inside it, the president at a desk quoting nineteenth-century poetry, drinking coffee, fiddling while Caracas burned.

He would never forgive them for it. If his relationship with the private media was already frayed, this set the tone of open hostility which he would maintain for the rest of his life. Chávez would take his revenge against more than one channel before his death.

His broadcast was over by around 5.30 p.m. In a symbolic gesture, he changed from his suit into military fatigues but on this occasion the uniform would not save him. As the deaths stacked up, the military high command who remained loyal to Chávez began to turn. The stress inside Miraflores was palpable. Chávez called his inner circle into a meeting to hear their thoughts before asking them to leave so he could reflect on his next move. One of them, the education minister Hector Navarro, recalls seeing as he walked out that Chávez had a handgun by his thigh and, once they'd left the room, he braced himself for a single gunshot from inside.

It wouldn't come. Sitting alone in his office, weighing his options, Chávez instead picked up the telephone and spoke to the one person whose advice he valued above all others: Fidel Castro. By all accounts, his trusted Cuban ally urged him not to 'immolate' himself. 'Save your people and save yourself, do what you have to do, negotiate with dignity,' said Castro. 'This won't end here.' The wily elder statesman of Latin American leftists wasn't wrong.

Months later, a controversial documentary, *The Revolution Will Not Be Televised*, by Irish filmmakers Kim Bartley and Donnacha Ó Briain, would be instrumental in shaping international opinion on the events of these chaotic two days. Broadcast on the BBC and Ireland's RTÉ, the film went on to win several awards but was also accused of being riddled with inconsistencies and of manipulating the chronology of the footage so that the confusing reality fit a staunchly pro-Chávez narrative. To this day, it is often quoted by supporters of the Venezuelan government as proof of a CIA plot or that the *Chavista* gunmen on the Llaguno Overpass were victims, not aggressors. Still, partisan though it is, the one thing the film did provide was unique access inside Miraflores and a glimpse of the high drama unfolding that night. Few moments were as tense as the military command arriving to demand the president's resignation.

From here, the rest of this story is well known. Chávez eventually succumbed to the pressure, which had allegedly ramped up to threats of airstrikes on Miraflores unless he stood down, and agreed to leave Miraflores for Fuerte Tiuna military base in custody. However, with Fidel's words still ringing in his ears, he didn't resign – at least, not as far as he and his cabinet were concerned. The military saw things differently. It fell to a high-ranking officer considered sympathetic to Chávez, General Lucas Rincón Romero, to tell an expectant, nervous nation that this extraordinary two-year experiment with a former coup leader in the presidential palace was over.

At almost 3 a.m., after Venezuela's bloodiest and most emotionally charged day since the *Caracazo*, General Rincón read a televised statement which stated, in suitably oblique language, that 'the president of the Republic was asked to resign his post, which he accepted'.

Chávez was later transferred to La Orchila, a military installation on a tiny island off the Venezuelan coast to be held while plans were made to allow him to travel to Cuba. Chávez often said he feared he would be plunged into the sea on the short helicopter ride out to La Orchila. It seems that if killing him was ever part of the plan, that was the moment.

As I made up for my late start in London that morning, Venezuelans awoke to huge uncertainty. Within hours, it was compounded by the ridiculous sight of the head of the opposition-led business federation, Pedro Carmona, swearing himself in as president. 'Pedro the Brief' as Chávez would later mockingly dub him, his name a synonym for usurpation and unconstitutionality. In a collective rush of blood to the opposition's heads, Carmona proceeded to arbitrarily wind up all the democratic institutions and appointments established under Chávez from the National Assembly to the Supreme Court, from the attorney general to the Electoral Council. Each announcement was greeted with huge cheers and whoops of victory from opposition figures in the room, giddy and drunk on power. Several military men were already feeling doubtful about where things were heading, among them General Lucas Rincón.

Other soldiers had stayed loyal to Chávez throughout. They included a young cadet at the Turiamo naval base, who fished out a note that Chávez had left for him in the bin before being taken to La Orchila, denying to the world that he had resigned. The note and its potentially explosive contents quickly made its way onto CNN. Chávez's wife, Marisabel Rodríguez, and his brutish vice-president, Diosdado Cabello – at that moment in hiding – were also getting the message out via the international media: Chávez had never stepped down. Unsurprisingly, private media channels in Venezuela opted to ignore those particularly crucial bits of information and broadcast cartoons and old movies instead.

The streets began to fill with angry and emboldened *Chavistas* demanding their leader be reinstated to his rightful place in Mira-flores immediately: *¡Queremos a Chávez!* they sang, 'We want Chávez!' They appeared in their thousands outside Miraflores and outside the state television channel, now theoretically in the hands of the opposition. The botched response from a hastily cobbled-together administration was further repression. Elsewhere, a rumour circulated that Vice-President Cabello was taking refuge in the Cuban Embassy in the Chuao district of Caracas and it was quickly surrounded by an angry mob of anti-*Chavistas*, the diplomats and employees trapped inside facing the real possibility of being harmed. The head of the Fourth Parachutists' Brigade and co-founder of the MVR-200, General Raúl Baduel, had had enough and began organizing a rescue mission to return his *Comandante* to power. Four helicopters headed out to La Orchila. As the heat rose, and the inevitable end became clearer to them, the coup leaders vanished from Miraflores and dissolved into Caracas, their brief moment in the sun over almost as quickly as it had begun.

When the helicopter carrying Chávez arrived back at Miraflores, it was greeted by an adoring, tearful crowd. He emerged, emotional and drenched in sweat, swept along on a wave of euphoria and vindication. 'He's back! He's back!' chanted the supporters at the gates. And from this night onwards he wouldn't be budged by anyone for the rest of his life. Once into some fresh clothes and in his seat in the presidential palace, Chávez wasted no time getting back on television. He wanted to reassure his followers that the moment had passed, and warn his opponents that he had survived it. 'The people arrived at this palace to never leave it,' he told the nation. Yet at times he also struck a conciliatory tone, promising to rein in some of his excesses, absorb the criticism and learn from the time he was out of office – all forty-seven hours of it.

He did learn, of course. But not in ways that the opposition wanted. He learned that military might was key to his continued survival and to that of the Bolivarian Revolution. Scores of mid-ranking soldiers were promoted, many to the rank of general. Within ten years, in fact, there were upwards of a thousand generals which lessened the likelihood of any one of them acting alone without being identified as a plotter by the rest of the top brass or Cuban spies strategically placed inside the barracks. Luis Herrera Ramírez, the young guard who had plucked out Chávez's note from the wastepaper bin and got it to CNN, was fêted by Chávez on live television as a model soldier. Army wages were regularly increased over the remainder of his reign in an effort to build up a loyal military class and the Cubans went on to play a key role in flushing out any dissent. Meanwhile, 13 April, the date of his reinstatement to Miraflores, was declared 'Day of National Dignity'.

He also learned that Washington was his bitterest enemy and Cuba, specifically Fidel Castro, his closest friend. The State Department and the White House had recognized Pedro Carmona with undignified speed and the US ambassador held talks with him during his fleeting self-declared presidency. The bilateral relationship, which was hardly healthy before April 2002, would never recover.

He learned that the privately owned television channels were traitors, and should either be turned over to *Chavismo* or turned off. Within a few years, he removed the licence of one of the country's oldest broadcasters, RCTV, which had split the screen during his 11 April *cadena*. Other channels were subjected to a different fate but would ultimately be silenced, too.

Mostly, of course, he learned he was more powerful and more popular than ever. Within the year, he would ride out another attempt to force him from office, this time via a three-month-long oil strike. When that also failed, he began to feel untouchable. He started to wield his power more ruthlessly against his enemies, beginning with the very people who had shut down PDVSA for weeks on end. Around half of the highly trained workforce was eventually dismissed. A new company would be created in its place, one that was '*rojo rojito*' as his energy minister, Rafael Ramírez, put it at the time, best translated as 'red through and through'. If the 2002 coup taught Chávez the importance of a loyalist military, the 2003 oil strike showed him the importance of a loyalist PDVSA.

In fact, after April 2002, loyalty was the only trait which really mattered to Chávez, far more than technical capacity, efficiency or transparency. A former presidential bodyguard with no background at all in finance or fiscal responsibility? No matter. You're now the National Treasurer with control over access to the Central Bank's foreign exchange reserves. If only that comment were an exaggeration. Chávez's friend and member of his security detail, Alejandro Andrade, was promoted to exactly that role. The *Comandante* had always felt guilty for having accidentally blinded Andrade in one eye during a game of *chapitas*, a form of baseball played with a beer bottle top instead of a ball. When 'One Eye' Andrade, as he was inevitably nicknamed, was eventually charged with money laundering in the United States in 2017, he owned dozens of racehorses, expensive cars, a luxurious property in Wellington, south Florida, and a $10 million Learjet registered in Delaware. Before he was sentenced to ten years in a federal penitentiary in Pennsylvania, Andrade confessed to US prosecutors that he'd taken more than a billion dollars in bribes over the course of just four years in the job. A billion dollars. By just one functionary. The loyalty over suitability equation was incredibly lucrative for certain well-placed *Chavista* officials.

Some suggest that Chávez always wanted the April conflict, indeed was looking for it. Certainly, he did little to harm that theory, in particular when he addressed Congress on the matter five years later, in 2007: 'What happened with PDVSA was necessary. It's not that we didn't generate it. We generated it. Because when I blew that whistle on *Aló Presidente* and began to sack people, I was provoking the crisis. When I named [my allies as] the president and the board, we were provoking a crisis. The opposition reacted as they did, and this is where we are today.'

To live in Venezuela in 2007 was to be in the presence of Hugo Chávez. Between wall-to-wall coverage on state TV and the scores of daily *cadenas*, he was absolutely everywhere, all of the time.

His appearances would oscillate from the jovial to the furious. Like an unpredictable father with a short temper, it simply depended what mood you caught him in. He could be genuinely funny or he could be in the blackest of moods, railing at the inefficiencies in his cabinet or the conspiracies lined up against him by the Americans. When he was at his upbeat, self-deprecating best, it was a little like watching a stand-up comedian in full flow. On one edition of *Aló Presidente* he described being trapped inside a half-finished motorway tunnel he was inspecting during a presidential visit to the provinces with a bad case of diarrhoea.

'Imagine being stuck, halfway in, halfway out, with those "physio-logical conditions", on live TV! Poor Chávez!' he roared with laughter, his devoted audience wiping tears of mirth from their eyes at their down-to-earth working man's president, the kind of guy who told bar stories about needing to take a shit at work. He made it look effortless and, unlike for most other politicians, it probably was – especially when connecting to Latin Americans from low-income neighbour-hoods or poorer socio-economic backgrounds.

In other moments, Chávez's television persona was far less jolly. He could be irate, unreasonable and foul-tempered, never more so than when discussing the 'imperialists' in Europe and Washington and what he saw as their interference in Venezuela's affairs. He told the German Chancellor, Angela Merkel, to 'back off, Mrs Chancellor. I won't say any more because she's a lady, just that: back off', over her comments that other governments in Latin America should dis-tance themselves from him. He habitually railed at 'damned' Israel, 'colonialist' Spain and 'fascist' Colombia. Pope Benedict was 'no ambassador of God on Earth, as they claim, for God's sake', he said. Christ didn't need an intermediary, he told the audience, as He lived in *el pueblo*.

In April 2010, I was on the receiving end of a Chávez tirade about the United Kingdom. In a joint press conference with President Putin during a visit to Caracas, I asked him how he thought the Obama White House would react to the multimillion-dollar oil and arms contracts the two men had signed. He visibly bristled.

'You're British, right?' he asked me instead of answering.

'Yes, Mr President,' I replied.

'But you live here in Caracas, correct?'

'Yes, sir.'

'Well, before we go any further: *¡Malvinas Argentinas!*,' he yelled to applause from the Venezuelan and Russian dignitaries in the room.

It was quite a surprise to hear the Falkland Islands/Islas Malvinas conflict brought up so tangentially in a question about Venezuelan arms purchases from Moscow but that was how he operated. 'Go ask your Queen how many jets and tanks she owns,' was his answer, urging me to find out from London before he would deem to answer any British reporter's questions about Sukhoi fighter jets and Kalashnikov rifles.

Naturally, though, his real cannon fire was saved for Washington. Whenever he was in doubt, he returned to the most trusted implement in his rhetorical toolbox: anti-Americanism. It wasn't difficult during George W. Bush's presidency, a man universally loathed in Latin America. Chávez dubbed him 'Mr Danger' over the wars in Iraq and Afghanistan: 'You are a donkey, Mr Danger,' he said on *Aló Presidente*, before repeating it 'in my bad English' so that the president might hear the insults in his own tongue. 'Coward, murderer, genocidal, alcoholic, drunk. You're the worst this planet has ever seen.' And so it continued for several minutes. President Obama posed a different challenge. He was young, black and progressive. Yet Chávez soon disassociated the man from the office of president – I'm sure Obama himself is a decent man, he said after he was elected, but the 'empire' is greater than him. Before long, that too descended into insults. Using scatological Venezuelan colloquial slang, he told Obama to '*vaya a lavarse ese paltó*'. At one deafening rally, he summarized his feelings towards all of Washington, shouting '*vayanse al carajo, Yanquis de mierda*', most politely translated as telling the Yankees to go to hell.

It was always a show, there was always a headline. The news agencies had to start picking only the most colourful and important comments from his broadcasts and simply stopped filing on the smaller incidents, they were so frequent. He was supposedly the subject of constant attacks, assassination plots and diabolical conspiracies by the imperialists hell-bent on removing him from the equation to take Venezuela's oil. Everything was set up as a David versus Goliath battle, with himself cast as the brave shepherd armed only with a slingshot.

In reality, he had a far greater armoury at his disposal – in the military and the judiciary, from the legislature to the streets. I was in the country when RCTV, his screen-splitting nemesis during the April 2002 coup, came off air. A crowd had gathered outside the station's headquarters to sing the national anthem, as it closed down for a final time, into a warm, moonlit sky. I weaved between them, recording their voices for a radio package, some bellowing out the lyrics in a kind of defiant chant, others singing through the tears, wiping their eyes in a melancholy lament. It struck me as an odd reaction to cry for a TV station best known for its melodramatic soap operas. But it quickly became clear they weren't mourning RCTV at all, rather the loss of a Venezuela they still recognized.

Right on cue, as the final strains of the anthem faded and the channel turned to bars and tone, radicals from the Bolivarian Circles came around the corner on motorbikes shooting in the air. The crowd scattered and I had a timely reminder, a few months before I moved to Caracas, of just how polarized the country had become, of how an argument over an expiring broadcasting licence could end in gunfire and panic.

For years, the private media outlets were essentially as Chávez had described them: run by a wealthy and powerful elite who enjoyed extensive control over public opinion and message delivery in Venezuela. After 2002, though, Chávez began to dominate the airwaves and rein in the newspapers. Some stations, like the Cisneros family's Venevisión, agreed to water down their anti-Chávez agenda to the point of complete dilution in exchange for the quiet life. Others, most noticeably the TV news network Globovisión, were eventually bought up in murky deals by Chávez sympathizers and strawmen and were turned into toothless, anodyne media outlets which posed no threat. At the same time, he created a network of local, national and even international pro-government programming from indigenous radio stations to the continent-wide Spanish-language network, Telesur.

By the time Nicolás Maduro was president, the media landscape in Venezuela was unrecognizable. At the height of his own constitutional crisis in 2019, one could flick through the domestic TV stations and find nothing but partisan news reports extolling the government's democratic credentials or pure fluff shows on pop singers and models. Extraordinarily, radio stations were even banned from mentioning Juan Guaidó's name, the head of the National Assembly who'd declared himself president and been recognized as such by more than fifty nations including the US.

Watching Maduro speak on the state channel VTV, I remembered a phone conversation I had with him following one of Chávez's most iconic moments. At the United Nations General Assembly in September 2006, Chávez entertained his natural showman on the world stage. A day earlier President Bush had delivered his speech from the same podium. It was a list of warnings and thinly veiled threats directed at Iran and Palestine, from Hezbollah to Hamas. 'Freedom, by its nature, cannot be imposed. It must be chosen,' he concluded, speaking at the height of the wars in the Middle East.

It set Chávez up perfectly. He gave a speech that was designed to infuriate and titillate in equal measure: 'Yesterday, the devil came here. Right here. And it still smells of sulphur today,' he told the packed chamber, to audible gasps and laughs of disbelief. Many delegates were delighted by his outrageous behaviour, maybe wishing they'd have dared say such things themselves. Chávez's words, as was no doubt always the plan, made headlines around the world.

That evening, I spoke to his foreign minister, Nicolás Maduro, who had accompanied him on the trip to New York. It was a long, meandering conversation, full of generic references to US imperialism and Yankee interference in Latin America and around the world. At the end, I asked him whether as foreign minister he would try to temper the president's comments or use more measured, diplomatic language than calling Bush 'the devil': 'Quite the contrary,' he replied. 'Comandante Chávez was right and is still right. Bush IS the devil. The devil-incarnate.'

That was the thing about Maduro: he had perhaps the easiest job in the government and he seemed to revel in it. His role was to travel the world and echo what Hugo Chávez had already said. It was a job which suited him and which he was actually pretty good at. He cut an affable figure, belly-laughing at Chávez's jokes and apparently happy where he was, acutely aware of his own political limitations.

★

The heat was stifling. Some had fainted as they waited in line and been ushered to the shade of a nearby tree. Oranges were being dished out and bottles of water. Troops marshalled the line but there was nothing for them to be wary of, no sign of anything except grief.

Every few moments, in a different section of the queue, someone would shout out '¡*Que viva Chávez!*' or '*Chávez vive, la lucha sigue*' meaning 'Chávez lives, the struggle continues' or some other hollow slogan. Music, soft by Venezuelan standards, was a constant background noise. There were the same revolutionary rap and salsa songs, combined with the dull hum of a dozen generators, which had been the soundtrack to every Chávez rally I had attended over the past seven years.

Yet this was no rally. Hugo Chávez was lying in state inside the Fuerte Tiuna military base and thousands of his supporters were queuing to catch a final glimpse of him.

Javier Castro was among them. I'd first met him a couple of months earlier in the car park of a state-run supermarket chain in the grimy, violent neighbourhood of El Paraiso, paradoxically meaning Paradise, in western Caracas. Javier was small and wiry and spoke with the rapid-fire intensity of a former drug addict-turned-born-again Christian. When he smiled, he revealed a chipped front tooth, the only outward sign of his shady past. We followed him on his motorbike to a half-finished socialist housing complex in nearby Montalbán. There had been grand plans to build two million homes within seven years in Venezuela. Forests of modern tower blocks and high-rise buildings shot up, providing tens of thousands of apartments, supposedly to be followed by vital neighbourhood amenities like subsidized shops and sports facilities.

Live on national television, Chávez had announced that by 2019 every single family in the country would have a 'dignified home'.[21] He called it 'the Great Venezuelan Housing Mission'.

'Today we're giving out across the country 1,704 new homes,' he said at one event. 'That brings us so far this year to 137,106 homes. Dignified, lovely and beautiful homes for our people.'

The reality in Javier's building complex was already much sadder. The construction had gone up quickly, then inexplicably ground to a halt. Swarms of mosquitos buzzed around pools of stagnant water and urine in the stairwells. From Javier's balcony we could see two half-finished towers and little sign of any new work since the presidential election. In fairness, they would eventually be completed and filled with state employees and military personnel but when I returned years later neighbours told me the buildings had never been connected to the gas mains and that *malandros* – gang members – operated in the blocks day and night.

Still, none of that mattered to Javier Castro who was genuinely in love with Hugo Chávez. He credited the president for getting him clean of drugs, for giving him a job, for providing him with an apartment.

'Chávez is my father. He's my brother, my best friend,' Javier managed to say before his voice faltered and the tears began to prick his eyes. At that time, the *Comandante* was in Cuba for a decisive cancer operation, the details of which were never fully revealed by either Caracas or Havana. All anyone knew was that it was bad and that he might never come back to power. As Javier showed me around the small apartment the government had donated to him as part of its social housing programme, he confessed that he could barely imagine life without Chávez.

'The revolution must be like this building: earthquake-proof,' he told me. 'Right now, we're experiencing a strong tremor [from Chávez's absence] but it won't collapse.'

In an emotional address to the nation before he left for Cuba, Hugo Chávez had described the surgery as 'absolutely essential'. A cancerous tumour 'about the size of a baseball' had initially been found in his groin in 2011 as he, ever the pitcher, had described it. It was removed in the first of three operations followed by several rounds of chemotherapy and radiotherapy in barely sixteen months.

Yet instead of recuperating as anyone else would, he went on a gruelling election campaign. He repeatedly criss-crossed the nation in an effort to defeat his young, good-looking and charismatic rival, Henrique Capriles Radonski, who presented Chávez with his first real test in a presidential vote since 1998. Especially an unwell Chávez. Polls showed that his poor health and uncertain future was a factor for undecided voters. In response, he was determined to show no sign of weakness, not a glimpse of vulnerability.

In fact, from the moment it was diagnosed, Chávez publicly played down and denied his illness. Following a particularly energetic campaign rally in Valencia, he brazenly dismissed his cancer to the Catalan journalist Carola Solé, saying, 'I don't even remember it' despite still being bloated from the chemotherapy as he spoke.[22]

The enduring image of that campaign – arguably of Chávez himself – was taken by the talented Reuters photographer Jorge Silva at the closing rally in Caracas. The heavens had opened, soaking thousands of red-clad supporters to the skin. Still, they weren't going anywhere. Chávez, too, stayed on stage, dancing with them in the tropical downpour as thoroughly drenched as they were. For someone who knew his immune system was on its knees, it was beyond foolhardy. Yet this was the final fiesta that none of them wanted to leave, a last goodbye from the man whose entire career had been built around a direct, unfiltered relationship with his supporters.

Jorge Silva later said it had taken him ten years to take the photograph he captured of Hugo Chávez that wet afternoon, the summation of his decade-long posting in Venezuela. He had managed to secure a spot beneath the main stage while the rest of the press pack moved to a supposedly more advantageous position for news images. At one point amid the cacophony of music and colour, he looked up and snapped Comandante Chávez as he paused in the rain. Head tilted back, eyes half closed and fixed to the mid-distance, his hands were clasped around the microphone at his waist, the raindrops framing him into a serene, almost Christ-like pose.

He was dying. And could hide it no longer.

For me, the moment it became abundantly clear that the braggadocio was futile and that Chávez knew he might not survive was about eleven months before his death, during Holy Week in 2012. At a Maundy Thursday mass in his home state of Barinas, a service was held to pray for the president's heath. His parents were there,

Elena and Hugo, his brother, Adán, his children and a few close comrades.

At one point, Chávez wearing a tracksuit, a rosary around his neck, took the microphone and began to exhort God to grant him more time on Earth: 'I say to God, if everything I've been through hasn't been enough, that I still had to live through this, then I welcome it. But give me life. Even if it be a burning and painful life, I don't mind,' he pleaded to a statue on the altar of Christ carrying the cross.

'Give me your crown of thorns, Christ, that I might bleed. Give me your cross, a hundred crosses, I'll carry them. But give me life, I still have things to do, Lord', the tears now streaming down his cheeks.

Even this supposedly private and personal event was broadcast live on state TV, his lowest emotional ebb turned into a campaigning moment. Whether that was tactically astute or a mistake is now irrelevant, but at the time it certainly seemed to me to reveal that the president was measuring his life in weeks and months rather than years.

Still, he won the election easily, beating Capriles Radonski by eleven percentage points. That Venezuelans would vote a dying man into power was testament to the unique place he held in their hearts. Anywhere else, anyone else, it would have been almost impossible. The electorate would have demanded to know his health status and, if it wasn't provided, assumed the worst and voted against him. Yet in Venezuela, with Chávez, it was the obvious outcome. He had no time to celebrate, though. The aggressive cancer was back, and he returned to Cuba for one last time.

After the surgery, an image – essentially a proof-of-life photograph – was released by Venezuela of Hugo Chávez with his two eldest daughters at his bedside, his tracksuit top zipped up to his neck, apparently hiding a tracheotomy scar. He'd survived but the painted grin was harrowing, not comforting. He was still alive, but barely.

The ninth floor of the Military Hospital in Caracas had been prepared for his return from Cuba. It had the latest apparatus installed and everything was ready for the convalescing *Comandante*. However, in a moment that summarized the dysfunction of his administration, power from the emergency generators didn't reach the ninth floor. The president's own brother, Argenis Chávez, was the president of Corpoelec at the time, the state electricity company, yet even he failed to deal with it properly. A hasty fix was made in time for Chávez's arrival.[23]

On the night before he died, an electrical blackout struck that part of the city and the doctors had to keep Chávez alive via artificial respiration using a bag-valve mask for almost half an hour. Apparently at the crucial moment, when the emergency generators were most needed, they didn't kick in automatically and couldn't be switched on manually. Chávez's days were numbered by then but being forced into manual artificial ventilation for so long almost certainly cut them shorter. The failings and incompetence that had characterized much of his administration, it seems, were present even in his final moments.

Just weeks after visiting his home, I bumped into Javier Castro again, this time in Fuerte Tiuna. He was wearing a black armband adorned with the tricolour of the Venezuelan flag, bought at a make-shift stand selling Chávez funeral paraphernalia. After several hours waiting patiently in line to view Chávez's body, the queue of mourners had been ordered by the soldiers to head home for the night. 'They say there were too many of us here so to try again tomorrow. I'll come back early,' he said with determination.

For those who endured the heat and the long wait, the final sight was both touching and macabre. After the frenetic first few days of reporting were over and many of the news teams who'd been para-chuted in to cover Chávez's death had left, I went back down to Fuerte Tiuna with a couple of friends who lived in Venezuela.

We stood in line, benefiting from the shorter queues at the end of a week of national mourning. Chatting to those around us, people had come from across Venezuela, bussed in from Anzoátegui, Falcon, Vargas, Bolívar and Chávez's home state of Barinas. The good-natured conversation among the *Chavistas* began to peter out the closer we got to the front and a more sombre mood took hold.

In the final few metres, we passed through a security check: 'Bags on the right, switch off your phones and put them away,' the soldiers barked. Watching the military issue terse instructions reminded me of seeing Chávez's courtiers become jittery in the moments before he entered the room. Even in death, I thought, he still had the power to make people nervous in his presence.

Finally, we trooped past his open casket. Inside, he lay dressed in full military regalia, a red *boina* on his head, a socialist soldier to the end. His lips were thick and dark, his waxy visage appearing almost plastic under the mortician's thickly coated makeup. Yet it was unmistakably him. The man who had filled the room with the sheer force of his personality was simply not there any longer. Famed in life for talking for hours, for constantly speaking out and never staying quiet, it felt incongruous to see Hugo Chávez finally silenced.

In front of me, an elderly woman was comforting her daughter and they propped each other up for support. We walked outside into the cool Caracas air and found everyone sitting slumped or in tears. I thought of the contrast it made with the scenes of complete hysteria I'd seen when the cortège passed through his most loyal neighbourhoods in Caracas. People had wailed and wept, were overcome with grief. They threw flowers at the coffin or tore off their red T-shirts and threw those; some even threw themselves at the hearse.

It was this adulation, this unconditional love which his political opponents could never quite understand about Chávez, much less recreate. Plenty of Venezuelans both at home and abroad will have raised a glass in celebration at his passing. They had longed for him to go years earlier – by any means, fair or foul. Yet the opposition could no more celebrate Chávez's death than the government could mourn his loss. There was another election to be held to choose his successor. Before he departed for Havana, the ailing president had told his supporters who he wanted to give the unenviable task of trying to replace him: the vice-president and long-time foreign minister, Nicolás Maduro.

'Elect Nicolás Maduro as president,' Chávez said on national television, spelling out every word. 'I ask that of you from my heart. He's one of the young leaders with the greatest ability to continue, if I'm unable to.'

Maduro, sitting solemnly next to Chávez as he spoke, looked as if he was going to be sick.

After his first few months in power, Nicolás Maduro's attempts to mimic Chávez's schtick were no longer funny. He had tried the same baritone voice, the same whimsical storytelling and folksy charm, he had recast himself as 'the Worker President' and his wife, Celia Flores, as 'the First Combatant'. But he simply couldn't pull it off. To most Venezuelans, it just never rang true. Even the ones who had adored Chávez – and were prepared to give Maduro the benefit of the doubt in accordance with his dying wish – were unconvinced. Meanwhile, Venezuela was paying for the poor impersonation, economically, politically and socially. Rampant inflation galloped into hyper-inflation with prices barely recognizable from one month to the next. The average family's monthly food basket of basic goods in early 2019 cost fifty times the monthly minimum wage.[24]

The security side of the collapse was frightening for those caught in the middle. The Bolivarian Circles, which had some teeth under Chávez, now morphed into something far more sinister and intimidating: armed motorcycle gangs called *colectivos*. In essence, they are paramilitaries at the beck and call of the Maduro high command. In particular, Chávez's enforcer – the former vice-president and head of the National Assembly, Diosdado Cabello, who had been alongside Chávez since the 1992 coup – is considered to be the man holding their leash, as much as anyone is. They're often employed alongside the security forces to 'defend the revolution', something they achieve through armed intimidation and often with bloody consequences. Protests are squashed in minutes as they arrive on their motorbikes, firing into the air or directly at the opposition demonstrators. Such political thuggery has been an enduring characteristic of Maduro's rule, a legacy for which Chávez cannot be excused, for having first allowed security in the *barrios* to spiral out of control.

The other body exerting violent repression when called upon is the 'Special Actions Forces', or FAES. If the *colectivos* can reasonably be considered paramilitaries, many Venezuelans would call the FAES nothing less than death squads. A unit of the National Bolivarian Police created by Maduro in 2017 to 'combat organized crime and terrorism', their capacity for violence is frightening. They're accused of carrying out summary executions across Venezuela with impunity and have been linked to hundreds of deaths. In a six-month period during 2017, they were responsible for almost a third of the killings in Caracas in which state forces were involved and almost two-thirds of killings involving the police force.[25] A Reuters investigation in February 2020 demonstrated that despite the fact that it is illegal for national police officers to have criminal records, some members of the FAES were convicted criminals.[26]

Meanwhile, abuses in Venezuela's jails worsened under Maduro, particularly for those arrested in street protests against his rule in 2014 and 2017. Many civilians received summary trials in military courts, were sentenced on terrorism charges by loyalist judges and sent to the dreaded detention centre at El Helicoide. Intended as a state-of-the-art drive-through shopping mall, El Helicoide is an iconic landmark in Caracas, a futuristic monument built under Marcos Pérez Jiménez to exemplify Venezuela as a forward-thinking, modern nation. After his overthrow, though, it sat empty, its luxury boutiques unused, an expensive white elephant of military rule. Gradually, successive governments began to move state agencies into the building, including the intelligence services, today called SEBIN, *Servicio Bolivariano de Inteligencia Nacional*.

The abuse of prisoners inside El Helicoide has been well documented by former detainees including an opposition congressman, Rosmit Mantilla, and a number of repentant guards.[27] They recount how the abandoned stores were used as torture cells where electrodes would be attached to inmates' testicles and teeth. Amid Venezuela's political crisis, Maduro supporters in Europe and the US are guilty of either wilful ignorance or of glossing over the mistreatment in this former capitalist temple but the practices that go on there are straight out of the 1970s military dictatorships' handbook.

The reality of a falling oil price, which had started to expose cracks under Chávez, began to reveal vast economic fractures and gaping holes of mismanagement. The government's main explanation for the disastrous state of the economy was that an 'economic war' was being waged on Venezuela by the United States. Yet that story quickly grew thinner than the Venezuelan people who were wasting away with each passing month through a scarcity of food. Underfunded public hospitals began to regularly admit patients with chronic mal-nutrition and starvation.

Ahead of a vote in 2017, I took a walk around part of the hectic, impoverished slum of Petare in eastern Caracas with Maribel Quiroz, a Catholic nun who runs a local primary school. Children had been fainting in class with nothing in their stomachs, Sister Maribel ex-plained, or skipping school altogether to find food. 'Hunger is a real problem which is hurting this community,' she told me as neighbours interrupted us every few metres to greet their local nun, dressed like them in jeans and a T-shirt rather than a habit.

'Hunger and crime,' she corrected. 'They're the two main issues here.' The school started to offer the neediest pupils a basic breakfast before class but were so inundated with famished children they'd been forced to limit the meals to the first 250 through the door.

Sister Maribel took me to meet the mother of a few of those kids, Edimar Armas, who lived nearby. We knocked on her door to find half a dozen children slumped on a broken sofa in front of the TV while a couple of older ones carried out chores in a cramped kitchen where a pot of black beans bubbled on a stove. At just forty-four, Edimar already had eight grandchildren and her job as a cleaner didn't come close to covering the family's basic needs. The stress was evident in her thin frame, and she acknowledged the situation was ageing her fast.

'This government once did a lot of things for many people,' she said, still conscious of not wanting to sound ungrateful to Chávez. 'But now it's being badly administrated. They raise the minimum wage, but then the food prices go up so much faster. I don't even get happy now when they say our wages are going to rise because I know it makes no difference.'

At the top of a road strewn with foul-smelling trash and with an open sewer of fetid water, we reached a small welding shop. A little red flag of the United Socialist Party of Venezuela fluttered over the entrance as the owner Edgar Pérez wiped his hands on his grease-smeared overalls and came out to greet Maribel. Despite having his political colours very clearly nailed to the wall, Edgar was also exhausted and hugely frustrated by the Maduro government.

'I've been doing this for thirty years and had this shop for twenty,' he said, insisting he could fix everything from cars to fridges. The struggle was in finding spare parts amid the scarcity, then being able to afford them with the hyperinflation. 'There should be equality here. I don't mean equality in the sense that we all have the same thing. But at least an equality of opportunities,' Edgar reasoned.

At the start of his reign, the people of Petare had voted almost unanimously for Chávez. Now none of them, from the nun to the mum to the mechanic, endorsed Maduro. Just three voices in a tidal wave of popular desertion since the heir ascended the throne.

Venezuela's oil industry was nationalized the same year that Hugo Chávez graduated the military academy, in 1975.

The price of a barrel of Venezuelan crude oil when he came to power two and a half decades later was just $8.43 a barrel.[28] By the time I moved to the country in 2008 it had reached an eye-watering $126 a barrel.[29] With production at that time still very healthy, around 3.2 million barrels per day (bpd), the country's oil income was immense. The profit margins were extraordinary: between 2004 and 2007, average annual growth in Venezuela stood at 9.7 per cent.[30] GDP per capita more than doubled between the year Chávez came to power and the year before he died.[31]

There was more than enough money to pay for the basic tenets of *Chavismo* at home and abroad. The socialist government wanted to fund large-scale social programmes in health, education and food distribution in Venezuela's poor neighbourhoods while propping up like-minded governments across the region. The state-owned oil company, PDVSA, became the piggy bank for whatever was wanted. When Hugo Chávez first said he needed a billion dollars for unspecified social projects, his economic advisers at the Central Bank turned him down. On hearing this, the then head of PDVSA and energy minister, Rafael Ramírez, simply created a massive unregulated slush fund for Chávez called FONDEN: 'Instead of one billion, I gave him one hundred billion,' he later claimed proudly.[32]

Tangible and meaningful poverty reduction was achieved in that time. The government's official figures claimed extreme poverty dropped from around 23 per cent in 1999 to single digits in 2011.[33] Even allowing for their hyperbole and creative bookkeeping, Chávez's biggest critics couldn't deny he was having a massive effect on the family budgets and monthly incomes of the poor. On a whole range of indicators, from school enrolment to child malnutrition, the government was claiming victory. Yet Chávez's Revolution was constantly accused of inherent clientelism and short-termist thinking, of being solely based on a high commodity price. The immediate benefits of pumping oil money into social programmes was obvious, critics said. But their next question was always: what happens when the oil price drops? The answer was deeply painful for millions of people and left many of them markedly worse off than before the self-proclaimed 'Bolivarian Revolution of 21st Century Socialism' ever started.

By 2018, the Venezuelan oil industry was in complete disarray. The price was a fraction of what it had been in those heady days a decade earlier and production had fallen to just 800,000 bpd. At the same time, annual inflation was galloping out of control, reaching almost 1.4 million per cent.[34]

The theft, squandering and mismanagement of the oil wealth were staggering. It amounted to the biggest robbery of natural resources and looting of national funds in modern Latin American history. For every shanty town lifted up and inspired to participate and organize by Hugo Chávez, there were scores of dishonest functionaries in government or the military siphoning off the wealth intended to help them.

Millions of people were pulled from poverty for a decade, maybe longer. But there were few roots of lasting change, precious little that addressed Venezuela's structural inequalities or vast wealth gap. The Revolution would be accused of always giving a man a fish rather than a fishing net. In fact, the government did give out nets. And outboard motors and boats and subsidized fuel. But the corrosive combination of corruption and controlled prices meant it was easier for the fishermen to sell their goods on the black market or use their launches to take tourists out to the beaches. Any supposed dream of creating a Bolivarian fishing flotilla fell as flat as most other efforts to diversify the economy away from oil.

Things only worsened once Chávez died and was replaced by his former foreign minister, Nicolás Maduro. To go from endless abundance and lavish excess to such crippling, dire need, from the potential for lasting social and economic success to complete chaos, has been ruinous for Venezuela. Oil production in 2019 dropped to pre-1945 levels[35] and Bloomberg estimated that the country's foreign currency reserves fell to just $800 million.[36] In the ensuing battle for the country's soul, hundreds of young Venezuelans lost their lives, dying face down in pools of blood on the asphalt of the streets they marched on to call for change. Students were gunned down rather than listened to.

Countless others, including many thousands of children, died in hospitals that were unable or unfit to treat them, often for preventable diseases. I was at a press conference in 2009 in which Chávez spoke passionately about the 'armies of street children and beggars' he used to see in the Venezuela of his youth, and how he'd all but eradicated that problem. Today, they're back, sitting outside restaurants in upscale neighbourhoods of Caracas and Maracaibo and Valencia, hoping for some leftovers or a couple of notes of worthless currency. As the national currency, the bolívar, lost more of its value over time, Maduro made the ultimate concession that the revolution's economic policy had failed: he began to dollarize the country.

Within a few years of the *Comandante*'s death, widespread malnutrition was back in Venezuela. Whole families – marginalized and ignored – went hungry in a throwback to times *Chavismo* proudly claimed were over forever. In a lot of homes, the kids only ate if their parents skipped a meal. People lost dozens of kilos in what was grimly dubbed 'the Maduro diet'.

Amid the poverty, millions of people have left. The Venezuelan exodus of the early twenty-first century is the biggest single migration movement in Latin American history. At its height, 5,000 people a day fled Venezuela into Colombia, opting to walk across the continent for the elusive promise of improved conditions abroad – as far afield as Bogotá, Lima, Santiago, São Paulo or Mexico City. Others stayed closer, settling in camps in the first towns they encountered after crossing the Colombian or Brazilian borders. Reaching Lima from Venezuela through a combination of walking, hitchhiking and bus rides is a journey of at least two weeks, spanning thousands of miles. It's a cold, fraught and dangerous trip which hundreds of thousands of Venezuelans have undertaken since 2016, pushing children in strollers or carrying them in their arms in the thin, damp mountainous air. Thousands more left their kids at home in the forlorn hope of reuniting someday under better circumstances.

Venezuela is a stark warning of what can happen when vanity and dogma outweigh pragmatism and common sense. Of when political polarization becomes so vicious that neither side will work with their opponents on the most basic questions of human necessity. Of valuing loyalty above all else, even when it means ignoring blatant cases of incompetence, corruption and greed. Of meddling in another country's internal affairs by both Washington and Havana.

It is an experiment that descended so quickly into anarchy, that went so terribly awry, that it can be hard to distinguish a viable solution. Meanwhile, those carrying it out still double down on the same losing hand that created the problems in the first place. Venezuela became the car wreck that the world can't take its eyes off.

Those who applauded Hugo Chávez often want to absolve him of much of the responsibility and reassure themselves that the blame for the kleptocracy lies squarely with his buffoonish, autocratic successor. For sure, Nicolás Maduro and his cadre must shoulder much of the responsibility for Venezuela's current malaise, yet that would be to underestimate the chaos he inherited, the impact of the policies put in place by his mentor. The anarchic, ad hoc and corrupt model they have created between them has turned Venezuela into perhaps the most entangled country in Latin America.

An untouchable political class was spawned under Chávez. Popularly referred to as the '*Boliburgues*', a portmanteau of Bolivarian and bourgeoisie, they used their unhindered access to state coffers to help themselves to billions in Venezuela's petrodollars. They used front companies and fake ventures to move the increasingly worthless local money, the bolívar, into hard currency at an astonishingly favourable exchange rate. Even when the dollar was reaching absurdly high numbers – hundreds, thousands, even hundreds of thousands of bolívars to the buck – they continued to get dollars at the barely credible official exchange rate available only to a select few, of 4.3 bolívars to the dollar. It was a licence to launder money and the *Boliburgues* took to it like a criminal cartel.

Alejandro Andrade, Chávez's former bodyguard-turned-Central Banker, was just one of the most egregious examples of thousands involved in the plunder and pilfering. The *Comandante*'s personal nurse, Claudia Patricia Díaz Guillén, who was inexplicably promoted to executive secretary of FONDEN, Chávez's war chest of oil money for social programmes, was eventually arrested in Spain and narrowly avoided extradition over the source of her multimillion-dollar income.

The Chávez clan themselves and Maduro's family were firmly at the centre of the *Boliburgues* bubble, spouting the increasingly insincere socialist rhetoric every day while living in a world of Chanel, Gucci, Louis Vuitton and Patek Philippe. It was obscene. And became more so as the economy tanked further and further, more millions plunged back into the poverty whence they came or worse, forced to leave the country altogether.

The roots of Venezuela's problems don't lie in *Madurismo*; they lie in *Chavismo* itself. And in Hugo Chávez. At his height, Chávez enchanted the Venezuelan poor and the international left in equal measure. Especially after the April 2002 attempted coup against him, one report after another in European newspapers painted him as a much-maligned Latin American hero, fighting for the rights of the poor while simultaneously sticking it to Uncle Sam:

'The chrysalis of the Venezuelan revolution led by Chávez, often attacked and derided as the incoherent vision of an authoritarian leader, has finally emerged as a resplendent butterfly whose image and example will radiate for decades to come,' wrote Richard Gott in the *Guardian* at the time.[37]

Things are always amplified in Venezuela, a place prone to exaggeration, where size and magnification is everything. Perhaps it's a curse of oil. But even if Gott's description had once been the case, that butterfly is now dying fast, its image not radiant but sullied and dull. Its death is a story of wilful corruption and profound incompetence, of repression and resistance. It's a story of faith, zealotry and the deification of one man.

It is the story of Venezuela's demise.

Francisco's hands trembled a little as he filled a glass beer bottle with gasoline. It was hard to see clearly through his gas mask and he was breathing hard from having run from the police and the National Guard. A group of his friends also had their bottles out and were readying them for the next onslaught.

Francisco had never been in the military, never fought or seen action. But it occurred to him that this moment – regrouping and rearming while surrounded by the enemy – must be what war was like. An engineering student, until now the only thing he had been fanatical about was football. Until Nicolás Maduro came to power.

His best friend, Arturo, a buddy since childhood, was next to him. Arturo had a sister with mental health problems and getting her the drugs she needed had become almost impossible. Arturo's ire at President Maduro had rubbed off on Francisco, and had forced him to recognize just how bad things had become. It seemed like everyone they knew had gone hungry at some point. Francisco had seen other students and elderly neighbours eating from the trash. Several friends who had tried to protest had been killed, shot in the chest as they advanced or in the back as they ran for their lives. Others had been picked up and thrown in jail, with no word of them since their arrests. It was 2017 and his country was fast descending into a dictatorship, like the ones his parents had talked about.

¡Basta! Enough. The two boys joined 'the Resistance', thousands of disillusioned and angry young people taking on the might of the Maduro machinery. Many had nothing but wooden shields and makeshift body armour to protect themselves from the tear gas canisters and live rounds being fired by the authorities. Some fashioned balaclavas out of their T-shirts to disguise their identity. First-year medical students acted as field doctors. Barely out of their teens, this was Venezuela's youth at its most *arrecho*, a Venezuelan word that means both furious and brave in different contexts. Francisco and Arturo had discussed it and decided that, if necessary, they were prepared to die for some pretty basic rights: to live in peace, to make sure there was enough to eat, to know that your vote wasn't being stolen.

This, though, was surely the final stage of the battle, Francisco thought, as the two friends embraced and ran back towards the riot cops, Molotov cocktails in hand and more in their rucksacks.

I met Francisco and Arturo, the names they asked me to use for them, a day later in a hideout in Caracas. There they showed me their cache of glass bottles to make more petrol bombs and told me of their plan to man the barricades with their classmates from early the next morning. There were just a few days to go before Nicolás Maduro's most arbitrary election yet – to create another assembly to write up a new constitution to replace the one that Chávez had put together to such fanfare in 1999.

The entire situation was farcical. Having been roundly beaten at the legislative elections in 2015, in which the opposition took two-thirds of the seats, Maduro initially recognized the result, then immediately started making noises about overriding parliament with a fresh constitution. He tried to justify his most dictatorial step to date by claiming, flimsily, that it had always been part of Chávez's master plan. Few believed him, and fewer still wanted it. The opposition coalition,

MUD, boycotted the entire process in an effort to deprive it of any legitimacy. Not that their absence was enough to stop the Maduro government from proceeding. All the opposition's nonattendance meant to Maduro was that this new assembly was about to be filled solely with *Chavistas*. It would be the very embodiment of a rubber-stamp organization. Even in the eyes of some high-profile Chávez supporters who began to desert Maduro on acrimonious terms, it was thoroughly illegitimate.

As someone who had covered numerous elections in Venezuela, under Chávez and after his death, this absurd vote struck me as the moment the mask finally dropped. All pretence by President Maduro and the inner circle to be playing by the rules of democratic government vanished. He evidently cared little what anyone else thought, either inside Venezuela or in the international community. The point had simply become to retain power for the sake of power itself. The sight of him dancing in the Plaza Bolívar after the hollowest and most cynical of victories, mocking an opponent who hadn't even entered the race, delivered one simple message: there was no way the PSUV would relinquish power to an opposition-controlled parliament. Not now, not ever.

'The country has been collapsing in every area you can think of: economy, education, security, food,' Francisco told me in the basement of their safe house, hours before trying to disrupt the vote with another street protest. 'Of course we're scared. Everyone who takes to the streets is scared,' they admitted. 'But we're in the final phase, we have to keep up the intensity on the streets. There's just a little left now until this is over.'

Yet, as is so often the case in Venezuela, there was still much further for the country to fall.

'The moment has come for the economic recovery of our country,' said Nicolás Maduro, in full presidential regalia, sash across his chest. He was flanked by Venezuela's top brass and his wife, Celia Flores, stood next to him in a white outfit with black buttons, her dyed-blonde hair perfectly ironed. In fact, apart from Celia, he was surrounded by soldiers on all sides as it was a ceremony to mark the eighty-first anniversary of the army, broadcast live on state TV.

He had hardly uttered two words of his next sentence when a loud explosion pierced the air. Maduro flinched, Celia Flores grabbed the person next to her and the Venezuelan military chiefs of staff instinctively ducked. A drone taped with C4 explosives had buzzed overhead before detonating out of range of the president but close enough to injure several troops.

On stage, Maduro's security detail covered him with bullet-proof blankets, trying to cocoon him from the threat and usher him offstage. The troops, lined up in neat columns, were spooked. First one soldier broke rank, then another, until the entire battalion was running in different directions heading for cover.

State TV cut the transmission. Whatever was happening wasn't meant to be seen by the nation. Those frenzied few moments in August 2018 appeared to be a bungled assassination attempt. Maduro's top ministers were quick to blame their enemies, from Washington to Colombian president Juan Manuel Santos to Venezuela's right-wing politicians. Within days, the arrests began, including a colonel and an opposition lawmaker, Juan Requesens. He was transferred to El Helicoide from where two videos eventually emerged, one of his supposed confession and another of him looking confused and dishevelled, wearing underwear covered in excrement, which provoked an international outcry at his treatment.

The drone explosion didn't seem a particularly sophisticated attack, but it had the effect of making Nicolás Maduro increasingly wary of everyone. He receded further and further from public view, limiting himself to live addresses from a bunker in Miraflores or posting videos featuring just a few handpicked supporters. On his rare appearances, a bullet-proof vest could be seen protruding from underneath his shirt, strapped around his wide frame. Washington kept up its relentless economic squeeze and the pressure on Maduro mounted from inside and out.

Despite having written a constitution in his own image shortly after taking power, in 2007 Hugo Chávez requested a host of sweeping changes to it. He called for unlimited re-election, to increase presidential terms from six years to seven and scores of other amendments. It was narrowly rejected by an electorate unsure of how such changes would benefit them. Chávez was a sore loser, calling the opposition's win '*una victoria de mierda*', and the following morning vowed he'd stand down by the end of his term. Still, his bad mood didn't last long and within the year he put the main question – the right of unlimited re-election – back on the table, this time with a sweetener for regional governors and mayors. Everyone would have the right to stand for office indefinitely.

On the second vote, with more regional backing to the 'Yes' campaign, there was no doubting the result. Chávez got the green light to stand for president as often as he wanted. It was a gift from the people he'd barely get to use. The first recipient of an unfettered right to repeated re-election was Nicolás Maduro.

He blew it, though. The oil price was already dropping and production was waning rapidly in the last years of Hugo Chávez's life. After 2013, however, the descent was precipitous. Wherever people turned, things were falling apart. From food security and inflation to provision of basic services and oil production, nothing worked as it should. It didn't even work as it had under Chávez: dysfunctional, but with some limited forward motion.

The truth is that the Bolivarian Revolution failed without the boom of petrodollars. Subsidized food wasn't reaching the poorest neighbourhoods, the minimum wage was well below the poverty line and hyperinflation rendered any state wage hikes pointless. When Maduro was hit with a thrashing at the polls, he redoubled his authoritarianism.

Following Chávez's example, serious presidential contenders found themselves '*inhabilitados*' – banned from public office over their finances or other irregularities – ensuring the opposition's strongest candidates couldn't stand. Respected international election observers were turned away with only pro-government groups allowed in.

When Maduro pressed ahead with the plan to defenestrate the

National Assembly, it inevitably led to confrontation on the streets.[38] The year 2017 was the bloodiest of either Chávez or Maduro's rule. Still Maduro didn't waver. In 2018, the opposition boycotted the presidential election, too. But that was a tactic that had previously failed against Chávez. Incredibly, given modern Latin American history, some began to openly call for foreign military intervention. Under the Trump administration, US sanctions in place on members of the Maduro inner circle were widened to the country's vital oil industry, only making economic matters worse.

By then, though, the *Chavista* economy was in freefall. Billions had been squandered in infrastructure plans, especially with the Brazilian construction firm, Odebrecht – a name synonymous with corruption in Latin America. Investigations into the firm's activities had brought down presidents and high-ranking politicians across the region. Former ministers and justice officials claim Venezuela had more money invested with Odebrecht than any country in Latin America and that investigations into its disappearance have been blocked.

The list of failed and abandoned projects in Venezuela is long and varied. It takes in everything from a stalled 2,300-megawatt hydroelectric dam at Tocoma to a third bridge across the Orinoco, from a metro line between Guarenas and Guatire to a Caracas–Valencia train. Each one of these paralysed projects represents the loss of billions of dollars. Taken together, they amounted to a kleptocracy.

Chávez's decision to value loyalty over ability saw the military in Venezuela tasked with managing the state's infrastructure from oil wells to agriculture. The problem, functionaries say, was that when things went wrong the military simply didn't have the technical capacity to fix them. Most of the electrical engineers or deep-sea oil drillers who did have the answers had been forced out long ago or had left the country in search of a living wage.

The pain of such underinvestment, corruption and ineptitude was most keenly felt in the provision of public services. Water provision had long been a problem for millions of Venezuelans. However, under Maduro the situation started to turn desperate as more and more days went by each month with dry taps. Venezuela's domestic electricity comes from its huge water resources, in particular the vast Guri hydroelectric dam in Bolívar state on the Caroni river. When the lack of maintenance at the plant reached a critical point, power cuts became more regular. The irony of rolling blackouts in a country drowning in oil was lost on no one.

In the middle of it all, facing the worst political crisis of his presidency, Maduro called a live press conference with the international media. He was battling the opposition over convoys of humanitarian aid from the Colombian border, something he said wasn't humanitarian aid at all but 'a covert invasion'. Anyway, he said, Venezuela didn't need it. Foreign aid was tantamount to 'begging'.

Mid-answer and in full flow, as he was comparing the Venezuelan right wing to the Chilean dictator Augusto Pinochet, the lights went out. Nicolás Maduro stood at the podium, startled and confused, in the dark in Miraflores. Aware of the metaphors being scribbled by the journalists, of the ridiculous sight of a blackout at the presidential palace unfolding live on TV, of his authority ebbing away before him, he reached for a cup of coffee and told his twitchy security men to calm down.

'*Está todo bien,*' he insisted. 'Everything's fine.'

BRAZIL /
LUIZ INÁCIO
'LULA' DA SILVA

'[Lula is] the most popular politician on Earth'

BARACK OBAMA

The heat in Mexico City was stifling. At altitude, the players were starting to tire, especially the Italians who had endured a bruising semi-final against West Germany. Brazil had taken the lead through a Pelé header after just eight minutes. Italy equalized shortly before half-time.

The 1970 World Cup final, being played in front of 110,000 fans in the Estadio Azteca, was in the balance. Or at least it was until the sixty-sixth minute. Gérson, a marauding, intelligent midfielder, picked up a loose ball outside the Italian area and drove forwards. He pulled back his powerful left foot and fired a thunderous shot past the despairing dive of Enrico Albertosi.

From there, Brazil didn't look back. Five minutes later, Gérson again took control. He arced the ball beautifully to Pelé who nodded it down for Jairzinho to bundle over the line: 3–1.

Then there came the goal which would live in the memory of Brazilians, of football fans everywhere, for decades. From Barcelona to Baku, from Rio de Janeiro to Rotherham, ask any self-respecting supporter to describe this moment and they will narrate what was probably the finest team goal ever scored in world football.

Brazil tenaciously held onto possession in a crowded midfield and fed the ball out to Jairzinho on the left wing. Surrounded by Italian defenders, he passed sideways to Pelé on the edge of the area. In an exquisite moment of hold-up play, Pelé timed his pass to perfection, duping the Italian defence entirely, to slot the ball into the path of the onrushing Carlos Alberto. The Brazilian captain didn't break his stride, connected seamlessly with the pass and planted an unstoppable shot into the net. Years later, Brazil's 1970 World Cup-winning team would be voted the greatest team of all time.[1]

Some 4,600 miles away in a cramped apartment in São Paulo, watching the match on a black-and-white television with a coloured filter paper in front of it – the poor man's colour TV – was a young football-mad metalworker from the northeastern corner of Brazil, tears streaming down his cheeks.

Luiz Inácio 'Lula' da Silva was the happiest he had been in his life.[2] He was recently married, and his young wife would soon be pregnant.

He had steady work as a lathe operator, earned a respectable wage and, to top it all, Brazil had just won the World Cup. Family life and work were truly harmonious for the first time since he had reached adulthood. Still, for Lula, such moments of happiness would prove fleeting. He was on the brink of a life of dizzying highs punctuated by episodes of crippling tragedy, a man who reached the pinnacle of power and popularity in Brazil but who lost more in a single night than most lose in a lifetime.

Lula's joy was always relative, a hard-fought happiness that was quickly tempered by the next setback. Even as he watched Carlos Alberto hoist the Jules Rimet trophy in Mexico City, his brief elation over a football match was deceptive. He couldn't have known it then but crushing disappointment and profound sadness were lying in wait.

In fact, he was just months away from his lowest ebb.

The tiny town of Caetés was a harsh place to grow up. Lula was born into abject poverty in the northeastern state of Pernambuco, the seventh child of eight, in October 1945. His upbringing was never easy or comfortable and, unlike Hugo Chávez, Lula doesn't romanticize his humble origins or remember his childhood particularly fondly. In the 1940s, few homes in the town had electricity or running water. Most families cooked on firewood and scratched a meagre living from the earth by growing 'rice, manioc and sweet potato'.[3]

His father, an illiterate farmhand named Aristides Inácio da Silva, left for São Paulo in search of work in the weeks before Lula was born. Indeed, Lula didn't even meet his father until he was four and only briefly lived with him at the age of seven. Instead, as was and remains so often the case in Latin America, child-rearing duties fell solely to the mother – Eurídice Ferreira de Melo, or 'Dona Lindu'. Photographs of her from the time show a woman with a world-weary face, a toughened *campesino* with a broad nose, thin lips and kind eyes. Years later, Lula would readily credit his indefatigable fighting spirit to his mother. He respected and loved her profoundly, a love matched only by his disdain for his absent father – though even in that case his anger eventually softened with age.

Aristides left for São Paulo on a flatbed truck known as a *pau-de-arara* (literally 'parrot's perch'), with a teenaged cousin of Dona Lindu's called Mocinha. Unbeknownst to Dona Lindu, Aristides intended to begin another family with Mocinha while working as a longshoreman in the port city of Santos in São Paulo state.

In his father's absence, the strong feminine presence was a key influence on Lula from a young age. The eldest children pitched in, too, helping to bring up the youngest as soon as they were considered mature. On a rare trip back to Pernambuco, Aristides picked up one of the kids, Jaime, and brought him back to São Paulo. From there, a lonely Jaime wrote to Dona Lindu and told her 'to come now', recalls his brother, claiming Aristides wanted them to join him.[4] The unwitting father couldn't even read the letter, and certainly wouldn't have agreed to his first family migrating south. Still, the grinding poverty in the northeast was becoming too much for Eurídice and Jaime's message was the excuse she needed to sell up and load the children on a *pau-de-arara* to São Paulo.

The journey south was tortuous. It took almost two weeks, from 10 to 23 December 1952. It is a daunting picture, the image of a mother travelling alone with so many children, sharing the cramped space with rough labourers and farmhands, eating little, sleeping less. 'We had to sell everything' to pay for the tickets, remembers Lula's older brother, Frei Chico. 'When you are kids, everything seems fun, but it was a very sad journey.' It left a lasting impression on the seven-year-old Lula, by then old enough to know that his life seemed destined to be one of enduring hardship. At that point, there were few prospects of much else.

If the journey on the *pau-de-arara* had been rough, the family's situation quickly became worse once they reached Aristides in Vicente de Carvalho – a poor district of Guarujá, a tourism and port town on São Paulo's coast. They found that urban poverty in Brazil is every bit as exhausting as the rural impoverishment they'd left behind. The key difference was that work, of a kind, was available. Everyone, including Lula, had to bring some money home.

Decades later, Guarujá would play a vital role in sealing Lula's political fate. Questions over the ownership of a triplex and whether Lula had received it as a kickback were ostensibly the reason given for his eventual imprisonment in a corruption probe. In the 1950s, though, a modern beachfront property was an unimaginably distant prospect. All the young boy knew of Guarujá's expensive apartments was that the shiny buildings on the seafront weren't good spots to sell his oranges, tapioca and *dolces* or to shine shoes. The businessmen who came out of them would rarely stop for him on their way to work and he'd be shooed away by the doormen. Instead he sold his wares to the workers at the quayside.

For Lula and his family these were hard years. For Brazil, too, it was a complicated and conflicted time.

In late 1952, when they made the journey south, the nationalist autocrat Getúlio Vargas was president for a second time. Born into a wealthy family of landholders in Rio Grande do Sul, Vargas had risen to prominence between the two world wars as Brazil rapidly became an industrial power. He enjoyed the typical stellar career of the elite, starting in the military before moving into law and then politics. Once he became an established figure on the national scene, he spent two years as Brazil's finance minister, serving under President Washington Luís between 1926 and 1928, before returning to his home state as governor.

For forty years, since the fall of the monarchy and the birth of the Old Republic in 1889, Brazilian politics had been dominated by the so-called '*café com leite*' (coffee with milk) agreements, the rotation of the presidency between the landed gentry of coffee growers in São Paulo and the dairy farmers in Minas Gerais. The alliance forged between politicians and rural elites from the two states ensured a *paulista* president was followed by a *mineiro* one for decades. By 1930, in the midst of the Great Depression and with fascism on the rise in Europe, tensions in Brazil had reached a crescendo. The plummeting price of coffee on the world market sent the economy into turmoil.

The political alliance between the *paulistas* and *mineiros* had broken down a year earlier as the São Paulo power base, led by President Luís, named their own candidate for the 1930 presidential election instead of the governor of Minas Gerais. This betrayal marked the end of the cosy agreements that held together the Old Republic.

On 1 March 1930, the *paulista* candidate, Júlio Prestes, beat Getúlio Vargas in the election, but he would never take office. The Liberal Alliance opposition parties immediately cried foul and refused to recognize the result. By 3 October, a revolution was underway in Brazil. State leaderships were forced out across the country and, with little bloodshed, the revolutionaries deposed Washington Luís in late October. On 1 November, a military junta handed power to Getúlio Vargas as interim president.

Vargas spent a total of eighteen years in power and became Brazil's most significant political figure of the twentieth century. He wasted little time in cementing his position. The 1891 constitution was suspended, Congress and state legislatures dissolved. In their place, state governors, under a newly created post of 'federal intervenor', would answer directly to Vargas, concentrating power in his hands. In an overture to the armed forces, he granted an amnesty to rebel officers, the *tenentes*, who had risen up against the corrupt agrarian rule of the 1920s. Yet it was his social reforms that earned him the title of 'Father of the Poor' from his supporters.

In an echo of Franklin D. Roosevelt's 'New Deal', he managed a route out of the economic crisis by strengthening Brazil's industrial base, making import-substituting industrialization the state's dominant economic policy. His was a nationalist and populist movement, one that favoured tax breaks and lower duties to stimulate the economy. The state became increasingly interventionist, mediating in trade disputes and centralising all regional decision-making. Vargas also deepened the growing divide between the richer south and the impoverished northeast – Lula's homeland – and rowed back on a promise of land reform.

However, the middle classes were growing wealthier and the poor were also finding steady paid work in industrial jobs. After 1932, when he crushed a brief *paulista* revolt, Vargas lurched further towards populist, anti-communist autocracy. Demands for a new bill of rights led to the creation of a Constituent Assembly and the writing of Brazil's first constitution by elected deputies in 1934. Until that point, women and the illiterate had been ineligible to vote, but the 1934 constitution widened the electorate by extending political rights to all adults.[5] It also introduced some key labour reforms including the minimum wage, an eight-hour workday and paid leave.

It was short-lived, though. Facing the prospect of having to stand down in 1937, as the constitution didn't permit a two-term presidency, the Vargas regime descended into a full-blown dictatorship. He delivered a radio address on 10 November 1937 in which, under the spurious pretext of a communist coup plot, he invoked a state of emergency and suspended parliament once again. It was an '*auto-golpe*', or a 'self-coup', in which he cemented his executive power by eliminating the legislature, the last-ditch statutory sledgehammer employed by tyrants and *caudillos* the world over.

Under his dictatorial powers, the 1934 constitution was ripped up and Vargas announced the creation of '*Estado Novo*', the New State, evoking the corporatist model of António Salazar in Portugal. All political parties were disbanded and the promised congressional elections were never held. Instead, the president assumed all legislative powers. Combined with a significant increase in police repression and brutality, Vargas ruled under a form of martial law throughout the Second World War. Following the outbreak of war in Europe, he at first prevaricated. Given the appeal of Benito Mussolini's fascist regime in Italy, the trade in cotton and other commodities with Germany and the existence of Nazi sympathizers among the Brazilian military, Vargas might well have sided with the Axis powers. However, despite overtures from the Third Reich, he kept Brazil neutral until 1941 when Pearl Harbor forced the hand of leaders across the Americas to row in behind the United States. Eventually Brazil played an important role in supporting the Allied victory.

Vargas established a number of crucial state entities in mining, oil, steel and manufacturing, including the mining giant Companhia

Vale do Rio Doce. He simultaneously kept the indigenous and rural population docile through a series of clientelist and paternalistic policies. However, after 1945 he could no longer cling onto unfettered power under the excuse of an international crisis. In fact, his term officially should have ended in 1943, and not long after the end of the Second World War he was ousted by a group of army officers.

By the time Lula and family reached the south in 1952, the 'Father of the Poor' was back. This time, Vargas had at least been elected via the ballot box. The intervening six years hadn't been easy on Brazil. His successor, Eurico Dutra, had distanced himself from the Vargas-era policies of nationalism and economic protectionism. Dutra drew Brazil closer to Washington and US interests and broke off diplomatic relations with the Soviet Union. However, the country was slipping further into inflation and the labour protections that Vargas had created for industrial and agricultural workers were being eroded. Meanwhile, Getúlio Vargas watched the Dutra presidency from the quiet of his home in São Borja.

When the opportunity presented itself to stand again, this time for the Brazilian Labour Party, Vargas took it and stood on an overtly populist platform, promising a return to his traditional nationalist and pro-labour policies. Much to the displeasure of some in the military, it worked. He won another term and took office in January 1951.

This time, his stint in power would be brief. He couldn't reverse the slide into rampant inflation and workers' wage hikes couldn't keep pace with the rising cost of living. Nor could he work with a pluralist and multiparty Congress. As he floundered, he tried to supplant his own brand of nationalism with a more virulent form of ultra-nationalism to maintain his popular support but immediately ran into opposition from the United States and the military. The president from Rio Grande do Sul, now constrained by parliament and the political parties, lacked the dictatorial might he'd enjoyed as a wartime *caudillo*. Brazil was slipping from his grip.

In the effort to shore up the Brazilian economy, he enacted one crucial measure during his second period in power. He founded Petrobras, the Brazilian oil and gas company, in October 1953. From its humble beginnings as a state-owned monopoly, producing around 2,700 barrels a day (bpd) in 1953, it became the biggest corporation in Latin America, producing over 2,000,000 bpd by 2010. The slogan around the Petrobras monopoly on extraction and new refineries was 'The Oil is Ours', a nationalist sentiment befitting a populist dictator.[6] The politician who became the real beneficiary of Petrobras and its exponential growth was at that time still just a boy, scrabbling around selling peanuts on the streets of Guarujá to earn a few cruzeiros.

The creation of Petrobras wouldn't save Vargas. The reality was that for a leader with the title of 'Father of the Poor', Vargas had delivered precious few tangible benefits to the working class. Lula, in fact, would later describe them as 'pseudo-benevolences' that were 'implanted in the workers' minds'.[7] To continue the rapid industrialization of Brazil, Vargas found himself in a dilemma. He either had to allow more foreign investment, as Dutra had done, which clashed with his nationalist rhetoric, or print more money, which caused inflation to rise and hurt the workers even further. The United States under Eisenhower was expressing serious doubts about Brazil and questioning whether to withhold much-needed development aid.

By the middle of 1954, he had another problem. Corruption in his inner circle was getting worse and was being exposed in the press. It was an effective stick with which to beat him. In particular, the investigations and revelations by one journalist, Carlos Larcerda, were hurting him badly. Seemingly without Vargas's knowledge, the head of his personal security detail, Gregório Fortunato, nicknamed the 'Black Angel', decided to take matters into his own hands. On 5 August 1954, Larcerda was standing in Rua Tonelero, a street in Rio de Janeiro, outside the offices of the newspaper he'd founded. A group of men drove up and fired at him from the car. He was injured but survived the assassination attempt, though his bodyguard, a former air force major, was killed.

It became known as the 'Crime of Rua Tonelero' and it would cost Vargas his job, and his life. It didn't take long to link Fortunato to the attack. The scandal was huge – the president's own bodyguard masterminding the murder of his critics. The armed forces gave him the blunt choice: resign or be ousted. But Vargas took a third option. On 8.30 a.m. on 24 August, Getúlio Vargas sat on his bed in his pyjamas in the Catete presidential palace in Rio, put a revolver to his heart and pulled the trigger. He left a note which read: 'They don't accuse me, they insult me; they don't fight me, they slander me and deny me the right to defend myself.'

When Brazil's most important and divisive figure of the twentieth century took his own life, it barely registered with the child who would become its most important and divisive of the twenty-first. Lula was too young in 1954 to be politically conscious. He didn't see the outpouring of grief on the streets, a sort of posthumous beatification of the late dictator, or hear the crowds chanting 'Getúlio' and the more affectionate 'Gegê'. With no television or radio at home, the kids only noticed that the adults were talking gravely, maybe overheard snippets of conversations about the president who had killed himself and perhaps caught sight of the funeral photographs splashed across the front pages of the newspapers.[8]

The family was preoccupied with more prosaic matters. It was increasingly clear to Eurídice that living with Aristides wasn't working. He had acquired a second family and a severe drink problem since moving south. Aristides was a mean drunk with a foul temper and his alcoholism made him unpredictable. There were often bouts of domestic violence, his hands raised against the children, in particular the twelve-year-old Frei Chico. Even in his seventies, Lula's older brother's face contorts a little at the memory as he describes being the victim of his father's violent mood swings. 'He used to beat us for pleasure,' he confirmed bluntly.[9]

Helped by the lucky discovery by one of the kids, Vavá, of an envelope stuffed with almost 6,000 cruzeiros on the street, some three years' worth of the minimum wage, Dona Lindu cut her losses with Aristides and moved the family sixty miles away to the sprawling urban hub of São Paulo.[10] Lula was about to begin again in the bustling, choking industrial heartland with which he would be closely associated for the rest of his life. The family moved into the backroom of a bar in the Ipiranga neighbourhood, popular with workers from the nearby factories.

Lula's formal education, what little he had, mainly took place in Guarujá where he had attended the public school. By the age of twelve his schooling ended altogether, and he started work at a local drycleaners.

As president, his signature domestic policy in Brazil would be 'Bolsa Familia', which pulled hundreds of thousands of children out of working in conditions similar to the ones he experienced as a child and back into formal education by substituting their income with a state benefit of around $55 a month. Ingeniously simple, the family's eligibility for the allowance was partly dependent on the child's regular attendance in class.

Yet there was no *Bolsa Familia* for the poor in the 1950s, and the cruzeiros Lula contributed to the family budget as a boy were vital, no matter his tender age. What he missed in formal education, though, he would obtain later in vocational training through SENAI, or the *Serviço Nacional de Aprendizagem Industrial*. An apprentice and training scheme established under Getúlio Vargas, SENAI trained men and women in the vital roles for the country's push towards industrial growth from welders and fork-lift drivers to Lula's trade of lathe operator. His two years in the SENAI programme were among the most contented of his youth. Still a teenager, he attended classes while learning to use an industrial lathe, earning a modest but steady pay cheque and making his family proud. He worked at a factory making screws before moving on in search of better wages.

Just as things looked to be settling down for Lula, he was beset by a personal disaster, one from which he would always carry a scar. Working the nightshift in a different factory, he accidentally crushed the little finger on his left hand in the press when a screw came loose. The story goes that he had to wait several hours until the day-shift workers arrived before he was attended to. He lost the finger and, though he received a modest compensation package, he had to adapt to having a nub where his pinkie had once been. Given the prevalence of industrial accidents at that time, he was lucky he didn't lose more than just his little finger.

As Lula contemplated life with nine digits, Brazil was facing its own turmoil: 1964 was a defining year for the country. Amid the bipolar Cold War politics shaping the region, the Brazilian military took power in a *coup d'état*. A disciple of Getúlio Vargas, the Brazilian Labour Party politician João Goulart – known as Jango – had been elected with a reformist agenda. Distrusted by Washington DC as a radical and a communist, in reality he was neither and his reforms were relatively moderate. They involved straightforward changes which many had been clamouring for not just in Brazil but across South America for decades: agrarian reform, more equitable distribution of land and property, further widening of the electoral base and reforms in education, banking and government.

The military, however, saw Jango as a dangerous leftist leading the country towards Soviet-style communism. Stoked by Washington's deliberate efforts to destabilize him, the situation came to a head in March 1964. The pithily titled 'March of the Family with God for Freedom' took to the streets, a demonstration involving hundreds of thousands of protesters from Catholic and conservative organizations across Brazil, funded by the US in an effort to overthrow Goulart.[11]

The ploy was successful. By calling for his impeachment and decrying his reforms as stepping stones to a communist state, the mothers and labour union members who turned out in protest in early March set the president's removal in motion. By 31 March, Jango was gone.

Those who backed military rule might have been happy to see Goulart forced out, but few would have imagined there would be no civilian government in Brazil for the next twenty-one years. Military rule was enforced by a series of 'Institutional Acts', seventeen in total, the first of which was issued just eight days after the coup. The first Institutional Act gave the executive powers to suspend individual, electoral and constitutional rights, and it hindered Congress from interfering with decisions taken by the president, a position bestowed upon General Humberto Castelo Branco.

Still, if that was a punch to the solar plexus, Institutional Act 5, or AI-5, was a knockout blow to what little that remained of Brazil's fragile democracy. Decreed on 13 December 1968 by Castelo Branco's successor, General Artur Costa e Silva, AI-5 sounded the death knell for Congress. In essence, the act meant that the president could dissolve Congress – or force it into recess, which Costa e Silva immediately did – and assume all legislative powers. The president could also arbitrarily remove public servants at will, including judges and politicians, and habeas corpus was suspended for political prisoners. The act also imposed strict censorship in the arts and on the press.[12] Hardliners took more and more control, and the increasingly repressive regime was met by student protests and labour strikes, carried out by some courageous men and women.

The morning after AI-5 was proclaimed, one newspaper found an ingenious way around the strangulation of free speech. On 14 December 1968, the weather report in *Jornal do Brasil* read: 'Weather black. Temperature suffocating. The air is unbreathable. The country is being swept by strong winds.'[13]

The editors clearly weren't referring to the day's meteorological conditions, which were warm and clear. AI-5 ushered in a period known as '*Os Anos de Chumbo*', 'the Years of Lead'. Torture, extrajudicial killings, death squads, kidnappings, the full gamut of repression of the classic South American dictatorship began in earnest. What began as an illegal organization called 'Operação Bandeirante – OBAN' joined together various police forces and military units against left-wing opponents before becoming codified into the state's feared repressive intelligence agency, DOI-CODI. Meanwhile, Brazil became a keen and willing member of the loathsome CIA-backed 'Plan Condor', a covert state terror operation co-ordinated with other like-minded and murderous military dictators in the Southern Cone, from Alfredo Stroessner in Paraguay to Augusto Pinochet in Chile.

The dictatorship's nationalist sentiment was neatly summarized in the uncompromising slogan it chose to promote the nation: '*Brasil, ame-o ou deixe-o*' – 'Brazil, love it or leave it'. It was a bad and dangerous time to become involved in politics, especially the confrontational left-wing politics of the labour unions. Yet by the turn of the decade, Lula had already made an impressive start to his own career as a trade unionist and had started to clench his left hand into a four-fingered fist.

In the summer of 1969, a twenty-eight-year-old journalist moved into a family house in a leafy hilltop district of Rio de Janeiro, Santa Teresa. Fernando Gabeira was a quiet tenant in a quiet community. Had his neighbours been a little more observant, they might have noticed Gabeira had rented a large space for a man with no obvious wife or children. They might have seen that he left the house infrequently, or observed the occasional comings and goings to the house of other young men and women in a series of unexceptional cars. Still, Fernando was careful. Nothing in particular stood out.

Behind the walls of the house, there was no family or kids' play den. In one room, specially insulated to avoid drawing undue attention to the noise, an offset printing machine was set up. There, Fernando's main journalistic function was to write and publish the pamphlet of the 8th October Revolutionary Movement (MR8), a radical left-wing dissident group that had taken up arms against the military dictatorship.

The innocuous location that Fernando Gabeira had selected was soon to be used for something far more daring than the clandestine publication of the organization's propaganda. The guerrilla group had decided they needed to make a statement: they intended to kidnap the US ambassador to Brazil.

Recently appointed to his post, Ambassador Charles Burke Elbrick had spent most of his diplomatic career in Europe. Barely in the country two months, he and his wife, Elvira, were still unpacking and caught in the initial whirlwind of a new posting, cocktail parties, receptions, ceremonial visits. On his fifty-seventh day in Brazil, 4 September 1969, the couple had lunch together in one of the first moments of calm they had experienced since their arrival. Afterwards,

Ambassador Burke left with his driver for the embassy. As Elvira was in the basement sorting through pairs of Levi's jeans, cupcakes and boxes of Revlon makeup for an upcoming fundraiser, her secretary came downstairs and interrupted her: 'Your husband has just been kidnapped.'[14]

On his route to work, the ambassador's limousine had been cut off by a Volkswagen blocking its path in a side street. Gunmen spilled out and forced themselves into the diplomatic car. They pulled out the car phone, shoved a tarpaulin over Elbrick's head and pushed him onto the floor at gunpoint. They made their getaway before transferring their hostage to a van and driving him to Fernando Gabeira's safe house in the hills. The ambassador's driver was left shaken but unharmed, and inside the car was an envelope containing the kidnappers' list of demands.

Chief among them was the release of fifteen unnamed political prisoners and the publication of the MR8's manifesto on television, radio and in newspapers. The military junta had forty-eight hours to deliver the ultimatums or the guerrillas would 'be forced to carry out revolutionary justice' and execute their prized hostage.[15] They never did carry out that threat, not necessarily because it was hollow but because the junta acquiesced to their demands. A list of fifteen political prisoners was placed in a supermarket suggestions box by Fernando Gabeira and the military government was instructed where to find it. At the same time, the MR8's three-page manifesto was being read out on the airwaves by newsreaders.

As for the US ambassador, experiencing rather more drama in the first weeks of his new posting than he might have expected, he was dealing with the pressure admirably. During his four days in captivity, he engaged the young guerrillas in conversation and Gabeira remembers they discussed topics like the Black Panthers in the US and how the youth were changing the nation. Plus they spoke of torture in Brazil: 'He was a little surprised. He was not informed of the torture in the prisons. He was, to a certain extent, innocent. For him it was incredible to see something so leftist, so clear. We spoke the language of revolution.'[16]

At some point, either in the car or the safe house, Charles Burke Elbrick had received a crack on the head, which his wife said never fully healed and which she blamed for his later ill health. In the end, once the political prisoners had been put onto a flight to Mexico as the kidnappers demanded, he was released into a crowd of football fans as they flooded out of the Maracanã stadium. He was dressed as he had been taken, minus his tie, and in his hands a gift from his captors: a copy of a book by Ho Chi Minh, with the inscription: 'To our first political prisoner, with the expression of our respect for his calm behaviour in action.'[17]

In large part, the kidnappers of the 8th October Revolutionary Movement were young, idealistic kids with little idea of how to organize a guerrilla movement. In fact, they almost took the Portuguese ambassador hostage by mistake, something Fernando Gabeira admits 'would have been the mistake of the century'.[18]

The released prisoners made it to Mexico, despite a last-ditch attempt by a group of military officers to stop their plane from taking off. From Mexico, the majority went into exile and refuge in Cuba. As for the kidnappers, several were arrested and two were tortured and killed in jail. Fernando Gabeira was fortunate. He spent just six months in jail, then bounced around a few countries in exile before ending up in Sweden. On his return to Brazil he wrote a book about the kidnapping, which became an Oscar-nominated movie, and entered traditional politics as a deputy for Rio de Janeiro in the 1990s. He eventually repented having kidnapped the ambassador. 'It is not a good souvenir to have. It was not a good thing that was done. In spite of the fact that we could release fifteen people who were being tortured and were in danger of being killed inside jail. But as far as the kidnapping is concerned, it is not a good form of struggle.'[19]

Lula, meanwhile, wasn't interested in joining the armed struggle. He opposed the dictatorship in all its guises, but an urban guerrilla movement was never going to be his choice of battleground. Rather, his political awakening came more from a desire to improve the conditions on the shop floor for himself and his co-workers. And from the dreadful tragedy that was about to strike his young family.

★

Having registered with the metalworkers' union in September 1968 – membership number 25,986 – Lula was persuaded to run the following year for the union's leadership, largely thanks to pressure exerted by Frei Chico. 'It wasn't easy to convince him, but it was important he do it,' the older brother said.

Lula got married that year. Maria de Lourdes Ribeiro was a neighbour in São Paulo who worked in a textile firm and had come to the city with her family from the interior of the state. The courtship was brief but happy and Lula and Lourdes were married in May. Lourdes apparently needed some reassurance about Lula's union activities, such were the fears of what a prominent labour movement position in a time of dictatorship might mean for the young couple.[20]

However, the danger to them lay not with the cruelty of Brazil's military men but the incompetence of its medical staff and the inadequacy of its hospitals. Lourdes became pregnant and in 1971 she was admitted to hospital with serious complications at seven months. The diagnosis was hepatitis, but it took far too long to reach that conclusion, precious time being wasted while she suffered and vomited violently. Lula later told the story of how he found Lourdes 'screaming and screaming' in the hospital ward 'without any assistance'.[21] On returning home to gather some clothes for her, he received a call to rush back to the hospital as his wife was having an emergency caesarean.

The end of this story is heartbreakingly inevitable. Both mother and baby boy died in childbirth. Just twenty-five, Lula was overwhelmed with grief. No matter how common such a terrible loss was, and still is in Latin America, there could be no solace, nothing to ease his suffering or his anguish for many months. One of the few lessons he could take from it was a political one: that the poorest in Brazil received sub-standard healthcare and were never treated as a priority. It was a bitter blow. But like spending a childhood working on the streets or losing an appendage, the experience moulded the way Lula thought and influenced his politics. Above all others, this moment of terrible loss shaped the young immigrant from the northeast and left its indelible mark on him.

'Look,' he said, taking a moment to find the right words when I asked him about Lourdes' death almost fifty years later, 'I think on many occasions God put his finger in my head.' He still mourned Lourdes to this day, he said, but 'I believe that the adversities that take place in our lives happen so we learn how to overcome them and find another way to live'.

Such a philosophical and phlegmatic attitude to death eluded Lula at the time. His brother remembers 'the very deep cut, a very violent impact' of the death of Maria de Lourdes and the unborn baby boy. The family rallied around him – even the feckless Aristides made a short reappearance to throw an arm around his son.

When he emerged from the depths of his mourning, Lula was back living in the family home with Dona Lindu. It became apparent to him that the only thing he had left to hold onto was his family and his comrades. He threw himself deeper into both. Union leadership wasn't an immediate answer to his grief, but it took on a new importance, especially after Frei Chico was arrested in late 1975.

Lula had been elected to the presidency of the metalworkers' union in April of that year although his older brother had traditionally been the more politically active of the two, becoming a member of the illegal Brazilian Communist Party (PCB) in his late teens. While Lula was away in Japan at a Toyota conference, Frei Chico was picked up and tortured by the military. Frei Chico remembers they were trying to get him to confess that the real reason for Lula's trip was to deliver a letter to an exiled Communist Party leader. Contacted by telephone in Tokyo, Lula was warned against returning to São Paulo by comrades in the union leadership. He ignored the advice and returned in order to prise his brother from captivity in an army barracks.

'They tried to pin things on him, to show he was a [communist] militant but they had nothing on him,' Frei Chico told me over bottles of cold water in a bustling open-air café in Curitiba. 'From that point onwards, he understood that this was really a dictatorship. I think it was fundamental for him in understanding that.'

One of Lula's best biographers, Richard Bourne, agrees that the torture and cruel treatment of his brother had a 'radicalising effect' on him: 'Frei Chico, the father of a family, had been working since he was ten years old. What possible order or ideology could justify the arrest and torture of men like him? Lula was simply revolted. At the same time, he lost most sense of personal fear.'[22]

I jokingly asked the older Da Silva brother if Lula's subsequent tumultuous career in politics was all his fault? Slightly chubbier than his brother, bald and sporting a grey moustache, Frei Chico gave a wry smile before answering.

'If you think that one's starting point comes from the participation of another, then perhaps that's true. But he never accepted being a communist or being a party activist. All he wanted was to work in the union.'

In the 1970s, the Brazilian economy got steadily worse. In particular, the wealth gap became a chasm. In 1970, the poorest 50 per cent of the population made do with 14.9 per cent of GDP. By 1976, their share had shrunk to just 11.6 per cent. Conversely, over the same period, the richest 20 per cent of society enjoyed an increase from 62.2 to 67 per cent of GDP.[23] The dictatorship's supposed 'Economic Miracle' was well and truly over.

In late 1977 and early 1978, there was palpable anger among workers who found their wages devaluing month by month. Furthermore, it was revealed that the military government had been lying about the inflation figures since 1973–4. With the minimum wage tied to inflation, it mattered a great deal to the factory workers – not just in the car plants but across Brazilian industry – that such sharp practices and dishonest bookkeeping was going on. By the estimate of Lula's union, there had been a 34 per cent shortfall and the staff wanted to see their missing back pay.

A couple of smaller 'stoppages' – the preferred term by those nervous of speaking about 'strikes' – were held in the Mercedes-Benz and the Ford factories in March and April of 1978.[24] They were a precursor to much wider and uncompromising industrial action that would last for months. On 12 May, workers in the Saab-Scania factory downed tools and wouldn't pick them up again for seven months. In some cases, they employed intelligent methods of striking, for example by sitting at their machines but without touching them. Eventually the pressure paid off. Part of the missing wages was recovered, around 20 per cent in some cases – although Lula felt they could have gone further: 'with a bit more freedom we could recover not just 34 per cent but 68 per cent, because the fundamental question is the lack of liberty. And it has to be won, it can't come through law.'[25]

It was painted as a wholly spontaneous, organic reaction to the pay issue, largely to protect the strike leaders from retribution, but the reality was that Lula, in fact the entire union leadership, was learning fast. How to organize, how to speak in front of crowds, how to connect. Even at the time he noted that the workers' win against the bosses was formative: 'For the first time I started to believe in words.'[26]

He also determined that clandestine organization wasn't for him. It might have suited Frei Chico and his Communist Party comrades, or Hugo Chávez in Venezuela, silently plotting in the barracks. But Lula thought that 'clandestine work is difficult... that union struggles must be in the open'.[27]

What seems clear, though, is that the strikes – or 'wage recovery campaigns' – did two crucial things. They showed that the military dictatorship could be forced to back down with sufficient organization among workers and ordinary people. And they thrust Lula onto the national stage. He appears in a television programme from the same year on *TV Cultura*, smoking profusely, his hair still chestnut brown and with a moustache rather than his later trademark beard. He comes across as inherently reasonable – undoubtedly a radical by the standards of Brazil's military dictatorship but calmly answering pre-recorded questions about union activities from members of the public in a talk show called *Vox Populi*.

In it, he gives the early indications of a plan beyond the union, the emergence of a political party for the workers and for the working class. With the de facto government still in place, he wasn't yet necessarily planning a presidential bid, but the idea of a Workers' Party was the logical next step. He saw a party as an extension of the clamouring for a voice he had seen among the metalworkers and the strikers, many of whom had risked their jobs to obtain a living wage from a government which had shown few qualms about torturing and murdering its opponents.

Years earlier, Lula had abandoned his own job at the lathe, as had the rest of the leadership, to focus more fully on professionalizing the union movement. The next phase, though, was to move beyond the shop floor and into national politics by forming the *Partido dos Trabalhadores*, the Workers' Party (PT). A variety of factors made it possible to form a political party. The military dictatorship had been weakened even before the wage recovery campaigns by the 1973 oil crisis. As the OPEC nations cut their production and sent prices up 400 per cent, Brazil racked up enormous debts to pay for its foreign oil.[28] Another oil shock was on its way in 1979.

The military dictatorship's economic woes and mismanagement were causing its popularity to plummet. Anticipating a backlash, the military began what was ostensibly a less harsh, less repressive phase known as the '*distensão*', meaning 'decompression', under the presidency of Ernesto Geisel. In turn, it would lead to the '*abertura*', or 'opening', a gradual easing of the military's vice-like grip over national politics. Political life in Brazil even during the *abertura* remained difficult and dangerous. Dissidents still risked their lives, students weren't suddenly free from police control and the country didn't become a model of democracy overnight.[29] Still, in 1978, the reviled Institutional Act 5 was lifted and, under pressure to allow greater public participation, the government passed the Party Reform Bill a year later.

As the seventies ended, and Lula took stock, he must have felt a spark of optimism once more. He had lost everything a young husband and father-to-be could lose at the start of the decade. The deaths of Lourdes and the baby had hollowed him out emotionally, threatened to destroy him completely for a time. Yet as he ushered in the New Year in 1980, his life was almost unrecognizable. He had remarried to Marisa Letícia Rocco Casa, a widowed administrator in a state school. Her late husband had been killed in a brawl and Marisa was bringing up her son alone. Once married, Lula legally adopted the boy. Over the next two decades, Lula and Marisa Letícia would share the entire journey from their modest apartment in São Bernardo do Campo to the presidential palace in Brasilia and would only be separated by death. When they met, Lula had also had a daughter, Lurian, from a brief relationship with another woman and soon their children together began to arrive. Two boys were born before 1980 and a third a few years later.

Beyond his stable family life, Lula had also scored his biggest political victories as union president. By February, the Workers' Party was a reality. It might have seemed unlikely as Marisa Letícia was cutting out red fabric to sew together the party's first flag, but Lula had embarked on a path that would eventually take him to the highest office in the country.

'The greatest musical show of all time,' the flyer proclaimed. Despite the hyperbole, 30 April 1981 promised to be an unmissable evening for those lucky enough to get their hands on a ticket. The line-up was a mouth-watering prospect for any fan of Brazilian music: Gonzaguinha, Luiz Gonzaga, Beth Carvalho, Fagner, Alceu Valença, MPB-4. The best of the country's rich tradition of samba, *forró* and *Tropicália*, all playing at the invitation and behest of the great Chico Buarque, perhaps Brazil's finest bossa nova musician and one of the country's most beloved sons.

The concert had a political tinge, too. It was being held to celebrate and usher in the following day, 1 May – the International Day of the Worker. By its very nature, the military government didn't like it. Still, the artists were determined to go ahead and the concert sold out quickly.

As the kids started to stream towards Riocentro, a huge convention centre in Rio de Janeiro – the largest in Latin America – two men stood apart from the bohemians and bearded beatniks in the audience. Guilherme Pereira do Rosário and Wilson Dias Machado weren't there for the music.

Sitting in a metallic-grey Puma GTE in the parking lot as the crowd began to assemble in the amphitheatre, the two men were DOI-CODI officers, code-named Agent 'Wagner' and 'Dr Marcos'. The only outward sign of their true identities, a sergeant and a captain respectively, was their military buzzcuts. The two-door sports car, with the false licence plate OT0297, had been seen earlier that day outside a restaurant as they ran through the final details of their operation over lunch. Most of the planning had taken place in the restaurant and the brothel next door.

The plan was to detonate four devices at strategic points around the convention centre to create as much panic and chaos as possible. One was to be placed near the stage while another would cut the lights and the power. With around 20,000 people at the event, those not caught in the explosion could have easily been crushed in the subsequent stampede for the exit. Fortunately, it didn't go that way.

Instead, as they drove the car into position, the device went off in Sergeant Pereira do Rosário's lap. He was killed instantly. Captain Dias Machado was badly injured and was carted off to hospital unconscious. The bomb intended for the electrical plant running the Riocentro was thrown into the right place by other operatives and exploded, but it didn't affect the show, which kept going. The audience were none the wiser until the very end of the show when the musician Gonzaguinha announced on stage that 'People against democracy placed bombs here that were to intimidate you.'[30]

Outside the concert, the press took photographs and film footage of the destroyed sports car with Pereira do Rosário's body still slumped in the seat, blood caked across his face. The photographers also got pictures of the remaining two bombs and apparently compromising documents inside the car before agents of the regime arrived and disposed of them. Visibly shaken, the concert organizer, Chico Buarque, said the bungled attacks were an act of 'cowardice without name'.[31] General Gentil Marcondes Filho, an army commander, appeared on the scene to say the investigators were doing their work but poured scorn on the suggestion this was an act of terrorism by the state, saying that was 'a very vague hypothesis'.[32] The security secretary for Rio, General Waldir Muniz, also added his more specific version of events. The two men, who he confirmed worked for the state security apparatus, were there precisely because they were attending to reports of an explosive device at the concert. He even recreated a snippet of their conversation in front of the media saying the sergeant had commented to the captain: 'Look here, a strange explosive', before it went off. Asked how he had gleaned such precise information from one dead man and an unconscious one, the general grew furious with the journalists shouting at them: 'What is this? An interrogation or an interview?'[33]

The official obfuscation would last a lot longer than a quick on-the-scene interview. The initial investigation was little more than a cover-up, sticking to the line that Pereira do Rosário and Dias Machado were answering a call about the bomb. That they were driving a car with false plates while supposedly on duty was quietly ignored and the case was archived. An amnesty law established after the fall of the military dictatorship covered crimes committed between 1961 and 1979. As the Riocentro attack didn't fall inside that period, a fresh investigation was opened at the end of the 1990s.

In this inquiry, six men, including retired Captain Dias Machado, were identified as being part of a radical DOI-CODI cell intent on blaming the attack on left-wing groups to justify a return to hardline policies. Greater funding would again flow towards their agency, they figured, if their false flag bombing had been executed successfully. Again, though, there was no comeback against the men involved. The statute of limitations was deemed to have expired and, once more, retired Captain Dias Machado and his co-conspirators rested easy. His last word on the matter was hissed at a National Truth Commission hearing in 2014, during the government of Lula's successor, President Dilma Rousseff – herself a torture victim of the dictatorship. Dias Machado's grey wavy hair was parted in the centre, his eyebrows still thick and black, dressed in a striped blue shirt, a picture of respectability. He said nothing throughout the proceedings, choosing not to incriminate himself further over his repugnant acts of three decades earlier. His only utterance was this statement: 'I have given full explanations to Military Justice three times and I was tried by the Supreme Military Tribunal. I gave testimony to the Public Ministry twice. It's all there.'

The Riocentro bombs showed that opponents of the regime were still operating in a deeply dangerous environment well into the 1980s. There had been other attacks and kidnappings by right-wing extremists and the car of one of Lula's union comrades, João Paulo Pires de Vasconcelos, was blown up in 1979. He narrowly escaped with his life.

Yet the explosions also marked the end of the dictatorship. The pact with the hard-line faction was that the investigation would be suppressed but that general elections in 1982 would go ahead. In them, Lula stood as a candidate for the governor of São Paulo – having now legally changed his name to 'Lula' to make it easier for voters to identify him – but fared poorly. The PT didn't do well nationally either as the nascent political party suffered its first major electoral setback.

Yet there was little time to lick their wounds. Instead, the party rallied around a new cause in 1984: '*Diretas Ja!*' It was a call to instate direct elections for the presidency and the kind of campaign Lula thrived on. A popular demand, one coming from below, to correct an injustice being carried out against millions of voters especially the illiterate and the poor. In a rare moment of unity, the opposition parties agreed to lend their weight to the campaign bringing hundreds of thousands out for rallies in São Paulo and Rio de Janeiro.

As the campaign reached its crescendo in April 1984, a state of emergency was declared in Brasilia with troops on the streets for several days ahead of a vote on the constitutional amendment by the deputies in Congress. Ultimately, the push fell short of the two-thirds majority required to change the law, but it was changed anyway the following May by Congress. Millions of excluded citizens could now vote directly for the president and political parties were legalized.

With the oxygen of its repressive control over Brazil's politics withdrawn, the ailing military dictatorship was finally dead.

Lula was now in a position to take a shot at the presidency. His national recognition was established – the public knew who he was, especially after he was elected as a PT parliamentary deputy in congressional elections in 1986. He had handled himself with dignity in some tough moments, both personally and politically. He rarely dwelt on these things, but he was proud of having risked his life through the union's activities under military rule and of fulfilling his promise to establish a Workers' Party. Everything he had done, he believed, showed he was not afraid to rub shoulders with the people.[34] He wanted to govern the country in a similar vein.

'Lula-lá, a star is shining, Lula-lá, the hope is growing' went the catchy jingle of his 1989 presidential campaign. Much like his run for the governorship of São Paulo, Lula had emphasized his everyman credentials, banking on the idea that voters wanted someone much like them at the helm. Unfortunately for Lula, they didn't. The long decades of elite rule still conditioned attitudes among Brazilian voters. They had been led to think of their leaders as exclusively educated, wealthy and white. Lula's more earthy appeal didn't yet translate to a mass audience in 1989.

The timing worked against him in many ways. In mid-November, he scraped into second place to ensure he would go into a run-off vote for the presidency against the conservative candidate, Fernando Collor de Mello. The fall of the Berlin Wall allowed opponents in influential sections of the media to paint Lula as part of a Cold War past which the world was rejecting. In the months preceding the election, Lula had travelled to a handful of nations including the Sandinista-run Nicaragua and Cuba where he met Fidel Castro. 'Lula and capitalism – changes promised by the PT divide Brazil', the rightwing magazine *Veja* ran on its front page ahead of the vote:

'In the final run up to the elections, there has never been a candidate such as Luiz Inácio Lula da Silva, nor has there ever been a real chance of a party such as the PT being elected to administrate the federal government apparatus... a party which comprises, within its various factions, trade unionists showing different degrees of aggressiveness, strike leaders and left-wing cultists who love praising Sandinism in Nicaragua, Fidel Castro's communism and class struggle.'[35]

The insinuation of *Veja*'s editors was clear: why choose an unreformed socialist for president as Brazil moved into the postmodern nineties? It was a position echoed by scores of other conservative commentators. Worse still, the Globo TV network, which televised the candidate's debate, in the days before the event was carried live, flagrantly manipulated the edit to highlight Collor de Mello's best moments and Lula's worst – anything to stave off a PT victory.

The final vote was on 17 December 1989 and Lula fared better than perhaps he would have expected when he first announced his candidacy. But he still lost by five percentage points. In the New Year, Fernando Collor de Mello was inaugurated as Brazil's first directly elected president of the post-dictatorship era. At just forty, he was also its youngest. Lula, though, had a new purpose.

By the premature end of his time in office, Collor de Mello was widely despised as a corrupt and grossly inefficient president. Even his own brother, Pedro Collor de Mello, played a role in his downfall. A journalist at the family-owned newspaper *Gazeta de Alagoas*, Pedro gave a lengthy interview in which he accused his brother of running a vast corruption ring. He said that President Collor de Mello was working in tandem with his campaign treasurer, a bald, moustachioed bank clerk of a man called Paulo César Farias – or PC Farias. The graft schemes the president and his frontman controlled ranged from shell companies in telecommunications to influence-peddling and generated hundreds of millions in bribes. The whistleblowing Pedro spilt the beans to the press so much that his own mother accused him of having gone mad.

'I don't just think PC Farias is the president's frontman,' Pedro Collor de Mello said in May 1992, 'I categorically affirm that he is.'[36] His brother's political fate was sealed. As public anger grew at his thievery, his neoliberal economic reforms and his inability to tackle hyperinflation, in September that year President Fernando Collor de Mello resigned hours before he was impeached. His vice-president,

Itamar Franco, took over for the remainder of his mandate. Collor de Mello's accomplice, PC Farias, fled to Thailand. Arrested and deported back to Brazil, he served two years of a seven-year sentence though fresh charges were pending when he and his young girlfriend were found shot dead in his beach house in Alagoas. The hasty conclusion of a botched investigation was that it was a 'crime of passion', a murder-suicide carried out by the girlfriend – despite ample evidence of foul play – marking another murky episode in Brazil's precarious democracy.

Two more presidential votes were held in 1994 and 1998. Lula was a candidate on each occasion and both times he lost out to Fernando Henrique Cardoso, an intellectual and former finance minister applauded for the successful introduction of the new currency, the real, over the cruzeiro. FHC, as he was known, reined in the rampant inflation and gave a sense of academic stability after the years of upheaval during the end of military rule and Collor de Mello's chaotic corruption. The tone towards Lula was perhaps more respectful under FHC, with fewer dirty tricks in campaigning, yet the business elites and the media conglomerates were still united in their opposition to the former strike leader.

Fernando Henrique Cardoso's campaign was well financed and well run, and the success of the Real Plan, the currency switchover, was obvious on polling day. On 3 October 1994, he recorded the largest margin of victory in a Brazilian presidential election, decimating Lula by two votes to one. He took 54.3 per cent of the ballots cast to Lula's 27 per cent. Henrique Cardoso's first term was popular enough for him to be re-elected with a similarly commanding majority four years later. He had extended a promising state-level social development programme, '*Bolsa Escola*', to the federal level which would later form the basis of Lula's *Bolsa Familia* – although the latter plan was more extensive and successful in terms of poverty alleviation.

Lula was finding it hard not to lose faith. By 1998, he had lost three consecutive presidential campaigns. He often fared better than the PT but for now there was no sense of him 'outgrowing' the party. Anyway, he didn't really have anywhere else to go and the creation of a breakaway Lula group would have been a strategic error. Instead, there was little choice but to gird himself for another final shot at it. 'I think Lula has something the rest of us don't,' laughed Frei Chico of his brother's three failed bids for president, 'and that's perseverance. It gives him a greater probability of achieving his objectives.'

Beyond just his tenacity and persistence, though, the region's political stars were realigning at the start of the twenty-first century. When Lula launched his 2002 campaign, Hugo Chávez had already broken through in Venezuela, viable left-wing candidates were cropping up in a range of South American countries and voters were crying out for something new. Lula's campaign slogan that year was 'Hope Vanquishes Fear'.

More than thirty years after joining the labour movement, more than twenty after founding the Workers' Party, after three failed bids for the presidency and countless days on the campaign trail, Lula was finally elected president in late October 2002. The margin of victory was huge, too, beating his conservative challenger, José Serra, by 61 to 39 per cent.

The scenes of his swearing-in ceremony on New Year's Day in 2003 in Brasília are a reminder of the extent of the popular reaction to Lula's win. Overjoyed kids, unionists and students celebrated with drumming and dancing and took over every corner of the Oscar Niemeyer-conceived seat of power, Brasília. Many of them had camped out for days ahead of the inauguration and travelled by bus from as far afield as Lula's home state of Pernambuco to witness the moment. It was an outpouring of the kind of hope he was referring to in his campaign slogan and which he reiterated in his opening remarks.

'The time has come to tread a new path,' he told the crowds outside and the millions watching at home.[37] Whether they were in the wealthy neighbourhoods or in the shanty towns of Brazil's big cities, whether they owned vast landholdings or were farm hands in the poorest villages, Lula promised 'a new style of government' and to change things with 'courage and care, humility and daring'.[38]

In retrospect, his speech on that 1 January morning did usher in a new style of governance in Brazil, one that strove to prioritize the poor more than any other administration in the post-dictatorship era. Yet to reach the presidential palace he had been forced to take steps akin to the old style of government. Under the influence of a talented but politically amoral campaign marketing guru called José Eduardo Cavalcanti de Mendonça, or 'Duda', Lula sharpened up his image, compromised on his message and toned down some of his most rigid demands. To the annoyance of many in the PT, he promised not to default on the national debt, a crucial issue as neighbouring Argentina slid into a deep economic crisis, the effects of which would be felt for years. Duda Mendonça's slick campaign videos created an image of a less fiery, more business-friendly Lula, of a man who remained in touch with the people but who had matured since his union days and was now ready for high office. He picked a wealthy self-made businessman from an evangelical party as his running mate. Together, these steps had the cumulative effect of easing the nerves of major foreign and national businesses and convincing a sizeable portion of the electorate that this former lathe operator had evolved and could now be trusted with one of the biggest economies in the world.

The section of the poor who had always been attracted to Lula was especially keen on one proposal in 2002: his hunger eradication plan '*Fome Zero*', meaning 'Zero Hunger'. It was present from day one, appearing in the opening speech as he promised to create the conditions for all Brazilians 'to have three decent meals a day, every day, without having to depend on donations from anybody'. Brazil could no longer tolerate so much inequality, he said, and his government was about to wage war on hunger, extreme poverty and social exclusion. 'Our war is not meant to kill anyone – it is meant to save lives.'

The Lula government quickly established the Extraordinary Ministry of Food Security and Fight Against Hunger to manage and direct the Zero Hunger project. Whatever else might have been achieved by Brazil at that time, either at home or abroad, this plan was the blueprint which underpinned Lula's administration.[39] It was composed of a variety of measures including the Food Acquisition Program (PAA), under which the state purchased its food stocks from family farmers, thereby bolstering the farmers' incomes and creating a reserve of supplies for use in other food security programmes. For example, in the National School Meal Programme (PNAE), which provided a free, healthy meal of decent quality with more fruit and vegetables. The biggest triumph, though, and today Lula's proudest legacy, was the family grant programme, *Bolsa Familia*. Considered 'the largest conditional cash transfer program in the world to date',[40] the modest but invaluable family stipend was predicated on a social contract between the family and the state which involved stipulations like compulsory school attendance for children and regular pre-natal visits.

The success of *Bolsa Familia* lay in the fact that it wasn't enacted in isolation but as part of a broader poverty eradication strategy. In addition to the Zero Hunger plan, there was also a huge push towards microcredits and soft loans to the poorest communities. There was a massive effort to build more universities and bring more Afro-Brazilians into higher education. Brazil's vast wealth gap, which for decades had turned the country into one of the most unequal nations on earth, was finally being tackled in a meaningful way.

Like most benefit systems, there was a degree of manipulation by some recipients of *Bolsa Familia* which opponents seized on, saying it encouraged laziness, dependence on state handouts and that it was unaffordable. But no matter what Lula's many critics said about the supposedly unsustainable nature of the programmes – itself a debatable point – the simple truth of the matter is that they worked undeniably well.

The percentage of Brazilian households living in extreme poverty fell from 17.4 per cent in 2001 to less than 9 per cent in 2008.[41] Few world leaders were able to cut their country's poverty rates by more than half at that time and Lula remains defiant about any criticism of that achievement, especially the accusation that he created an unsustainable and clientelist system:

'That's what the Brazilian elite say. Every time that you develop policies of social inclusion, the intellectuals of the right wing come along and say you're being a populist. They would say, "Lula can't spend on *Bolsa Familia*, Lula has to build bridges and roads." And I'd answer: "If the people ate cement or ate asphalt, that would be my priority. But people eat beans, rice, flour, bread. So the priority is to give them food. Once they have food, then they will be able to build the roads and the bridges that we lack in Brazil."'[42]

Over the course of his presidency, the UN heralded *Bolsa Familia* as a blueprint for other developing countries to imitate.[43] The funds were primarily given to the female head of the household – the Dona Lindu figure – and, by empowering millions of women like her across Brazil, Lula's own life experiences were again evident in his social development policy. *Bolsa Familia* and *Fome Zero* were very personal crusades for Lula: 'Hunger is a disease,' he told me. Eradicating it in Brazil was the cross on which he would hang his presidency and stake his popularity.

Yet it is also clear that without the spike in global commodities prices, Lula's social programmes would have been almost impossible to introduce so widely. The oil giant Petrobras, Brazil's largest company, was fundamental to the economic boom. In 2006, the discovery of a huge, untapped oil field in the pre-salt layer, a geological formation created by the breakup of the supercontinent Gondwanaland, became the region's biggest oil discovery of the past few decades. Initially called the Tupi oil field, it later became known as simply the 'Lula oil field' – supposedly for the word 'squid' in Portuguese, but Petrobras was fooling no one. As the number of platforms and oil rigs increased, it became Brazil's most productive oil and gas field, generating some 30 per cent of the country's production.[44]

'Pre-salt oil is a passport to the future,' said Lula at the time. 'It should go on educating the next generations, culture, the environment, fighting poverty and developing technology and science.'[45] The benefit of the wealth creation wasn't confined to the poorest, though; far from it. The middle class grew fast and, inevitably, the richest got richer, too, albeit slightly more slowly than the rest of society. As the

Brazilian poverty expert Ricardo Paes de Barros clarified: 'The incomes of individuals in the lowest decile of the income distribution is growing at Chinese rates, while the income of the richest decile grows at German rates.'[46]

It all made Lula wildly popular among certain sectors in society. Adoration of him rivalled that of Hugo Chávez in neighbouring Venezuela. The extent of that idolization became clear to me in one of the most remote parts of Brazil I have visited.

The boat to Codajás leaves early, before the morning has completely broken over Manaus, the capital of Amazonas state, deep in the rainforest. As the sun rises across the river, it reveals the intersection of the Amazon and its mighty tributary, the Rio Negro, a clearly defined line in the water where the earthy black Rio Negro mingles with the coffee-coloured Amazon. As the motorboat headed out from the port, I settled in for an uncomfortable trip. Six hours of relentless river journey beckoned, as we began to push upstream to Codajás. Beside me in the boat that morning were local *ribeirinhos*, river-dwellers who inhabit the banks of the Amazon and whose lives have changed little over the past fifty years. Sitting together in small groups were mothers and children who had gone to Manaus to sell their fish, pick up supplies or to visit family in the city.

As we picked up speed, river life flashed past in a collage of fleeting images: a village on stilts, rickety wooden homes called *palafitas*, cement and breezeblock evangelical churches as the Seventh Day Adventists and Pentecostals continued to colonize even the furthest Amazonian outposts. We overtook paddle steamers and party boats playing samba, part of the inexorable penetration of tourism into the deepest reaches of the globe. Then, eventually, the trip settled into a monotonous rhythm of dense forest, a solid wall of thick green on either side interrupted by the occasional sight of a group of women washing clothes and kids splashing in the water.

Codajás is known as '*A Terra do Açaí*', 'the Land of Açaí'. It is one of Brazil's main centres of production of the tiny berry, the super-fruit on which the town's income is based. As I disembarked the boat, bending double to stretch out my back and aching limbs, I was approached by a bespectacled man with weathered skin. As the only foreigner on the only boat from Manaus that day, I can't have been hard to identify. '*Eu sou Carlos Crispim*,' he said with a friendly grin, holding out his hand.

Carlos Crispim Rodrigues was the then vice-president of the Mixed Cooperative of Products and Regional Fruits of Codajás – though I hear that today he has risen to become its president. He was one of the leaders of the town's açai co-operative and my guide to the rainforest and the town. We began with a short journey by 4x4 into the forest. It didn't take long to reach a point where the jungle was so thick that walking and hacking with machete was easier than driving. Carlos took me to a point where the açai palms were abundant, the small blueberry-like fruits hanging heavy in bundles at the tops of the trunks. A member of the co-operative quickly shinned up the palm with incredible ease, his only harness a loosely bound piece of cloth between his ankles, to harvest the fruit, the lifeblood of the town.

The bundle of berries he brought back down had become much more valuable to Codajás in recent months. It was May 2008 and the Amazonian fruit's anti-ageing, antioxidant properties had been extolled by Oprah Winfrey and Gwyneth Paltrow, the first celebrities to kick off a new health fad. Suddenly the humble açai was hip, the Amazonian cure-all being ordered in Manhattan and Milan in everything from smoothies to facials. For Carlos and the agricultural collective in Codajás, the new-found thirst for their product, the trendiness of açai, was a uniquely profitable opportunity. With the world suddenly demanding a fruit that had been quietly feeding families in the Amazon for centuries, the price had risen eightfold in a matter of months. A credit line from the Lula government had helped the co-op to buy a processing machine from a German company, a loud, rattling metal contraption which stripped the açai berries from their stems and funnelled them into sacks for export.

The plant grew wild with next to no human intervention, no pesticides or neatly planted orchards or machination beyond the noisy sorting machine. It was as organic a product and as local an industry as perhaps exists in Brazil, yet it was opening up to a globalized world of the super-rich, of people thousands of miles away craving antioxidant creams made from exotic jungle fruits. After the tour, Carlos and I sat and drank beer as the sun went down near a gaudy monument to the açaí farmer erected in the main plaza. Carlos told me about the town's annual açaí festival, how hundreds of tourists descended on Codajás to enjoy the music and the stalls serving the berry as a juice or an ice cream or liquidized with a sprinkling of tapioca on top.

We also talked about Lula, Carlos's eyes nearly glazing over in appreciation at the 'Worker President'. 'None of what we've done here would be possible without him,' he told me. 'He's helped the poor a lot out here', motioning with his arm to the green expanse that lay beyond the town. There were pictures of Lula and campaign posters for the PT spread all around Codajás, and the co-operative had one up in its small factory. These people had voted Lula into power in 2002 and had voted him back in 2006. They were far removed, thousands of miles, from the industrial belt of São Paulo, Lula's traditional heartland, yet they shared with their fellow workers the sense that 'one of theirs' was at the helm, a sentiment which was sweeping the region from Chávez in Venezuela to Evo Morales in Bolivia.

Still, my river journey up the Amazon was in the early part of Lula's second term, when his position as president was firm, when he stood on solid political ground. He was basking in the popularity that came with sustained economic growth, genuine poverty reduction and prioritizing the poor. Before then, though, he had almost come completely unstuck. In his first term, a scandal engulfed his administration, threatened his party and looked set to bring an abrupt end to the presidency he had sought for so long.

The well-dressed man ushered his guests into two revolving office chairs opposite him. The black-and-white video, being filmed by one of the guests with a tiny camera hidden inside a briefcase or strapped to his body, wobbled wildly as he sat down, then settled into focus.

Across the desk, the well-dressed man's striped tie was in a full Windsor knot and on his wrist he wore a nice-looking watch with a leather strap. The three men chatted a little and, niceties dispensed with, quickly got down to business. The guest doing the secret filming reached over the desk and handed the well-dressed man a bundle of notes folded in half. The well-dressed man didn't count the money but simply pocketed the wad – 3,000 reais, at the time worth around $1,200– into his suit jacket.

With his confidence won, the well-dressed man started to talk, openly and irresponsibly. He was Maurício Marinho, head of contracting and administration at Correios, the Brazilian postal service. He thought his guests were legitimate businessmen, keen on trying to get their company onto the post office's official list of computer equipment suppliers. 'It's very easy,' he tells them. The man at the top had him 'covered', he bragged. 'He speaks to me, he doesn't leave messages.' Not only was it possible to buy a company onto such a list but the tenders could be rigged. Yet the 3,000 reais bribe was just the start. He went on to lay out details of something far more politically explosive.

Though Lula had won the presidency by a country mile in 2002, his PT parliamentarians had fared less well. In order to form a functioning government, he had made non-ideological alliances with a variety of minor parties including the PTB, the Brazilian Labour Party. According to the loose-lipped Marinho, the PTB had been able to place its people at the top of the postal service and a utilities company as a political sweetener for its alliance with the Lula government. As Richard Bourne described: 'The PTB was then milking bribes from these state enterprises in a systematic fashion; in one case... the enterprise was required to produce 400,000 reais (roughly $200,000) a month for the party.'[47]

Unfortunately for Maurício Marinho, he wasn't speaking to a couple of company directors looking for an illicit helping hand but to a lawyer, Joel Santos Filho, who was being paid by a disgruntled businessman to film the meeting – either to expose the corruption or to blackmail him over it. It wasn't long before the whole thing snowballed. In a front-page splash in its 18 May 2005 edition, *Veja* magazine published the contents of the video and exposed the link to Roberto Jefferson, a director at Correios and leader of the Brazilian Labour Party in Congress. His relationship to the Lula government was key. Historically, the PTB had been the party of Getúlio Vargas before being disbanded by the military dictatorship. By 2005, the reborn party was headed by the opportunist Jefferson, who had previously backed Collor de Mello and whose primary interest was proximity to the government of the day for the potential lucrative openings it would bring. Plenty in the PT had had their doubts about aligning with the likes of Jefferson and the PTB in the first place. Now, facing an inevitable expulsion from Congress, the stripping of his parliamentary privileges and a possible prison sentence, Jefferson chose to go down fighting. Guns blazing, in fact.

He went to the newspaper *Folha de São Paulo* and laid out the entire unsavoury business, blow-by-blow and naming names. In essence, he set out the details of a vote-buying scheme in which the PT was paying out a monthly payment of 30,000 reais to specific deputies in exchange for their support in parliament. The scandal became known as the *mensalão* – the big monthly payment – and Brazilians began to follow every twist and turn of the subsequent investigation. The funds had apparently been funnelled through an advertising agency with close ties to the government, but the scandal quickly spread to every murky corner of Brazilian political life from lobbyists to illegal gambling to the mafia. It emerged that Duda Mendonça, the publicity guru whose PR work had been so crucial in getting Lula elected, had been paid with money from offshore accounts. Things got especially weird when the assistant to the brother of the PT president was found trying to flee Brazil with $100,000 stuffed down his underpants and more in his hand luggage.

At the very top of the PT, Jefferson implicated the party's president, José Genoino, its treasurer, Delúbio Soares, and Lula's chief of staff, José Dirceu. One of the political prisoners released by the kidnapping of the US ambassador, Dirceu was a founding member of the Workers' Party and about as close a comrade as Lula had at that time. The heads rolled. All three men resigned and, in time, they were sentenced to prison along with many others over the *mensalão*. Unsurprisingly, the question asked over and over throughout the scandal was: how much did Lula know?

He claimed he'd known nothing. His closest allies, even those facing some serious jail time over the affair, consistently argued he was unaware of what was happening and wasn't party to the illegal monthly stipends. Nevertheless, the calls were growing by the day for him to step down, barely halfway through his first term. As was his traditional response when his back was against the wall, as it most certainly was over the *mensalão*, Lula came out fighting: 'In the history of the republic, no government has done even twenty percent of what we are doing to counter corruption. No one has more moral and ethical authority than I do,' he retorted after the scandal came to light.[48]

This early scandal wouldn't claim Lula's scalp. In the sweep of deputies and politicos drawn into the sleazy, grubby mess, he avoided any lasting stain although his reputation was damaged. If it wasn't for the popularity of the social programmes, the economic boom he was still enjoying as China bought up Brazil's beef, soya, steel and oil, the *mensalão* might have ended very differently for Lula. It served, however, as a forewarning about corruption in his government. But it was not heeded.

As Jean Charles de Menezes left his flat, number 17 Scotia Road in Tulse Hill, south London, there was a slight urgency in his step. It was a little before nine-thirty in the morning and he had to get to Kilburn, on the other side of the city, to fix a broken fire alarm. The twenty-seven-year-old Brazilian was an electrician, a good one, and had been in the UK for three years sharing the poky apartment with two cousins, Vivian and Patricia. Recently life in London had been going well for Jean Charles. The British capital wasn't an easy city to adapt to. The southeastern districts – Tulse Hill, Brixton, Stockwell, Camberwell – were a long way from his birthplace in rural Minas

Gerais, and even from São Paulo where he had moved as a teenager to find a job. But there was a fairly large Latino community in that part of London and he had found work doing something that he was talented at, so much so that he was able to send money back each month to his family in Brazil.

Dressed in a light denim jacket and jeans, he was unencumbered that morning as he'd left his tool belt with a colleague. But as he emerged from the block of flats on Scotia Road, he was being watched by undercover armed police.

London was on edge. It was 22 July 2005, just two weeks after Islamist terrorists had torn three underground trains and a double-decker bus apart in suicide attacks on 7 July. Fifty-two people had been killed that day and, although Londoners were showing their traditional stoicism in the face of adversity, people were uneasy. Another co-ordinated attempt to bomb the city's public transport system had failed the day before, on 21 July, but had further heightened tension across the city. One of the group which had attempted the latest bomb attacks, Hussain Osman, also lived at the block on Scotia Road – at flat number 21, four doors down from Jean Charles – and it was being staked out based on a gym membership card found among the bombers' belongings bearing that address.

When Jean Charles walked towards the bus stop to travel to Brixton tube station, any one of a series of momentary decisions could have saved his life. The surveillance officer, code-named 'Frank', who was tasked with filming the comings and goings on Scotia Road, had taken that exact moment to relieve himself into a bottle, missing the chance to record Jean Charles' face as he exited the block and allowing an assumption that Jean Charles was Hussain Osman to gather pace. The officer, 'Ivor', who followed the Brazilian didn't intercept him as he boarded the bus or question him about who he was or where he was going. Instead, he noted that the suspect had 'Mongolian eyes.'[49] The police further convinced themselves that de Menezes was their man when he briefly stepped off the bus, noticed that Brixton tube station was closed and got back on to continue to the next stop, Stockwell. It was, the officers concluded, an attempt to throw them off the scent. Again, none of them approached him or did anything to establish whether they were tracking an Islamist suicide bomber or a Brazilian electrician.

There, as he swiped his way onto the Underground with a valid pass, and in possession of a valid permit to be in the country, he picked up a free newspaper to read on his journey to work. Once settled in a seat, it took seconds for the firearms officers following him to burst onto the Victoria Line train. Another few seconds for 'Ivor' sitting near the Brazilian to point him out to his onrushing armed colleagues, 'Charlie 12' and 'Charlie 2', by yelling 'he's here'. Another second or so to pin de Menezes back down as he stood up in confusion. Then thirty seconds for the officers to fire a total of eleven shots in three-second intervals at Jean Charles, hitting him seven times in the head and once in the shoulder. At no point, a witness later testified, did they identify themselves as armed police.

It then took about twenty-four hours for the police to definitively conclude that the electrician from Gonzaga in Minas Gerais was not Hussain Osman, an Ethiopian-born extremist intent on killing and maiming his fellow Londoners. It would take another year for the Crown Prosecution Service to announce that no officers involved in the shooting would face criminal charges and another two and a half years after that for an inquest to return an open verdict into the death of Jean Charles de Menezes. Throughout it all – from an inquiry by the Independent Police Complaints Commission (IPCC) to a hearing in which the Metropolitan Police Service was found liable under the Health and Safety at Work Act 1974, even an appeal against the British government at the European Court of Human Rights – the de Menezes family remained a dignified presence, unwaveringly demanding justice for their son, slain through mistaken identity.

It was a complex moment for Lula to navigate, too, one that perhaps revealed that his diplomatic and foreign policy skills extended beyond merely slapping the shoulders of like-minded Latin American leaders. In March 2006, just eight months after Jean Charles had been riddled with bullets in Stockwell, Lula arrived in London for a state visit. It contained all the trimmings and finery that the British

Establishment could offer: inspecting the Guard of Honour at Horse Guards Parade, a carriage ride with Her Majesty Queen Elizabeth II, a state banquet hosted by the Queen at Buckingham Palace. It was an extraordinary moment for the boy from Pernambuco, who had buffed shoes and sold sweets on the streets, who had operated a lathe and led strikes in a factory in São Paulo. The image of him being fêted by Prime Minister Tony Blair, the Prince of Wales and a variety of other dignitaries wasn't lost on a domestic audience back in Brazil either. Here were Europe's wealthiest and most privileged hoping that some of the stardust of the developing world's most renowned leader after Hugo Chávez might rub off on them.

Afterwards he held a meeting with Tony Blair where the death of de Menezes was brought up, with Lula pushing for greater action by the UK. There had been suggestions from some quarters of the press that extrajudicial deaths at the hands of the police were so common-place in Brazil's big cities that the Brazilian government would be wise not to cast stones. Lula was having none of it: 'We want there to be justice, and the family deserve all the support of the British and Brazilian governments to clarify what happened,' he said in the press conference afterwards. The distraught and mourning family, who had earlier rejected Blair's condolences, met Lula at the airport before he left the UK. His origins not so different from theirs, he connected with them in a way no politician had since Jean Charles was killed. 'Lula told us he would be following the case very closely', Jean Charles's cousin, Patricia, said of a meeting the family defined as 'very productive' and 'very, very positive'.[50]

Jean Charles de Menezes was the victim of individual error, collective confusion, mistakes, poor judgement, negligence and prejudice. His killing in 2005 might have been just one more complicated moment in a long political career, one of many over Lula's eight years in office. Yet it captured Lula's new-found ability to operate seamlessly at both ends of the scale – on the global stage with the cream of British society and among *o povo*, the people who were put down, abused – even killed – by the power structures and the apparatus of the state. One suspects Hugo Chávez wouldn't have been able to pull off such a masterstroke of diplomacy, to leave both Downing Street and a grieving family from Minas Gerais with the same sense of seriousness, approachability and honesty. His effect extended well beyond Europe, too. He was greeted by crowds of adoring supporters in twenty-one African nations on twelve trips to the continent while in office.[51]

'I think they treated me well,' Lula told me in 2019 of his relations with Blair, Brown, Chirac, Obama et al., 'because I was the only president at the G20 or inside the G8 meeting who had known hunger, who had suffered poverty, who had lived in terrible conditions. I would look around the room and ask myself "which of these presidents has woken in the night to find their home flooded, under a metre and a half of water, full of rats and cockroaches and faeces?" None of them.'

'They understood that I was the only one from the shop floor, from the factory, who had suffered hunger and unemployment and they treated me with great respect. And I respected them in return. Although my mother was illiterate, that was something I learned from her: that respect is good.'

Sepp Blatter attempted to instil some drama into the announcement, but it wasn't easy when everyone already knew the name inside the envelope. FIFA had ruled that the 2014 World Cup would be held in South America and, after Colombia withdrew its bid, only one possible destination was left. Still, Blatter went through the rigmarole of the announcement, slowly removing the card to reveal 'Brazil' as the host nation.

President Lula, flanked by national coach, Dunga, and former player-turned-politician Romário, took the trophy from Blatter, handling it gingerly, perhaps wary of the supposed jinx in touching the prize before the match had begun. Still, no need for bad omens, Brazil would surely win on home soil. Everyone smiled.[52] It was a major international vote of confidence in his administration and in Brazil. Another would follow a couple of years later, arguably bigger and more prestigious, when the International Olympic Committee chose Rio de Janeiro to host the 2016 Summer Games.

These were moments Brazilians could be proud of. Realistically no other nation in the region, barring perhaps Mexico, was capable of handling two such global events, especially in quick succession. If the military dictatorship had used the 1970 World Cup to engender nationalist sentiment at home and divert international attention away from their crimes – to deflect tough questions and add a sheen of respectability – Lula's intention was exactly the opposite. It was to draw attention to what was happening in Brazil, to revel in the country's status as almost the sixth biggest economy in the world, to enhance its growing international profile and celebrate its music, culture and sport.

By this stage, Lula had ridden out the worst moments of his presidency. The *mensalão* scandal was behind him. Another, which broke around the same time, involved his son, Lulinha, who was in cahoots with the sons of one of Lula's old union buddies, Jacó Bittar. The young men created a mobile phone games company called Gamecorp and the accusation against Lulinha was that, in a circuitous way, the company had received funding from state entities and that he profited from his father's state visits to whip up international investment. Lula has always claimed his son got rich through his own hard work and keen business acumen. Few believed him. Yet nor could they necessarily muster the energy to get especially angry – at least at that stage. To a weary public in Brazil, the idea that the president's family and inner circle had enriched themselves during his tenure felt depressingly normal. While it was disappointing that Lula had turned out like so many other politicians in that regard, turning a blind eye to the nefarious practices going on around him, he certainly wasn't any worse than previous presidents – especially figures like Collor de Mello.

In fact, at home his popularity was at an all-time high, something which probably prevented the Gamecorp scandal from escalating. Internationally he had successfully trodden a fine line, staying friendly with and supportive of Hugo Chávez while being careful not to alienate Washington, under either George W. Bush or Barack Obama. I saw Lula in Caracas around this point on one of his regular visits to

Chávez. At the time, Venezuela's socialist president was at his most demagogic, changing the constitution to allow indefinite re-election. Lula was naturally asked his thoughts on the idea and whether he was considering doing the same in Brazil. After all, Colombia's conservative president Alvaro Uribe was already making noises in Bogotá about a similar constitutional amendment which would allow him to stand for a third consecutive term.[53] I remember Lula batted the question away with a smile and a generic answer about it being an issue for the Venezuelan people to decide. Yet when not sitting right next to Chávez, he had been a lot more categorical: 'When a political leader begins to think he is indispensable, and cannot be substituted, a little dictatorship is born,' he said in 2007.[54] While clearly allies, Lula and Chávez never saw completely eye to eye and, as his time in office was winding down, Lula marked clear water between them – taking care not to criticize his leftist neighbour for decisions being voted on by Venezuelans.

Doubtless, had he been allowed to run, Lula would have won a third term with relative ease. Polls suggested as much. Instead, he chose a successor. But his choices were limited by scandal. José Dirceu was so deeply embroiled in the *mensalão* debacle that he was facing jail and other logical choices within the PT such as former finance minister Antonio Palocci were ruled out over different corruption charges, including a bizarre allegation of frequenting a house of ill repute and then leaking the financial records of the main witness – the doorman – to the press. Lula settled on Dilma Rousseff, an uncompromising former left-wing guerrilla who had been tortured for three weeks and jailed for three years by the military dictatorship. She had come into Lula's orbit as an energy adviser and, thoroughly taken by the smart and opinionated Rousseff, he surprised many when he made her his energy minister. In 2005 she was appointed his chief of staff, cementing her position as part of his closest fraternity. She was also made chairman of Petrobras's board of directors, a position of great clout in Brazil, though her seven-year tenure would eventually cost her dearly.

As Lula's heir apparent, Rousseff promised to extend his popular social policies and won the 2010 presidential election in a second-round run-off. Her supporters were overjoyed as she became Brazil's first woman president. However, a bumpy and tumultuous few years lay ahead. As Lula handed over the presidential sash with an affectionate embrace and a kiss, Dilma's vice-president was Michel Temer, leader of the Brazilian Democratic Movement party, the PMDB. His choice as running mate was a concession in order to build a workable coalition. It was a marriage of convenience destined for the most acrimonious of divorces.

A leading political journalist in Brazil once told me that the biggest issue with Dilma – beyond the fact that she wasn't an astute and experienced political operator but an obdurate ex-militant who was inflexible with cabinet colleagues and opposition parties alike – was her relationship with Lula. 'He thought he could control her,' my friend told me. 'But a former president can't control a new one, and Lula made a big mistake thinking he could.' It was an example of Lula's ego getting the better of him, of believing that everyone would bend to his will and that the future was guaranteed if people did as he saw fit.

Dilma simply wasn't that kind of political animal. She didn't even like politicians especially, only dealing with them where strictly necessary, and certainly didn't like having her opponents as part of a coalition. Her lack of a background in electoral politics, initially seen as refreshing, soon came to be portrayed as naïveté and a lack of sophistication. She squeaked back into office in 2014, winning re-election by just 3 per cent. However, questions about her past role as chairman of the board of Petrobras were getting louder. She had presided over the board of directors during the period under investigation by the biggest graft probe in Latin American history, called '*Lava Jato*', or Operation Car Wash.

The political vultures were circling and just weeks after her inauguration for a second period in office, she faced huge, crippling nationwide protests over the corruption allegations. Dilma wouldn't serve out the entire term. The picture for Lula was growing bleak, too.

*

'I think the experience of death is easier for people to theorize than it is for people to live with.' Lula could barely finish the sentence, his voice cracking and turning falsetto on the final few words. He was learning to live with the experience of death once again or, rather, to live without the person he loved the most. Marisa Letícia, his second wife and his companion since 1974, had died of a stroke on 3 February 2017. She was just sixty-six.

At a memorial mass one year later, Lula delivered the tearful, moving eulogy, dressed in a dark tunic with red and yellow stripes and a Chairman Mao collar. On his chest was a single star, the symbol of the party he had formed with Marisa Letícia at his side, the first activist long before she became the First Lady. News reports spoke in their usual grave tones of an 'untimely death' but that didn't capture anything like the shock that Lula felt at losing his wife of forty-three years so suddenly. On the stage at the memorial, it was clear he was still barely holding it together twelve months later. Every one of his seventy-two years seemed suddenly to have caught up with him.

Once Dilma had taken power, Lula should have slipped into the relative anonymity of a post-presidential existence, enjoying his family, working the occasional well-remunerated public speaking engagement, perhaps taking up a role at the UN. Instead his troubles were only just beginning.

First, he had his own health issues to contend with. Diagnosed with throat cancer in 2011, doctors found a tumour on his larynx. With Hugo Chávez having also been diagnosed with a cancerous tumour a few months earlier, their most vitriolic enemies on the right saw it as some kind of divine retribution for having taken Latin America to the left. Nothing could have been more absurd. In the subsequent bouts of chemotherapy, Lula fared better than Chávez. The cancer hadn't metastasized and, although his hair fell out from the treatment, making him resemble his brother Frei Chico more than ever, he managed to overcome the illness within six months.

The source of Lula's greatest problems wasn't health-related. They were political. As the drum for Dilma's impeachment grew louder in her second term, so the net of Operation Car Wash ensnared her mentor. *Lava Jato* began as a much narrower investigation into a seemingly localized money-laundering scheme being run by black-market money dealers called *doleiros,* who used small businesses like petrol stations and car washes to launder their ill-gotten gains. The criminality was first exposed at a car wash in Brasilia, hence the name. Yet in a matter of months it had grown to reveal the true extent of political corruption in Brazil and across the continent. The laundered funds were tied to an executive at Petrobras, specifically the director of refining and supply, Paulo Roberto Costa, and soon the entire house of cards came crashing down.

Lava Jato revealed a vast web of slush funds and hush money, often paid in the form of expensive watches, lavish gifts and luxury cars. At its height, investigators found that there had been 'more than $2bn siphoned off Petrobras in bribes and secret payments for contract work, $3.3bn paid in bribes by the construction firm Odebrecht, more than 1,000 politicians on the take from the meat-packing firm JBS, 16 companies implicated, at least 50 congressmen accused, four former presidents under investigation'.[55]

The politicians and wealthy businessmen involved came from across the political spectrum, from large and small parties, from all political colours and from every region of the country. However, as the investigation deepened, the biggest names to be accused hailed principally from Lula's PT and the PMDB. As the governing party and its main coalition partner, they were the two parties with the most power and influence during the period the crimes were committed. The heat on Dilma, for her role as the head of the Petrobras board of directors while this bribery and corruption was taking place, was turning up by the day. Ironically, the *Lava Jato* investigation was only made possible in the first place by the appointment of an independent attorney general by the Rousseff government in September 2013.[56] The more *Lava Jato* picked up pace, the more that the presiding judge, Sérgio Moro, based in the city of Curitiba, grew in fame. In the favourable sections of the press, which were in the majority, Judge Moro was painted as a heroic anti-corruption pioneer, some kind of Brazilian Eliot Ness exposing illegal practices in business and in parliament, no matter which vested interests they might bring down. The reality of Moro's supposed impartiality, however, would emerge several years later. In a sensational exposé by the online newspaper *The Intercept*, the investigative journalist Glenn Greenwald and his team published Moro's encrypted chats on the Telegram mobile app with the *Lava Jato* prosecutors, including the lead prosecutor, Deltan Dallagnol.[57] It appeared that throughout the trial, Judge Moro was providing the prosecution with everything from tips and strategic advice to help in shaping media strategy, in an attempt to keep them on course to bring down Lula. In one exchange, Moro said to one of the prosecutors: 'Maybe, tomorrow, you should prepare a press release explaining the contradictions between his testimony and the rest of the evidence or with his previous testimony. Since the defence already put on their little show.' 'We can do this. I'll talk to the group,' answered the prosecutor.[58] In another, speaking directly to Deltan Dallagnol, he suggests the best order to issue search warrants and carry out interrogations for maximum effect. Moro refused to acknowledge most of the conversations and claimed a private dialogue with the prosecution was normal. Yet it looked like meddling and interference on a grand scale, by the presiding judge himself.

The revelations threw into question the validity of the most important conviction he handed down, that of ex-President Lula – the chief scalp he'd claimed through Car Wash. They also cast fundamental doubts about Moro's fitness for office, but by then he had been made Brazil's justice minister. Many of Moro's supporters stayed loyal even after the leaks, arguing that the extent of corruption under *Lava Jato* was so vast, so all-encompassing, that the ends justified the means. Dilma and Lula had to pay, they said – from Internet chat forums to the floor of parliament – and nothing was going to divert the effort to see them jailed or disgraced.

Undoubtedly a great deal of wrongdoing went on during Dilma's ill-fated time at the helm of Petrobras and during both of their presidencies. Exactly how much either of them knew, however, is an argument which will echo in Brazil long after both have gone. The difference for many Brazilians lay in whether they had merely turned a blind eye, a commonplace in Latin American politics, or actively ordered and knowingly benefited from corruption. *Lava Jato* caught political fish of all sizes, many of whom had direct knowledge of what was happening. Yet having enmeshed hundreds of minnows and bottom feeders, several well-placed prosecutors and an influential judge were then only interested in reeling in Lula.

By late 2015 and early 2016, the clamour for Dilma's impeachment reached fever pitch. The economy was tanking as the corruption scandal continued to worsen. Street protests paralysed the major cities, the electorate became angrier, and her popularity fell to a single digit. By March 2016, the PMDB definitively broke the coalition with the PT and began to support the impeachment process against her. Their party leader, Vice-President Michel Temer, was due to take her place if she was removed so it was in their interests to see the president forced out.

Within a few months, she was gone. Formal proceedings for her impeachment began in April, she was suspended in May and then unceremoniously voted out of office by a 61 to 20 majority in the Senate in August, ostensibly for cooking the books in the national budget. As the congressmen and women were casting their ballots on Dilma's impeachment, there was a momentary flash of the malicious turn that Brazil's politics would soon take: a far-right deputy for Rio de Janeiro, Jair Bolsonaro, dedicated his 'yes' vote to Carlos Brilhante Ustra, to gasps and genuine dismay in the chamber. Brilhante Ustra was the head of the DOI-CODI, the military dictatorship's feared and despised torture unit which had tortured President Rousseff herself as a young woman. Other moments captured the absurdity of the process, with numerous deputies accused of far more heinous crimes than Rousseff voting with grand words and great gravitas about weeding out corruption to remove her from power. Her supporters in Brazil and elsewhere in Latin America called it a coup, saying she was ousted for not calling off the investigation as it claimed one politician after another.

Temer took over as acting president, yet he was even more compromised and tainted than Dilma and his popularity was negligible from the start. Named repeatedly to investigators as having received bribes and co-ordinated the transfer of illegal slush funds into his party's coffers, by 2019 he, too, had been arrested. He wouldn't be the only former president caught in the dragnet of *Lava Jato*.

Throughout the impeachment process, Lula was under the microscope. One the highest ranking politicians arrested in a sting operation was the leader of the PT in the Upper House, Senator Delcídio do Amaral, who opted to co-operate with the state prosecutors in exchange for leniency. As investigators interrogated him, he swore to Lula's active involvement. In fact, Amaral accused Lula of masterminding the entire dirty business. Lula denied it, naturally, saying Amaral was trying to save his own skin. Yet the mud continued to be thrown.

It wasn't long before some of it stuck.

The chant was loud, continuous and defiant: *'Lula Livre! Lula Livre!'* At that moment, Lula was still free but the hours were ticking down. Lines of police were standing by, waiting for the order to go in and get him. The crowd's other main slogan *'Cercar, cercar e não deixar prender'* was a call to 'surround, surround [the building] and don't let them arrest [him].' The stand-off had the potential to turn ugly if it wasn't handled carefully. The building in question was the headquarters of the ABC metalworkers' union in São Bernardo, Lula's stronghold for almost fifty years and now the site of his last defiant stand before jail.

'I'm being prosecuted,' he told them from the stage. 'But I have said clearly that I'm the only person to be prosecuted over an apartment that isn't mine.' It was 7 April 2018, a Saturday. Some of the most committed supporters had been blocking the entrance to the building since Thursday.

Lula's voice was hoarse and aphonic. He looked tired and emotionally spent. Little wonder; not only was he about to go to prison, it was all happening on Marisa Letícia's birthday, his first without her.[59] Yet despite his grief, there was no sign of any wavering in the bravado that had defined him over the past five decades. He was Brazil's first working-class president and wasn't about to be carted off to jail without first underlining the hypocrisy – the rank hypocrisy – of what was happening to him. In a nation where the political elites had stolen from the state coffers for decades, had sucked the nation dry, had given money and positions of power to their friends and their children, *he* was the first former president to be convicted for corruption? It was almost laughable, he said, a show trial in a kangaroo court.

He singled out the Globo media group, the Federal Police, the prosecution and, his particular nemesis, the sentencing judge, Sérgio Moro. All of them had lied: 'Not one of them has the courage or sleeps with the calm conscience or the honesty and the innocence with which I sleep. None of them.'

This was the culmination of *Lava Jato* and the Brazilian right's crowning moment: one leftist president impeached, another about to be imprisoned. Lula confirmed to the anxious crowd that he would hand himself in but insisted he had nothing to fear. He was not a thief.

'What they do not realize is that the more they attack me, the more my relationship with the Brazilian people grows,' he growled over the microphone. Lula swept through a mass of handshakes and hugs, back into the building of his political roots. Even the soundtrack was an echo from his past, the jingle from his first electoral campaign in 1989 ringing out over the loudspeakers.

The accusation that would bring him down also came from his past: Guarujá, the city he had reached as a boy after twelve days on a flatbed truck heading south. It was his alleged connection to a triplex – apartment #164-A in the 'Solaris' building to be precise – which prosecutors claimed he had received as a gift from a Brazilian construction company, Grupo OAS, in exchange for lucrative contracts with Petrobras. Later on, further charges would be added related to more than a million reais' worth of renovations and improvements to a farmhouse that he and his wife used. To Lula and his supporters, it was all an orchestrated attempt to jail him. They insisted that not even his ownership of the now-notorious beachfront property had ever been definitively proven by the investigators.

'There are only four people who know what truly happened: God, me, Moro and Dallagnol,' he told me a year later, almost shaking with anger. 'I dream of meeting Moro and Dallagnol in a debate some day so that, on live TV, they can apologize to the Brazilian people.'

We were speaking inside prison in Curitiba. After several months of pestering and patience, a formal request to a judge to interview a prisoner and a late-night flight from Havana, I was in the capital of the state of Paraná and the centre of the *Lava Jato* investigation, where he was serving two separate jail sentences totalling twenty-five years for money laundering and corruption. Kept in solitary confinement for twenty-two hours a day, as we chatted Lula asked me to speak up. He was becoming deaf in one ear, he explained, and it wasn't easy to hear me as our seats were kept the regulation ten metres apart.

'I'm waiting for them to explain what is the crime that I have committed. Dallagnol is the liar-in-chief of this country. He must have to take meds to sleep at night!' Lula spat out the words.

The prison in question is actually a Federal Police station, tucked at the top of a hill in a residential neighbourhood of the city. Ironically, there is a bronze plaque in the building's lobby with Lula's name on it, marking the inauguration of the police station which happened during his presidency. The day of my visit was a grey morning with cold, crisp air, the city snarled up by commuter traffic. Outside, a small group of the most committed Lula supporters had occupied a patch of ground across the road and adorned it with red PT flags, and posters. Vendors were selling mugs, T-shirts and badges with *Lula Livre!* written on them, and musicians were singing and strumming protest songs on the guitar. 'We were previously camped out in the middle of the street,' Florisvaldo Fier, more commonly known by his nickname Dr Rosinha, told me, 'but we had to move because of a judicial order so we started to rent this space.' A distinguished-looking retired medical doctor with a bushy white beard, Dr Rosinha was one of the original founders of the PT and is now the party's president in Paraná. He explained how the activists had held their protest in the space since the very first moment Lula was imprisoned, sitting out from 8 a.m. to 7.30 p.m. every day. 'The right-wing turned up too and the police broke it up, using real violence against us with batons and rubber bullets,' the doctor recalled. Eventually, though, they were left largely to their own devices.

A red sign stood in the centre of the camp with the number 508 written in white letters, the number of days Lula had been imprisoned when I went to see him. 'Lula knows we're here,' said Dr Rosinha and insisted they would stay in the makeshift camp until he was released.

Inside, after being taken through two layers of security, we were shown into a soulless meeting room with harsh strip lighting where the police allowed Lula to conduct his occasional media interviews. We busied ourselves setting up cameras, lights and microphones while we waited. It was a strange moment. Normally when I've interviewed a president or former president in Latin America, it was in some kind of ostentatious surroundings – either the presidential palace, a palatial hotel suite or their hacienda where they whiled away their twilight years reminiscing on their glorious achievements of their time in office or the outrageous injustice of their dismissal.

Talking to Lula, however, was a very different prospect. He was one of the founders of the Pink Tide, the left-wing movement in Latin America I'd spent the majority of my professional life reporting. In its simplistic version, he was portrayed as the more reasonable counterweight to the impulsive and reckless Hugo Chávez – though that characterization rarely captured the reality of their dynamic or that of Brazil and Venezuela. I'd met him before at press conferences and international forums but hadn't expected our first face-to-face interview to be conducted like this, with him behind bars in the country where he once counted on personal approval ratings in the high eighties.

There was a little flurry among his legal team and the police officers, and then Lula strode in, his hair wispier than I remembered, dressed from head to toe in black and navy blue, box-fresh black-and-white Nikes on his feet. Or, rather, prison-cell fresh. Little opportunity to scuff your shoes when you spend twenty-two hours a day inside the same four walls.

I rose and he came to greet me – a concession the police had granted him for behaving properly with previous interviewers – and although I put out my hand, he went in for a bear hug. A standard Latin American greeting perhaps but, one suspects, also his sly way of bringing me onside before we even started recording. Maybe that's too cynical. As I put it at the time, after so long in isolation it was hardly surprising he was in need of some human contact.

We sat down, microphones clipped on, cameras rolling, I barely had a chance to formally introduce myself before he began to vent his spleen about Sérgio Moro and the lead Car Wash prosecutor, Deltan Dallagnol. He soon extended his wrath to the Globo media network, Michel Temer, the 'coup' against Dilma; the list went on. The *Lava Jato* prosecutors should be ashamed of themselves, he said, for the latest revelations. Overnight, new phone chats had come to light in which they apparently mocked the deaths of Lula's wife, his brother and, most reprehensibly of all, his seven-year-old grandson, Arthur, who had died of meningitis a few months earlier.

'They don't have to apologize to me, I'm a very experienced man who has been through much in my life. But what these people need to do is apologize to the Brazilian people,' he railed, 'for the lies that they have been telling for so many years.'

He was working hard not to let hatred consume him, he said, given that he had so much time alone with his thoughts. I pulled a little further at that thread. How was he dealing with being in solitary confinement in a cell for so long?

'There is a certain tranquillity here. I'm alone in a room, the only people I can see are the lawyers, the family – every Thursday – and the prison guards when they come to take my meals and so on,' he described. 'I'm very alone.'

Was the solitude beginning to mess with his mind, I persisted: 'No,' he responded defiantly. 'I talk to myself,' he added with a half-laugh. 'If there's no one to talk to, I talk to myself to make plans because there's a lot of things to do when I leave here.' Lula was permitted to receive pen drives with articles and information on them from his legal team and had domestic television channels, but not cable, in his cell. He was reading a lot, he said, and was 'taking care' of the Workers' Party from inside jail.

Yet more than just caring for the PT from prison, he apparently still ran things from his cell. Which candidates would stand for state governors, what policy position was going to be taken on key issues, what response to give to the latest attacks, which were the most important international solidarity links to nurture, almost anything of consequence was run past Lula first for his green light. From the start of his second term onwards, when Brazil's economy was booming and Lula's popularity at its peak, the Workers' Party effectively became the Lula Party. The first and most obvious sign of that was his hand-picking of his successor, deciding that Dilma Rousseff was the heir apparent rather than allowing the Workers' Party itself to choose its own.

That paled into comparison, however, with his decision to run for office from inside jail in 2018. He had already announced his candidacy while still free and had begun to travel the country searching for re-election. Opinion polls suggested he'd win comfortably and an incredible comeback looked feasible. However, the noose of the corruption probe was tightening fast. His arrest in April 2018 made his election impossible and almost immediately his main opponent, the former army captain Jair Bolsonaro – the ultra-conservative congressman who had shown such contempt and malice towards Dilma when voting for her impeachment – pulled into the lead.

For the majority of politicians around the world, at that stage the race would have been over. They'd have accepted that, by fair means or by foul, this particular election was gone and would focus instead on their own, more pressing legal battle. Instead the PT announced that Lula would remain the candidate even from prison. By all accounts, his tiny cell became a campaign headquarters as he remained adamant that an election win would resolve everything – remove him from incarceration and return him to the presidential palace. Voters appeared to agree. If he was deemed eligible to run, an important caveat, he was back in the lead in most opinion polls. Lula could still legitimately claim to be Brazil's most popular politician, even from behind bars.

Eventually, though, in late August the judiciary stepped in. It would be unconstitutional for a jailed candidate to run, the judges of the country's top electoral court decided, and barred Lula from the race. Even the UN Human Rights Committee had urged the court to let him run but their plea was ignored. Lula's legal team described the judgement against him as 'lawfare'.[60] Lula and the PT dawdled for another week and a half before he eventually agreed to step aside for Fernando Haddad, his vice-presidential candidate and, crucially, a free man, to stand instead. The timing was terrible. Even with Lula's backing, Haddad had next to no time to make an impression on the electorate before October's vote. He managed to push Bolsonaro to a second-round run-off but it was to no avail. The ex-military officer with strident sympathies for the dictatorship was sworn in as Brazil's president on 1 January 2019.

Hoisted on the shoulders of a supporter, Jair Messias Bolsonaro floated above the throngs, waving and smiling, grabbing hands and punching his fists in the air. He had plenty to be happy about. Since Lula had been ruled out of the contest by the electoral court a week earlier, he had become the front runner for president. Now, information was being leaked from Lula's camp that he was prepared to accept defeat and step aside for his running mate. Bolsonaro's biggest threat was nullified. With the vote to be held in little over a month, the aggressive populist seemed to be in a commanding position to become Brazil's next leader.

He was in Juiz de Fora in the state of Minas Gerais for a rally and the street was packed with his supporters as he was carried over the crowd, who showered him with applause and encouragement. The event was informal, the nationalist candidate wore faded blue jeans and a yellow T-shirt with green trim, the colours of the flag, with the slogan: '*Meu Partido É O Brasil*' – 'My Party is Brazil'.

So many in the crowd were wielding their mobile phones that when his attacker came near, Bolsonaro probably thought he was just another supporter seeking a selfie. Yet Adélio Bispo de Oliveira wasn't brandishing a cell phone but a knife. Before the politician had a chance to comprehend what was happening or his security detail had time to react, Bispo de Oliveira had plunged the blade into Bolsonaro's fleshy belly and yanked it out in an instant. Jair Bolsonaro winced sharply and grabbed his stomach, doubling over in pain. In the ensuing confusion he was bundled into a waiting car and rushed to hospital. His assailant was grappled to the ground and taken into custody.

By the evening, representatives of the Bolsonaro family, in particular his sons, were briefing that he was stable but significantly weakened. He wouldn't be able to return to the campaign trail for the time being, possibly not even before the first-round vote. He had lost around 40 per cent of his blood in the stabbing and the wound to his intestines had been life-threatening. Had Bispo struck his blow just a few centimetres higher, he might easily have pierced the candidate's heart and altered the course of Brazil's politics in the process.

Ultimately that was his intention, to stop Bolsonaro from becoming president. He was profoundly mentally ill and had developed an obsession with the extreme right-wing, anti-gay and pro-military congressman. His family said they had lost contact with him, such was the state of his illness, and in due course a judge would acquit him on mental health grounds and order that he be held in a psychiatric facility indefinitely.

As for Bolsonaro, the attack slowed him down but didn't halt the momentum that would see him elected to the top office in the country. Millions of voters were seemingly unconcerned about his virulently homophobic language, suggesting he would prefer his son be dead than be gay. They weren't put off by his misogyny, either, saying of a particular congresswoman that she was 'not worth raping; she is very ugly'. They appeared unfazed by his dire approach to human rights or the environment or indigenous peoples. They ignored or, worse still, agreed with his attitudes on race, climate change or Brazil's violent military dictatorship. He relentlessly banged the drums of militarization and evangelicalism. The country's dangerously overcrowded prisons were 'wonderful places... [where] those who rape, kidnap and kill are going to suffer,' he said. It hurt millions of Brazilians, cut them to the bone, to see such a man not just connecting to a large audience with this hateful rhetoric but actually winning the presidency with it. To those who voted for him, it mattered not at all to hear these radical provocations. Quite the opposite. The more outrageous he became, the louder he blamed Lula, Dilma and the Workers' Party for Brazil's ills, the more they lapped it up.

The irony was that he could only become president by relying on a sizeable portion of Lula's traditional voters. On election day, a significant number of Brazilians must have made the calculation that they would have voted for Lula but, given that he wasn't available, they were going to cast their ballots for Bolsonaro instead. On the surface, that appears a self-defeating and illogical conclusion. Yet the cult of personality was well rooted in Brazilian politics by then. For all his obnoxious pronouncements, Bolsonaro managed to tap into a rich seam of support through a combination of *caudillismo* and machismo. Criticism of him became 'fake news' and his barefaced lies became 'telling it like it is'. In such an inverted reality, many confused his repeated sexist and homophobic slurs as 'forthright honesty'. The entire package was all wrapped up in the most repulsive form of (white) nationalism, one which before long would see Bolsonaro claiming 'Indians are undoubtedly changing... They are increasingly becoming human beings just like us' or his culture minister using excerpts from a speech by Joseph Goebbels while Wagner played in the background.

The easy definition of Jair Bolsonaro as 'the Trump of the Tropics' became a cliché, but such a throwaway line failed to capture the kind of populist Brazil was dealing with. It didn't appreciate the extent to which this wasn't some kind of Brazilian version of a politically inexperienced reality TV star and real-estate mogul. Bolsonaro knew parliament, he knew the military. He had spent years spouting the same kind of language which was suddenly appealing to voters at a national level. He was a purely Brazilian construct who most closely resembled his ally Trump in their use of Twitter, their reliance on the shock factor of their words, their denial of climate change and their neoliberal economic policies which favoured corporations and the wealthy.

Once in office, the comparisons were sometimes closer with President Rodrigo Duterte in the Philippines as he pushed hard-line security legislation. In a country already blighted with widespread extrajudicial police killings, especially in the poorest favelas and shanty towns, Bolsonaro said he hoped criminals would 'die in the streets like cockroaches'.[61]

Internationally, things weren't much better over the course of his first year. Apart from Trump, with whom his relationship blossomed, elsewhere he ruffled the feathers of leaders around the world, nowhere more so than in France and with President Emmanuel Macron. In part, the spat between them was personal as well as political. President Bolsonaro had commented on and laughed at a supporter's derogatory meme on social media about the appearance of Macron's wife, Brigitte. The incident was childish, puerile and offensive, and President Macron said he felt sad for Bolsonaro and for Brazil. 'Brazilian women are probably feeling ashamed of their president,' he told a news conference. By then, though, the two men were already at loggerheads over the wildfires destroying swathes of the Amazon in August and September 2019.

It was depressingly predictable to see Jair Bolsonaro explicitly deny there was even a problem in the Amazon and instead accuse concerned European nations of having a 'neo-colonialist agenda'. The motivations of the G7 Group of Nations in the Amazon are clearly not always altruistic and there is obviously a certain hypocrisy in hearing European nations call for urgent action on the rainforest when their own forested lands were destroyed centuries ago. Still, putting aside the global need for conservation, Bolsonaro denied it on a nationalist level, that it was a hindrance to development and growth, one imposed by outside. The crisis in the Amazon was evident in late 2019 and, as the rainforest crackled and burned, the

Bolsonaro government's combination of inaction and indifference did not amount to a coherent environmental policy.

I saw the Amazon fires for myself, recording the view from above in a light aeroplane with Greenpeace. The environmental NGO took me on one of their monitoring and mapping flights in the state of Rondônia. As we flew out to the region in flames, we passed areas of verdant forest and saw evidence of the constant encroachment of pasture for cattle grazing. The forest was being cleared little by little, the lead Greenpeace activist Danicley de Aguiar yelled at me over the rattle of the plane's twin engines, starting with the most valuable tropical hardwoods and then using fire to clear the much-weakened jungle.

'We're getting close,' Danicley shouted, motioning out of the window on the left side of the plane as thick plumes of white-grey smoke, ash and dust came into view. Suddenly visibility reduced to almost nothing. The pilot tilted downwards and swooped over the burning forest to give us a closer look and to afford our cameraman a chance to film some of the worst of the damage. A wall of flames tore through the rainforest, consuming hundreds of hectares of dense jungle and reducing them to a scorched and blackened wasteland. We spent the best part of three hours over the affected area. The stench and residual smoke inside the plane became so bad the pilot had to periodically climb to let in some fresh air. At no point did we see anyone doing anything to tackle it. It was as demoralizing and disheartening a sight as I can recall in more than two decades of reporting in Latin America, during which time I have witnessed some shocking environmental abuse taking place in numerous nations. But this, the Amazon on fire under the stewardship of Jair Bolsonaro, was truly disturbing.

It was disturbing, in part, because he was denying it was even happening. But also because his policies included reducing funding for forest protection agencies. The fires we saw were happening in supposedly protected national parks and indigenous lands. Yet Bolsonaro has repeatedly said he favours greater deforestation, development, agriculture and mining on that territory. At its most egregious, the denial of the damage taking place was breathtaking. There was a constant sense from Bolsonaro and his cabinet that nature was there to be dominated, to be brought under control, that any gesture towards protection of the country's vast natural resource was a form of weakness. Rather cut, burn, mine, exploit at will what God has provided to use, a feature of right-wing discourse around the world. Anyone who raised their voice against such a position inside his administration found themselves cut down along with the tropical hardwoods. In August, the head of the Brazilian National Space Research Institute, Ricardo Galvão, was sacked after the agency showed with satellite imagery that deforestation was on the rise, something Bolsonaro had dismissed as lies.

It wasn't just wildfires either. A couple of weeks later, I was back in a light aircraft with the Brazilian environmentalists, this time in a different Amazonian state, Pará. Here the story was less one of fire – although it remained a massive, uncontained problem in the state – but of gold. As we arced over the sea of green once again, the immense scale of the rainforest was astonishing, as it had been from the boat in Amazonas or from the air in Rondônia. Before long though, ugly scars began to spoil the landscape.

Open wounds of run-off and slurry pockmarked the earth below us, the canopy ripped away by illegal gold miners known as *garimpeiros*, and, in its place, pools of foul water contaminated with mercury. The heavy metal leaches into the subsoil and the water system, poisoning the fish and killing animals. It is one of the most harmful human activities currently polluting the ecosystem, once again taking place on what was theoretically protected indigenous territory. In particular the Yanomami were being inundated by illegal miners, often under attack by armed men forcing them from their lands, not just in Brazil but in Venezuela, too. Jair Bolsonaro was actively arguing for the *garimpeiros* to be legalized, not penalized. He had made swingeing cuts to FUNAI, the government agency protecting the 305 indigenous tribes in Brazil which account for around 900,000 people. Indigenous lands were a hinderance to agribusiness and mining and all the benefits of development that indigenous people actually wanted, Bolsonaro brashly claimed, in order to no longer live 'like prehistoric men with no access to technology, science, information, and the wonders of modernity'.[62] He repeatedly said he would not demarcate 'one square centimetre' of indigenous territory before later admitting he misspoke: he meant to say 'not one millimetre', he clarified.

Sitting next to me on the flight was Arnaldo Munduruku, a seventy-one-year-old leader of the Munduruku ethnic group who quietly surveyed the damage to his people's land below, occasionally pointing out of the window to make an observation or ask a question of the Greenpeace activists. 'It makes me want to cry,' he said after we'd been flying over the mined region for more than an hour. 'It's so ugly, what they're doing. The fish can't survive this.'

I asked Arnaldo what he made of Bolsonaro's plans to use the backing of a handful of pro-government indigenous people as a means to open up their territory. Inside the small plane, the indigenous leader almost did begin to cry, his eyes pricking with tears of frustration at the flagrant abuse. 'The government should respect our land. Bolsonaro shouldn't touch our lands. Our land is sacred. We won't accept anyone on our land. It's where we are born and die. The Munduruku people did not come from another country. We were born here in Brazil.'

Once again, the Guarani, Yanomami, Tikuna, Guajajara, his own Munduruku, even the uncontacted Awá, had to ready themselves to fight a brutish, uneducated government in Brasília.

What did you expect? asked Lula rhetorically, his prison guard mutely standing watch and listening. 'Bolsonaro is ideologically guided by a man who thinks the Earth is flat.' This was a reference to Bolsonaro's political guru, an eccentric conservative polemicist and self-styled philosopher, Olavo de Carvalho, who lives in Virginia. His website, 'Mask-less Media' (*Mídia Sem Máscara*) railed against 'media lies'. On his Twitter feed, he drops such pearls of wisdom to his followers as *'Fascista É O Cu Da Tua Mãe'*, roughly translated as saying 'Your mother's ass' to the constant accusations he was a fascist. A former communist who swung to the far right, among his more repugnant views, delivered via his YouTube account, is the absurd claim that the Nazis were a left-wing party and that Brazil's military dictatorship was 'too soft', its 'mildness' allowing for the perpetuation of 'leftist lies' and indoctrination.[63]

In short, if Bolsonaro is supposed to be a kind of Trump of the Tropics, then Olavo de Carvalho is Brazil's Steve Bannon. In fact, much as the comparison between Bolsonaro and Trump lacks depth, drawing a parallel between Olavo and Bannon works little better. Their resemblance lies, perhaps, in their ideological influence over their respective presidents. While that sway soon waned for Bannon as Trump moved onto other yes-men, Olavo remains a crucial voice in Brazil's presidential ear. In particular, Bolonsaro's children are huge fans of de Carvalho and managed to secure for him the top distinction from Rio de Janeiro's state legislature and latterly an official award of honour at the federal level once their father was president.

The different influences on Bolsonaro's presidency also include the evangelical church – from individual believers to prominent celebrity pastors – with evidence to suggest he would have almost certainly missed out on the presidency without their support. They saw in Bolsonaro a leader who was going to return 'traditional values' – read ultra-conservative values – to Brazil, even if he did begin to worry them by retweeting a bizarre pornographic video of a golden shower at the Rio carnival. Such things were toe-curlingly embarrassing for millions of Brazilians who wanted a head of state who would act like one, not look for fights with everyone from the gay community to the French First Lady at every opportunity. Yet the car-crash presidency was just getting started.

For Lula, languishing in solitary confinement, it was like an endurance test. After being forced out of a race he was almost certain to win, he had to watch as his replacement was beaten. Then Bolsonaro named the neoliberal economist Paulo Guedes as his finance minister. Guedes was an openly declared admirer of the economic shock therapy of Augusto Pinochet's Chile, where he had lived for a time in the 1980s. The analogy between Bolsonaro and the most reviled of

Latin American dictators was being voiced as a genuine concern by his opponents. Most galling of all for Lula, Bolsonaro appointed his nemesis, Judge Sérgio Moro, as justice minister.

'When you're alone in a prison cell, like I am, with no one to speak to, then your anger, your rage, the hatred inside you can harden.' Lula was being disarmingly honest. 'I can't let hatred consume me. I don't want to be angry with anyone. I don't want to leave here with anger or rage. I see this as something I have to go through. If God has decided to test me, I hope I can pass the test.'

Hatred is an important word when it comes to Lula. As the years pass since his time as president, it is easy to forget that the other side of the coin of the adulation and adoration he was held in by the poor was a profound hatred by the elites of Brazil. Towards the end of his tenure I was a guest at a wedding of a wealthy family in Niterói, a city just across the bay from Rio de Janeiro. 'Everyone here will pretty much hate Lula so be careful when talking politics,' my friend warned me as we went in. She was right. Apart from her lawyer father, an inherently reasonable man in his seventies who applauded Lula's strides on poverty reduction, everyone else seemed to wish a pestilence on the man. I was surprised by the virulence of their loathing. Yet over the water in Rio's poorest *favelas*, one would have heard the exact opposite sentiments.

I was reminded of how a minor Brazilian celebrity, Lilian Aragão, the wife of a comedian, prompted an outcry with an online video in which she complained about how the country's airports had turned into 'bus stations' with passengers having the temerity to board flights 'wearing flip-flops'. Obnoxious in the extreme, her comment revealed the resentment among the wealthiest in Brazil's sharply demarcated and stratified society, in which people refer to each other using an alphabetized class system of A- to E-class based on gross monthly income, education levels and occupation.

Lula disrupted these established norms. Under his presidency, the C-class grew from 66.5 million people in 2003 to 116.7 million in 2015.[64] Racial quotas were introduced in the universities and the number of Afro-Brazilians enrolled in degree courses tripled.[65]

Unemployment rates were among the lowest in the country's history. Even if it was based on a high oil price and a seemingly insatiable appetite for its commodities, Brazil became the seventh largest economy in the world during his time in office, and did so in the middle of a global economic crisis.

It would be too simplistic to suggest that Lula's enemies simply used 'the damn apartment' in Guarujá, as he refers to it, as a coffin in which to bury his achievements. Once the legal process against Lula was exposed as so fundamentally flawed – presided over as it was by a judge in cahoots with the prosecution, often guiding the legal case against him – then even some of his long-standing and most vocal opponents began to cry foul. For example, the right-wing magazine *Veja* put some of its journalists to work alongside the reporters at *The Intercept* website to uncover details of Sérgio Moro's apparent collusion with the state prosecutors. Still, even though the case against him was evidently compromised, I have heard journalists broadly sympathetic to Lula and his cause say he has legitimate questions to answer about the scale of the corruption that took place on his watch.

In his cell, he apparently remained completely unbowed about questions of his own culpability. He was a victim, he insisted, the target of a co-ordinated conspiracy. 'Will, I want you to know you're interviewing a political prisoner, an innocent man,' he told me at one point during our conversation.

Yet in his hours of solitude, alone in a boxy cell day after day, he must surely have spent time grappling with his past. Lula is brash, confident and unwavering, but not entirely devoid of self-reflection. He must have surely identified the times he, perhaps knowingly, perhaps not, skated on ice that was too thin or flew too close to the sun. Maybe he didn't consider his mistakes to be huge ethical transgressions, especially given those of his predecessors. If so, he either allowed a sense of invincibility to get the better of him or simply chose to look away at the pertinent moment – whether over the *mensalão*, his son's questionable business ventures, the Car Wash or that 'damn apartment'. Asked whether he'd been guilty of falling in love with power, of even partly facilitating the rise of Jair Bolsonaro by perpetuating a political system built around one man, Lula interrupted the question: 'I'm sorry, pardon me. But you must have been talking to my enemies. You must have been listening to a band of criminals', before launching into a long diatribe about how he had stepped aside from the union leadership in 1978 and similarly left the presidency in full compliance with the constitution, even while enjoying an 87 per cent popularity rating.

Sitting in the cheap cafeteria opposite, the sun on our backs, his biggest supporter, Frei Chico, chatted in Curitiba's brisk afternoon air having visited his brother in jail, and reflected on all the factors that had led them to this point. He, too, had been imprisoned and was aware that perhaps he'd pushed Lula into politics too early. I wondered if he ever wished the aged brothers were back in São Bernardo enjoying a cold beer in retirement together after a simpler and less stressful career as factory workers. Fewer intoxicating highs but the lows less low? Frei Chico shook his head. He believes that their paths were decided the moment Lula began to excel in the metalworkers' union: 'Lula did something that he has always done in his life. He worked looking people in their eyes.'

The impoverished background, the loss of a finger, the death of his wife and child: any one of the sharply painful experiences Lula endured as a young man might have prompted a less determined character simply to fold and accept defeat, to opt for the safer path of an existence in blissful obscurity. Instead, Lula went on to lead one of the most extraordinary lives in modern Latin American political history. The shoeshine boy who became president, he is unquestionably Brazil's most significant politician of the past half-century, his impact comparable to few others to have governed the country.

Barack Obama famously described Lula as the most popular politician in the world. Lula insists it was an exaggeration and was seized upon by critics to paint him as a populist. 'I think it's necessary to separate populism from popularity,' Lula said. 'You can have 100 per cent of popularity without being a populist. I don't consider myself a populist. I consider myself a leader who dared to govern with the people, who was not afraid of the people.'

The interview ended and Lula hugged and shook the hand of everyone in the room. 'I'll see you all soon,' he grinned before being escorted back to his cell.

BOLIVIA /
EVO MORALES

'I know you've come to kill me. Shoot, coward,
you are only going to kill a man'

ERNESTO 'CHE' GUEVARA

In Indian folklore, when Julián Apaza Nina was born in 1750 in the Aymara bastion of Ayo Ayo, two vast and beautiful condors landed on the sweeping mountain range opposite the town. One represented the Quechua people, the other the Aymara, and they were a sign that Apaza Nina would grow up to become an important man for the two indigenous communities. Whether truth or fable, the boy fulfilled the prophecy symbolized by the majestic Andean birds. He became Túpac Katari, the warrior who led the largest Aymara insurgency against the Spanish in South America.

In the 1770s, the Royal House of Bourbon in Spain began to instigate reforms and redraw the territorial boundaries in the New World. Over the eighteenth century, the Spanish colonies in the Americas had become richer and more prosperous than their European masters. The intention of the Bourbon Reforms was to restructure the administrative system they had inherited from the Habsburgs while simultaneously raising greater revenue for the crown.[1]

On the advice of José de Gálvez, the inspector general of the Viceroyalty of New Spain, the crown began to carve up the region into new territories. The Viceroyalty of Rio de la Plata was created from the huge Viceroyalty of Peru, as the distance from Lima was creating difficulties for the outlying cities and administrative districts. Upper Peru, which included a large part of today's Bolivia, was the main centre of silver mining in the empire. Under the reforms, its riches began to be shipped to Spain via a more direct route from Buenos Aires rather than west from Peru or Chile.

The new system angered the criollos[2] and the Indians alike. The Spanish imposed a greater tax burden on the indigenous populations and the wealthy criollo elites were tired of having their lucrative status quo upset by the Europeans. The Indians, descendants of the great Inca empire of the past, were resentful of the despised *mita*, or forced labour, in the silver mines in Potosí. Spain's brutal subjugation and control had lasted for two centuries and independence movements led by Simón Bolívar and Antonio José de Sucre would soon take hold across the region. First, though, a series of defiant indigenous uprisings between 1780 and 1783 challenged the power of criollos and

Europeans. The two biggest were a rebellion of Quechua peoples commanded by Túpac Amaru II in Cuzco and an Aymara uprising led by Túpac Katari in La Paz.

The Quechua leader, Túpac Amaru II, was born José Gabriel Condorcanqui. He was a *kuraka* – an Inca provincial magistrate – and a bilingual merchant, who spoke both Quechua and Spanish. He claimed direct descent from the last Inca king, Túpac Amaro, who had been beheaded in 1572 for attempting to drive the Spanish out of the Neo-Inca State. Descended from the same bloodline, Condorcanqui began to redefine himself as an eighteenth-century Inca warrior and changed his name to Túpac Amaru II in honour of his revered ancestor. His wife, Micaela Bastidas, and his son, Hipólito, were also important generals in the uprising. In November 1780 they captured, tried and executed a local Spanish administrator in the city of Tinta on charges of cruelty. With the gauntlet laid down to Spain, Túpac Amaru II formed an indigenous army and launched an attempt to take control of the royal Inca city of Cuzco.

Despite the scale of the rebellion and ferocity of the indigenous peoples' anger towards the Spanish, and the killing of *caciques* and burning of towns loyal to the crown, the uprising failed to lay siege to Cuzco. Spanish reinforcements arrived from Lima and Túpac Amaru II, Micaela Bastidas and several other leaders were betrayed and rounded up. They were publicly executed in Cuzco's main plaza on 17 May 1781 in the most gruesome fashion. Túpac Amaru II was forced to watch as his wife was executed first, then his son, then other family members and allies.

The Spanish first cut out the Inca warrior's tongue and ordered that his arms and legs be tied to four horses, which were driven to the four corners of the plaza. His body refused to split so he was quartered by the sword, and his head sliced from his torso, executed in the same plaza in Cuzco where his ancestor and namesake had been beheaded two hundred years earlier.[3] The body parts were sent to cities in the region loyal to Túpac Amaru II as macabre warnings. His head was despatched to Tinta, the birthplace of his rebellion.

In Upper Peru, the man whose leadership had been foretold as a child by the flight of a condor was leading an equally ambitious and daring insurrection of the Aymara people. Julián Apaza Nina renamed himself as Túpac Katari and fought alongside his fearless wife, Bartolina Sisa. With an army of 40,000 warriors, they descended on La Paz and installed Katari and Bartolina Sisa in a royal court they established in El Alto, the high plateau perched above the city. They held La Paz for 184 days before the crown broke through the siege lines and overpowered the defenders. Tens of thousands died in the battle and Túpac Katari met a fate almost identical to that of his Quechua brother in Cuzco: he was drawn and quartered, his limbs despatched around the empire as a warning and a threat.

Before he was murdered, Túpac Katari uttered the words which have lived on in Bolivia and the whole of South America as a symbol of defiance, dignity and rebellion in the face of an unjust European power: 'A mí solo me mataréis, pero mañana volveré y seré millones' – 'You can kill me, but I will return, and I will be millions.'

The name Túpac Katari endured after his grisly execution. In the mid-1980s, the Túpac Katari Guerrilla Army (EGTK) was born. An armed group of disparate members, from Trotskyists to rural indigenous activists, they sought social justice in Bolivia through a political ideology they called 'Katarism'. The group was engaged in its first acts of sabotage when the government of the former leftist revolutionary Jaime Paz Zamora (in power from 1989 to 1993) clamped down on them hard, arresting most of its top leadership.

Among those detained was the group's co-founder, Álvaro García Linera. He would spend almost five years in prison without being formally sentenced for his role in the abortive armed struggle. The prisoners later testified that they were tortured in jail. When García Linera was released, he began to tether his political future to that of a young coca growers' union leader from Cochabamba.

That relationship would take them both to the seat of power in Bolivia, and fourteen years in the presidential palace. In the process, the coca farmer would be regarded by his supporters as nothing less than the modern incarnation of Túpac Katari.

*

Rebellion is hewn into the mountains of Bolivia. Its very name comes from The Liberator, Simón Bolívar, whose struggle for an independent Latin America freed swathes of the continent from Spanish rule – from Venezuela to Ecuador, Panama to Peru. Bolivia was emancipated in August 1825 and renounced the colonial title of Upper Peru.

'If of Romulus, Rome. Of Bolívar, Bolivia,' said the deputy for the department of Potosí, Father Manuel Martín Cruz, as a new name for the nation was proposed. Yet the Andean country's mineral wealth and natural resources have always made it attractive to foreign powers, and vulnerable to interference and intervention. Exploitation is a thread that stretches through Bolivian history from the excava- tion of the conquistadors' first silver mine in Potosí to the favourable terms obtained by multinational energy companies in the twentieth and early twenty-first centuries. The quantity of silver ore in Potosí was so great, perhaps the largest seam of silver ever discovered, that the mountain it was extracted from was called 'Cerro Rico', or 'Rich Mountain', by the Spanish. It was also termed 'the mountain that eats men' as so many workers died in its mines.[4]

Such enduring exploitation, however, has brought with it revolt and unrest. And rebels.[5] On 3 November 1966, a bald, unassuming-looking Uruguayan businessman in thick-rimmed glasses called Adolfo Mena González stepped off a flight from Montevideo to La Paz. His pass- port was stamped with no fuss and he entered Bolivia like any other visitor. He wasn't, though. The passport was false and the visitor was Ernesto 'Che' Guevara, slipping into the country clandestinely to foment armed struggle across South America, starting in Bolivia.

The Argentinean-born Marxist revolutionary had been a guerrilla commander in the Cuban Revolution and, after they took power in 1959, Cuba's minister of industry and president of the National Bank. Yet the ministerial life, even as part of a communist government led by Fidel Castro, was never for him. He had already participated in the civil war in Congo, supporting the pro-Lumumba rebels in their war against the Mobutu regime, a disastrous experience that left

him disillusioned and pessimistic about the chances of exporting revolution to Africa.

With the bitter aftertaste of that failure still in his mouth, Che returned to Cuba for a final meeting with Castro and to say goodbye to his wife and children. Bolivia was his redemption or his ruin, his last chance to create the 'two, three, many Vietnams' around the world that he sought.[6] Various comrades and confidants urged Che Guevara not to travel to South America, imploring him to see that the Bolivia expedition was a suicide mission. He chose to travel anyway.

Within three days of arriving in Bolivia, he reached the Ñancahuazú region, a remote and inhospitable corner of jungle in the department of Santa Cruz. There he joined forces with the woefully undermanned National Liberation Army of Bolivia (ELN) as they prepared to launch a rebellion to topple the government of President René Barrientos. From the outset, the attempted overthrow was beset with difficulties. The local Communist Party never supported the revolutionaries and barred its members from joining Che's ranks. Broken radio equipment cut off all communication with Havana and they had completely misread the extent of the peasantry's appetite for revolution. Che and the Ñancahuazú Guerrilla found themselves trapped and their situation worsened by the day. Taking on the Bolivian army alone would have been hard enough, but the ELN were unaware that a team of CIA-trained commandos and elite US Rangers were directing the Bolivians' anti-insurgency effort.

Sitting in his den in Miami exactly forty years later, the walls plastered with anti-Castro paraphernalia, over iced tea the man who led that CIA mission retold me the story of his search for Che Guevara. Félix Rodríguez is a Cuban-born exile who participated in several of the CIA's more ignominious Cold War episodes. He was there at the Bay of Pigs, the catastrophic invasion of Cuba by anti-Castro mercenaries, and was wearing a black guayabera shirt bearing the logo of the *'Brigade 2506 Veterans' Association'* when we met at his home. He was also in Nicaragua, helping to covertly arm the Contra right-wing paramilitaries and he testified at the inquest into Colonel Oliver North's role in the debacle.

It was a warm October morning in 2007 when I met Rodríguez. Greying and portly, he pulled out his book of memorabilia and began to show me photos and keepsakes from his time as an anti-communist CIA agent on the hunt for the world's most famous guerrilla. Inside the yellowing and fragile pages of his logbook from October 1967, his expenses had been meticulously recorded and kept within the CIA's stipend of $14 a day. He had ripped out a page from Che's code book, supposedly designed by the Chinese government, with a new encryption for each message. There were more morbid mementos, too: the wad of tobacco from Che's last pipe. And locked inside his safe, no longer to be shown to visiting journalists, a Rolex watch – a parting gift from Fidel Castro to every Cuban on the Bolivia mission – prised from a guerrilla's limp, dead wrist.

On the ground in 1967, Che Guevara and the Bolivian rebel group scored a few initial minor victories over the Bolivian army but they were outnumbered and outwitted. They became further isolated and their numbers dwindled, and on 7 October an intelligence unit was tipped off by a farmer that voices were coming from a ravine known as Quebrada del Yuro where no one was supposed to be camped out. The military surrounded the area and opened fire on the depleted guerrilla force. It was a rout.

Che was injured in the right leg and, when the troops reached him he put up his arms and said, 'Don't shoot! I am Che Guevara and I am worth more to you alive than dead.'[7] They took him to the tiny village of La Higuera and left him bound and bleeding on the dirt floor of the schoolhouse. The CIA agent Rodríguez untied Che and attempted to interrogate him but was met with a defiant silence: 'Whenever I asked him questions that were of tactical interest to us, he would smile and say "you know I cannot answer that".' Somewhere along the line a humiliating photograph was taken outside the mud-brick class-room. Che Guevara stands bedraggled, his hair and beard matted, his clothes ragged with rough leather bindings instead of boots on his feet. Next to him stands a twenty-six-year-old Félix Rodríguez, a smirk forming at the corners of his mouth for having scored such a victory over Castro.[8]

On the morning of 9 October 1967, Rodríguez spoke to Bolivian high command and asked for instructions. Their rudimentary code was 500 for Guevara, 600 for dead, 700 for alive. Over the crackly line, the order came in: 500, 600. Félix Rodríguez, fully aware of the gravity of what he had just been told, asked for confirmation. The same communication came back: 500, 600. He went back to the schoolhouse to confront his prisoner. As he walked in, both men knew what was coming next. In the CIA man's version of that moment, the only one that's available, he apologized to Che, saying there was nothing he could do, they were orders from above. Félix Rodríguez says Che turned 'white like a piece of paper' before composing himself and answering: 'It's better this way, I should have died in battle.' Guevara supposedly handed him his pipe and told him to give it to one of the soldiers who had treated him well. Félix Rodríguez pocketed the pipe and asked him if he had a final message. 'Tell Fidel he will soon see a triumphant revolution in America', which Rodríguez took to be sarcasm over having been abandoned in the Bolivian jungle for the revolutionary cause, 'and tell my wife to remarry and try to be happy.'

Rodríguez left the room and spoke to Sergeant Mario Terán, a Bolivian solider who was waiting outside and had volunteered to do the deed. He gave Terán clear instructions – to aim at the neck down so that the bullet wounds in his torso would make it appear that Guevara had been killed in battle.

As Sergeant Terán stepped nervously into the schoolroom, Che challenged his executioner to carry out his sentence. 'I know you've come to kill me. Shoot, coward, you are only going to kill a man.'[9] With the first volley of his rifle, Guevara was hit in the chest and began to writhe in agony on the floor. A second burst finished him off. Sitting on a bench nearby, Félix Rodríguez took a note of the time: it was 1.15 p.m.

Che Guevara's corpse was carried out by helicopter to the nearby town of Vallegrande where nuns washed the body before soldiers placed it on a trolley in the washroom of the local hospital. His bullet-ridden torso exposed, Che was laid out on the gurney, bearded and Christ-like, his eyes open. Journalists and photographers arrived, as well as a throng of curious locals, to confirm with their own eyes the rumour that 'El Che' was dead. However, his killing would need more than just a cursory visual confirmation. To rebuff any suggestion from the Cubans that his death was a fabrication, the Bolivians took his fingerprints, a plaster-cast death mask of his face and, grotesquely, cut off his hands and placed them in formaldehyde.

The body, missing its hands, was dumped into an unmarked grave and buried alongside a handful of other dead guerrillas. The Bolivian military and the government then obfuscated and lied for the next thirty years, implying it was buried deep in the jungle and couldn't be found. Its precise location would have remained a mystery but for the tenacity of one journalist, Jon Lee Anderson, as he researched his brilliant and exhaustive biography of the Marxist revolutionary. In late 1995, he elicited a confession as to Che's whereabouts from a former Bolivian general who had been one of the soldiers who had quietly buried Che in the middle of the night. After Anderson published his scoop in the *New York Times*, the Bolivian government launched a search amid an international media frenzy. Eventually, their efforts led to a site at an airstrip on the outskirts of Vallegrande. When they excavated, they found the skeletal remains of a number of men. One of the sets of bones was lacking its hands.[10]

The skeletons were exhumed by a joint Cuban-Argentinean forensics team, placed into coffins and taken to Cuba. In a solemn private ceremony, attended by Fidel and Raul Castro, Che's family and his closest comrades, the remains were installed in an ornate mausoleum in Santa Clara. The interment at once undid the Bolivian high command's effort in 1967 to deny Che Guevara a dignified final resting place or a shrine which his supporters could visit.

Félix Rodríguez, now in his late seventies, still dines out on his Che story on university campuses and among the anti-Castro Cuban-American community in Florida. After the execution, there had been some discussion over Guevara's final possessions, the soldiers well aware that one day they would be worth good money. Though he wanted it for himself, Rodríguez gave Che's pipe to Sergeant Mario Terán, who had insisted it was his by rights for having pulled the trigger. Rodríguez handed it over, looking him in the eyes and telling him it was his 'so he would always remember his deed'.

As we walked in his leafy Miami garden in 2007, I asked the ageing, cynical former CIA agent whether he harboured any regrets about the events in Bolivia in 1967. 'Yes,' he smiled grimly, his eyes narrowing. 'I should have kept that pipe.'

One of Che Guevara's biggest miscalculations was to think that the peasant poor were ready to rise up in Bolivia. Seven years before Castro's revolutionaries took power in Cuba, Bolivia experienced a leftist revolution of its own in April 1952. The Nationalist Revolutionary Movement, or *Movimiento Nacionalista Revolucionario* (MNR) in Spanish, overthrew the army, an exceptionally unlikely situation in post-war Latin America. Most leftist uprisings in the region were uprooted before they had a chance to take hold. Yet in Bolivia, young conscripts felt no great loyalty to their government and weren't prepared to fire on the citizenry as ordered. Instead, the revolutionaries of 1952 governed alongside the main workers' union, *Central Obrera Boliviana*, to bring a raft of universal rights to the rural workers.

Under President Víctor Paz Estenssoro, they freed *campesinos* from bondage, nationalized the mines and instigated an extensive land reform programme albeit under a 'state capitalist' model which continued to favour foreign businesses.[11] Still, they ended the practice of forced labour, and estates with low productivity were completely redistributed. They established universal suffrage, removing literacy and property requirements, which increased the electorate fivefold overnight. Almost uniquely in Latin America, the peasantry had won social gains that made them a very unreceptive audience for a conventional Marxist appeal to the rural poor outside the cities.

It was into this post-revolutionary rural context that Evo Morales was born in 1959 in the tiny Aymara village of Isallawi. His father, Dionisio, buried the placenta according to indigenous custom, in a quiet, shady spot to protect the baby's health and return the placenta's spirit to the Pachamama, Mother Earth.

Lula had grown up poor in Brazil and, to a lesser extent, so had Hugo Chávez in Venezuela, but neither had a childhood quite as tough as Evo Morales'. Born Juan Evo Morales Ayma, he was one of seven siblings, though just three would reach adulthood. In fact, his mother, María Ayma, almost died from postpartum haemorrhage giving birth to him.[12] The boy fought his way into the harsh world of late 1950s rural Bolivia and grew up in a single-room adobe home in an impoverished hamlet so small that it appeared on few official maps. Isallawi lies in the Orinoca Canton in the Oruro department, a dry and inhospitable region on the western shores of Bolivia's second biggest lake, Lake Poopó, around which small fishing and farming communities had grown. Like many indigenous children in the South American countryside, he was expected to work from a young age and was responsible for herding the family's sheep and llamas on the Altiplano. His was a life of pre-dawn starts and long working days, and Evo's family survived on the maize and quinoa they produced and the drinks his mother made by boiling fruit peel.

His youth wasn't spent entirely in Bolivia. In April 1966, when Evo was just six, his father took him and his older sister, Esther, to Campo Santo, a town embedded into the red-rock canyons and grandiose valleys of northern Argentina, some fifty kilometres from the city of Salta. Dionisio was one of thousands of Bolivians to make the journey into northern Argentina in the mid-1960s in search of back-breaking seasonal work harvesting the region's extensive sugarcane fields.

A photograph of Evo from the time shows a serious-looking boy in a cap, his strong features set in a semi-frown, with the appearance of being old before his time that is common in Latin American children who have grafted alongside their parents from a young age. He spoke no Spanish and found it tough to adapt at primary school. 'I didn't speak Castellano,' he recalled on a trip back to the town in 2014. 'I was a closed-off Aymara. I sat at the back, behind all my classmates. My teacher would speak but I didn't understand a word.'[13]

The teacher was Elva del Valle Kutny, who Morales met again on his return to northern Argentina on the presidential visit to where he 'started with the ABC'. Kindly and patient, del Valle coaxed some

animation out of the timid indigenous boy, encouraging him to speak Spanish and interact with the other children: 'Perhaps she could see I was shy, scared. She'd pull my hair, pinch my cheeks and say "Evito, Evito". That was the only thing I understood.'[14]

Despite his tender age, Evo wasn't excused from work in Argentina any more than he had been in Bolivia. After school, he would roam the streets of Campo Santo with a box of flavoured ice-lollies, selling them for a few pesos each to the thirsty sugarcane workers. With that relentless work, learning basic Spanish and playing football – a passion which endured all his life – Evo had come out of his shell somewhat by his seventh birthday. His father later took them back to Bolivia and their highland *ayllu*, an indigenous concept of territory involving a network of shared land, customs and festivals.

Morales progressed to high school at the Agrarian Humanistic Technical Institute of Orinoca and finished all but the final year. For his university studies, his parents sent him to Oruro, the nearest major city, where he worked as a bricklayer and in a bakery to earn money so that he could study. In the end, he didn't graduate, not because he didn't finish his exams but because he lacked the funds to pay for the necessary paperwork to receive his final diploma.[15] By 1977, Evo's formal education was complete.

As a young man, Morales moved away from Orinoca and from the department of Oruro altogether. At that time, the very idea that he was destined for high office – in fact, would preside over Bolivia as its longest-serving president – would have been absurd and risible to his friends and family. Yet even when he became more closely associated with a different part of the country, the Tropic of Cochabamba, he would always value the dusty outpost of the Altiplano where he was born, the place where his father ceremonially made his first connection to the earth.

Orinoca is easier to reach than it used to be since the road into the town was surfaced with asphalt, although the only regular bus service runs just twice a week. The *pueblo* is made up of a mere 243 homes, of which fewer than 80 have running water and only 12 are connected to the sewerage system.[16] Yet on 2 February 2017, Evo gave the town what he considered an appropriate gift: the biggest museum in the country. Amid the mud-brick shacks and unpaved dirt streets the gleaming, modern buildings of the 'Museum of the Democratic and Cultural Revolution' sit inside a sprawling 11,000-square-metre complex. It took around four years and $7.25 million of state funds to complete. It is a vast, colourful fortress of concrete and metal, divided into three wings, each named after a different animal from Bolivian mythology.[17]

The halls contain 13,000 objects including Pre-Columbian pottery and artefacts from Tiwanaku, an ancient indigenous city near Lake Titicaca. However, while half of the museum is dedicated to the historic memory of the native cultures of Bolivia, the other half is dedicated to one man, the town's most famous son. Opponents dubbed it the 'Evo Museum'.

Evo wept as he cut the ribbon at the inauguration on that crisp February morning in 2017.[18] He was dressed in a multicoloured poncho embroidered with his name and the town's in white lettering. A garland of coca leaves and flowers was placed around his neck and he wore a wide-brimmed hat with the words '*Evo Presidente 2020–2025*' emblazoned on it. Indigenous music played and goat-horn bugles were sounded as Morales unveiled a bronze plaque in front of thousands of well-wishers and the press.

The collections inside were eclectic. They contained four statues to Evo as well as countless paintings and photographs of his development from local boy to coca growers' union leader to president. In one of the rooms, eighteen football strips either worn by Morales or donated to him by players like Argentina's Lionel Messi adorned the walls. In another room there were scores of his hats. Even a trumpet he used to play in the imperial band was encased in a glass cabinet. Some in the town were thrilled with the new addition, confident that it would put Orinoca on the tourism map. They hoped to siphon off some of the nearly quarter of a million annual visitors to the immense Salar de Uyuni, the largest salt flats in the world, located a couple of hours' drive south. Other locals were sceptical and saw the entire project as an enormous expression of vanity.

His supporters rebuffed any criticism of the multimillion-dollar construction, though. The museum had 'almost divine' significance, said one cabinet minister, Carlos Romero, as it was located in Evo's birthplace: 'There is a concentration of energies here, where the leader of the biggest revolution that has existed in Bolivia was born.'[19]

As Private Morales stood on guard duty outside the presidential palace in La Paz in late 1978, the country was in upheaval. The occupant of the Palacio Quemado, literally the Burned Palace, had changed three times in almost as many months.[20] The incumbent was General David Padilla Arancibia, though, like many men who had sat in the chair behind the doors that Morales was protecting, he wouldn't last for long.

General Padilla's seven-and-a-half-month stint as Bolivia's leader came about in response to another military man who had taken power by force. Hugo Banzer had studied in some of the most prestigious academies for young South American military cadets in Argentina, Brazil and the United States. They included Fort Hood and the notorious US Army School of the Americas, synonymous with counterinsurgency training and teaching of the arts of repression during the Cold War. With a military junta in charge in Bolivia in the mid-1960s, Banzer rose to the rank of colonel and was given his first ministerial position as the minister for education. His taste for politics grew in tandem with his lust for power. By 1970 a socialist military leader, Juan José Torres, popularly known as JJ, was in office and Banzer began to plot against him. The Nixon administration, to which Banzer had established ties during his time as Bolivia's military attaché in Washington, let it be known that a change of leadership would be welcome, given that JJ Torres was siding with peasants, unions and students against the interests of major US energy companies.

Hugo Banzer's first coup attempt flopped and he was forced to flee to Argentina. However, his next uprising, on 22 August 1971, was better planned and successfully removed Torres from office.[21]

Installed as the country's de facto leader, he directed the bloodiest presidency in modern Bolivia, known as the *Banzerato*. The seven years of his rule were characterized by the extreme repression of students and unionists, social organizations, indigenous groups and the clergy. Opposition to General Banzer wasn't just curbed, it was crushed. Left-wing political parties were banned while two right-wing parties provided him with the civilian political support he initially needed to create a veneer of legitimacy. By 1974, the pretence was over. He outlawed all political parties and banished their leaders, including the conservatives who had first backed him.

The Banzer dictatorship was brutal in other ways, too. He enlisted the help of a Nazi war criminal in hiding in Bolivia, Klaus Barbie – the 'Butcher of Lyon', who had famously tortured the French Resistance leader Jean Moulin to death – to advise the security services in interrogation techniques. Thousands were imprisoned and tortured, hundreds killed or 'disappeared'. More than thirty years later, when the sentry on duty, Evo Morales, inhabited the Palacio Quemado himself, contractors would find a series of rooms, known as the 'horror chambers', in the basement beneath the interior ministry. There the Nazi-trained interrogators subjected their prisoners to Barbie's repulsive methods – from electric cattle prods applied to the testicles or teeth to flooding the floor with water and running a current through it, electrocuting the victims. Evo's government tore back the false walls to reveal a maze of corridors and rooms containing pieces of bone, archives and documents, the vestiges of Hugo Banzer's atrocities hidden for decades beneath the government's home office.

When eventually a combination of pressure from the Carter administration and public opinion demanded a return to civilian rule, Hugo Banzer allowed elections to go ahead in 1978. His plan was to step aside for a hand-picked successor – General Juan Pereda – cultivate the image of a politician rather than a dictator for a few years and then return to power via the ballot box. It didn't go quite as he had hoped.

The vote-rigging in favour of General Pereda over a left-wing former president, Hernán Siles Zuazo, was so egregious and flagrant that there were 50,000 more votes cast than there were names on the electoral register. Before Banzer could act, Pereda did. He overthrew the reviled dictator and took power for himself. Despite initial assurances of a fresh election, when no clear timetable for a new vote was forthcoming, it was the turn of General David Padilla to swoop in and remove Pereda from the picture. General Padilla immediately set a date for an election, keen to bring back a vague semblance of democracy to the presidency.

That, then, was the backdrop against which Evo Morales did his two years of military service. A photograph from the time survives and it is a captivating image: Guardsman Morales in his olive-green uniform and white metal helmet with 'PM' for *Policia Militar* stamped on it, standing upright and alert in the cold night air of La Paz. Few of the politicians and dignitaries who scurried around the presidential palace during those frantic months will have given a second glance to the indigenous conscript on the door. Yet he would go on to become more important in Bolivia's political history than any of its short-lived military leaders.

The *Wiphala* flag is comprised of forty-nine squares in the colours of the rainbow in a seven-by-seven patchwork. The colour of the longest line – the seven squares running diagonally across the centre – varies for each of the different *suyu*, or quarters, of the Inca empire. The colour for the *Qullasuyu*, the southern Inca province which includes modern Bolivia, is white to signify time, dialect, harmony and change.

Evo Morales would court controversy over the *Wiphala*, a symbol of indigenous identity and pride, when he gave it 'dual-flag' status under the new constitution of 2009, making it the equal of Bolivia's national tricolour flag. Some of his most vociferous critics, particularly in the opposition stronghold of Santa Cruz, refused to raise the flag over local government buildings and would not accept its elevation to a national symbol alongside the red, yellow and green of the country's nineteenth-century standard.

Yet despite the protests, the *Wiphala* flutters over Sucre and Potosí and La Paz and is displayed in ways previously unimaginable. It hangs in the presidential office inside the Palacio Quemado and adorns the left sleeves of the uniforms of the Bolivian police. There is in fact scant evidence of the banner's ancient origins beyond some fabric found at the archaeological site at Tiwanaku, but it became a rallying cry for Aymaran identity in the 1970s to bolster the symbolism of emerging indigenous and *campesino* organisations.[22]

The story of how Evo Morales took the *Wiphala* and planted it firmly at the heart of the nation's most powerful institutions, from Congress to the military to the presidential palace, is an astounding one, given his origins and the challenges faced by the peasant movement he led. His remarkable journey began with his own relocation from the Orinoca Canton to El Chapare, a tropical region north of the city of Cochabamba.

In 1980, after Evo finished his military service, life in the Altiplano was especially dire. Always a harsh place in which to eke out an existence, a period of extended drought and sharp drops in temperature brought on by the El Niño meteorological effect had caused crops to fail and livestock to die. It was enough to persuade Evo's parents to move on.

Like tens of thousands of others in similar circumstances at the time, they chose to settle in El Chapare. The weather and environment in Cochabamba couldn't have been more different from their village of Isallawi. Its temperate humid rainforests stretch for miles along a wide tributary of the Amazon, and it is far removed from the dry, windswept lunar landscapes of the Altiplano. Yet despite the jarring change, the Tropic of Cochabamba quickly became the family's new centre of gravity:

'Although leaving their ancestral home, which had seen at least four generations, might seem a drastic step for the Morales family,' says Morales' biographer, Sven Harten, 'it fits the notion of the *ayllu* as discontinuous territory that connects different *pisos ecológicos* such as the Altiplano, the valleys (Valle Alto) and the tropical zones of the Yungas and the department of Cochabamba.'[23]

The family cleared a ten-hectare plot of land and planted crops they had no previous experience of – rice, citrus, papaya, banana and, of course, coca. The coca leaf would shape Evo Morales' future completely and by extension Bolivia's. The verdant mountainsides, fertile soil and temperate climate of Cochabamba provided the ideal conditions for its production. From this moment on, Morales would be associated with the coca plant, considered sacred by the region's indigenous peoples, and with the polarizing politics of its cultivation.

Those politics were wreaking havoc in Bolivia at the time the family was finding its feet in their new home. Rooted in indigenous culture, traditional Andean uses of coca include the making of coca tea or chewing the leaves to combat altitude sickness, abate hunger and as a mild stimulant. Millions in the Andes use the plant on a daily basis, masticating a thick, saliva-soaked wad of leaves stored in their cheeks. In its natural form, the coca leaf releases a harmless buzz or a slight sensation of alertness with none of the jitters of caffeine. Although it has potential uses in hygiene products and foodstuffs, the coca industry has never generated significant amounts of money in the legal economy. Yet it is also the key raw material in the production of cocaine – and it was cocaine that put another military leader in power in La Paz in 1980.

After the violence and chaos of the Banzer years, the election that year failed to produce a clear winner. Following a brief civilian government followed by another, even briefer military one, an interim president was installed: Lidia Gueiler Tejada, Bolivia's first woman president and, oddly enough, the actor Raquel Welch's cousin. In her capacity as transitional leader, she steadied the ship until another election on 29 June 1980. The vote again produced no outright winner but the leader of a left-wing alliance, Hernán Siles, had a strong enough lead to expect to be confirmed as president by a session of Congress.[24] Before the deputies could take their seats, however, another of Lidia Gueiler Tejada's cousins, the commander of the army, Luis García Meza Tejada, launched a violent coup and installed himself as dictator.

The putsch was known as the 'Cocaine Coup'. Carried out by officers angry at the investigation into their roles under Hugo Banzer, it was heavily funded by drug-trafficking groups who had infiltrated the highest ranks of the Bolivian military. Though General García Meza's time in power wouldn't last long, it was especially violent and bloodthirsty. Again, the fingerprints of Klaus Barbie were evident in the brutality of the regime's repression. General García Meza even appointed the Nazi interrogator as a lieutenant-colonel in the Bolivian military. Hundreds more were killed or disappeared, among them the celebrated novelist, journalist and congressman Marcelo Quiroga Santa Cruz. It was a return to the worst years of the *Banzerato*. Again, the press was gagged and political parties banned. As the general population suffered under the army's draconian rule, the military dictatorship was buoyed by Jimmy Carter's poor showing in the US election. The regime was hopeful that a Republican victory would bring them Washington's backing for their pro-US, anti-communist policies.

However, the taint of cocaine clinging to García Meza was too much even for the Reagan White House. Increasingly isolated and unable to suppress public opposition completely, General García Meza stood down in August 1981 and fled Bolivia.[25] There followed one more repressive and bloodstained year before the army finally gave way to civilian rule in 1982 and returned to their barracks. They would stay there for the best part of four decades.

Evo Morales, adapting to life in the tropical forests of Cochabamba, was not imprisoned or physically harmed during the dictatorships. However, the Cocaine Coup did have one crucial influence on him. In 1981 García Meza's soldiers came through the tiny jungle enclave of Senda Bayer in the central Chipiriri district. For reasons lost in the wanton violence of the era, they took exception to one peasant farmer, a coca unionist who refused to buckle when the drunk soldiers tried to make him confess to being a drug-trafficker. Laughing and mocking the unarmed *campesino* as they dragged him from his home, the troops doused him in gasoline and burned him alive in front of the villagers. Evo said the sadistic murder became 'forever recorded in my thoughts and in my conscience', and the 'horrendous crime' stiffened his resolve to join the indigenous and peasant political movement.[26]

*

Coca was included in the United Nations' Single Convention on Narcotic Drugs in 1961. The UN likened the coca plant to the opium poppy and included this unequivocal passage about its control: 'The Parties shall so far as possible enforce the uprooting of all coca bushes which grow wild. They shall destroy the coca bushes if illegally cultivated.'[27]

Twenty years later, with Reagan's war on drugs at its height, the coca-growing peasants, or *cocaleros*, of El Chapare found themselves the target of policies devised in Washington and accepted by the civilian government in Bolivia. The new era of hostile, moralistic and insensitive attitudes to the cultivation of coca coincided with Evo's first steps into indigenous politics. He joined his local *cocaleros* union and was appointed as its sports secretary, largely because of his obsession with football. However, his time inside the coca growers' *sindicato* would involve much more than organizing soccer matches.

The *sindicato* was where Evo found his voice. He learned to speak Quechua, the other main indigenous language to his native Aymara, and to speak in public, first as the sports secretary and a few years later as the local union leader. He developed oratorical skills which, while lacking the fiery and ornate rhetoric of Chávez or Castro, chimed well with the Aymara and Quechua community he served, verbalizing the injustices they felt on a daily basis. He has often said that the role of the union leadership is one of service – that the members command while the leadership merely adheres to the collective will: 'The most important principle... is that the bases rule. This means that the *dirigentes*, the leaders, have to listen and follow what the grass-roots decide.'[28] The ideal was crystallized in the concept of '*mandar obedeciendo*', or 'to lead by obeying' which would feature heavily in Evo's political discourse as he rose in the union.[29]

The *sindicato* in indigenous communities has a great influence over social matters large and small. In fact, it is often considered the most important social institution beyond the family.[30] Evo went further, seeing the *sindicatos* as the alternative to an indifferent and often hostile Bolivian state: 'The unions have turned the Tropic of Cochabamba into a "mini state". The union is the one which solves the question of health, education and survival. This organisation has strengthened in the absence of the state and become the maximum authority of a participatory democracy.'[31]

An incredible degree of patience is needed at the *sindicato* assemblies. Everyone present is afforded the right to speak if they wish. Meetings can stretch over many hours as delegates and members of the community wait to have their say. Held inside a draughty gymnasium or cultural centre, the indigenous women – or *cholas* – sit wrapped in shawls, layered skirts and traditional bowler hats, the men in jeans and wellington boots. They will listen, argue and chew coca leaf until a consensus is reached. Yet the long discussions aren't just hot air: they can have a real bearing on peoples' lives from resolving territorial disputes and internal squabbles to issues over coca production quotas or unpaid membership dues. It is Andean grassroots decision-making at its most elemental and Evo Morales became a master at it during his time in Cochabamba.

He would show real empathy with his audience. While some might drift off or lose concentration during the hours-long debates, Evo remained alert throughout and was adept at recalling and clarifying even minor points of order. People appreciated that he was both meticulous and inclusive. Evo developed the ability to win people over with his persuasive language rather than trying to drown out or silence his critics.[32] Leadership rotates inside the *cocaleros* unions and most male members will hold some form of secretarial role in the organization during their lives. However, Morales' obvious bargaining and consensus-building skills saw him repeatedly re-elected over older, more experienced comrades.

By the late 1980s, the anti-narcotics campaign of the government of President Víctor Paz Estenssoro – in power for his fourth and final time – and the Reagan administration entered a new and violent phase. Villa Tunari is a remote Amazonian town that is little more than a smattering of boxy homes and stores on the banks of the Espíritu Santo River, surrounded by dense national parks. Eco-tourism has turned the place more recently into a launching point for river tours or expeditions into the rainforest. However, in late June 1988, barely 1,500 people lived in Villa Tunari and most of them survived on coca production.

Coca growers across Bolivia were incensed over a proposed piece of anti-drug legislation, Law 1008 or 'Law on the Regime Applicable to Coca and Controlled Substances'. It capped the maximum area for legal coca cultivation in the whole of Bolivia at just 12,000 hectares. In Cochabamba alone, the *cocaleros* worked 49,000 hectares that year with an overall total in Bolivia's two main coca-growing regions – Chapare and Yungas – of nearly 60,000 hectares.[33] Coupled with a large-scale and aggressive eradication programme, individual coca farmers and the growers' unions were under attack. Undoubtedly part of the yield from those 60,000 hectares was destined for the cocaine trade, although identifying exactly how much has never been easy. The key difference with coca production in Colombia, for example, is that in the latter country there is almost no ancestral or ceremonial or mildly medicinal use of coca, and it is principally grown for sale to the illegal drug trade. In Bolivia, the US-backed coca eradication drive was seen as part of a centuries-old repression and mistreatment of indigenous peoples and their customs.

In large part, the coca eradication programme was carried out by a 1,000-strong anti-drug division of the Bolivian police called UMOPAR, or Mobile Police Unit for Rural Areas. Known as the Leopards, they received training inside Bolivia from the DEA and the US army's Green Berets and more senior officers were sent to Fort Benning in Georgia for further instruction.[34] They were also supplied with US helicopters to support their work on the ground. As a former BBC correspondent based in Bolivia at the time put it, the DEA claimed to be merely facilitating the Bolivian government in their anti-drug endeavours, but it was 'quite clear that they call[ed] the shots'.[35]

UMOPAR was responsible for a wide range of interdiction duties from breaking up cocaine-processing labs to seizing *pasta*, the coca-based raw material for cocaine, and other precursor chemicals.

However, they extended their remit to become a repressive security force in the rainforest, and were accused of rampant human rights violations against coca growers and their families from torture to theft and thuggery.[36] Well-equipped and well-trained, they dominated policing in the coca-producing regions of Bolivia and operated with an impunity which came from having influential friends in the government and the US Embassy in La Paz.[37]

On 27 June 1988, the UMOPAR arrived by helicopters and police vehicles at Villa Tunari where a group of *cocaleros* had been mobilizing since May over the imminent passage of Law 1008 through Congress. So far, the coca growers' demand that they be consulted over the anti-drugs law had been ignored. The community had learned that the local UMOPAR unit planned to use chemical herbicides stored nearby to destroy their crops and had gathered at the town's police post to try to sabotage the operation. Things quickly turned violent. With the protest taking place in an area defined as illegal for coca cultivation, the trigger-happy rural police agents had the justification they needed to repress the demonstration. They used automatic weapons and fired live rounds into the crowd of *cocaleros*. Film footage from the day shows indigenous men and women scattering in all directions at the sound of gunfire. UMOPAR officers in camouflage fatigues struck the protesters in the head with the butts of their weapons. There are pictures of bleeding and injured women, one shot in the belly, and of men being forced at gunpoint into stress positions on the ground.

A dozen members of the *cocalero* community were killed at Villa Tunari in the massacre, with hundreds more injured. Evo Morales witnessed it all:

> There were shots fired and someone was killed. So people began to get angry. I remember that the [union] leadership was worried and then another comrade, a woman, was killed. The troops arrived by land and air, in helicopters. I don't know if they fired tear gas or bullets but as some comrades were running, they fell into the river and drowned… we had to pull out their bodies.[38]

In July of the same year, Evo Morales continued his ascent up the ladder of the *cocaleros'* union and was appointed executive secretary of the Federation of the Tropic. In the wake of the violence at Villa Tunari and the inevitable approval of Law 1008, all six federations in the Chapare region unified into a single co-ordinating council. In time, Evo was made president of the 'Six Federations' committee, too.[39] On the first anniversary of the violence at Villa Tunari he made a speech which brought him to national attention. The youthful Aymara leader, who appeared in an alpaca sweater, jeans and windcheater, spoke in limited Spanish but with unfiltered fury about the deaths of his *compañeros*, the corruption and cruelty of the UMOPAR officers and the unwelcome presence of *gringo* forces on their lands. He ended his speech with the line '*¡Causachun coca! ¡Wañuchun yanquis!*' Long live coca! Death to the Yankees! It was a fitting introduction to an audience beyond Cochabamba.

There would be repercussions for such language. The next day, a group of UMOPAR agents, unimpressed with Evo's speech, ambushed him and beat him severely. He was so badly hurt the officers thought they had killed him and left him for dead on a hillside.[40]

The name Copacabana immediately conjures up images of the famous stretch of beach in Rio de Janeiro, of good-looking young Brazilians sunbathing or playing volleyball on its white sand. Yet landlocked Bolivia has a Copacabana of its own, and it, too, is a beach resort. After Bolivia lost its access to the sea to Chile in the War of the Pacific (1879–83), the only shorelines in the country are those around Lake Titicaca. Tourists head to Copacabana, near the border with Peru, to take boat tours on the shimmering lake or horse-ride across the rugged hills surrounding the picturesque town. Every February, ornately dressed groups of Andean dancers and besuited brass bands fill its cobbled streets for the three-day festival of its patron saint, the Virgen de Candelaria. Thousands of pilgrims from Bolivia and Peru come to drink, dance and party outside the sixteenth-century basilica and celebrate the final day with the herding of a hundred bulls down the town's main thoroughfare.

In April 1995, Evo Morales was in Copacabana, though not for pleasure cruises or fiestas. He was spending the night in a freezing cell, on a military base near the town, together with a group of other indigenous rights activists and coca unionists. They were interrogated and insulted all night. Their arrest came as the police rounded up the *cocalero* leaders who were considered troublemakers or potential armed insurgents. Among them was a Peruvian pro-coca activist, Ricardo Soberón, who would become the anti-drugs czar of his country some years later. In the early hours of the morning, between rounds of questioning, the commander of the base came to reassure Soberón that, as a foreigner, he'd be fine. 'We like Peruvians,' the soldier told him, and mentioned that his wife was from Arequipa.

'The problem,' the official added, 'is that shitty Indian [*indio de mierda*] over there', nodding in the direction of Evo Morales, apparently asleep, his face covered by his hat. Evo removed the hat and without missing a beat retorted: 'Officer, this "shitty Indian" is going to be your president.' The soldiers collapsed in howls of derision.[41]

The anecdote is revelatory in a number of ways. It exposes Evo Morales' growing self-confidence by the mid-1990s. He was at first quite a timid man and initially not attracted to the idea of leadership. He certainly embarked on union politics with few intentions of becoming the figurehead of the movement, though it was one he believed in wholeheartedly. However, after more than a decade in union politics, he had risen to the leadership of the Six Federations, the most important coca growers' organization in the country. Any residual shyness was gone, replaced with a robust self-assurance.

More importantly, the story reveals that Evo already had bold political and personal aspirations to hold the highest office in Bolivia. In order to do that, he and the indigenous coca growers' movement required what they would call a 'political instrument' – a new political party.

'We are eternal voters for the traditional parties and they the eternal governors, yet they fail to resolve our social problems,' he said to the press.[42] Faced with such dire need and abject poverty in the indigenous communities, and the continued state repression of coca production, the *cocalero* leadership wanted to create their own mechanism for political change. It would be fully indigenous and *campesino* in character and would take on the traditional parties on their own turf: in Congress, the Senate and, eventually, the presidential palace.

Evo acknowledged that, despite the experience of some of the *sindicato* leaders in organizing meetings and union activities, they weren't natural politicians. Yet he believed that apparent inexperience was a distinction which should only drive them forward: 'It's important to create a political instrument, not only to defend coca and the coca growers, but also to defend the country, the national sovereignty, the natural resources, our human resources. The rural poor have the right to conceive our own development. We want to fill the void which exists because under every government we have been kicked, killed, doused in gasoline.'[43]

Bolivia's then president, elected in 1993, was Gonzalo Sánchez de Lozada, a wealthy US-educated mining businessman who had served as planning minister in the government of Víctor Paz Estenssoro in the late 1980s. Widely known as 'Goni', his accented Spanish, spoken with an American drawl, also earned him the nickname '*el Gringo*', especially among the rural poor. He dressed the part of a slick Washington lobbyist in expensive tailor-made suits, silk ties and gold cufflinks. In September 1994, the *cocaleros* – furious at the lack of movement over the draconian laws on coca production – decided to make their presence felt with a vast march on La Paz. The plan was for hundreds of thousands of demonstrators to follow the 600-kilometre route of an attempt to enter the city a decade earlier by striking tin miners. Known as the March for Life, it had been a large, noisy demonstration – thanks in large part to the miners' disconcerting habit of tossing small sticks of dynamite on their protests.[44] But the police repression was so bad that the organizers, including the main mining union leader, Filemón Escóbar, called it off just sixty kilometres from their destination, fearing a bloodbath.

On the March for Life II, the coca growers learned from the mistakes of their mining comrades and managed to evade the police roadblocks.

The indigenous poor streamed into La Paz in droves, descending from the steep hillsides into the bustling business district and cobblestoned colonial centre bringing commerce and traffic to a standstill. They chanted '*vida, coca y soberanía*' meaning 'life, coca and sovereignty' outside government buildings and refused to budge, despite police intimidation.[45] Initially the pressure seemed to work, with Sánchez de Lozada agreeing to abandon the DEA-backed policy of forced eradication of coca.[46] Yet it soon became clear he would have promised almost anything to clear the protesters out of the city. A programme to push *cocaleros* towards alternative crops was widely despised as the agricultural produce they were obliged to grow – pineapples, bananas, passion fruit, palm hearts and peppers – was much harder to cultivate than coca and would quickly rot in Cochabamba's muggy climate.[47] Such policies only seemed to further underscore to the Indians the need for their own party.

However, Sánchez de Lozada did at least change the electoral rules so that new parties and independent candidates could stand. Evo Morales had again boosted his national visibility through the second March for Life. His face frequently appeared on TV and in newspapers, his thick, dark hair and well-defined features increasingly familiar to a national audience. His words were capturing wider attention, too. Evo was soon being heralded by the anti-globalization movement from activists in Seattle to the Zapatista rebel leader in southern Mexico, Subcomandante Marcos, to the obstinate French farmers' unionist, José Bové.[48] With his political star rising, Evo adopted a more sophisticated and polished rhetoric which revealed two broader intellectual influences.

The first had much in common with 'Katarism', the Bolivian indigenous movement named after the slain Aymara chief, albeit fused with 'European-style pacifist and ecologist currents'.[49] In this conception, the Indians were the protectors of the Pachamama and the indigenous model of 'living well' – in Quechua '*sumak kawsay*', in Spanish '*buen vivir*' – was held up as a harmonious alternative to the carbon-based global economy, which sought to destroy their homelands, rip up their coca plantations and force them to work for pittances in the mines or gas fields.

The second key ideological influence on Morales was Che Guevara. He travelled to Cuba in 1992 where he paid homage to the late Argentine rebel leader and had hoped to meet Fidel Castro. Although he wasn't granted an audience on that particular trip, the two men would later meet on numerous occasions and Cuba would become as much of an influence on the Aymara *cocalero* leader as any specifically Andean ideas. Evo Morales emphasized the concept of 'Two Bolivias', as Latin American historian James Dunkerley explains it, a view of the country that was often reduced to 'a model of dichotomous relations: international neoliberals v. exploited nationals; whites v. Indians; oligarchs v. subalterns; global models v. local experience etc'.[50]

An example of this hybrid of ideologies can be seen in the swearing-in ceremony of the committee members of the Congress of Six Federations, of which Evo was head. The members had to swear to 'comply with what the Congress says... in the name of the Father, in the name of the Mother, of the Pachamama, the leaders of the past, Atahuallpa, Túpac Katari, Comandante Che Guevara, and all those *compañeros* who have died to defend the union and the coca leaf.'[51]

In essence, for Evo, there were the people – *el pueblo* – who were disenfranchised, marginalized and isolated from public life, and there were the white, European gatekeepers of Bolivia's natural resources who used the country's riches to perpetuate themselves in power. In 1994, he saw the two Bolivias in direct conflict with one another, and believed there had to be an adjustment – not via armed struggle, as that had already failed under Che and many others, but a reckoning delivered through such overwhelming popular support at the polls that the opponents of *el pueblo* might never again return to power.

The *cocaleros'* first 'political instrument' was the Assembly for the Sovereignty of the Peoples. A broad coalition of rural workers' unions and indigenous women's groups, the coca growers were just one voice among many inside the ASP, which was formed in 1995 at a noisy congress in the lowland city of Santa Cruz. It was headed by Alejo Véliz, the leader of the largest and most influential peasant union in Bolivia, the CSUTCB or the 'Unified Confederation of Bolivian Peasant Workers'. Véliz was born in the Cercado province of Cochabamba, a region of alfalfa and maize crops, and came of political age while training to be a teacher in the 1970s. Invariably dressed in a black leather jacket and a wide-rimmed black sombrero, he cut a dashing, charismatic figure. And he was an astute political animal.

In the wake of the March for Life II, Evo Morales was becoming known as Bolivia's leading rural workers' rights activist and he quickly grew in importance in the ASP. His supporters touted him as its future leader and the obvious choice as its presidential candidate. However, his candidacy was far from guaranteed. Other figures in the indigenous movement staked a strong claim, in particular Alejo Véliz who was older than Evo and had years more union experience. There emerged an obvious split between followers of the two men, *evistas* on one side and *alejistas* on the other.

There were divisions, too, between the *cocaleros* and the other main workers' unions including from the extractive industries like mining and organizations of non-coca-growing peasant farmers. Thousands of miners who had lost their jobs in Goni's austerity cuts had become coca farmers in order to survive. Their priorities, in particular the question of overturning the government's anti-coca policies, differed from those of their former mining comrades. In Bolivia's entrenched indigenous and peasant politics, it was a dispute that caused some rifts that would last for decades – not least between Morales and Véliz.

Still, with the 1997 election approaching, it was no time for disunity. So the ASP put up candidates under the banner of the United Left, a largely defunct left-wing party.[52] Alejo Véliz stood for president, Evo Morales for Congress. Largely thanks to the well-oiled political machinery of the *cocaleros'* Six Federations, the United Left/ASP performed well in Cochabamba. Evo was elected to parliament in a landslide, one of four congressional deputies for the United Left in the Chapare, and formally made his breakthrough into national politics.[53] However, the party's showing elsewhere was weak. Alejo Véliz obtained just under 4 per cent of the vote, barely scraping 80,000 ballots in the presidential race.

Following the election, Morales' rupture with the ASP was inevitable. Véliz accused Morales of campaigning against him while the *alejistas* had voted for Evo and his candidates.[54] Although it smacked of sour grapes, many Evo voters had undoubtedly ticked the box of a different party's candidate for president. Either way, the relationship had broken down irreparably. Véliz expelled Morales from the party and he took his legions of followers with him.[55] Evo is quoted as having told his allies: 'We, then, are going to make the Political Instrument for the Sovereignty of the Peoples, they can keep the (ASP) name.'[56]

In what appears to have been an effort to prevent the group getting off the ground, the National Electoral Council wouldn't recognize the 'Political Instrument' as a party. However, as the United Left had for the ASP, another minor party came to Morales' rescue. Its name was *Movimiento al Socialismo*, meaning Movement Towards Socialism, whose acronym 'MAS' had the added advantage of meaning 'more' in Spanish. MAS was originally a splinter group of an extreme right-wing and fascist party. By the mid-1990s, it had barely participated in any elections and was a party in little more than name. Still, it was registered with the Electoral Council and its handful of remaining members voted to hand over the party's name, logo and registration to Evo Morales' movement. From a fringe irrelevance, MAS would become the biggest party in Bolivia.

MAS was not an immediate success. Extraordinarily, given his past crimes, the winner of the 1997 election was the former dictator, Hugo Banzer. While his second presidency wasn't a reprise of the unbridled torture and murder of the 1970s, the *cocaleros* were immediately back on the defensive as he instigated another extreme eradication policy called 'Coca Cero', Zero Coca. Fortunately for the peasant movement, Banzer's second coming wouldn't last. His government was hampered by allegations of corruption, nepotism and the ghosts of his violent past. He had to answer uncomfortable questions over new evidence which shed light on his role in Plan Condor, an illegal pact between the South American dictators of the 1970s for the kidnapping, torture, extradition and murder of leftist political opponents in exile. In the end, it wasn't another coup or even a democratic vote that finally forced Banzer out. It was the ravages of lung cancer, which first hastened his resignation in August 2001 and killed him a year later.

In the election of 2002, Evo Morales stood for the presidency for the first time. The field included two ex-presidents, Gonzalo Sánchez de Lozada and Jaime Paz Zamora, but Evo ran them close. He beat everyone except Goni, the former president with the *gringo* accent, and took more than 20 per cent of the vote. In fact, Goni only received 40,000 more ballots than Morales. However, under Bolivia's antiquated electoral rules, whenever no candidate secured more than 50 per cent of the ballots, Congress would cast the deciding vote. After a marathon session, in which deputies from MAS and another indigenous party, *Movimiento Indígena Pachakuti*, railed for hours over Sánchez de Lozada's record in office, the decision unsurprisingly went against Evo. Still, as the defeated candidate, he was at least made a congressional deputy again, and would galvanize the opposition to a second Goni presidency both inside parliament and on the streets.

He wouldn't have to wait long. Tensions were brewing long before Sánchez de Lozada took the oath of office. As is so often the case in Bolivia, the issue was the exploitation of the country's natural resources. Bolivia is South America's poorest nation, yet it has the region's second largest reserves of natural gas after Venezuela. The impending conflict was over a proposed pipeline which would pump natural gas via Chile, specifically through a northern port called Mejillones, for export to the United States. To all manner of poor Bolivians, it felt like a perfect storm of insults. First, the port was in Chile. Bolivians have never forgiven their neighbour for taking away their access to the Pacific in the nineteenth-century war. Many Bolivians argued for a pipeline to the port of Ilo in southern Peru instead. In addition, the consortium of foreign companies exploiting

newly discovered gas reserves had negotiated terms which meant that Bolivia only stood to make around 18 per cent on each cubic metre of gas sold. Billions of dollars' worth of Bolivian natural gas would earn the country at most a sum in the low hundreds of millions. Lastly – but equally gallingly to the left – the gas was destined for the United States, prompting accusations that Bolivia's *gringo* president was merely serving his masters in Washington.

Whether they were supporters of Evo and MAS or otherwise, many citizens saw the entire venture as another grievous example of Bolivia's natural riches being 'stolen' by white foreigners from under their very noses. With the previous clashes over the state's coca eradication policies still fresh in the memory, the anti-pipeline protests began almost from the start of Sánchez de Lozada's presidency. Within a year, they were so widespread and violent that the period became known as '*la Guerra del Gas*', 'the Gas War'.

Strikes, roadblocks and pitched battles with the military were common in much of the country by mid-September 2003. One of the worst-affected areas was El Alto, the 800,000-strong city which lies in the mountain mist above La Paz. Behind its labyrinth of bare-brick, low-income houses lies a fortress of radical indigenous activism and fervent support for Evo Morales.[57] The city's protests and blockades were effective in shutting down the fuel supply to La Paz which began to run low on basic goods. An increasingly desperate President Sánchez de Lozada ordered the military to get the fuel tankers into La Paz by any means necessary and authorized the use of lethal force. The protesters of El Alto refused to back down and the result was carnage. At least sixty civilians were shot by the army, their bodies strewn across the streets or desperately carried into the nearest houses by their comrades in a vain effort to save them.

In another town in the department of La Paz, eight-year-old Marlene Rojas Ramos, in two pigtails and a knitted pink sweater, was playing inside her home when a bullet came through the window. It pierced her chest. The indigenous family of six kids was trapped for hours inside their cramped concrete shack while the siege continued outside, their younger sister fighting for her life. Marlene bled out in her mother's arms.[58] The details of her killing were in every newspaper and on every television screen in Bolivia and were the final insult for a weary, angry and disgusted population. Sánchez de Lozada's administration quickly unravelled. His vice-president resigned, his governing coalition collapsed and, despite a last-ditch attempt by the US State Department to stand by him, on 17 October 2003 'El Gringo' handed a resignation letter into Congress and boarded a flight to Miami.

After the chaos, killings, coups and collapses of successive governments, Bolivians were ready for a lasting change. From Hugo Banzer to Luis García Meza to Sánchez de Lozada they had been mistreated and ill-served by the men who had occupied the Palacio Quemado for the past fifty years and wanted someone completely different.

Evo Morales was certainly that. Rather than fluent English, he spoke Aymara, Quechua and the limited Spanish of Bolivia's native peoples. He didn't wear designer suits, he dressed in farmer's jeans and a windbreaker or, on special occasions, a poncho, sombrero and garland of flowers. He wasn't educated at West Point or the School of the Americas but in the coca fields of Cochabamba. Instead of trips to Washington, he visited Libya, Cuba and Venezuela and at the height of the war in Iraq he condemned the United States as a 'terrorist nation'.[59] After twenty-five years on the front line of indigenous politics, eight of those years as a congressman, no one in Bolivia could say they didn't know who Evo Morales was by the time of the 2005 presidential campaign.[60]

His campaign slogan had to portray Evo as a president for *el pueblo* and not the foreign energy companies, to differentiate him from the 'white European elites' he was running against. It had also to underline the indigenous concept of '*mandar obedeciendo*' – of leading by obeying the will of the masses. In the end, they settled on just two words: '*Somos Presidentes*' – 'We're Presidents'.

Combined with his tireless campaigning, it worked magnificently. In every town and city he visited, huge crowds turned out. They included his core indigenous and peasant supporters of *cholitas* in

layered *pollera* skirts and miners in MAS T-shirts, elderly retirees and university students on campuses. He crossed the nation talking to the Aymara and Quechua people in their own languages in the highland towns of his native Altiplano and to the Guaranies in the eastern lowlands. He even attempted to make inroads in the traditional conservative opposition stronghold of Santa Cruz de la Sierra. Yet he never toned down his message. On the final day of campaigning, Thursday 15 December, Evo Morales stood on stage at his closing rally in La Paz in a brown poncho holding an Aymara Indian staff and promised to be 'Washington's worst nightmare'.

On the Sunday before Christmas 2005, the same rural and urban poor, students and professional middle classes who had attended his rallies queued patiently at polling stations in every corner of the troubled Andean nation. Turnout was huge, with almost 85 per cent of the electorate casting their votes. Morales won, in an unprecedented landslide. It was the first outright victory – with no need for Congress to cast its controversial deciding vote – since the National Revolution in 1952. Evo took 54 per cent of the votes, some 26 percentage points ahead of his nearest rival, Jorge 'Tuto' Quiroga. No president in modern Bolivian history had achieved such an electoral result. His journey, from the son of an impoverished llama shepherd to the democratically elected president of Bolivia was astonishing, especially given Bolivia's historical treatment of its indigenous poor.

While Lula and Hugo Chávez had to overcome racism to win in Brazil and Venezuela, defeating an anti-northeastern bias in Lula's case and a generalized bigotry towards darker-skinned mestizos in Chávez's, neither one could claim to have defied racial prejudice like Evo Morales. He was the first indigenous president in a majority indigenous nation in the Americas since independence from Spain. The comparisons being made by his tens of thousands of delirious supporters celebrating on the streets of La Paz and Cochabamba weren't to Lula or Chávez, they were to Nelson Mandela and the ANC in South Africa. Dancing and weeping with joy, they yelled into reporters' microphones above the noise of the celebration, saying that Evo had overturned 500 years of racism and discrimination perpetuated by a white leadership against an ethnic majority. They had been excluded and subjugated for centuries purely on the basis of their language, customs and the colour of their skin. Just decades earlier, they said, indigenous people weren't even permitted to enter the Plaza Murillo, the central square opposite the Palacio Quemado, where they were now celebrating his victory. 'With Evo, things will be different,' they insisted.

Dressed in a white polo shirt with green trim, tucked into formal black trousers, Morales came on stage in Cochabamba to tell his most faithful supporters – the coca growers of the Chapare – that although the counting was still going on, Jorge Quiroga had accepted defeat and congratulated him. Exhausted but elated, he spoke with a rasping voice into the microphone in deliberate, direct sentences:

> The indigenous movement from its inception is not exclusive, it's inclusive. This is what we live by. Our government will end discrimination, xenophobia will end, hate will end and so will the discrimination to which we have historically been sub-mitted. We want to live together in so-called diversity, changing the neoliberal model and ending the colonial state.

The crowd erupted into deafening cheers.

Evo Morales had two inauguration ceremonies. The first took place a day before the official event in La Paz, some 3,800 metres above sea level on the frigid, windswept Andean plains. At the pre-Columbian archaeological site of Tiwanaku, tens of thousands of Indian support-ers waved the *Wiphala* and watched as Evo, dressed in the ceremonial white robes of an Aymara elder and holding the staff of indigenous authority, was anointed *Apu Mallku* or Supreme Leader of the Aymara people. He was then purified with sacred water.

Many of those at the ruined ancient city simply couldn't believe he'd pulled it off. 'Before, all of our uprisings were against the government, the economic model, against imperialism,' said Julio Salazar of the *cocaleros*' federation. 'But now, we are the government.'[61]

The following day, few such solemn religious rites were evident during the presidential swearing-in ceremony in Congress. It wasn't entirely without indigenous symbolism, though. Rather than the sombre ties and dark suits of each of his predecessors, Evo wore a specially designed collarless black jacket embroidered with Andean motifs. His eyes brimmed with tears as he received the presidential sash, the first time it had sat across the chest of an Indian since Upper Peru became Bolivia. It was an undeniably historic and long overdue moment and one which few of the older generation of indigenous men and women ever thought they'd live to witness. Hugo Chávez and Lula were there as well as Thomas Shannon, President Bush's Assistant Secretary of State for Western Hemisphere Affairs. Later, Shannon and Morales held cordial talks with both men discreetly overlooking Evo's earlier 'nightmare' rhetoric.

During his speech, in which he switched between Spanish and Quechua, Evo called for a minute of silence for the ancestral Inca martyrs. He praised Fidel Castro to warm applause from the MAS deputies and representatives of the Latin American left, and called Chávez and Lula his 'brothers'. Lastly, Evo received the staff of military command, making him the first Captain General of Aymara origin that the armed forces had ever known.[62] Once the event was over, President Evo and Vice-President García Linera strode outside, beaming, to join their euphoric supporters. From the podium in the clear-blue morning of a new era, his voice booming through the loudspeakers, Evo had one basic message for them: 'This democratic, cultural fight is part of the fight of our ancestors, it is the continuity of the fight of Túpac Katari, it is a continuity of the fight of Che Guevara.'[63]

President Evo Morales' feet had only been under the desk for 100 days when he made good on one of his biggest and most important electoral promises. On 1 May 2006, Evo issued executive decree #28701 ordering the 'nationalization' of the country's oil and gas reserves. For journalists and photographers, the decree came with some strong images: troops were posted to the country's energy installations and oil fields. Pictures of Evo Morales standing next to heavily armed Bolivian soldiers in front of the chained gates of an oil field operated by the Brazilian giant Petrobras made front pages around the world. To the outside world and to his support base, it looked as though the president was wasting no time in resetting the unequal relationships with the multinational firms who had profited so richly from what had been termed the 'capitalization' of the country's energy resources in the 1990s.

Strictly speaking, what happened wasn't a nationalization at all. In fact, Evo specifically stated 'This is not an expropriation' as he issued the decree.[64] He didn't throw out any foreign energy firms nor did the Bolivian state take over their operations – as Fidel Castro had done in Cuba forty-five years earlier. A more accurate term for Bolivia's 'nationalization' might be the 'enforced renegotiation' of the oil and gas sector. In the 1990s, primarily under President Gonzalo Sánchez de Lozada, the state-run energy company *Yacimientos Petroliferos Fiscales Bolivianos* (YPFB) was broken up. The various parts were sold off at bargain prices and accompanied by a generous slashing of tax and royalty rates for energy exploitation.[65] What President Evo's decree #28701 did was to try to make sure that YPFB took back control over those different consortiums through a majority share and a managing interest. Government revenues from the oil and gas fields shot up, from as little as 18 per cent to between 50 and 82 per cent. Morales gave the foreign oil companies six months to renegotiate their terms, but he had already turned the tables on them in a single move.

'Foreign investors will receive a reasonable profit,' insisted President Evo, 'but the huge profits that left this country without resources, this country so poor… have ended.'[66]

It was a courageous yet calculated move. A decade or two earlier, a left-wing president in Bolivia who sent troops to foreign-run energy installations probably wouldn't have lasted a year. But a variety of factors combined to protect Morales. His tremendous popular support at the polls just three months earlier certainly helped, his appointment as the country's first modern indigenous president having been welcomed around the world as a sign of democratic progress in Bolivia. And times had changed. The international situation made Cold War-era military coups and interventions deeply problematic, with the US embroiled in Iraq after a disastrous invasion and little appetite for further foreign policy adventurism. Naturally, British Petroleum, Repsol, Enron, Shell and Petrobras strenuously objected to the government's 'unilateral attitude' and threatened to take Bolivia to court.[67] However, in the end they relented. They reasoned that the decree still allowed them to make considerable profits via 'mixed companies' – joint public-private ventures where the state holds majority ownership – without becoming entangled in the kind of protracted litigation taking place between Exxon Mobil and Venezuela over Chávez's energy policies.

Furthermore, to the annoyance of some on the left, Evo paid the energy companies for their lost revenues and latterly for the takeover of some of their filial companies. The payback wasn't as handsome as the foreign firms would have liked. In total, the Bolivian government paid out $828 million in compensation to twelve energy companies, including Shell and Pan American Energy LCC – barely a quarter of what they had initially asked for.[68] Nevertheless, a policy which involved anything less than Castro-style expropriation prompted leftist critics to decry the entire process as 'fraud', 'hollow' and 'pseudo-socialism'.[69] They particularly resented the repurchase of the country's two largest oil refineries from Brazil's Petrobras: Guillermo Elder Bell in Santa Cruz de La Sierra and Gualberto Villarroel in Cochabamba. In the weeks before the May Day announcement, Evo had negotiated a price of $112 million for the two installations in a deal that gave Petrobras legal guarantees and permitted the Brazilian energy giant – alongside Repsol and Total – to continue operating 83 per cent of Bolivia's gas reserves and 86 per cent of its oil reserves.[70]

Nevertheless, Evo would continue to call it a nationalization for the rest of his time in office and for many millions of poor Bolivians the distinction mattered little. They loved the hard-nosed new approach to the multinationals. And the funds it generated. Over the next decade, YPFB estimated that the move brought in $31.5 billion to the public coffers. In the ten years before the decree was issued, Bolivia's energy contracts had generated a mere $2.5 billion.[71] It was an important victory for the MAS government, fulfilling its promise to 'take back sovereignty' over its natural resources and use the profits for social programmes and infrastructure.

During the initial flush of success in 2006, Morales set off on a whirlwind tour of four continents, Latin America, Europe, Asia and Africa – particularly memorable for the media's obsession with an item of the president's clothing, a multicoloured alpaca sweater called a *chompa*. At bilateral meetings with the Spanish king Juan Carlos, or the Chinese president Hu Jintao, Morales wore the stripy maroon, blue, white and green jumper that stood out next to his counterparts' drab grey suits and ties. The press loved it and briefly tried to turn him into a fashion icon, sending reporters to find the textile factory in La Paz that made the *chompa* sweaters.

Amid the Western media's mildly offensive mockery of his fashion choices, Evo's words on his trips to Europe's capitals were often lost. Addressing the European Parliament in Brussels that May, he clarified his position on the energy decree: 'nationalization is not expropriation,' he told the MEPs. 'I understand that your companies need a return on their investments, but you cannot own the resources – the state will control them.'[72]

Over time, the Workers' Day nationalizations became something of a tradition. On 1 May 2008 he took over the country's largest telecommunications company, Entel, from a subsidiary of Telecom Italia. The following year, it was the turn of Air BP, a division of British Petroleum, and on May Day 2010 he picked off four power companies, including one belonging to France's GDF Suez.

'We're recovering the energy, the light, for all Bolivians,' he said as he announced the move in Cochabamba.[73]

The European companies began to lose their patience. They said the climate in Evo Morales' Bolivia was too uncertain for fresh investment, so he was forced to look both further afield and closer to home for new energy partners: Gazprom of Russia, Mexico's Pemex and Venezuela's PDVSA. In another snub to Washington, in late 2009

President Morales and the Iranian president, Mahmoud Ahmadinejad, connected via video conference to remotely inaugurate the first office of the National Iranian Oil Company in Bolivia.

'Coca is green, not white like cocaine.'

Evo Morales held up a single coca leaf before the delegates in the UN General Assembly. 'This is the coca leaf that represents the Andean culture, a coca leaf that represents the environment and the hope of the peoples,' he told a packed chamber in New York in September 2006. 'It isn't possible that the coca leaf is legal for Coca-Cola yet the coca leaf is illegal for medicinal uses in our country and around the world.'

The UNGA had heard a lot of presidents over the past few days but nothing quite like Evo Morales, who produced leaves out of his jacket pocket and berated the US over a crop that many of the delegates had never seen before.

'Yesterday I heard a report by the government of the United States which says they won't accept coca cultivations and they will place conditions on us to change our ways. I want to say with great respect to the US government, we are not going to change a thing, we don't respond to blackmail or threats.'

Apart from the nationalization of Bolivia's energy resources, Evo's other great promise to the people who had voted for him was to defend the cultivation of coca. He had a debt to the Chapare region in particular, a debt he couldn't leave in arrears for long.

The essence of his policy, often repeated during his presidential campaign, was '*Coca, sí, cocaína, no*' – 'yes to coca, no to cocaine'. Within a year of taking office, Evo had extended the acreage of legal coca cultivation from 30,000 to 50,000 hectares. Each *cocalero* family would have the right to grow one cato – a plot of 1,600 square metres – of coca. More importantly, he ended the forced eradication programmes carried out by Bolivian rural patrols with DEA funding and training. They wouldn't be necessary, he insisted, as the *cocaleros* themselves would be responsible for controlling the production and eradicating illegal crops. They had decades of experience in self-government, he argued. For example, if a union found a family had exceeded their one cato quota, they would have their entire crop destroyed and would be banned from planting coca for a year. A repeat offender would be barred permanently from coca growing by the *sindicato*.[74]

Despite being criticized by the DEA for giving free rein to his union members, there was a certain logic to Evo's policy. The union was already the main organ of social control and punishment in the coca-growing communities. And many hundreds of thousands of *cocalero* families had little intention of defying the law. In the Chapare and other coca-growing regions like Yungas, where Morales had also extended the area under legal cultivation, most were simply grateful to be able to grow coca again without the threat of violence or forced eradication. Limiting their cultivations to 1,600 square metres seemed a small price to pay for peace in the relations between the state and the farmers of the highlands.

The government also made a simultaneous effort to promote legal uses for coca so that *cocaleros* weren't tempted to sell their crops to the illegal drug trade. Morales spoke of plans for a state-owned factory to process coca on an industrial scale, making products like toothpaste, shampoo and soap. A commission of advisers was set up to research the viability of other coca-derived products – from herbal teas and food supplements to paper.

None of it went down very well in Washington. It was destined to be a difficult relationship from the start. As MAS had been growing in strength and heading towards an election victory, the US secretary of state, Condoleezza Rice, told a Senate Foreign Relations Committee that the Bush administration was 'very concerned' about the possibility that the Bolivian party was being funded by Hugo Chávez. Furthermore, when Morales held his first talks in the Palacio Quemado as president with the US ambassador to Bolivia, David Greenlee, the American diplomat raised doubts about several cabinet appointments, including the choice of Felipe Cáceres, a *cocalero*, as the anti-drugs czar. Morales flatly rejected the ambassador's concerns, in a clear message that Washington's envoy no longer had the influence inside the presidential palace he once enjoyed.[75]

Morales had some fun at their expense, too. In March 2006, he met Condoleezza Rice in the Chilean city of Valparaiso on the fringes of Michelle Bachelet's inauguration as president. Throughout their twenty-five-minute meeting, President Morales stressed his government's position that 'coca isn't cocaine' while she urged him to work with the US 'to counter the drug trade'. At the end, Morales gave Secretary Rice a charango, a ukulele-like Andean instrument with five pairs of strings. The US chief diplomat happily strummed away on it for the cameras, to the horror of her staff, not realizing that the back of the guitar was lacquered with coca leaves. Evo Morales was displaying a penchant for the theatrical well before Hugo Chávez presented President Obama with a copy of the Uruguayan Marxist Eduardo Galeano's *Open Veins of Latin America*. Despite her spokesman's claims that 'the gift was well received' and that they 'certainly hoped to bring it back' to Washington, the coca-embossed guitar never made it onto the plane.

The United States has never had much of a sense of humour when it came to Bolivia's *cocalero* president. However, two events in the space of two months in the autumn of 2008 saw the bilateral relationship effectively collapse. The first, in September, was the expulsion of the US ambassador to Bolivia, Philip Goldberg.

The eastern lowland city of Santa Cruz de la Sierra is actually quite far from the mountain range from which it derives its name. The Andes split the country in two – both geographically and also as a symbol of historical, ethnic and political division. 'In Bolivia, when one speaks of east and west, it goes well beyond just cardinal points', a long-time resident of Santa Cruz told me.

Santa Cruz is everything the Chapare coca-growing region is not. It is Bolivia's main business hub, its most populous city (over one and a half million people live there, while La Paz contains around one million) and it has grown rich from oil, soya and real estate. Instead of the bleak, crater-like valleys and harsh terrain of the Altiplano, its skyline is a mosaic of gleaming modern tower blocks and residential apartment buildings. The city is growing outwards as well as upwards, as gated communities with armed private security guards spring up beyond the outer ring road that was once the city's boundary. Santa Cruz attracts some 70 per cent of Bolivia's migrant population, and its professionals and educated classes are served by good jobs, schools, universities and a functioning public transport system. The Viru Viru International Airport is the gateway to São Paulo, Buenos Aires, Panama City, even Madrid. It sits on a vast esplanade outside the city where ñandúes, a native species of Andean ostrich, and *tatúes*, armadillos, run free. *Cruceños*, as the people of Santa Cruz are called, have always felt a class apart from the indigenous rural Bolivians of the Altiplano and the grittier urban poor of La Paz and El Alto. Never was that distinction better illustrated than by the crass comments of Bolivia's contestant for Miss Universe in 2004. Gabriela Oviedo, a long-limbed, slender *cruceña*, explained to the judges that not everyone in Bolivia was 'poor, very short people and Indian'. To the utter disbelief and indignation of her countrymen, she reassured the panel she was 'from the east, where... we're tall, and we are white and can speak English'.[76]

Miss Oviedo's ill-advised comments might seem a frivolous example, but they highlight a certain superiority felt by the people of Santa Cruz towards their fellow Bolivians. Among the wealthiest '*frates*', a term derived from the fraternities of US campuses where many rich *cruceños* were educated, the upper classes gather over good whisky to hatch business schemes and support one another's political campaigns. And they formed a powerful and entrenched opposition to Evo Morales. From late 2007, that opposition escalated significantly. Santa Cruz and four other departments held local referendums calling for more autonomy from La Paz. While few envisaged complete secession, and still firmly identified as Bolivians, what they did want was greater control over their own resources. When Morales nationalized the energy industry, the idea that La Paz would dictate how much of that income would trickle down to Santa Cruz was abhorrent to many *cruceños*. They wanted their own police force, their own tax systems and judiciary. They wanted to manage their own hydrocarbon resources and land.[77] They wanted the same kind of autonomy that a US state has from Washington DC. But Bolivia doesn't have a federal system, and introducing one overnight would be deeply destabilizing, and Morales wasn't about to grant the richest regions of the country – governed by his biggest critics – the freedom to do as they pleased.

In 2008 there were large-scale strikes and demonstrations in Santa Cruz and the other would-be breakaway regions, Beni, Pando, Tarija and Chuquisaca. Protesters threw rocks and sticks of dynamite at riot police, who responded with tear gas. The governors of the rebel departments warned Evo they were prepared to cut off the gas supply unless he ceded to their demands. Instead, he sent troops to protect the energy installations in the region. On 10 September, demonstrators managed to successfully attack a pipeline and cut the provision of gas to Brazil. Some twenty people were killed during the unrest, mainly in the department of Pando during clashes between opposing groups of supporters.

On the same day, Morales threw the US ambassador out of the country. Ambassador Philip Goldberg had openly held talks with the breakaway governors and Evo Morales accused him of trying to foment a 'civil coup'. 'The ambassador of the United States is conspiring against democracy and wants Bolivia to break apart,' he said from the presidential palace. 'Without fear of anyone, without fear of the Empire, today before you, the Bolivian people, I declare Señor Goldberg, US ambassador, *persona non grata*.' Speaking for the Bush administration, Thomas Shannon called the move 'lamentable' and 'a big mistake' but Goldberg returned to the US. In retaliation, the Bolivian ambassador in Washington was expelled so quickly it's a wonder the two men didn't bump into each other at the airport.

Barely a month after Goldberg's departure, a second expulsion monopolized the headlines. The US Drug Enforcement Agency asked for permission to fly an AWACS radar plane on an anti-drug reconnaissance flight over Bolivia, with a particular focus on the Chapare, Morales' own heartland coca region. The request was denied. Bolivia informed the DEA that they needed no help controlling their coca crops and insisted that the government's 'zero cocaine but not zero coca' policy was working. Within weeks, Evo accused DEA agents in Bolivia of 'political espionage' – in short, of spying on him. The anti-drug agency was banned from carrying out any further operations in Bolivia, bringing to an end a relationship which had formed the basis of drug interdiction efforts in much of South America for more than thirty years. All DEA agents were asked to leave the country.[78]

Washington's response to the eviction of its staff was swift. It added Bolivia to a list of states that had 'failed demonstrably' to meet their counter-narcotics obligations. By declaring Bolivia uncooperative in the war on drugs, Washington could also suspend tariff preferences for Bolivian imports. The US 'certification' – which linked trade to a commitment to tackling drug trafficking – was the 'blackmail' Evo had referred to when he produced a coca leaf from his pocket at the UN General Assembly.

Three years later, the DEA caught up with the man who had been head of Bolivia's anti-narcotics operations at the time their agents were thrown out. General René Sanabria was arrested in Panama over charges that he had attempted to smuggle 144 kilograms of cocaine into the USA. He was accused of being the *capo* of a drug-smuggling ring made up of a dozen Bolivian police officers. Evo Morales dismissed the arrest as a crude attempt by Washington to smear him and his government's '*coca, sí, cocaina, no*' policy. But in Miami, a sobbing and repentant General Sanabria was sentenced to fourteen years in a federal prison for masterminding a vast cocaine-smuggling conspiracy.

Right hands on their hearts, their left hands raised, tens of thousands of Evo supporters were wrapped up against the damp air of a February morning in El Alto, the chill cutting through their hats, ponchos and jackets. On stage, Evo Morales and Álvaro García Linera were dressed in full presidential garb – Morales wearing his trademark Andean jacket with the Mao collar, the presidential sash across his chest. Besides them were representatives of all the main social organizations and unions in the country as well as visiting friends like Venezuela's foreign minister, Nicolás Maduro, and the Guatemalan Nobel Peace Prize winner, Rigoberta Menchú.

It was 7 February 2009. 'Do you swear to respect and make respected the new Political Constitution of the State?' Evo asked the crowd. 'Yes, I swear,' they answered in unison. Morales signed the new Carta Magna which had been approved by a huge majority in a referendum two weeks earlier. The ceremony was taking place in the wet open air of El Alto and not 'inside the four walls of Congress', he told them, because 'we have nothing to hide'.

'El Alto on its feet, never on its knees! Bolivia on its feet, never on its knees,' he yelled, to cheers from the congregation thronging the avenues of the 'rebel city', where scores had been killed just five years earlier in the Gas War. Evo was laying on the 'ancestral legacy' rhetoric thick, invoking dead martyrs and referring to 500 years of struggle against the 'oligarchy'. Yet he was right to call it historic: it was the first time Bolivia had a constitution that had been approved in a popular vote.

'Some groups have permanently tried to remove me from the palace,' he said, his speech punctuated by the constant crack of fireworks overhead. 'You know that some groups have constantly tried to kill me. Now I want to say to them: you can remove me from the palace, you can kill me, mission accomplished with the re-foundation of a new, united Bolivia.'

On that February day, when only the rain prevented the party in El Alto from continuing into the evening, Evo Morales officially turned Bolivia into the unitary 'Plurinational State of Bolivia'. The move granted different degrees of autonomy to the country's nine departments as part of the negotiations to end the violence in the breakaway regions that had been going on since the end of 2008. It also made Bolivia a secular country, officially ending the Catholic Church's constitutional hold over the state. It clarified the division between Sucre as the official capital, but La Paz as the Plurinational State's legislative and executive seat of government, in essence its de facto capital. It permanently codified the claim against Chile to the Pacific coast that Bolivia had lost in 1883 but specified that it would only be restored through 'peaceful means and the exercise of sovereignty'. Coca was protected as a 'cultural patrimony' under the constitution and it was recognized by law that 'in its natural state it is not a narcotic'.

Judges would be elected rather than picked by Congress, land-ownership was limited to 5,000 hectares and the electoral system was changed. Should no presidential candidate gain more than 50 per cent of the vote, the process would advance to a second-round run-off rather than a vote in Congress, in line with most of the rest of Latin America. Evo wove in a little something for himself on that front, too. The president would be allowed to stand for one consecutive re-election. In theory, Morales' first term ran from 2006 to 2011. However, as the new constitution was approved, he called for fresh elections in 2009 which he was predicted comfortably to win. He argued that the new constitution was like pressing a reset button so that, assuming he won the 2009 election, it would be considered the start of his first term, not his second. The move conveniently erased, for legal purposes, the three years he had already spent in office. To pacify his furious opponents, Morales agreed not to seek re-election in 2014.

It was always likely that Evo Morales would seek to create a con-stitutional mechanism allowing him to stand again. One five-year term simply wasn't going to be enough for him. In 2009, his star among his supporters could hardly have been brighter. Beyond the removal of the DEA and the US ambassador, all of which played well with his base, his policies were incredibly popular. The coca growers were happy with the larger area permitted for cultivation, albeit with some regional tensions within their movement. Improved healthcare provision, popular social programmes and a rise in the minimum wage were helping poor and indigenous communities across Bolivia. Monthly payments were available to support the families of students and the state pension was increased. Evo followed the lead of Chávez and Lula in using high global commodities prices to bolster national development and tackle extreme poverty. This economic strategy had worked in Venezuela and Brazil at the first crest of the Pink Wave, and it was working to great effect in Bolivia.

World Bank data showed that Bolivia's GDP grew by around 4.9 per cent a year during his first term.[79] These numbers were backed up by the International Monetary Fund. Neither of the Washington-based financial institutions could be said to have been sympathetic to Evo's socialist agenda, yet they acknowledged economic growth when they saw it. The billions brought in by the energy nationalizations and contract renegotiations were pumped into poverty reduction and real strides were made in lifting the poor out of misery. By 2018, Bolivia was globally recognized as one of the countries which had most effectively reduced poverty over the past decade. Extreme deprivation was down by more than half, from 38.2 per cent in 2005 to 15.2 per cent in 2018, while poverty in general was down from 60.6 per cent to 34.6 per cent over the same period.[80]

Responsibility for these advances was invariably credited to Evo Morales. Even when other 'revolutions' and leftist political movements in the region floundered, he appeared to show that a government could apply socialist policies and still strengthen the economy and undo centuries of racial discrimination and prejudice in the process. It is worth noting that despite the headway Evo made in tackling poverty, Bolivia remained the poorest country in South America. Nonetheless, he was lauded in the international media for his policies and at home the applause was translated into votes.[81] He won every election during that period with consummate ease. He triumphed in a recall referendum in May 2008 (there was an 83 per cent turnout, and Morales took 67.4 per cent of the vote), the constitutional referendum in early 2009 (90.3 per cent turnout, the new constitution was approved by 61.4 per cent) and the subsequent presidential election in December 2009 (with a staggering 94.3 per cent voter participation, Evo was returned to power with 64.2 per cent of the total vote).

The opposition despised him but they couldn't question his legitimacy. No previous president had achieved these levels of voter participation, or such margins of victory. On winning another term in office that would last until 2014, Evo felt emboldened as never before. He promised to accelerate the implementation of his socialist agenda. His critics groaned, and were determined to oppose him at every turn. But of all the changes introduced by the 2009 constitution, it wasn't the declaration of Bolivia as a secular state, the cap on land-holdings or the sacred status of coca that would eventually throw the country into disarray. It was the new rules on presidential re-election.

The cable car, painted a bright shade of fire-engine red, lifted off from El Alto towards La Paz, gliding effortlessly down over the precipitous mountain slope. In the cabin was Passenger Number One of a service that would move an estimated 18,000 passengers an hour. At some 4,000 metres above sea level as it soared over breezeblock homes and dirt-brown football pitches, it was the highest cable car system in the world. The cab sailed over the snarled traffic on the motorway – Autopista Héroes de la Guerra del Chaco – which links the twin cities. The view across La Paz was spectacular, the city laid out in its hazy, dysfunctional glory beneath the snow-capped peak of Illimani, the highest mountain of the rugged Cordillera Real range. After a smooth ten-minute ride, the cable car dropped rapidly, coming to a stop at the Taypi Uta Central Station in La Paz.

As Passenger Number One – President Evo Morales, naturally – stepped out of the cabin, there was applause among the workers and government ministers waiting at the station. The journey was short, but that was the point. It was designed to save hundreds of thousands of commuters several hours a week as they travelled from El Alto to La Paz, and back home again at the end of their shifts. It would connect the periphery to the hub and bring the people from the hillsides into the urban centre. The government called their metro system in the sky 'Mi teleférico', or 'my cable car'.

It was cheap, too, just three bolivanos, around 45 US cents, for a single journey. Less if you used a smart card to connect between two different lines. It wasn't cheap for the government, though. At a cost of $234 million, it was one of the most expensive cable car lines in

South America, only outstripped by Rio de Janeiro's costly failure, a gondola system built before the 2014 World Cup and shut down soon after the 2016 Olympics, the ghostly, empty cabins abandoned and the metal cables suspended for years above the favelas of Complexo do Alemão.[82]

Yet few of the people entering a cable car in La Paz were complaining about the comparatively high price of a kilometre of track. Everyone from students to street vendors to office workers was simply glad to see a transit system that seemed designed to serve their needs. 'I'm speechless,' said one of the first passengers accosted by the media on the opening day. 'It's awesome: the quiet, the view, the Illimani. It's perfect.'[83] Photographers fell over themselves to snap *cholas* inside the cabins, their flowing skirts and bowler hats set against the gleaming new cars, the archetypal image of 'indigenous tradition meets Bolivian modernity'. There was something quite wonderful about some of South America's poorest people riding to work on a system originally conceived so that the world's wealthiest skiers could reach the slopes of the Alps. For most passengers, though, none of that mattered. It was just faster and more comfortable than the bus.

The system was built by the Austrian transportation firm Doppelmayr, though there was no tender process. It was a 'turnkey' operation: the firm was granted the contract without competition and handed the project back to the government in a fully completed and operational state. All Evo needed to do was turn the key to fire it up. Financed through a sizeable loan from the Central Bank, Evo inaugurated Phase One in 2014: the red line, the yellow line and the green line – the colours of the Bolivian flag. Soon, the rest of the palette was added: purple, blue, sky blue, orange, white, brown, gold and silver. Together they formed the longest *teleférico* in the world and cost Bolivia around $23.5 million per kilometre. It was far more expensive than similar cable car systems in Cali in Colombia, Ecatepec in Mexico or Ankara in Turkey which were installed for closer to $13 million a kilometre.[84] The government said the second phase would cost over $500 million to complete, though some estimates believe it ran closer to $700 million. However, the government was quick to point out that the unexpectedly high popularity of the cable cars would see them recoup the Central Bank loan ahead of schedule.

When one sees the gondolas whirring efficiently overhead, it's hard not to be impressed by such a feat of engineering, ambition and urban planning in a nation as poor as Bolivia. At rush hour, thousands of people buzz around the cable stations to dive onto the first available car and float home through the clouds. The cars are safe, well maintained and quiet. I was struck by the sense of achievement and the collective pride at having built a transport system that serves both the valley and the plateau. These projects often collapse in Latin America under the weight of corruption, defective installation and mismanagement. Rio's did – and so did the San Agustín Metrocable line in Caracas, both built by the tainted Brazilian construction firm Odebrecht.[85] La Paz's system not only worked, it was popular. It instantly became one of Evo's cornerstone pieces of infrastructure, a project that would leave his imprint on La Paz and El Alto for decades to come.

Still, if the cable car transit system was the project which brought him praise and acclaim – except among the El Alto taxi drivers' unions – another of his pet infrastructure projects created a permanent and irreparable crack within the indigenous movement. It was also a transport project, but in this case it was a highway cut directly through a national park. The plan was for a 300-kilometre-long road to link the departments of Cochabamba in the centre of the country and Beni in the northeast. Around 65 kilometres of the road would bisect the Isiboro Sécure Indigenous Territory and National Park, or TIPNIS, an area of rainforest the size of Jamaica and rich in biodiversity and wildlife. The government's own statistics stated that the freshwater ecosystem teemed with some 3,000 species of plants, 850 native mammals and reptiles and 470 species of birds.[86] It was also an autonomous indigenous territory. Yet Evo was adamant that the road was needed to bring development to the two regions and to facilitate trade with Brazil. Agricultural produce from Beni would be distributed via Cochabamba, which brought the added advantage to Evo Morales of bypassing the opposition stronghold of Santa Cruz. The public works minister said that Beni and the TIPNIS were 'enclosed' without the transport link and insisted that the section of highway due to pass through the park would be constructed with due care for the environment.

It didn't seem that way to the roughly 14,000 people of the Chiman, Yurucare and Moxos ethnic groups who lived inside the biosphere. The idea of earthmoving equipment gouging paths or digging tunnels through half of their territory was intolerable to them, especially coming from another Indian. Evo dismissed their objections out of hand. The road would be built, he said in June 2011, 'whether they like it or not'.[87] Just as the diggers and bulldozers were being readied to rumble into the forest, a march on La Paz began. Hundreds of representatives from the tribes of the TIPNIS set out from Beni, a small but vocal mass of environmentalists, trade unionists and indigenous people who opposed what they saw as an attack on the Pachamama. They were men and women who had twice voted Evo into power, the last time just two years earlier, and they were now converging on their leader's presidential palace holding placards calling for him to change his mind or step down.

At one point, the marchers seized the country's foreign minister, David Choquehuanca, who was there to try to negotiate with them, and forced him to guarantee their safe passage past a police roadblock. But at the tiny town of Yucumo at the foot of the mountains in a protected national park, the fraying tensions with the security forces snapped. The protesters were halted by riot police and, following a stand-off that lasted several days, hundreds of officers charged the marchers' camp using tear gas and batons. The demonstrators claimed four people were killed and an unconfirmed rumour ran around that one of them was a baby. The government insisted there had been no fatalities. Neither side disputed, however, that there had been hundreds of arrests, injuries and untold damage to Evo Morales' reputation.

Here was the revered Indian president – the *Apu Mallku*, Supreme Leader of the Aymara people – ordering his goons to crack heads and detain peaceful indigenous protesters. Or so it looked to many observers watching the images on television. The pictures showed

Indian men, women and children being forcibly removed and hit with nightsticks by officers clad in helmets and green uniforms. The news reports brought much wider sympathy to the TINPIS people's cause. These were people of the forest, people who survived on hunting, fishing and farming, they were Evo's people. Had he forgotten his past so quickly? Had the massacre at Villa Tunari or his own beating at the hands of the UMOPAR officers escaped his memory? Could he no longer recall the Gas War in El Alto or the countless times he, too, had faced tear gas and batons or spent nights in jail? Perhaps his sacred commitment to the Pachamama had slipped his mind, his harshest critics insinuated, after so many rich lunches and trips abroad on private jets.

Some of Evo's faithful were so shaken by the events at Yucumo that they turned against him for good. His trusted interior minister, Sacha Llorenti, was forced to stand down while his defence minister, Cecilia Chacón, resigned in protest at the police repression. 'This is not the way!' she wrote in her resignation later to him. 'We agreed to do things differently.'[88] It was a sentiment shared by many in the rank and file of MAS, too. Protests against the state violence were held in La Paz and urban Evo voters found themselves turning out to welcome their rural brothers as the TIPNIS marchers passed through their towns, handing out bottles of water and holding up their children to cheer them on their way.

Loyalists organized their own marches in support of the road. The economic argument favoured them, they said, and they were tired of being told that as indigenous people they couldn't develop the resources with which they were blessed. However, the indigenous people's right to consultation over any development that affected them was enshrined in the very constitution Morales introduced in 2009, and the people of the TIPNIS said they were never once asked about the road. Furthermore, the vast majority of those supporting Evo were from his traditional *cocalero* base in the Chapare, fuelling suspicions that the real reason he was so determined to persevere with project was to favour the *cocaleros*. The road offered a chance to enter the sparsely populated TIPNIS and open up the national park to coca farming. The territory was already subject to illegal land grabs by coca growers from the president's core region of support and it looked to many – both inside and outside the native people's movement – that Evo Morales favoured some Indians over others. He was accused of increasingly representing just a select group of Aymara and Quechua coca farmers from the highlands.

The pictures of riot police hitting and tear-gassing unarmed indigenous protesters shook Morales. He called off the road construction and offered to hold a referendum on it in the two departments concerned, Beni and Cochabamba. It soon became clear that such a concession wouldn't be enough for the people of the TIPNIS, who vowed to continue their march. In the face of what was becoming the biggest protest movement of his presidency, Evo apologized profusely for the repression, saying:

I want to ask the victims' families to forgive us. To forgive me. There was no instruction from the president nor did we ever think things would happen in this way. As we too have been victims of repression on many occasions, I want to send them a fraternal greeting.[89]

Some of the chants in the demonstrations in La Paz in support of the TIPNIS tribes were striking. Crowds of people got as close as possible to the presidential palace, a ring of security forces keeping them at bay, and shouted 'Evo, fascist!' and 'Evo, lackey of Brazil's big business' because a Brazilian development bank was funding the road.[90]

Even though he shelved the plans, Morales wasn't about to abandon his road altogether. Six years later, he signed a measure that removed the legal protection or 'inviolability' of the TIPNIS national park and allowed him to press ahead with his highway. At a ceremony in one of the regions due to benefit from the road and surrounded by placard-waving groups of loyalists, he didn't miss the opportunity to label anyone who opposed the construction as 'colonial environmentalists' and 'enemies' of the indigenous peoples.

'They are not interested in the indigenous movement having electricity or roads. They are not interested, but they use the indigenous movement, they use the environment to live well.'[91]

He had said in 2011 the road would happen whether they liked it or not. By removing the park's legal sanctity, it seemed that he would be as good as his word. But in the process, something important in his movement had broken and it wasn't entirely clear if he would be able to fix it.

Evo's pact with the opposition not to stand for president in 2014 was a promise he wouldn't keep. In fact, he may well never have had any intention of keeping it. Why would he when opinion polls were giving him an unassailable lead?

First, he had to deal with the bothersome issue of the constitution. It stated that only one re-election was permitted. A year and a half before the vote, the constitutional court ruled in his favour and declared that Morales' first mandate of 2006–9 didn't count. Initial polls gave him a narrow victory in the first round – a shade over 40 per cent with a ten-point advantage over his nearest opponent. In the end it was nothing of the sort. Neither the TIPNIS road debacle nor a bitter conflict over gas price rises, called the *gasolinazo*, had affected his popularity. He took 61 per cent of the vote with almost 90 per cent of the electorate turning out to cast their ballots. In terms of the popular vote, he was even slightly up on five years earlier.

The economy was still booming – in fact, it had grown by 6 per cent in the election year alone. The government-funded social programmes were having a genuine impact on people's lives, and there were visible improvements in health, social security and access to higher education. While the bubble burst in Venezuela following the death of Hugo Chávez, the South American socialist economy managed by one of his pallbearers was still making headway. Evo had always been accused by his opponents of being little more than a satellite of Chávez, a mindless disciple of his late friend and of Fidel Castro. The robust improvements in poverty statistics, verified by everyone from the UN to the IMF, rebuffed that charge. When he had come to power more than a third of his compatriots lived in extreme poverty. When they went to the polls in 2014, that was down to one in five. What's more, as far as they could see, he'd paid for it with revenues taken from foreign energy companies. No wonder they still voted for him.

I got my strongest sense of that unwavering support not at a rowdy pro-Evo rally but in the tiny village of Choritotora, high in the Andes south of La Paz, where Aymara families worked the parched brushland for potato and quinoa crops or grazed sheep and llamas. I was there with the family and friends of a former BBC journalist, Lola Almudevar. Lola had moved to Bolivia around the time Evo took power and taken to the country instantly, displaying the enthusiasm and zest of the young and fearless in her journalism. Her writing centred on Bolivia's neediest, especially its indigenous women, whose causes she championed on the airwaves and in her newspaper articles. On her way to cover a story, the taxi she was travelling in with a Reuters journalist ploughed into the wreckage of two trucks involved in an earlier accident on the road to Calamarca. The taxi driver's wife, who had come along for the ride, was killed instantly. Lola died on her way to the hospital.

In the two years since her death, her loved ones in the UK had mourned her and kept up her association with the Andean nation. By holding cultural events in her native Nottingham, they raised enough money to build 'Centro Lola', a women's centre on a windy expanse of land near Choritotora. The location had been carefully selected to serve the widest catchment area of tiny Aymara communities possible. We were in Choritotora for its inauguration. It was an emotional and moving day, full of celebration for Lola's life rather than tears over her death. Gifts of Andean textiles were exchanged for Nottingham lace between the two sets of women, and fireworks and music began when they cut the ribbon to the centre. The Aymara women danced with Lola's mum, Monica Stoppleman, outside their bright new orange-and-red community centre, the indigenous mothers all too aware of what it meant to lose a child.

One of Evo Morales' social programmes involved sending a health-care visitor out to the region more regularly to weigh the newborns, vaccinate the infants and offer new mothers post-partum support. Previously the midwives and doctors had to travel to each remote community individually and see the mothers in their homes, said a local woman, Jostina Chuquijuanca de Soria, her Aymara translated into Spanish for my benefit. Now they could come to the Lola Centre for properly organized visits. 'The most important thing about this centre is that we're protected from the sun and the rain,' she added.

I remember how Jostina explained that Evo's government had given them funds in exchange for taking their children to monthly health checks and ensuring the older ones attended school. It had an echo of Lula's *Bolsa Família* in Brazil, but adapted to the Andean context. The state's natural gas revenues also paid for workshops on domestic violence and children's nutrition. 'Also for children's early stimulation programmes,' Jostina said, 'where we learn how to play and work on making toys.' The paint was barely dry on Centro Lola and already a picture of Evo Morales was up on the wall. The women adored him for the programmes that benefited their community and gave their kids a fighting chance of making it past two years old. It struck me then, visiting Bolivia as a correspondent based in Chávez's Venezuela, that the two men were perhaps most similar in the way they were loved by their most ardent supporters. It was a faith that transcended politics. If Evo had asked Jostina and the other Aymara women of the communities around Calamarca to vote for him for a third, fourth, even a tenth time in succession, they would have done so without a moment's hesitation.

By 2014, Morales had alienated some indigenous supporters, that much was clear. Yet when they were faced with a choice between an indigenous president or a return to the kinds of men who had governed Bolivia in the past, it simply wasn't a choice. The opposition was as fractured as it ever had been and had no coherent alternative to Evo. In the hours after his third successive election victory, Evo Morales sat down with the BBC and insisted that *this* would absolutely be his last term in office. 'There is no need for Evo to be president until 2025,' he said, falling into his increasingly disconcerting habit of referring to himself in the third person. He maintained he'd given no consideration to changing the constitution to allow a fourth term of office.

'My big desire is to go back to Chapare, improve my farm, maybe build a couple of cabins to welcome former presidents,' he said.

It was about as sincere, it turned out, as the last time he'd promised not to stand again for the presidency.

'Do you agree with the reform of Article 168 of the Political Constitution of the State so that the president and vice-president can be re-elected two times in a continuous manner?'

The question was only answerable with a cross for 'Yes' or for 'No'. As they marked their ballots, millions of Bolivians who turned out on 21 February 2016 had mixed feelings about this referendum. It was a vote on whether to grant President Morales and Vice-President García Linera the right to stand again. Under the 2009 constitution, they had already had their one re-election and they were fast approaching the end of the second five-year term allowed by law. Added to the almost four they served before the new constitution, they would have been in power for fourteen unbroken years by the time they stepped down in 2020. A good innings by any standard, and unheard of in modern Bolivian history.

Yet the voters might still grant them five more years. Evo Morales and Álvaro García Linera just needed more of them to mark Yes boxes than Nos in this plebiscite, known as the '21F' after its date. The vote was hugely controversial. The traditional opposition voices led the charge against Evo, although the 'No' campaign was a surprisingly broad church. Even within MAS and on the left, many weren't convinced that another Evo term was the right move. They ranged from former MAS allies like the mayor of La Paz, Luis Revilla, and the governor of the department of La Paz, Félix Patzi, who had set up a new centre-left *Soberanía y Libertad* party. Their open disgust at the flagrant attempt to stay in power was balanced out by kinder calls for him to step down, for example from the ex-MAS prefect Rafael Puente.[92] 'It is precisely those of us who value Evo for his political intelligence, for his valour and his capacity for leadership who should be in agreement that if our current president needs anything it is to return for a time to what we call "the bases", to return to his home and his community for a few years.'[93]

For the 'Yes' campaign, Álvaro García Linera espoused the argument that Evo had become 'irreplaceable', a supreme leader in the Fidel Castro vein, and even resorted to apocalyptic language to force his point home: 'There will be wailing and the sun is going to hide, the moon will disappear and everything will be sadness for us', he said of a possible future without Evo at the helm.

In the final two weeks of campaigning, the mudslinging suddenly intensified. Much of it revolved around Evo Morales' former girlfriend, Gabriela Zapata, with whom he had allegedly fathered a child. She was a top executive at the China CAMC Engineering Company, which had received government contracts worth over half a billion dollars. A journalist, Carlos Valverde, denounced the alleged influence-peddling implied by these payments and Evo found himself on the back foot over corruption and his personal life just days before the referendum. At first he claimed he barely knew Gabriela Zapata. Photographs of the two of them at carnival quickly surfaced. Then, in a plot twist straight from a South American soap opera, Morales said they'd had a son but that he had died at birth – something she initially denied.[94] Gabriela Zapata was eventually sentenced to ten years in prison over the illegal use of public funds, falsifying documents and money laundering.

Evo tried to blame the muckraking on the United States, saying its embassy had passed the information to Valverde. Yet phantom love child aside, the misuse of public funds seemed so blatant that pointing the finger at a Yankee diplomat just wasn't going to wash for many voters. Undoubtedly hurt by the scandal, Evo Morales lost the referendum by just 2.6 per cent. It was his first electoral defeat in ten years, but it stung worse than he could have imagined. He went into a dark mood, sequestered in the palace, and barely spoke to anyone but his closest advisers. When he emerged from his foul temper several days later, Evo was defiant. 'We respect the result, that's part of democracy… We lost a battle', he accepted, 'but it's not like we're defeated.'

He certainly wasn't. He had one final constitutional card left and, even in the face of this narrow but clear defeat, he intended to play it. In his quiet moments, when he wakes before dawn as he has since his childhood and has a few undisturbed minutes to himself, Evo Morales may look back on this decision and regret it. To countless observers he seemed to have been presented with the ideal opportunity to retire at the top of his game. The economy was still growing over a decade after he first took office and inflation was low. If he had walked out of the presidential palace as planned in 2020, his economic and social achievements would surely have remained in the electorate's rose-tinted memory above any errors or misjudgements. Then, after a few years back in Cochabamba, he could have returned to power, rejuvenated and newly in touch with his indigenous base.

However, taking a break wasn't something he was prepared to countenance. Instead, his team embarked on an ill-advised online and media campaign to redefine 21F as 'the Day of the Lie', attempting to gain traction with the idea that the vote lacked legitimacy. Then he turned to a supportive and compliant constitutional court. To the disbelief and outright fury of many 'No' voters, the judges granted Evo the permission he sought to stand again. They abolished term limits and justified it on the preposterous grounds that not being allowed to run for president for a fourth consecutive term was a violation of his human rights.

Print journalists were filing their first drafts in time for the morning editions. Their copy was laden with conditional speech, as the vote count was still going on, but most felt confident enough to predict the race was heading to a second round in December. The historians among them noted that it would be the first time Bolivia had ever gone to a second-round run-off in a presidential election. Previously, Congress made the final decision and since 2005 Evo Morales had won every vote by such a margin that no second round had been necessary.

Not this time, though. At a little after 7 p.m. on 20 October 2019, the Supreme Electoral Tribunal (TSE) began to publish its preliminary results. Morales was in the lead in his bid to hold office for a fourth consecutive term but not by enough to avoid a face-off with his nearest challenger, former President Carlos Mesa. Then, at 7.40 p.m., with almost 84 per cent of the votes counted, something weird started to happen.

The updates from the Electoral Tribunal froze. On Bolivian television, the presenters started to get jumpy. 'What is happening?' they nervously asked their studio guests, who knew no more than they did. The Organization of American States (OAS), acting as election observers, publicly urged the TSE to explain the confusion. The Electoral Council's head said they had stopped publishing preliminary results because the official results were coming in and 'we can't have two sets of results at the same time'. Evo, however, appeared in a jubilant mood inside the main hall of the Palacio Quemado. Injudiciously, he told his cheering supporters that victory was assured once the votes were in from the most remote parts of Bolivia.

'The rural areas are going to keep guaranteeing this process of change,' he said over the chanting and applause. The TSE stayed silent for almost a full day. Nothing more was announced, no updates given, no new figures. Bolivia was in electoral limbo – a dangerous condition for a country so prone to political instability, especially given just how upset some people were that Evo Morales was standing in the first place. If he was seen to be trying to 'steal' the vote, the situation would turn ugly.

At 7.30 p.m. on Monday the 21st, exactly twenty-four hours after they stopped publishing results, the Electoral Tribunal held a press conference in a hotel. If things had been moving steadily towards a second round before the information blackout, they had now suddenly turned on their head. Evo was miraculously 10.14 per cent ahead, the magic margin required for an outright victory, with 46.86 per cent of the vote to Mesa's 36.72 per cent. With only his traditional strongholds left to declare, the TSE was claiming that President Morales had avoided a run-off and secured his coveted fourth consecutive term.

All hell broke loose. Carlos Mesa called for his people to take to the streets until the authorities agreed to a second round. The OAS said it was 'worried' about the 'drastic and inexplicable change' in the Tribunal's result. The Bishops' Conference in Bolivia expressed concern, along with the European Union, Washington, Brazil, Colombia – all of them casting doubt on the process and calling for a second round. Jumping to Evo's defence were Venezuela and Cuba who recognized his win immediately and congratulated him on his 'historic triumph' over 'neoliberal oppression'.

On the streets of La Paz and Santa Cruz, people were raging. As far as they were concerned, the twenty-four-hour shutdown was an obvious stunt by Morales to stave off the possibility of defeat. In reality, Evo might still have won a run-off, as it was by no means clear that the opposition would coalesce into a single, unified anti-Evo vote in December. Yet that hope was lost amid the sound of smashing glass, angry chants and the whistle of tear gas canisters fired by riot police. Triggered by unverified videos circulating online showing unknown civilians supposedly hoarding boxes of voting papers, opposition demonstrators set fire to electoral offices in cities across the country and ceremonially burned ballots in the street.

Evo went on television and reverted to the language of revolutionary fear. 'A *coup d'état* is under way. The right wing prepared the coup with international support.' Bolivia was in turmoil, the antithesis of the stability that five more years of Evo's rule was supposed to bring. Days of violence stretched into a week, and then two weeks. Three people were killed in clashes between rival supporters. Students occupied their university buildings and major arterial roads were blocked by flag-waving opposition voters. Each day brought new eruptions in La Paz, Sucre, Santa Cruz, Potosí and Cochabamba. No region was immune from the chaos. In one small town, Vinto, the MAS mayor was publicly humiliated by demonstrators who marched her through the streets barefoot, drenched her in red paint and forcibly cut off her hair.

The tone had changed. The protestors didn't want a second-round run-off between Evo and Mesa anymore. They smelled blood, and were openly calling on Evo to resign. On 8 November, there was a key intervention. Rather than repress the protests, a breakaway group of police officers joined them instead. Videos emerged of uniformed policemen waving the Bolivian flag alongside the demonstrators to chants of 'Freedom!' and 'Policeman! Brother! Together in the struggle!' As a large group of armed, masked officers joined an anti-Evo demonstration, the government's description of the events as a coup attempt no longer seemed so far-fetched.

Evo Morales had spent the morning of Saturday 9 November in the presidential residence in the San Jorge neighbourhood of La Paz, surrounded by his inner circle. The walls were closing in on him. He had barely slept since the police mutiny had begun. The Organization of American States was due to publish its preliminary report on the election debacle the following day and it was likely to make uncomfortable reading for him. It would say that there were 'irregularities', 'clear manipulation' and that 'the first round of the elections held on 20th October should be annulled and a new electoral process should commence'.[95] Morales managed to get the secretary general of the OAS, Luis Almagro, on the phone but he had already refused to postpone publication of the report until tensions calmed and now he wouldn't budge. He would soon stop taking Evo's calls altogether. As far as Morales was concerned, the Washington-based organization was just pouring gasoline onto a wildfire.

The night before the OAS report came out, Evo was alone in the residence. News from the streets was getting steadily worse with the military saying it would not 'confront the people' who were calling for his head. During another sleepless night, he began to make phone calls in the small hours of Sunday morning. The first was to his long-standing right-hand man, Álvaro García Linera, who reportedly pledged his allegiance 'to the end'.[96] Evo then asked his communications minister to gather the press at the presidential hangar in El Alto airport at first light. When the OAS report came out, it included another damning judgement: '[it was] statistically improbable that

Morales had obtained the 10 per cent difference to avoid a second round.' Evo stood in front of the assembled media to tell the Bolivian people that, in light of the findings, he was calling a fresh election in the coming weeks. He made reference to 'new political actors' but crucially didn't rule out that he or his vice-president would stand again. It was a fatal flaw.

By the time he sat down afterwards for an interview with the leftist television network Telesur, it was already becoming clear that his concession wasn't enough to placate the protesters. It was one of Evo's biggest miscalculations to think that he could pacify the streets. They wanted nothing short of his removal from office by this stage and the offer of a rerun of October's vote was an affront to them. They didn't have to wait long for what they wanted, though. Sunday 10 October 2019 will go down in Bolivian political history. With the police in revolt, the army refusing duty and his political allies abandoning him, Evo was isolated. Experiencing a moment of profound existential crisis, he returned to the place where it all began: the Chapare region in the Tropic of Cochabamba. Before leaving, he shed tears at the hangar in El Alto, tightly hugging those who weren't joining him. The moment had the feel of a decisive defeat. Even some of the military personnel at the airport had stopped saluting him. The presidential jet flew him to the town of Chimoré where he formed a kind of war cabinet from the reduced group of trusted lieutenants and confidants who had travelled with him, including the vice-president, García Linera and the health minister, Gabriela Montaño. In the coming hours, other ministers resigned and made their escape into exile or threw themselves on the mercy of foreign embassies.

Evo's inner circle barely had time to form a plan before the institution that has so often shaped Bolivia's fate entered the fray. The military decided that Morales' moment in the sun had passed. With the simplest of threats, the high command brought a decisive end to almost fourteen years of socialist governance. The head of the armed forces, General Williams Kaliman, appeared in his uniform on television, flanked by his top brass, to 'urge' Evo to resign. In a scene reminiscent of Latin America's dramatic Cold War overthrows,

General Kaliman said in measured tones that, in the face of the 'escalating conflict', Morales should stand down. Or, as he put it, should relinquish his 'presidential mandate to allow the pacification and maintenance of stability for the good of Bolivia'. With the country's other top generals standing behind Kaliman or sitting menacingly on the table next to him as he delivered the message, it was clear that this wasn't merely a request.

Morales knew that he was beaten. His home in Cochabamba had been ransacked, his sister's home had also been wrecked and if he didn't leave Bolivia very soon he might well be killed. With no police or military backing, and his popular support staying indoors, fearful of a bloodbath on the streets, he had no choice but to accept Kaliman's ultimatum. Looking thoroughly exhausted and emotionally drained, Morales stood at a podium in Chimoré, flanked on either side by members of the coca growers' unions and the indigenous movement that had first brought him to national prominence.

'I am resigning,' Evo Morales said looking grave and frightened and sad, clasping the microphone with both hands as if at prayer. 'I want to tell you, brothers and sisters, that the fight does not end here. We will continue this fight for equality, for peace.' He wouldn't let the moment pass without apportioning blame to his opponents for what he said was an old-school overthrow orchestrated from Washington. 'There has been a civilian, political and police coup,' he maintained. 'My sin is to be indigenous, a union leader and a coca grower.'

Evo's next and most immediate problem was that he had to leave Bolivia in one piece. The presidential plane was naturally no longer at his disposal. Mexico stepped forward to offer him political asylum, which he promptly accepted. The Mexican government sent a plane to Lima where it was to refuel and await permission from Bolivia to enter their airspace and pick up the now former President Morales. After a tense hold-up in Lima, the Bolivian military – who were clearly running things in La Paz – gave Mexico permission to send its aircraft to Cochabamba and take Evo away. Once the plane landed in the jungle airport, Evo Morales walked across the runway with Álvaro García Linera, tears streaming down their faces. Amid final hugs from their emotional supporters, some of whom were openly wailing at the forced departure of their leader, Evo tried to force a smile onto his tear-stained face as the two men stepped onto the Mexican aircraft and into exile.

'*Fuerza*,' his followers told him as he boarded, 'have strength, you'll be back soon.'

The Mexican foreign minister, Marcelo Ebrard, described Morales' trip back to Mexico as 'a journey across Latin American politics.' The only viable route entered the airspaces of some radically different governments and the Mexicans had to engage in some convoluted negotiations to ensure Evo's safe passage. They co-ordinated with the Bolivian military chiefs in La Paz, the right-wing government of President Jair Bolsonaro in Brazil and the governments of Peru, Ecuador and Paraguay. Even the Peronist president-elect of Argentina got involved. Some eighteen hours after leaving Cochabamba, the plane touched down in Mexico City. Evo half emerged from the plane, waved, and then stepped back into the cabin, seemingly confused as to the correct protocol for a former president. Marcelo Ebrard, on the tarmac to greet him, beckoned him out and Bolivia's longest-serving leader officially went into exile in Mexico, part of a long tradition that includes Leon Trotsky in 1936, Spanish Republicans after Spain's Civil War and a pre-revolutionary Fidel Castro.

'You have saved my life,' Evo said with genuine appreciation once firmly on Mexican soil.

Morales swiftly embarked on a series of media interviews and banged the same constant drumbeat: he had been forced out in a military coup for having the audacity to nationalize energy resources, for being socialist, for being Indian. It wasn't a hugely sophisticated analysis, but it would be the only one he would deliver to anyone who asked. Clearly, the immediate cause of his ousting was the contested election and the vote count debacle. Across Latin America and the rest of the world, the left portrayed Evo as the victim of a *coup d'état*, one manufactured by the OAS and carried out by the Bolivian military and the far right.[97] Much of what Evo said during those first raw days in Mexico was undeniably true. His economic record in office was self-evident and so were his efforts to destigmatize indigenous identity in Bolivia. It was also true that the most conservative forces in the country had wanted to force him out from the very beginning.

Yet the reasons he was forced to request asylum in a city 3,000 miles away from his home were manifold. At least in public he was unwilling to accept almost any part of the blame himself. In truth, even once Evo had secured the controversial right to stand in the 2019 election, he was struggling. In 2014, Morales had been re-elected with more than 60 per cent of the votes cast. In 2019, he was straining to reach 45 per cent. In those intervening five years, the fissures in the indigenous movement that emerged over the TIPNIS highway had fractured into wide, ugly cracks. In particular, the impoverished department of Potosí, whose Rich Mountain had been exploited for centuries for every last ounce of its silver ore, felt more disconnected from Evo Morales than ever. As the silver ran out, the miners continued to risk their lives in search of zinc, dynamiting inside narrow tunnels and dying from the lung disease silicosis, known among them as simply '*mal de mina*', 'mine illness'. The life expectancy of a mine worker was just forty years old.

Now Potosí had a new curse: lithium. It is the mineral in insatiable demand for batteries and cell phones and hybrid cars. The government hoped that China's endless thirst for lithium for its electronics factories could bolster the Bolivian economy as the price of natural gas levelled out after the commodities boom. Potosí boasts the largest single lithium deposit in the world. It sits beneath the hauntingly beautiful, crystalline-white crust of Salar de Uyuni, a salt flat so large it can be seen from space. It is a place that takes the breath away, its fine powder stretching out across the plateau to a seemingly limitless horizon. Salar de Uyuni forms part of the 'Lithium Triangle' which includes sizeable deposits in northern Argentina and Chile. Chile's pro-business government has long allowed foreign mining companies to extract its copper, so pivoting to the export of lithium came relatively easily. Meanwhile, Salar de Uyuni lay largely untouched.

In 2018, Evo signed a contract with a German firm, ACI Systems, to build a plant for the industrial use of lithium to produce battery components, primarily for China. ACI Systems promised investment of more than a billion dollars in the deal but the indigenous and mining groups of Potosí were furious at their meagre share of the arrangement. They demanded an increase of up to 11 per cent of the royalties saying that once again the government in La Paz was in cahoots with a foreign company to extract Potosí's riches and give local people nothing in return. Much like the anger over TIPNIS, the fact that it was an Aymara president who cut the deal made the betrayal all the worse.

The people of Potosí instigated a civic strike over the Morales government, a protest lasting more than fifty straight days. As primarily Aymara and Quechua Indians, Morales would have been counting on Potosí's vote in 2019. But many turned their backs on him, angry with what they saw as his mistreatment of the Altiplano, the region of his birth.[98] Evo also saw the hand of lithium in his political downfall but in a very different way. He blamed the unrest and his eventual eviction from the Palacio Quemado on the United States, saying they wanted Chinese state-run firms and the German company out of Bolivia in order to obtain the lithium deposits under Salar de Uyuni for themselves.

'I'm convinced that it's a lithium *coup d'état*,' he said, 'and then a coup against Evo and all our economic policies.'[99]

However, lithium wasn't the only element behind his removal. A classical rather than a chemical one, that of fire, also played a part. In late 2019, as Brazil's right-wing president, Jair Bolsonaro, came under global scrutiny for his blasé and botched response to the huge Amazon wildfires, Evo Morales was also the subject of intense criticism over conflagrations in Bolivia. The Chiquitania forest is a region of tropical savannah in Santa Cruz, the lowland department in eastern Bolivia. It is of huge environmental significance as it connects the Amazon and the Gran Chaco, two of the most important eco-regions in South America. As the fires raged out of control on the Brazilian side of the border, great swathes of the Chiquitania forest were also going up in flames. As many as two million hectares were destroyed in less than a month. Around half the losses took place in protected areas, rich in biodiversity. Evo wasn't just attacked for his handling of the crisis, which was considered ponderous and poorly co-ordinated. He was also rounded on by environmentalists over legislation he passed earlier in the year to allow farmers the right to use 'controlled burning' to clear land for their crops. It was intended as an easy gesture to help secure the rural vote in an election year but the consequences in terms of the loss of the country's precious forests were huge. During the crisis, a group of scientists from the College of Biologists in La Paz estimated that it would take about three hundred years to regenerate the local ecosystem.[100]

Morales initially turned down offers of international aid, especially a super-tanker plane from the United States to dump water on the affected region. The decision only made his publicity effort – appearing in the affected area dressed in fire-retardant clothing and spraying water at the smouldering earth with a thin hose – seem all the more ineffectual and out of touch. Worse still, his cabinet made comments that seemed to come straight from Bolsonaro's mouth. The defence minister, Javier Zavaleta, blamed shadowy 'saboteurs' for playing a 'macabre game': 'We put out the fires and there are people behind us that are starting them again… We cannot control wildfires like this.'[101] Evo backtracked, accepting some international support, and suspended campaigning for a little while. However, the timing of the crisis before the election cost him votes.

In essence, though, his fall in support wasn't caused by either lithium or forest fires. His grip on economic management had been weakening. Annual growth had slowed to a more modest 4 per cent despite a massive increase in government spending on infrastructure projects and social programmes. Public debt climbed rapidly, with the World Bank figures showing an increase from 38 per cent of GDP in 2014 to 53 per cent by the time Bolivians went to the polls. In addition, foreign exchange reserves were down by almost half and the budget deficit grew to 8 per cent.[102] It wasn't the picture of unfettered economic growth it had been a decade earlier and, although he had done a huge amount to pull people from poverty – for which he deserves great credit – there were also many millions for whom life was as tough in late 2019 as it had been the day Morales first took power. One of his earliest rivals, Alejo Véliz, put it simply in an interview with a Bolivian newspaper about halfway through Evo's time in office: 'We continue to be inside a neoliberal economic model… for the peasants their markets haven't grown.'[103]

None of that might have mattered if Evo Morales was still in his pomp as a leader. However, after more than thirteen years, the gloss was beginning to rub off the supposedly 'irreplaceable' leader. Certainly, some who had voted for him in the past felt that granting him five more years – president until 2025 – was simply too much. While his style hadn't drastically changed since his *cocalero* union days, observers who had watched Morales for a long time said that he had lost something of his empathetic tone the further he travelled from his roots. Rather than capture the injustices felt by the poorest every morning as they struggled to make a living, his speeches were now peppered with the same hollow socialist rhetoric of Venezuela or Cuba, increasingly filled with meaningless *lemas*, or slogans, rather than inspiring the crowds with his own real-life experiences.

Some feared it was because he was no longer having any ordinary experiences. Evo consistently referred to himself in the third person – like Caesar. Even people in the Chapare began to complain that he seldom visited them anymore and when he did grace them with a quick visit they 'cannot get close to him'.[104] In fairness, the rings of security, press and political entourage that accompanied him were the same for almost any other president in Latin America. But Evo wasn't supposed to be just any president. He was supposed to be one of them – a peasant farmer just like them only sitting in the Palacio Quemado because they had put him there. In fact, wasn't the original slogan for his campaign *Somos Presidentes* – We're Presidents? By the 2019 campaign, the line on his supporters' lips was markedly different: 'Evo or No one.'

*

Two days after Evo's hasty exit from the country, the road from El Alto airport down to La Paz was an obstacle course, littered with breezeblocks, burning tyres and twisted sections of metal fencing. My taxi driver, Hector, a young indigenous guy with sharp, inquisitive features, was incredibly adept at weaving fast through the narrow gaps between the barricades. It was barely 4 a.m., bitterly cold and pitch dark as we descended into the city below.

Hector invited me to sit up front with him to feel the benefit of the weak current of warm air flowing from his dilapidated dashboard. His woollen hat pulled low below his ears and forehead, he patiently answered my incessant questions about the tumultuous past forty-eight hours. 'Over these weeks of protest, El Alto was basically quiet,' he explained as we swerved around another concrete slab in the road. 'But they started to take to the streets on Monday and, *puta*, look at it now. They've trashed it.' Was he glad or sorry to see Evo gone, I asked him a little hesitantly. Hector almost winced. 'I'd say this was a coup. I would have voted for him again,' he confided. 'He might have made some mistakes and maybe it was an error to try to stay on. But he wasn't doing so bad. The growth in Bolivia was good. And he was the only president who cared about the *campesinos* and the poor.'

Hector was born into the same rural poverty as Evo, he explained, and his parents still worked the land cultivating corn, maize and potatoes in the province of Larecaja, north of La Paz. He was now fully westernized and said he only really spoke Aymara when he went home to visit his folks. Hector had come to the sprawling urban hub for his military service and after he left the barracks in 2015, he began studying automobile engineering. He had built a life with a girl from his college and was now a father of two. Driving a taxi at night was a good way to supplement the family income, at least until he could find a steady job in the car industry. It had been almost impossible to work this week, though, Hector said. Besides the danger of driving around during an unofficial curfew, petrol was increasingly scarce and rising in price by the day. Some of Evo's more radical supporters had attempted to cut off fuel supplies to La Paz in protest at his forced resignation.

Sunrise brought the prospect of more violence. The street protests before Evo's dramatic departure had been calling for him to go. The demonstrations since then were demanding he come back. A protest march was due to begin in El Alto, so we attempted to weave our way back up the road as best we could. Our driver stuck a small *Wiphala* on his radiator, his own sign of solidarity with the protesters, which he also figured might help us get past the roadblocks. It worked at a few. At others, the car was whacked on the hood by pro-Morales demonstrators unimpressed at the sight of a *gringo* camera crew at a time like this.

After twisting our way around El Alto's narrow streets and ramshackle neighbourhoods, we found a vantage point across the valley. La Paz stretched out below us, Bolivia's seat of power glistening in the sun beneath the resplendent Illimani mountain. In the distance, indistinct chanting could be heard, occasionally drowned out by the crack of fireworks or dynamite. Suddenly, the crowd came into view over the brow of a hill: a mass of men in hats, boots and ponchos, women in brightly coloured *pollera* skirts, kids who struggled to keep up with their parents. The people of El Alto, one of the supporting pillars of Morales' power, were streaming down in their thousands into the sister city below. They were livid at his expulsion and united in their demand that the interim government stand down at once.

We drove down to meet the marchers. Primarily Aymara and Quechua speakers, they were making their feelings known in Spanish, the chant now clear and defiant: *'¡ahora sí! ¡Guerra civil!'* they bellowed – 'now, yes, it's civil war!' Leading a group of marchers was Jesús Rojas, an Aymara man in his sixties and one of the founders of the CSUTCB peasant workers' organization. Jesús was dressed in a rubyred poncho and jet-black hat, and his voice was almost breaking with rage when he spoke. Yet beyond his obvious anger over the military's hand in Evo's departure, he was particularly upset over the opposition demonstrators' disrespect for sacred indigenous symbols. A day earlier, video footage had emerged of anti-Evo protesters burning the *Wiphala* and stamping on it. Many indigenous people were deeply offended and worried about where it might lead. 'We're angry, we're furious,' he yelled at me through a mouthful of chewed coca leaves, his eyes blazing, 'especially at the police. The *Wiphala* is of the *Qullasuyu* [the southeastern province of the Inca empire]. It's of the Aymara, of the Quechua, of the thirty-six ethnicities of the *Qullasuyu*. They cannot step on it or burn it. They are to blame for all of this.'

Once the marchers reached the Plaza San Francisco in La Paz, they joined forces with pro-Evo groups from other departments bussed in from across Bolivia the night before. On spotting our microphones and equipment, dozens wanted to speak on camera, grabbing us by our jackets and implored us with tears in their eyes to '*[decir] la verdad*', to 'tell the truth'. This was a coup, plain and simple, they said. They all echoed a few basic points: Evo had been forced out by the military in violation of the constitution and the opposition was working with Washington to try to kill their elected leader. As we were speaking to a woman in a brown shawl with a gold front tooth, tear gas canisters suddenly whistled over our heads and into the crowd. It seemed like they were targeting the group talking to the press. Young men grabbed the projectiles with damp cloths to protect their hands from the hot metal and threw them back at the riot police. Everyone scattered, coughing and spluttering, to get out of the line of fire. As soon as the protesters regrouped in a side street, their chants started up again, even more defiantly: '*la wiphala se respeta, ¡carajo!*' – 'respect the *Wiphala*, dammit!' The troops patrolling the streets on foot and in armoured vehicles carried live rounds as well as tear gas.

In the days after Evo Morales left for Mexico, the initial power vacuum was filled by the military. However, the high command was adamant that the army didn't intend to run the country in the long term. In a hastily arranged session of parliament, the little-known second vice-president of the Senate from an obscure opposition party, Jeanine Añez, was sworn in as interim president. The ceremony was farcical. She took the oath of office before a nearly empty chamber with the MAS deputies prevented from entering the building by a security cordon outside. Afterwards, interim President Añez walked the short distance into the Palacio Quemado holding up a bible in a bizarre, evangelical procession with her supporters shouting, '*La Biblia volvió al Palacio*', 'the Bible has returned to the Palace'.

A few days later I was the first journalist to secure a face-to-face interview with the new Bolivian leader in the Palacio Quemado. Inside the president's office, there were unmistakable signs of Evo Morales everywhere. Two large pieces of indigenous art hung on the walls and *Wiphala* flags were draped in opposite corners of the room. A space hadn't yet been found for a new flat-screen plasma television so it sat unplugged on the floor. The room had the feeling of a recently vacated study with the previous occupant's imprint still lingering before the new owners had had a chance to redecorate. The heavy, ornately carved presidential desk made of tropical hardwood was unchanged, and Añez settled into the president's luxurious studded leather chair as if she'd been occupying it for five years, not five days. Her dyed-blonde hair was perfectly ironed and meticulously arranged for the camera, her make-up impeccable. Dressed in a designer outfit, she was trying to show she was everything that Evo was not.

I asked her about her oddly staged and overtly religious entrance into the presidential palace. What exactly was that? 'A manifestation of faith,' she answered flatly. 'When Evo Morales came to power, he is an atheist man [sic]. So he didn't want anything related to the church and to faith. But we are women of faith, Bolivians are people of faith. So it was very significant to us that the Bible was in the palace as a symbol of reconciliation and faith.' But surely Bolivia is still a secular state, I said. 'That was an imposition from the Movement Towards Socialism and you have to understand that they took advantage during all these years to impose things on the Bolivian people because they had the votes [the majority] in parliament.'

The clip of her baffling and inexplicable logic over the separation of church and state went viral. In the rest of our conversation she insisted she hadn't been installed via a coup: 'Of course not. These are different times.' And she denied deleting a series of racist tweets about indigenous people from her Twitter account:

Those tweets were fake… I've never been racist. I'm just a normal woman, from a small village in a poor part of the country [Beni]. I think these negative attitudes came from Evo Morales and his government who divided the country and spread hate and racism. Our society has never been so divided.

She also praised the actions of the police who were coming under international criticism for the number of dead and injured protesters. A day after our interview, Jeanine Añez signed Decree 4078 on that wrought wooden desk. It officially gave members of the armed forces immunity from criminal prosecution over any deaths that took place during their operations in 'the defence of society and maintenance of public order'. Her decree caused an international outcry. The following day, seemingly liberated by the stroke of the presidential pen, Bolivian security forces shot and killed nine local people in the town of Sacaba during a protest. Añez had given the army carte blanche to shoot at will – and they had gleefully accepted it. Two weeks later, as the protests began to subside, Decree 4078 was repealed.

One afternoon during their first week in power, the interim government took journalists around the 'Casa Grande del Pueblo', an imposing $34 million presidential residence built by Evo Morales directly behind the Palacio Quemado. The looming twenty-nine-storey tower was hugely divisive, with many seeing it as an unnecessary eyesore in the colonial heart of La Paz and another expensive vanity project akin to the Evo Museum in his birthplace on the Altiplano. The transitional government wanted the public to see where their money had gone. The new communications minister breathily narrated live for Bolivian television as she took journalists from room to room, as though entering one of Saddam Hussein's palaces after the fall of Baghdad or exploring a fugitive drug lord's recently vacated mansion. She took the camera crews into Evo's bedroom where his Andean jackets and embroidered shirts still hung in the wardrobe, his books stacked on his shelves with titles like *The CIA Against Che*. There was a helipad on the roof and a private lift, the minister exclaimed excitedly, as the photographers poked around Morales' bathroom. The jacuzzi, sauna and spa room were evidence enough, the conservative media declared, that Evo Morales was nothing like the humble coca grower he claimed to be.

A few weeks later the interim government did much more to Morales than just rummage through his bedroom. On 19 December 2019, they issued an international arrest warrant for him on charges of sedition and terrorism. In exile, he remained defiant, calling the charges 'unjust, illegal and unconstitutional'. However, he knew that a return to Bolivian soil would put his freedom at real risk, not for a night or two behind bars but possibly years, if anyone other than MAS was in power.

The young taxi driver Hector wasn't available to take me back to the airport in El Alto after some of the most intense days I have ever spent in Bolivia, so I travelled with a man called Rolando instead. Like his colleague, he was incredibly dexterous when it came to finding a path through the rubble on the road to El Alto. Things had calmed a little as the interim government began to impose its will. Protests were fewer and lacked the energy of ten days earlier. But the pro-Evo radicals of El Alto were still trying to shut down the fuel supply to La Paz.

Rolando was older, more jovial and more cynical than Hector, especially when it came to the subject of Evo Morales. It was time for him to go, Rolando said decisively, cleaning his glasses with one hand as he drove. He accused Evo of being *aferrado al poder*, of clinging to power, and was firmly of the belief that he had lost touch with the people. The taxi driver's criticism of his former president was relentless as we climbed the deserted road to the airport, the air becoming thinner as we slalomed around the piles of bricks and burned-out barricades. I had spoken to protesters and the president, to analysts and politicians, to journalists and street vendors about the crisis. Yet it was the ageing, balding taxi driver Rolando who delivered the most visceral analysis of Evo Morales just as I was getting out of his cab: 'He lived in the *Tierra de las Maravillas*, he was Evo in Wonderland!'

★

Almost a century and a half ago, Bolivia lost its access to the sea. The War of the Pacific left a deep and painful wound on the Bolivian national psyche. It is a cut that will not heal or scar over time as its perpetually landlocked status continues to hold the country back from further development. It must export its silver, zinc, soya and lithium through Chilean ports like Arica and Antofagasta. Although it was granted free transit and use of the ports under a 1904 treaty, Bolivia is uncomfortably dependent on the victor of that humiliating nineteenth-century conflict. Eighty per cent of Bolivia's imports enter via its neighbour and any serious dispute between the old enemies could leave Bolivia almost entirely cut off.

Diplomacy has so far proved fruitless. In 1975, during a brief restoration of diplomatic ties, Chile's brutal dictator Augusto Pinochet approached his equally loathsome counterpart in Bolivia, Hugo Banzer, with a proposal. He would return a thin stretch of coastline to Bolivia in a land swap that would also improve Chile's access to freshwater. However, the deal involved a small part of Peru's territory and the complex proposal for three-party ownership soon collapsed. Evo Morales had hoped relations with an understanding left-wing ally in Chile, Michelle Bachelet, might break the impasse but again it came to naught. Even when Bolivia took its border dispute to the International Court of Justice in The Hague, the final ruling in 2018 went Chile's way, as the judges decided that the Chileans were under no obligation to negotiate over the issue. Bolivia, it seems, was destined to remain without an ocean.

Through it all, Bolivia has maintained its navy. With no sea on which to sail, on every 23 March, the Day of the Sea, the Bolivian navy run exercises on the sparkling blue icy waters of Lake Titicaca instead. Countless journalists have filed witty articles or tongue-in-check radio reports about South America's landlocked navy. Yet, in reality, there is nothing funny about these sad fleet manoeuvres. The image of Bolivia's armada going around in circles on the plate-smooth surface of the sacred lake is a tragic not comedic one. The nautical drills of sealess sailors are a tangible example of a country that has been tossed by political winds and treacherous currents for centuries.

Statistically, nowhere in Latin America has had more coups than Bolivia. In the 195 years since independence from Spain, it has experienced a staggering 190 coups, attempted coups and revolutions.[105] Whether the removal of Evo Morales was the 191st will divide Bolivians for years. To millions on the left, the debate is redundant – it was a classic coup in the Cold War military tradition, they say. Case closed. Others, and by no means just the country's 'elites' or 'oligarchy', believe the military acted in the interests of the people. They point angrily at Evo's fourth attempt to stand for president: the referendum, his inability to accept a 'No' from the people, the constitutional change to remove term limits and finally the inexplicable twenty-hour-hour shutdown of the vote count.

Whatever one's judgement of this thorny debate, Bolivia is a country in which things are never quite as they seem. In their fascinating and informative book on Bolivia, Linda Farthing and Benjamin Kohl wrote about the 'Aymara concept of *ch'ixi*, which recognises that something can be simultaneously white but not white and black but not black'. Yet *ch'ixi* cannot be defined as what 'we can simplistically observe as grey, but in fact it responds to the logic of a third state: it is and is not black and white and not grey either'.[106]

Evo's Bolivia – as the authors aptly named their book – can be arguably said to occupy this third space. Not a 'third way' in the Blairite sense, but a different conceptualization of politics and society and culture that spring from an Andean worldview. The word *caudillo* is inaccurate to describe Evo Morales. It invokes a more militaristic figure than is appropriate for a man whose political roots lie in the cultivation of the coca plant. Yet it would be equally naïve to fail to recognize that he became steadily more autocratic over his fourteen years in power. Evo Morales the icon was the sole prism through which his political project passed. A 'third state' perhaps – neither *caudillo* nor a strict social democrat and not even something in between. Rather, a combination of all of those things at once, a uniquely Aymaran response to a unique moment in Andean political history.

Whatever is written or said about Evo Morales following his forced resignation/overthrow, there are some undeniable truths that should not be overlooked. His economic record and achievements in poverty reduction have been well documented and, while they were starting to wane by 2019, they created a legacy which few would have questioned had he left office without attempting to cling on for a fourth term. Yet even more important is what he did to redefine the concept of indigenous politics in Bolivia and across Latin America. In his 2006 victory speech, Morales said: 'In the world there are large and small countries, rich countries and poor countries, but we are equal in one thing, which is our right to dignity and sovereignty.' He wouldn't relinquish that concept at any stage, even in exile. In power, Evo Morales' main international concern was to challenge the dissonance between the wealthiest and poorest nations.

Especially at the start of his tenure, it went hand in hand with his main domestic priority: to tackle 'Bolivian apartheid'. The term had first been used to describe the country's imbedded racial discrimination in 2000 by Felipe Quispe Huanca, a *campesino* leader known as '*el Mallku*', or' the Condor'. He used the idea of a Bolivian apartheid to illustrate the two Bolivias: 'one modern, of *criollos* with money and the other backward, of peasants and indigenous poor, the first with rights, the second with aspirations of having rights.'[107]

Evo Morales attempted to break the boundaries between those two Bolivias, at least for a time. His faithful vice-president, Álvaro García Linera, has written extensively on the issue of the 'hatred of the Indian' and attributes their exit from power principally to enduring racist attitudes in the country: 'Racial hatred is the political language of [the] traditional middle class,' he wrote in the first days of their exile.[108] Evo's rise came about through an awakening from a 'popular slumber' over these attitudes, argues García Linera, which saw 'an extraordinary acceleration in the pace of mass political activity.'[109]

And yet, when the end came for Evo's fourteen-year rule, it wasn't entirely a surprise. Although he had always claimed to govern under the indigenous principles of '*buen vivir*', or 'good living', some of his original supporters who voted against him in 2019 clearly felt *he* was the only one living well – inside a gaudy tower with a multimillion-

1. **February 1992**. Hugo Chávez addressing the media following his unsuccessful coup attempt. It was during this brief televised speech that he made his now infamous *'Por ahora'* comment.

2. **April 2002**. President Hugo Chávez is returned to office two days after he was ousted from the Palace of Miraflores and arrested by the military in Caracas.

3. **October 2012**. Hugo Chávez closes his final presidential campaign in Caracas. He was already in the late stages of the aggressive cancer that would take his life five months later.

4. **March 2020**. President Nicolás Maduro, Chávez's hand-picked successor, has little of his mentor's outsized charisma but counts on the backing of Venezuela's armed forces.

5. **March 1979**. Luiz Inácio 'Lula' da Silva lifted by metalworker colleagues after a union rally in his heartland of São Bernardo do Campo.

6. **November 2008**. (*below left*) Lula successfully trod a fine diplomatic line between alliance with Chávez and dinner at the White House with President George W. Bush.

7. **January 2019**. (*below*) Far-right President-elect Jair Bolsonaro and his wife travel to the National Congress for the 38th presidential inauguration.

8. **September 1998**. Leader of Bolivian coca farmers and government deputy Evo Morales is carried by supporters after arriving in La Paz to end a 24-day march from El Chapare.

9. **November 2019**. At the behest of the military, Bolivia's first indigenous president Evo Morales announces his resignation after fourteen years in power.

10. **September 2010**. President Rafael Correa wears a gas mask after striking police fired tear gas to keep him inside their Quito headquarters during negotiations over benefits.

11. **February 2017**. President Rafael Correa (left) and Lenin Moreno (centre) celebrate Moreno's victory in the presidential election in Ecuador. The two men would fall out soon after.

12. **September 1984**. U.S. President Jimmy Carter (centre-left) meets with members of Nicaragua's junta, including Daniel Ortega (centre-right), at the White House.

13. **July 2019**. President Daniel Ortega and his wife, Vice-President Rosario Murillo, at the commemoration of the 40th anniversary of the Sandinista Revolution in Managua.

14. **March 1961**. Cuban revolutionary leader Fidel Castro at a sugar plantation near Havana. From rural roots, he became Washington's greatest regional adversary from the Cold War into the 21st century.

15. **May 1980**. Refugees from Cuba stand on the deck of their boat as they arrive at Key West, Florida. More than 100,000 Cubans fled the island during the Mariel Boatlift.

16. **December 1994**. Hugo Chávez and Fidel Castro meet for the first time at José Martí Airport in Havana. The two went on to have a close bond until Chávez's death in 2013.

17. **September 2008**. Fêted as a new generation of socialists for Latin America, Hugo Chávez, Evo Morales, Lula da Silva and Rafael Correa join hands after a meeting in Brazil.

dollar price tag, built and paid for with the public purse. In one of his earliest trips to Europe as president, Evo Morales told the European Parliament that 'three cosmic commandments have brought me this far'. They were Ama Sua, Ama Hulla and Ama Quella, meaning don't steal, don't lie and don't be weak. Unfortunately for Evo, many Bolivians felt he and his administration had strayed from those indigenous ideals, especially the first two.

What's more, he had started to believe, along with his most sycophantic yes-men, that he was indeed irreplaceable. He began to believe the obvious hyperbole of his re-election campaign. Evo had fallen ill to the 'sickness of power', a Bolivian political analyst in La Paz told me over coffee: 'hubris'. Or, as a Bolivian friend put it to me, '*le endulzaron la oreja a Evo mucho, hermano*', his advisers poured honeyed words into his ears. It was a journey, often at breakneck speed, from 'We're Presidents' to 'Evo or No one'.

In Mexico City I caught up with Evo Morales at an event in the Autonomous University where he was due to address left-wing students, social organizations and indigenous groups from Mexico's southern states of Oaxaca, Chiapas and Tabasco. I had managed to squeeze my way backstage and exchanged a few words with the exiled former president before he addressed his audience, who were growing impatient to hear their star speaker. Evo looked exhausted and a little lost, a fish out of water in North America. Despite the warm reception, he had the look of a man who hankered for home. Indigenous music specially composed for his visit was performed and then a slew of people spoke before Evo, from well-known Mexican leftists to Álvaro García Linera.

Finally the man the crowd had been waiting for got up and walked to the podium. He had arrived from Bolivia in nothing but a short-sleeved polo shirt but somewhere along the line a beautiful hand-made Andean jacket, of the kind he liked, had been produced for his media interviews and public appearances. '*Hermanas y hermanos*,' he began. Suddenly a group of people at the back of the auditorium, next to the television cameras, burst into the Bolivian national anthem. As they waved the Bolivian tricolour flag and sang louder and louder, it dawned on the rest of the audience that they weren't overenthusiastic Evo supporters but opponents, critics of the great man who had infiltrated their event to interrupt his speech. In response, Evo's fans began to chant his name to drown them out.

I stood behind Morales at the podium recording the unfolding chaos as he paused his speech and folded his hands, the noise too great to continue. The guest of honour was caught in the middle of the cacophony. On one side, the flag-waving opponents bellowed out the nineteenth-century hymn entitled '*Bolivianos, el Hado Propicio*' – 'Bolivians, a Most Favourable Destiny'. On the other, his admirers repeated their chant over and over and over until the protesters were forced from the hall:

'Evo! Evo! Evo! Evo!'

ECUADOR /
RAFAEL CORREA

'We can't lose with ballots what we've won with rifles'

ELOY ALFARO

ECUADOR /
RAFAEL CORREA

'We can't lose with ballots what we've won with rifles'

ELOY ALFARO

The origins of modern Ecuador are steeped in blood and gold. Around the year that Columbus set sail from Spain to forever alter the course of the Americas, an Inca warrior, Rumiñahui, was born. Roughly translated from Kichwa as 'stone face', Rumiñahui was the half-brother of the last Inca emperor, Atahualpa. Atahualpa's father was Huayna Capac, the 'Sapa Inca', meaning the 'Only Inca', ruler of the Inca empire, '*Tawantinsuyu*'.[1]

When he died of smallpox in 1524 – a disease introduced by the Europeans that had ravaged Mexico and was sweeping south into the Andes – the empire was divided between his two sons.[2] His named heir, Huáscar, reigned over the southern part from the royal city of Cuzco while Atahualpa ruled the northern portion as the appointed governor of Quito.[3]

Peace held between the two brothers for several years, but soon civil war broke out. There ensued a long and violent campaign as the northern armies loyal to Atahualpa gradually wrested control over the empire from Huáscar. As the civil war reached its conclusion, the Spanish conquistador Francisco Pizarro, an uneducated former pig farmer from Extremadura, journeyed south from Panama with around 170 men and just over 60 horses.[4] Atahualpa was on route to Cuzco, where his brother, Huáscar, was being held captive, to install himself as the sole ruler of *Tawantinsuyu*. Pizarro knew Atahualpa was camped near Cajamarca, in what is now Peru, so he marched into the city with barely a hundred men and sent emissaries and a translator to Atahualpa to invite him to talk.

Minded to meet the European invader in person, perhaps intrigued by the horses – an animal never before seen by the Inca – Atahualpa arrived in the plaza in Cajamarca in full regal splendour:

As the sun declined on the evening of Saturday 16 November 1532, Atahualpa entered the empty square of Cajamarca on a magnificent litter borne by 80 nobles and escorted by 6,000 men; thousands of warriors in full battle order had been drawn up on a plain outside the city awaiting further orders.[5]

Pizarro's men were hidden in empty buildings surrounding the royal party and had concealed their small artillery pieces. They, too, were awaiting their signal. In the end, it came from the church.

Vicente de Valverde, the Spanish priest with Pizarro's party, walked into the centre of the square and approached Atahualpa's gold-encrusted litter carrying a cross in one hand and his prayer book in the other. There the Dominican friar stood before the Inca king and delivered the Requirement, the words devised under the Catholic Kings as the theological and legal justification for conquest. 'I am the priest of God and I teach Christians the things of God and in the same way I come to teach you.'[6]

Valverde passed the breviary to Atahualpa who, never having seen a book before, leafed through it and then threw it to the ground. That was all the priest needed: 'Come forth, come forth Christians, and attack these dogs our enemies who do not want the things of God.'[7] The Spaniards emerged from their hiding places and opened fire on the Inca with their cannon and matchlock muskets. They tore into the crowd on horseback, cutting down with their long steel swords the noblemen and the soldiers who protected the Emperor Atahualpa. They fired on the Inca army amassed outside the city, too, and annihilated their ranks with lances and swords, resulting in thousands of dead. Atahualpa was in the hands of the invaders.

Atahualpa underestimated the Spanish plans for domination of the New World and believed that they could be persuaded to release him in exchange for a vast ransom in gold and silver treasure. Held in a room in Cajamarca, which would become known as the 'Ransom Room', Atahualpa offered to fill it with gold and two more with silver in exchange for his life, a trade Pizarro readily accepted. The process of bringing the gold figurines, ornate jewellery, finely spun vases and headpieces from across the empire took three months. In that time, Atahualpa ordered his men to kill his recently defeated brother, Huáscar, to prevent him from exploiting his vulnerability.

The Spaniards melted down the gold treasures into ingots to be transported to Europe. Under the terms of their agreement, Pizarro should then have set Atahuapla free. But one of his fellow conquistadors, Diego de Almagro – who had invaded Peru along-side Pizarro but would later be his bitter rival for control of the Inca capital, Cuzco – urged him to kill the imprisoned ruler. Pizarro was eventually persuaded by the argument that Atahualpa posed a grave threat to the conquistadors if he were released or allowed to live. What came next was one of the infamous tales of treachery, deceit and murder that stained the Spanish conquest of the Americas with the blood of its native peoples.

Atahualpa was given a show trial, presided over by Pizarro, in which he was deemed to be guilty of various crimes from revolt to idolatry and his brother's murder. He was sentenced to be burned at the stake, a fate that the priest Vicente de Valverde would commute to death by garrotte if he acceded to being baptized. Fearful of the consequences in the afterlife of having his body burned, Atahualpa agreed and was baptized as 'Francisco', after Pizarro, in the moments before his death.

In the same square in Cajamarca where he had been captured by the European invaders, the last Inca emperor – Atahualpa, the son of Huayna Capac, ruler of *Tawantinsuyu* – was murdered by strangulation. The decision to kill him rather than send him into exile caused great dismay, even among many Spaniards in Peru. But doubt and remorse counted for nothing. The Spanish crown and the church had sent out a powerful message to anyone contemplating insurrection. They were still exposed to attack from Atahualpa's loyal northern armies. In particular, from Rumiñahui – his warrior half-brother – who was on route to the Ransom Room with a huge amount of gold from Ecuador, the most mineral-rich part of the Inca empire, when he learned of Atahualpa's death. He ordered the gold he was transporting and the remaining treasures from Quito to be buried deep in the Llanganates mountain range or thrown into a lake. Rumiñahui also destroyed anything that might have been of use to the Spanish en route to Quito, from armouries to storehouses. He torched the city itself and ordered the women of the temples to flee. Those who refused were killed to preserve their dignity from the rapacious Spaniards.

Eventually, the Inca warrior known as 'Stone-Face' was captured while defending the stronghold of Quito. Before he was (inevitably) executed, he was tortured for hours, perhaps days. But Rumiñahui refused to speak a word about where he had stashed the gold. His half-brother Atahualpa's treasure remains hidden in the mountains of Ecuador. Or so the legend goes.

The history of Latin America was shaped by blood and treasure, particularly by the obsession with silver and gold and the continent's many mineral riches. The themes of fraternal betrayal, of plunder and of quenchless greed continue to plague today's Ecuador. The driving force now, however, is not for gold but for power.

Before it shut down in tough economic times, there was a bar in Quito's chic cultural quarter of La Floresta called '*el Pobre Diablo*', or 'the Poor Devil'. A converted factory packed with hip craft-beer drinkers listening to live jazz, on one wall was a portrait of every single president who had ruled the Republic of Ecuador since independence in 1822. Under each picture, a small brass plaque showed their dates in power. If ever there was an illustration of the country's political instability and volatility, it was the Poor Devil's wall.

There were dozens of them. Many of the terms in office were shockingly brief, the presidents barely lasting weeks – 23 August to 2 September 1947 was the tenure of one head of state, followed immediately by another lacklustre leader who fared little better: 2 to 17 September.

Yet through it all, one man kept reappearing on the Ecuadorean political landscape: José María Velasco Ibarra. The hardy perennial of Ecuadorean politics, he served as president in the 1930s, 1940s, 1950s, 1960s and 1970s. On only one of those five occasions did he complete a full term in office. In total, he spent some thirteen years as president, making him Ecuador's longest-serving leader – at least until Rafael Correa burst onto the scene in the mid-2000s.[8]

Born into wealth in 1893, José María was the eighth son of twelve. Just four of them would reach adulthood. His father, Juan

Alejandrino Velasco, was a civil engineer of Colombian heritage from the Esmeraldas province, and his wife, Delia Ibarra, an old-fashioned and traditional *quiteña* (a woman of Quito) who home-schooled the boy, unlike her other children who all attended formal classes.

Having graduated in jurisprudence, José María Velasco Ibarra quickly made a mark in Ecuadorean public life. He studied in Paris in 1930 and wrote columns on electoral fraud and democracy for *El Comercio de Quito* under the pseudonym 'Labriolle'. On his return to Ecuador he launched himself more completely into politics, becoming first a parliamentary deputy, then the vice-president of the Chamber of Deputies, and finally its president, all before he turned forty. From there, the next logical step was the presidency of the Republic.

In his first campaign, in 1933, Velasco Ibarra made a fundamental change to the way politics is conducted in Ecuador. With the illiterate ineligible to vote, the electorate was only around 20 per cent of the population in the 1930s. Turnout was sometimes barely 3 per cent.[9] Nevertheless, Velasco criss-crossed the nation, visiting pueblos that had never seen a politician from Quito, to whip up their support. Dressed in austere dark suits and thick horn-rimmed glasses, his oratory rather than his scholarly appearance beguiled the crowds. Ostensibly standing for the Conservative party, his was a personality-driven campaign unconstrained by traditional party affiliation. Velasco Ibarra won easily with some 80 per cent of the votes cast, the largest margin of victory ever recorded in an Ecuadorean election.

As president, he called for the break-up of state monopolies and attempted to push a land-reform programme through the legislature to divide the largest land holdings among the peasantry.[10] His economic reforms thwarted by Congress, he became increasingly autocratic, locking up opponents and gagging the press. As he tried to force the measures through, the bald, bespectacled Velasco Ibarra was denounced as a dictator by the military and deposed. He went into exile in Colombia.

In exile, 'the Great Absentee' – '*el Gran Ausente*' – as he was known, came to represent the solution to all Ecuador's problems. War had broken out in Europe and tempers in South America were fraying, too. Ecuador was embroiled in a month-long border war with Peru in which it lost a large part of its national territory. It would be a key theme of the 1944 election, for which Velasco Ibarra secured the support of a broad coalition of opposition parties, from conservatives to communists, called *Alianza Democrática Ecuatoriana* (ADE). Using typically nationalist tropes, he promised to take back the territory surrendered to Peru and his campaign milked nostalgia for the brand of rudimentary populism he had displayed during his short time in power. It was an effective tool to stir up sentiments against the Liberals. Slogans for his 1944 campaign made outlandish promises that 'With Velasco' there would be more sugar, meat and even peace with Hitler.[11]

The weight of public support for Velasco grew as he embarked on another tour of every corner of the nation. Huge crowds greeted the man leading what became known as *La Revolución Gloriosa* against the Liberal Party and the *carabineros*, a deeply unpopular and repressive elite police force. The era of the Glorious Revolution 'was particularly important', writes Carlos de la Torre, one of the foremost authorities on Latin American populism, 'since it marked the beginning of mass politics in Ecuador'.[12]

Velasco Ibarra managed to create a conception, says de la Torre, that '[he] is the deserving leader because he is like the people. He has suffered and he is pure.'[13] In terms of an appeal to Ecuador's poor, it was hugely effective. José María Velasco Ibarra would be the dominant force in Ecuadorean politics for the next thirty years. By turns deposed and reinstalled by the military, the traditional power in Ecuador, he held office in every decade until his death in 1979. The populist ideals of *Velasquismo*, however, would long outlive him and would be harnessed particularly effectively by one man almost three decades later.

Akela called the troop to attention. The sixers quickly shuffled their patrols into line, puffed out their chests and straightened their backs, impeccable in their freshly pressed beige-and-green uniforms. Scout Group 14 met every Saturday afternoon in the patio of the Colegio San José, a Lasallian school in Ecuador's second city of Guayaquil. At first glance, it was an odd marriage: Robert Baden-Powell, father of the colonialist-era youth movement, and the Vatican's patron saint of educators, Jean-Baptiste de La Salle.

Yet there was a natural congruence between the Scout Promise to do one's duty under God and de La Salle's ideals of the 'Brothers of the Christian Schools'. And in Guayaquil in 1970, the San José schoolyard was the most convenient space the troop could hold their weekly meetings.

The boys stood silently in their neat little rows, their neckerchiefs and woggles in place, as Akela introduced their newest cub. Just seven years old, Rafiquito was officially a year too young to join the pack. But such was his determination to enlist and pitch in with the older lads that the Scout leader decided to make an exception. It was the start of a lifelong commitment to the movement for the young Rafiquito, a slender, inquisitive boy with thick, carefully combed dark hair, whose full name was Rafael Correa Delgado. In time, he would rise to lead a Scout patrol, then form his own unit, Group 17, at a different school. Even into his mid-twenties he would still travel with the troop to Europe for international Scout jamborees.

Yet for all his commitment to the fleur-de-lis and the scouting cause, he would not be awarded their top honour, the Wood Badge, until years later as president of Ecuador.[14] For Rafael Correa, the Scouts represented all that was good and right. Honour, service, rigour, discipline, hierarchy – all of it combined with adventures in the Andean nation's great outdoors. Correa found order in the world of nautical knots, bonfires and camping badges, and a camaraderie that would endure for decades. It would eventually extend to making one of his fellow Scouts his vice-president.

'You can't imagine the happiness it brings me to be in this hall with you, my Scout brothers and sisters,' Correa told a packed auditorium of the 25th InterAmerican Scout Conference in Buenos Aires in 2013, 'to recall the happiest moments of my childhood and adolescence.'

Latin American Scouts could count on his government in Quito to preserve 'a profound scouting spirit'.

In impassioned tones, a sky-blue-and-white neckerchief of the Argentine troop knotted loosely over his suit and tie, he urged them towards politics. 'Dear young people, we should all be political. A Scout should be political. Obviously not in terms of party politics, but in the etymological sense: to look for and to be concerned for the public wellbeing and the common good.' They were the embodiment, he told them, of the Scout's code: to leave the world a little better than you found it.

Such lofty ideals were far from the young Rafiquito's mind when he persuaded his dad to take him over the road to the Scout troop on that Saturday afternoon in 1970. They lived opposite the San José school and Rafael used to watch the Scouts out of the window. At the age of seven, he just liked the look of their rough-and-tumble games and was jealous of their smart uniforms.

The plane's wheels screeched onto the tarmac in Miami. Most passengers breathed a quiet sigh of relief at having landed safely after a long flight from Quito. For one passenger, though, tucked away in economy, the hardest part of the journey was just getting started. Rafael Correa Icaza's heartbeat quickened, a film of perspiration began to form and his shirt stuck to his back. No matter that he'd made this trip before, what he was doing was always an inherently stressful experience.

On this occasion, 18 September 1968, all his worst fears were realized. The suspicious look from the customs agent, the tap on the shoulder, the courteous yet categorical 'follow me please, sir'. As Rafael stood before his luggage, laid open in front of him, waiting for the inevitable discovery in his suitcase, he may well have been mentally weighing up the costs and benefits of this brief foray into criminality. On the plus side, it brought in some decent cash – in hard currency, US dollars – and allowed him to provide for his family during tough economic times in Ecuador. Plus, although he wouldn't necessarily have admitted it out loud, he had always expected himself to achieve more in life than he had so far. A series of unfulfilling administrative jobs hadn't met the ambitious expectations he'd had for himself as a younger man. In truth, life as a drug mule made him feel like he wasn't just another provincial nobody from Los Ríos.

Yet as the officer pulled out the two kilo-bricks of Andean cocaine from his bag, the limitations of his plan were self-evident. Rafael was about to be sentenced to five years in a jail in Atlanta. His kids – Fabricio, Pierina, Rafael and Bernardita – were eight, seven, five and four. The prolonged absence of their father at this sensitive age would leave a lasting mark on the children, one which other people would later call a stain.

As a man, Rafael Correa Icaza, or 'Fiche' as he was called by his family, had his defects – he was impulsive, quick to anger and often pig-headed. Yet, as a father, he always tried his best. He was attentive and devoted towards his children. In particular, given that he dropped out of secondary school for a rougher education on the streets, he placed especial emphasis on their schooling. He would take the children on long hikes to inculcate them with a knowledge of Ecuador, its landscape and its social history. The family home was a cultured one; journalists, musicians, writers and artists were frequent visitors. His sons, Fabricio and Rafael, paint a picture of 'a brilliant guy though he never finished high school… a self-taught, voracious reader'[15] and a man with 'a complex temperament, who always challenged authority in both its forms: the law and he who exercises it'.[16]

Although the Correa Delgado family resources were always stretched thin, Fiche himself had originally come from money. His own father, Rafael Antonio Correa Jurado, had once been a wealthy owner of a hacienda in Los Ríos called El Palmar but ran the business into the ground through poor decision-making and ill-advised invest-ments. Consequently, Fiche's life was one of poverty and transience, having lived in several different parts of the country by the time he moved to Guayaquil aged fifteen. There he met Norma Delgado, the handsome second daughter of the Delgado Rendón family. She was a devout and pious Catholic and distantly related to 'el Viejo Luchador',

Eloy Alfaro Delgado, Ecuador's revolutionary leader at the turn of the twentieth century. A strong, athletic volleyball player, Norma was captain of her school team. She began dating the tall, dark-haired and striking young man who had moved into her neighbourhood. The two were born in the same year, 1934, and, like Rafael, Norma didn't finish high school. In her late teens, she found secretarial work in a construction company in Guayaquil and the two married in a simple church ceremony in 1958. Their first child, Fabricio, followed a year later.

The first-born son in the Correa family was always called Rafael, a tradition which had traversed the generations. The line of Rafaels stretched back to the eighteenth century to a Chilean nobleman, Rafael Correa de Saa. His son – Rafael, too, of course – was the one who first moved the family to Ecuador. In his stubbornness and innate defiance, Rafael Correa Icaza bucked the naming convention. Angry at his father over some transgression, he refused to continue the tradition. When a second son was born to Rafael and Norma in 1963, the boy's grandfather wisely approached his daughter-in-law instead and asked her to carry on the lineage. Not one to perpetuate a family rift, she dutifully complied. The son was named Rafael Vicente Correa Delgado, the seventh Rafael.

Besides the two boys there were also the two girls. The first, Pierina, younger than Fabricio but older than Rafael, was studious, inquisitive and bright. The youngest, Bernardita, was the baby of the family and went by the affectionate nickname 'Bananita', meaning 'little banana'.

A lengthy separation from his kids in an Atlanta penitentiary was a horrifying prospect for Rafael Correa Icaza. His relationship with Norma had swung back and forth over the years but he'd certainly never intended to lumber her with bringing up four children on her own. Added to that, a conviction for drug smuggling left a permanent stink, and he didn't want to contaminate his children's lives with the shame of it. Fiche vowed they wouldn't know, at least while he was serving time in the US. Rafael recalls with fondness how his dad had given him books and written the family 'beautiful letters' from abroad.[17] As far as the children were concerned, *papá* was simply 'working' in America.

The younger Rafael laboured under that belief until he was eighteen. His mother eventually told him the real story. Fabricio heard it straight from his father. During the years her husband was absent, Norma sustained the family by cooking and selling lunches that Fabricio, and later Rafael, carried in metal containers to a handful of regular customers after school.[18] After Rafael Senior had served three and a half years of his five-year stretch, he was granted time off for good behaviour and deported back to Ecuador. His reintegration into the family wasn't easy, however.

His experience in a US jail had changed Fiche. To this day, his children describe how their father had tried to better himself in prison by working out, learning English and giving up cigarettes. Fabricio says he came back to Ecuador looking muscular and fit. Yet he was changed for the worse, too, angrier and even more volatile. Though he attempted to reconcile with Norma, it was clear that the relationship was broken. Fiche soon moved out.

Norma wasn't a vengeful woman nor would she be an uncharitable ex-wife. She actively involved the children's father in many aspects of their lives after their separation, inviting him to the main family gatherings, birthday parties, and even to spend Christmas together. Despite what the distance and the jail sentence had done to their relationship, Fiche and Norma remained good friends. 'They were childhood friends and probably never should have got married in the first place,' reflects Fabricio. 'But these are things one understands when one's older.'[19]

If it was a shock for the teenage Rafael Correa to find out that his father was an ex-convict and a drug smuggler, he didn't hold it against him. Correa reserved his ire not for the sins of his father, whom he painted as an unwitting victim of circumstance, but for the United States.

'It's not the drug mules [to blame],' he said to me of his father's criminal past, his voice rising a little, 'it is the war on drugs that punishes poverty.'

Correa Senior's time in prison was, at least for a while, the family's dark secret. However, the story would come out several decades later, once Rafael Correa was president. The truth of his father's time in the US was known about in certain parts of the Ecuadorean press but was never published.[20] However, on the eve of an important referendum in 2007, an opposition parliamentary deputy, Luis Almeida, blurted out the facts of the case in order to weaken Correa. Another of his critics, former President Lucio Gutiérrez, soon added to the smear campaign by labelling the president the 'son of a criminal'.[21]

Incensed, Correa defended his family's name on his weekly radio programme: 'I have nothing to hide. I had a tough childhood. What fault is it of mine what my father did forty years ago?' he asked rhetorically. He railed at Luis Almeida, who had first divulged the information, calling him a 'scoundrel'.[22] In response, he was applauded in Ecuador for mounting a robust defence of his father's peccadillos. People were broadly sympathetic to his argument that his father's time in jail had been the result of poverty, desperation and an unjust US policy of harsh sentences for minor crimes.

Today, Correa likes to make the comparison between the US-led 'War on Drugs' and Prohibition in the 1920s. When the illicit production of alcohol led to mafia violence inside '*Gringo-landia*', as he called the United States, when those killed were '*gringos*' and not Latinos, then the politicians relented and retracted their draconian ban. In the case of illegal narcotics, the opposite is true. The dead are Latin Americans, the violence is in Latin America, 'so they continue to criminalise and to punish,' he reasoned, jabbing a finger in the air.[23]

A few months after his father's criminal record had been used as a stick to beat him with, Correa began to act on the logic of his analysis of North American hypocrisy. In autumn 2007 he formally requested that the legislature grant a pardon to Ecuadorean mules jailed for carrying two kilos or less of cocaine – the same amount Fiche had smuggled forty years earlier. The day before he left office a decade later, Correa finally implemented the law by executive decree. Some 3,000 drug mules serving jail sentences similar to his father's were released.

Reflecting on the pardon, Correa quoted the left-wing Uruguayan writer Eduardo Galeano on the imbalance between supply and demand for illegal drugs between Latin America and the United States: 'We put up the dead, they put out their nostrils.'

In 1995, Rafael Correa's father killed himself. He never saw his son rise to the most powerful position in the country and join a select group of left-wing leaders who were changing the region and making headlines around the world.

'My father was someone who deserved a better life', Correa told me with an almost imperceptible shake of the head, some two and a half decades after his father's suicide. The seventh Rafael was considered to be much like his father in character – sharing an unyielding, almost blinkered vision of the world. It meant the two of them butted heads often, as his father had with his grandfather. He was the son who felt the loss most keenly.

Yet his father's suicide wasn't the episode that most deeply affected Rafael Correa. Just eleven months older than Bernardita, Rafael was closest to her in age and affection. On 28 May 1976, Bernardita's school day was cut short. A classmate asked her mother if Bernardita could come over to play, and the mother asked Norma's permission. Norma was doubtful – she knew her youngest was headstrong and could be hard to control. Still, faced with a complicated day because of the abrupt cessation of classes by lunchtime, she relented.

Wearing a small lilac swimming costume, Bernardita headed down to the pool inside the condominium complex. The friend's mother was either absent or not sufficiently vigilant, and the Correa Delgado family's youngest, Rafael's baby sister, drowned face down in the pool. When Fabricio received the fateful call he ran desperately to fetch his father and they made their way to the hospital where she had been taken, still unclear as to her condition. 'She died,' was the blunt response of the nurse when they reached the clinic. '*Bananita*' was gone. She was just twelve.

'I think it marked me more than anything else, the tragedy of my sister,' Rafael Correa reflected over our second cup of black coffee in a cafeteria in Belgium. 'It was tough when she died, a hard blow.'

Fabricio, who had dashed to the hospital with his distraught father, agrees it was especially hard on his younger brother. 'Pierina and I were at an age where we would go on holiday with our aunts and uncles or on trips with our cousins. The youngest two were the ones who spent most time together and with my mother.'

He says the family's faith pulled them through. '[Bernardita] became like a saint. For me she's my guardian angel watching over me, over my children, over my grandchildren.' While Rafael Correa's childhood was not necessarily the dirt-poor struggle of some Latin American political leaders – Evo Morales in Bolivia or Lula da Silva in Brazil, for example – he certainly experienced his fair share of family suffering before he reached puberty.

As Rafael Correa reached his teens, he had lost a sister, watched his parents divorce and would find out in due course that his father had trafficked cocaine into the US. Yet those experiences seemed to give the sensitive boy a certain steel which he began to focus into leadership qualities.

If the Scouts provided an outlet for his craving for authority, so did school. His forthright and outspoken nature saw him named president of the Cultural Association of La Salle Students (ACEL), a role that led him into frequent clashes with the teaching faculty. In one particular act of defiance, the headteacher took him to task over the tone of his speech for the school's anniversary ceremony. In the face-off between teacher and student, Correa was told that if he wasn't happy he could leave. He promptly turned on his heels and walked out.[24] The incident almost cost him the chance to graduate. Fabricio credits himself for smoothing things over with the headteacher and enabling his younger brother to get his high school diploma.

Rafael had acquired a taste for student politics and would continue to pursue positions of power at university. He attended the Catholic University in Guayaquil (UCSG), an elite and fairly new private school in Ecuador. More middle-class young people were starting to enrol alongside those from Guayaquil's wealthier families. Correa was studying economics and rose to become the head of the Economics Faculty's Students' Association, and then the president of the *Federación de Estudiantes* – the entire student body. It was his first real experience of political influence. Every week a few students from the *Federación* would meet the rector and other key teaching and administrative staff to discuss pertinent issues. Rather than just a talking shop, the student representatives had a meaningful say over decision-making.

An example laid out by Correa's unofficial biographers, Mónica Almeida and Ana Karina López, was over the introduction of the *pensión diferenciada*, the weighting of tuition fees according to family income. The scheme by which the poorest students pay less than the richest remains in place in UCSG today and is essentially unchanged from the programme Rafael Correa devised in 1985. At the request of the rector, and as both the student president and an economics major, Correa was sent to Quito to examine a similar scheme in the other large private Catholic university in Ecuador, PUCE. He was also given permission to examine the university's balance sheet, to see where the money to fund the weighting scheme might come from. He roped in other students from a range of different disciplines, law, finance and the department of student wellbeing, to come up with a proposal which was ultimately adopted at UCSG. Still, Correa and his contemporaries didn't benefit from the new model as it didn't come into force for three more years.[25]

At least one of Correa's detractors from that time denies that he was fighting the corner of the neediest students as their president and says that he was merely acting on orders from the university hierarchy. Yet regardless of whether Correa had helped to force the issue, or the institution had always intended to adopt a more socially conscious approach to fee paying, the *pensión diferenciada* can perhaps be considered the first win of his fledgling political career.

The Cold War was still far from over and was evident even in Ecuador's student politics. Socialists or left-wingers were simply 'communists', with little subtlety in the differentiation between them. Few would claim Rafael Correa was a leading figure of the left as the head of Guayaquil's Catholic University's student body. However, he did discover one key instinct that he would employ years later in office: loyalty to a very tight group of carefully trusted political allies. Correa's truest friends and confidants came from his home, his Scout troop, his school and his university. Even a number of his opponents at university made it into his cabinet. Eventually, however, that fealty to his inner circle would help bring him down.

By his own account, the experiences that truly moved Rafael Correa and decisively shifted his politics were still to happen. They would take place outside the university, in the thin air of the picturesque but poor mountains around the Quilotoa volcano.

'What is the indigenous problem?'

The question put to him on a stand at a jobs fair stopped the twenty-four-year-old Rafael in his tracks. Until then he'd been going through the motions, wandering around the hall, picking up leaflets from banks and accountancy firms and for postgraduate courses abroad. When one of the country's key social development issues was raised in such stark terms, he realized he had no answer.

'I didn't know. I just stood there, thinking to myself: how can I have just graduated as an economist but not be able to answer the question "What is the indigenous problem in Ecuador?"'

As was so often the case with the devout young graduate, he turned to the church for answers. Specifically, he went back to the Lasallian Brothers and the director of the order in Ecuador, Father German Delgado. He asked the priest to send him to one of their indigenous missions. Most of the Lasallian missions were in the Amazon. However, Correa wasn't sent to the jungle but to the Andes:

'Zumbahua. I'd never heard of it in my life. So I got my rucksack and I went to live there for a year.'

The town of Zumbahua lies in the mist and clouds of the Latacunga region of Cotopaxi, some 3,500 metres above sea level. A handful of streets which peel off a wide central avenue, its setting is what lends the town its charm. It lies in a valley surrounded by imposing green hills and jagged Andean cliff faces. The difficult elevation and the village's poverty make it a rare stop for tourists, though some pass through, dressed in stout walking boots and lurid waterproof jackets, to hike along the trails to the nearby crystalline waterfalls or to visit the bustling handicrafts market on a Saturday. For Rafael Correa, it was perfect: a small, self-contained village where people 'cultivate crops through the rocks, without water and in the dust'.[26]

Its relatively remote location was ideal to find the space he sought away from the life he'd been leading. He had achieved a more than decent mark at university, bumped up considerably by the strength of his final thesis on support for the small business sector as an alternative source of employment in Guayaquil – a theme he would develop in postgraduate research abroad.

While his course mates and friends had launched into careers in banking and finance, he felt both a duty and a need to spend a year of volunteer work in education, social development and religious instruction. It was a learning experience for him, too. He learned colloquial Quechua and his facility with the language would serve him well in years to come. Yet it would be harsh to suggest that his time in Zumbahua was some kind of carefully calculated rung on the ladder to high office. Speaking of his time in the region, Rafael Correa visibly softens as he recalls a time and place which he remembers fondly, with his university studies freshly completed and the world opening up for him.

The town he arrived in was, and still is, one of the poorest in Ecuador. Many homes were made of adobe and had zinc roofs or were thatched with straw. Some had dirt floors and the children suffered from treatable conditions like malnutrition, intestinal illnesses or Chagas disease. The vast majority of the population was illiterate and Rafael Correa's job, among others, was to teach mathematics and Spanish at a basic level so that people could complete their primary education. He also administered the local mill, leading to more than one disagreement with the indigenous workers over the accounting for bags of ground maize, barley and grain. Always the Scout, in his spare time he would take his rucksack and trek through the magnificent hillsides to the nearby Quilotoa Lagoon, a stunningly beautiful crater-lake in the hollow of the dormant volcano. Though he had long suffered from a painful right knee and was no Alberto Spencer – Ecuador's greatest footballer – at the best of times, he still enjoyed a kickabout with the men on the town's dirt pitch.

The year in the Andes was crucial to the making of Rafael Correa. He undoubtedly milked it later on in campaign material and on the stump but, that aside, it seems clear he learned something about the realities of life for Ecuador's Quechua-speaking population of which he had hitherto been ignorant.

In the process, he found the answer to the question posed to him at the careers fair. The 'indigenous problem' was not just a curious minor aspect of Ecuadorean society but was fundamental to it. The dusty barren earth out of which the families of Zumbahua struggled to produce a living had once been fertile valleys, he learned. 'But during the Conquest, the landowners expelled the indigenous people and sent them to the poorest lands.'

This process of marginalization and impoverishment had continued unabated through the centuries, he argued, and was being accentuated in the modern context by a misplaced understanding of indigenous culture. 'Mestizos and Europeans think indigenous poverty is part of their culture, that it's folkloric. Please, spare me,' he told me with his trademark sarcasm. 'They say "don't give them new homes, don't change their huts with dirt floors because it's part of their culture". No, it's not. It is part of their poverty.'

Correa's time as a well-meaning but naïve economics graduate in Zumbahua left a deep impression on him. When I met him miles from the Andes in that half-empty cafeteria in Belgium, it took Correa just seconds to become animated once more about the issues still facing the town more than thirty years after he first turned up in the remote indigenous community wearing an earnest look and a brightly coloured rucksack.

'Zumbahua was the best post-graduate course I ever did,' he said.

*

Louvain-la-Neuve – the site of Correa's more formal post-graduate course – is a strangely soulless university town about forty-five minutes by train from Brussels. It is pedestrian in the sense that it is a slow-moving, provincial town, and it's pedestrian in the truest sense, too, with its entire city centre cordoned off from traffic, which is directed underground instead. As I stepped off the train and climbed the stairs from the grey, sunken station I mingled with a throng of French-speaking Belgian students wearing backpacks and sneakers, lighting up cigarettes in the brisk morning air and unlocking their bicycles.

The red-brick new town was built in the early 1970s as a result of the linguistic divide between the Flemish and Walloons. The Catholic University of Leuven had been French-speaking since its inception in 1834. In an increasingly bitter row in the 1960s, Flemish nationalists, who were Dutch speakers, protested against the dominance of French, and this spilled over into wider violent student protests in 1968. The dispute was eventually resolved, if not amicably, then at least peacefully with the original Catholic institution splitting in two. The Dutch-speaking university remained in Louvain near Flanders while the French-speakers created a new campus near Brussels, Louvain-la-Neuve.

Rafael Correa arrived there as a postgrad in the autumn semester of 1990. Louvain-la-Neuve has grown and is no longer solely a university campus, but one gets the sense of a place where little has changed since the intense Ecuadorean economist lived austerely in the local student accommodation. Today the town's other biggest attraction is the Musée Hergé, a museum of several floors dedicated to the life of Georges Remi, the celebrated Belgian illustrator better known for his pen-name Hergé, the creator of the adventurous and perpetually young journalist, Tintin.

Rafael Correa owes a great deal to the peculiar Belgian new town, beyond the diploma he received. In Louvain-la-Neuve he met Anne Malherbe Gosselin. The story goes that they met by chance in the stairwell of her student halls of residence as he was looking for a friend. She jokes that it was his striking green eyes which first attracted her to him. 'It was, as they say, at first sight', she later told Ecuadorean television, although that may well have been a line for the cameras at the height of his first campaign.[27] She was studying physical education, her wiry, athletic frame making her a formidable competitor in a variety of sports. Malherbe was the daughter of a high-ranking NATO chief and from a very different family background to Correa's. The two began dating and, despite the obvious cultural differences, they soon found they had much in common, from a passion for the outdoors to a shared political worldview. Even as a handsome student, Correa was never considered much of a lothario in his youth. Still, he could be incredibly charming when he chose. Anne comes off in public in Ecuador as aloof and distant, but she fell for the passionate Ecuadorean with a penetrating gaze and sharp sense of social justice. For Rafael, someone who was perhaps always yearning for a stable relationship and a family, a lasting commitment was the logical next step. They married first in a civil ceremony and then with a full church wedding in 1992.

The thesis Correa submitted in Louvain-la-Neuve extended his previous examination of the role of small businesses in Ecuador. After he graduated, they returned to Ecuador where their lives would soon change drastically from the ones they had led as students. Even when they reached the pinnacle of Ecuadorean society, Anne made no secret that she largely preferred her life prior to her husband's decision to launch into politics.

Of course, Correa didn't jump directly onto the campaign trail on his return from Belgium. There was still much to come in his political development before he was sufficiently well positioned to take a run at the presidential palace, the Carondelet. He began with a return to academia by teaching at his alma mater, UCSG in Guayaquil, though the city's humid coastal climate never sat well with Anne's European sensibilities. So he left his home town and the couple moved to Quito where she adapted more easily to the subtropical highland air and could pursue her own career in education.

Rafael got a job at the University San Francisco of Quito (USFQ), the institution in which he would form the basis of his career as an academic. One former colleague says students were divided into two camps over Correa as a tutor: they either detested him or adored him. Polemic, decisive, argumentative and deeply divisive, his traits as a professor would later become accentuated on a national scale as president. He would constantly clash with senior faculty staff over university policy. Although, in truth, for a school considered conservative and right wing, Correa was always given complete freedom in his classroom.

His teaching was by no means Marxist, remembers one of his postgraduate students. Rather, he was a Keynesian and a social democrat with a keen sense of economic justice and inequality. His lectures were thick with his own moral outrage although his former student felt they lacked a coherent structure or a clear syllabus. Set readings would include Rosa Luxemburg and the Argentine economic theorist Raúl Prebisch, but from 2004 he often quoted *Confessions of an Economic Hitman*, by John Perkins, an autobiography in which the former engineering consultant claimed to tell 'the shocking inside story of how America REALLY took over the world'. Challengers and dissenters in his audience were often subjected to savage takedowns in front of their classmates, and some who attended his seminars recall being crushed by his powerful skills of argument and persuasion. In roughly equal measure, economics students at USFQ relished his teaching, this lecturer who encouraged them to adopt habits of independent, critical thought, or saw him as an onerous, pompous egomaniac who lacked intellectual rigour and whose classes they would find any excuse to avoid.

Meanwhile, his home life was stable and secure. They had three children: Sofia, Anne Dominique and Miguel Rafael. While Sofia was three, Anne Dominique still a baby, and, a little before Miguel Rafael was born, Correa was given another secondment to an international university. This time he went to the United States. As president, the airbrushed version of his curriculum is that he won a competitive national contest to study at the University of Illinois while only paying the same fees as applied in Ecuador – the funding part of a bilateral education agreement. His detractors doubt the veracity of that claim, suggesting that his position as a lecturer at USFQ gave him an unfair advantage over other students to gain the prestigious grant. In truth, Rafael Correa's stock as an economist was rising fast in Ecuador and his name would have been among the outstanding candidates for a chance to study abroad, given his record up to that point.

From 1997, he spent three years in the US Midwest, enduring its stiflingly hot summers and near-Arctic winters in the sister cities of Urbana-Champaign. He embarked on his PhD, again with a focus on regional wealth inequality, under the title 'Three Essays about Contemporary Latin American Development'. The thesis tackled questions of structural reforms, monetary union in the Andean Community and a quantitative analysis of the Washington Consensus in Latin America.[28] It was no small feat for someone whose English was far from fluent. But his tutors remember a dedicated and hardworking student, and Correa clearly enjoyed his time in the United States. The two children were in a good primary school and nursery respectively and he was putting his indefatigable energy towards something that carried real prestige in Latin America: a doctorate from a prominent US institution. Such a qualification remains highly sought-after by young academics in South America and confers a gravitas on them, deserved or otherwise.

The University of Illinois degree would certainly stand Rafael Correa in good stead, especially when he later criticized the United States as he could claim that his condemnation came from personal understanding of American society. Yet there is a certain irony in the image of Rafael Correa – a man notorious for his vehemently anti-American rhetoric and long speeches railing at Washington – walking around the Urbana campus, latte in hand, living for three happy years in the belly of the beast.

The house speciality at the Rinconcito Ecuatoriano restaurant and bar in Murcia is *morada colada*, a traditional Ecuadorean drink of spiced fruits, purple maize and herbs. Their menu is packed with typical Ecuadorean meat and seafood dishes and at Easter the owners serve up *la fanesca*, a soup from their homeland made of broad beans, corn, chickpeas and dried cod.

The lively city in Spain's southeastern corner is an odd spot to find Ecuadorean restaurants, yet it is peppered with them. And you don't just hear Ecuadorean-accented Spanish in the bars and hotels. The fertile valley around Murcia is sometimes called 'Europe's Orchard' for its extensive orange and citrus groves. Ecuadorean migrants make an important contribution to Spain's agricultural economy as farmhands, forklift operators and import-exporters. In Murcia itself, shops and small businesses with a link to Ecuador sell everything from floor tiles to furniture.

A glance at a local website advertising seasonal workers and domestic staff is mostly full of the CVs of unemployed Ecuadoreans: 'Offered: Ecuadorean agricultural worker, 25 years old, extensive experience in picking broccoli, peppers, cauliflower, lettuce, celery, oranges, tangerines and tractor driving.' Or: 'I am a 26-year-old Ecuadorean woman, serious and responsible with a great desire to work, with experience and my papers in order. I offer domestic services for a full- or half-day, childcare or care for the elderly. Available immediately.'

Marcela Carrilla remembers when she was one of these desperate applicants. She comes from Ambato in Ecuador's central Andean valley which, in a coincidental echo of Murcia, is nicknamed 'City of Flowers and Fruit' and the 'Garden of Ecuador'. Marcela had a career as a beeper and pager salesperson, selling businessmen the latest in 1990s technology. The impetus for her to leave her country at the turn of the twenty-first century was the same as it was for the owners of the Rinconcito Ecuatoriano or any of the roughly half a million Ecuadoreans who arrived in Spanish cities at the time: the dreaded 'dollarization'.

In 1997–8, Ecuador's Pacific coast was devastated by the effects of the El Niño phenomenon. Caused by a fluctuation of surface ocean temperatures in the Pacific, the westward trade winds weakened along the Equator and brought a concurrent warming of the waters along the coast of northern South America.[29] The thriving marine ecosystems of Ecuador and Peru were destroyed and their fishing industries decimated. In addition, El Niño brought extensive flooding, rainfall and coastal erosion. Crops and agricultural harvests were ruined. The problems spread to the oil industry with a barrel of Ecuadorean crude selling at a mere $6 a barrel. The economic outlook in Ecuador in 1998 was extremely bleak.

The country was already in a precarious position before the atmospheric and meteorological conditions conspired to make matters worse. External debt was estimated at around $13 billion, some 64 per cent of GDP.[30] The president of Ecuador at the time was Jamil Mahuad, a Harvard graduate of Lebanese decent. He presided over economic ruin. An estimated 70 per cent of the urban population lived in poverty while half the banks and financial institutions in the country teetered on the brink of collapse. Mahuad's government promised to bail them out using the Central Bank's dwindling foreign currency reserves. When one institution, Filanbanco, threatened to go under, the government propped it up to the tune of $600 million to stop the sucre, Ecuador's weakening currency, from devaluing further. Soon, the entire house of cards began to collapse.

Bank after bank needed bailouts, some seeking to offload the cost of their catastrophic mismanagement onto the public purse, sucking up more of the country's precious dollar reserves. The end of 1999 saw a severe recession.[31] Inflation rocketed to 100 per cent annually and the sucre devalued from 16,000 to 26,000 to the dollar in a matter of days.[32] Banks closed their doors, and assets and accounts were frozen in an effort to halt capital flight, sparking predictably furious protests. Faced with few workable options, in the first days of 2000, President Mahuad announced the demise of the sucre, which would be replaced by the US dollar. The upper-middle classes and elites in Latin America have long kept their money in dollars in bank accounts abroad, and were largely protected from these radical measures. However, the poorest found that their meagre savings in sucres, which had already lost most of their value, were suddenly worth next to nothing.

'It was like trying to pay for things with bits of blank paper,' recalls

Marcela Carrilla. With the country in full-blown economic melt-down, no one was buying her beepers and she started planning to leave Ecuador. For Mahuad, there was no time to plan his exit. Days after announcing the dollarization, he was unceremoniously forced from the presidential palace after two years in office by a massive protest movement led by indigenous people and supported by the military.[33] He promptly fled the country.

Marcela saw no choice but to join the growing exodus to Spain. A mother of two, a girl and a boy, she left them behind with a grand-parent while she flew to Madrid on a tourist visa. There, she slipped into the shadows and joined the vast black-market workforce of Ecuadorean casual labourers, farmhands, waiters, chambermaids and nannies. She and her husband, the father of her youngest child, found work wherever they could. He waited tables in bars and found work on building sites, while she cleaned hotel rooms: any job where a blind eye would be turned to their lack of official paperwork. The family spent seven months apart before cobbling together enough cash to bring the boy over from Ecuador. Marcela's elder child never made it over. 'They changed the rules just weeks after my son got in.' Thousands of Ecuadorean families experienced this kind of family separation. Another 500,000 had made it to the United States and there were many more scattered around countries like Italy, Portugal and other parts of Latin America.

An amnesty offered by the Spanish government a few years later allowed Marcela the chance to regulate her immigration status and become a legal permanent resident. Her son is now a Spanish citizen. They were tough years, though. She separated from her husband and had to bring up the boy alone on a cleaner's salary in the Spanish capital. When the credit crunch took hold in Europe, and Spain's economy began to spiral into crisis, many Ecuadorean immigrants began to return home. By that stage, Ecuador was picking up again thanks in part to a high oil price and a new, dynamic president in Correa. Still, Marcela chose to wait it out in Madrid and now feels vindicated in her decision. 'There's no perfect life in Europe and there's no perfect life in Latin America,' she says of the choices she made.

'We're better off here because another crisis could strike Ecuador at any time. It comes in waves or circles.'

For Rafael Correa, who watched the chaos unfold from distance while studying in Illinois, dollarization was the key moment that hardened his rejection of neoliberalism. His view about the economic shock therapy was only confirmed once he moved back home and saw its consequences up close. In time, though, people's anger towards dollarization eased. By 2005 the dollar had helped provide Ecuador with a certain fiscal stability. In fact, by the time Correa ran for president, the US dollar was so popular that one of the main accusations made against him was that he would 'de-dollarize' the country and bring back the sucre. Whatever his true feelings, Correa denied that he had a problem with the *gringo* currency circulating as Ecuador's legal tender.

After Illinois, Correa returned to the University San Francisco of Quito with a new swagger. Now an economist with a PhD from the US, he had more confidence in his convictions and was more sure-footed on campus, both as a teacher and an academic. Inevitably, given his irascible character and petulant tendencies, it led to more clashes with the chancellor, a personal vendetta he would carry into his presidency. Ecuador had changed, too. While still far from being a politically stable nation, it was perhaps at least on more solid ground following the painful experience of dollarization.

One man in particular was having a significant influence on Correa around this time. The economist Alberto Acosta entered Correa's life a little before he moved to the United States and on his return to Ecuador began playing a greater role, and could even be described as a mentor. He was the black sheep of a wealthy Quito family, the arch-leftist from a staunchly conservative tribe. While Correa studied in Belgium and the United States, Acosta spent time in the universities of Cologne and Bonn. By the time they met, Acosta was already becoming politically active and was one of the founders of a left-wing indigenous party, Pachakutik.

Different in appearance and demeanour – Correa imposing and intense, Acosta bespectacled and bookish – they were kindred spirits over the 1990s and early 2000s. When they returned to Ecuador, with Acosta working at a German-funded organization for social democracy, Correa regularly invited him to speak at seminars for his postgraduate students. They later collaborated on a book. However, soon they would be working on much more than academic papers together. Acosta was a key architect of the 'Citizens' Revolution', the movement that catapulted Rafael Correa onto the global stage.

In April 2005, simmering political tensions in Ecuador were coming to a head. The current president was Lucio Gutiérrez, the former general who had led an uprising to depose President Jamil Mahuad during the economic chaos of 2000. Having been jailed for a few months for his role in Mahuad's ousting, he was allowed to stand in the 2002 presidential election, and won with a broad coalition of left-wing, indigenous parties. In Venezuela just two years earlier another former military man who'd attempted to take power by force had subsequently won at the ballot box. But Gutiérrez was a very different and more short-lived political beast than Hugo Chávez.

First, he surprised, angered and alienated his left-wing partners by quickly jumping into bed with George W. Bush on the reviled Free Trade Area of the Americas plan. His fragile alliance started to crumble and, before long, broke up completely. He formed another coalition with the conservative Social Christian Party, but it could not hold. In the meantime, he presided over a corrupt and weak administration that failed to fix the social inequalities and economic distortions worsened by dollarization. By late 2004, impeachment proceedings against him collapsed, but the eventual outcome in a country renowned for its angry mobs forcing unpopular leaders from the presidential palace was inevitable.

In an effort to play down the significance of the protests, Gutiérrez told the press a 'group of outlaws' had attacked his home. The demonstrators gleefully adopted the label and coined the term 'the Rebellion of the Outlaws' for their anti-Lucio movement. He attempted to cling onto power by stuffing the Supreme Court with crony judges. But as the protests grew, his decision to declare a state of emergency was the final straw. Congress disobeyed the order, thousands of demonstrators, especially indigenous protest groups, refused to leave the streets until he was gone, and the armed forces publicly withdrew their support for the president.

On 20 April, Lucio Gutiérrez was flown from La Carondelet by helicopter to the Brazilian ambassador's residence where he stayed until safe passage out of the country could be negotiated. In the process, Gutiérrez's vice-president, Alfredo Palacio, was made president. He needed a cabinet, and fast. For finance minister he turned to an outspoken young academic who had already done some advisory work for his office, which had prompted rumours of a 'shadow cabinet' being formed by Palacio well before Gutiérrez was ousted.

Rafael Correa made the leap from lecture halls to halls of power just two weeks after his forty-second birthday. He wouldn't return to academia until his mid-fifties. Inside the ministry, he set about his task with his usual energetic, whirlwind work ethic. If he had grown accustomed to a lack of sleep as a father of three small children, it served him well. Colleagues attest that he began to operate effectively on just a few hours' sleep a night.

He attacked a controversial fund for external debt commitments, called Feirep, which absorbed some 10 per cent of the national budget and channelled hundreds of millions of dollars towards servicing loans from the IMF and the World Bank. Just a month into taking up his office, he appeared before parliament to argue for that debt burden to be reduced to free up funds for social programmes. Feirep didn't make 'technical or ethical sense', he argued, and he marked himself out as the rising star in Palacio's administration.[34] He wanted to renegotiate government bonds and work more closely with Chávez's Venezuela on energy issues, was critical of the mining and energy ministry and positioned himself firmly alongside the leftist social movements, the unions and the indigenous peoples, speaking Quechua in public to flaunt his credentials. These were the values he had been forging with increasing clarity as he wrote his doctorate and began teaching. However, he was – and remains – acutely aware of which way the political winds were blowing. With Hugo Chávez reaching the zenith of his power in Venezuela, he wasn't the only regional figure in South America at that time to look towards Caracas and start thinking ahead. Venezuela snapped up $300 million of the new bonds, causing an irreparable rift between finance minister and president in Quito.

It took a little over three months before there was a definitive rupture with Palacio. When Correa resigned as finance minister, it was accompanied, as might be expected, by a rhetorical flourish. In his resignation letter, he admonished the president, telling him he 'didn't understand your anger over international commitments supposedly made by me without your knowledge.'

'I feel the real problem,' he continued, 'is the strong pressure which exists to impede any relationship with a brother nation like Venezuela and, as corollary of that, distrust in my work as Minister of the Economy.'[35]

It was canny on a variety of levels. He had only spent 106 days as finance minister but in that short time he had made a significant impact on the national consciousness. He could be confident that the Ecuadorean people weren't going to look on him as erratic or fickle for his decision to resign. Palacio would go through as many as thirty-three ministers in just twenty months in office.[36]

His resignation sent two clear messages. One to President Hugo Chávez in Venezuela, that he had a real ally in the US-educated now former economy minister in Quito. Another to Ecuador's poor and indigenous, many of whom had watched Venezuela jealously for several years as Chávez funded lavish social programmes with oil money while thumbing his nose at Washington. And they asked themselves why they didn't have a similar leader in Ecuador.

'¡DALE CORREA!'

The line flashed up at the end of a campaign spot accompanied by the sound of the crack of a belt. The wordplay in Spanish was the main slogan of Correa's 2006 presidential election campaign –

meaning both 'Go for it, Correa' and 'Give them the belt' or 'Give them a lashing'. What it lacked in subtlety it made up for in effectiveness. People wanted nothing more than to take the belt to the current crop of politicians running Ecuador and give them a hiding. This young dashing former finance minister was offering to do just that.

He would turn up on stage carrying a belt which he would wave around like a whip, his supporters roaring in approval. They, too, held their belts up high, in a mildly intimidating threat of the retribution and punishment that was coming for the country's political classes and entrenched elites. In a TV advertisement aimed directly at Ecuador's young people, Correa appeared in chinos and a garish luminous-green polo shirt, the campaign colour of his new political group, Alianza PAIS, to urge the youth 'not to let the same old dinosaurs age your hearts'. We've got them on the run, they know they're done, he said to the camera surrounded by a multiracial group of twentysomethings in jeans and T-shirts yelling '¡Dale Correa!'

Behind the scenes, his bid was being pushed hard by Vinicio and Fernando Alvarado Espinel, brothers and PR strategists who ran the publicity and marketing for Correa's campaign. Friends of Correa's from his time at the Lasalle school, they came up with such videos and slogans for the Citizens' Revolution and emphasized the use of YouTube and the Internet. Meanwhile, a number of politicians were stoking the flames of Correa's belief that he could emerge from relative obscurity to become the most powerful man in the country in barely a year. Two figures were particularly influential, Paula María Romo and Juan Sebastián Roldán, both of whom would assume ministerial positions in his administration. All this was unfolding to the disbelief and quiet horror of Anne Malherbe, Rafael Correa's wife, who had never wanted to live with a president but, rather, the forceful academic she fell in love with. It was one thing to marry an ambitious young economist. Quite another to become the First Lady of a South American country you barely know. So disconcerting, in fact, that Malherbe refused to take the title of *Primera Dama* when the moment came. There are few interviews from the time with her available, as she opted to focus on the children and her own work in education once her husband launched his presidential bid. In one of them, she explained, in fluent, French-accented Spanish, why she intended to reject the title of First Lady if he won.

'I don't see the point and nor does Rafael,' she told an interviewer on Ecuadorean television. 'Those two words "First Lady" make no sense. I don't think there's any "first ladies" in this world,' she argued,[37] an approach which risked alienating the electorate by appearing to snub one of the most influential titles in the land. But Anne's mind was made up on the subject. In the same interview, she was also quizzed as to why she hadn't turned out in support of her husband during his campaign and was repeatedly asked about his temper, the presenter openly insinuating he had too short a fuse for high office. As Correa's seemingly unstoppable run gathered pace, though, Malherbe was the one who showed her temper. On at least one occasion, she was rumoured to have held an all-out shouting match with Romo and Roldán, insisting they leave her husband in peace.

But he didn't want to be left in peace. He wanted to be president of Ecuador. Even after only a short stint as a minister, he was convinced he could do the job better than the likes of Mahuad and Gutiérrez and Palacio and all the other *farsantes* – con men and phonies – who had occupied La Carondelet over the past twenty years. He tore into them during the televised presidential debates, his quick temper very obvious on live TV. However, even that was turned into a virtue by Alvarado's PR team, spinning it as an example of his 'passion for the fatherland'.[38]

On election day, it wasn't just the youth vote that brought Rafael Correa the presidency. It was also the indigenous voters and the elderly and the disabled and the vast numbers of poor. The race went to a second-round run-off in November between him and Álvaro Noboa, a banana magnate and the richest man in Ecuador. The choice couldn't have been starker. It felt to voters like a decision between one of those 'same-old dinosaurs', the very wealthiest example of the powerful, established elite who had plunged Ecuador into its current mess, or the person promising to give them the whipping they all deserved.

In early twenty-first-century Latin America, that was no choice at all. Even the attempts by Noboa's camp to smear Correa as a rabidly left-wing Ecuadorean version of Hugo Chávez probably did him more good than harm, such was the clamour for change. He took 57 per cent of the run-off vote and was sworn in as president on 15 January 2007. Chávez, Lula and Evo Morales attended the inauguration as well as the Iranian president Mahmoud Ahmadinejad.

Ecuador had been through a decade of political upheaval. The country had rattled through eight presidents in just ten years, three of whom were ousted from power by angry street protests. One of them, President Abdala Bucaram, nicknamed 'el Loco', was even declared mentally unfit to rule in 1997 after just a year in power.

People yearned for stability, for order. They were about to get it with Rafael Correa, the fiery economist from Guayaquil with a pro-gramme based on redressing the country's inequality and helping the neediest. At that stage, however, they didn't realize just how much he would dominate the political space – and their lives – for the next ten years.

Alianza PAIS had grown into a political party for the election but its roots were in a leftist civil organization set up in the late 1990s by figures like Alberto Acosta and Ricardo Patiño – who would later be named Correa's foreign minister – in response to dollarization. Part of Alianza PAIS's first promise was to write a new constitution. If any evidence were needed that the new administration was going to uproot the institutions of the past, the creation of a Constituent Assembly in 2007 was compelling proof.

In an echo of Chávez, his increasingly close ally in Venezuela, Correa also used his inaugural speech as president, the sash still draped over his right shoulder, to announce a referendum on the new assembly that would rewrite the constitution. The new body was 'vital to limiting the power of the traditional parties', he told the chamber, in effect confirming its demise.[39] The deputies, however, were braced for it. During the election campaign, Alianza PAIS had taken the bold decision not to challenge for a single seat in Congress. Their only campaign was the presidential one. It was risky, but it paid dividends. First, it freed up funds for Correa's bid which was ultimately successful. Secondly, it showed the electorate that Correa and Alianza PAIS were serious about removing the existing legislature once they took office. He would have no majority – nor even a minority government – because as soon as he won, the current parliament was finished. It gave a certain coherence to his strategy and was wildly popular in the polls.

The popularity of Congress was already in the doldrums. Seen as a corrupt, compromised and untrustworthy body, Ecuador's people had the least positive view of its legislature of any country in Latin America.[40] Despite the public rejection of Congress and the over-whelming calls for a new constitution, the country's twentieth in its history, the parliamentary deputies weren't about to vote for their own execution. Amid backroom wrangling, an agreement was reached so that enough parliamentarians voted in favour of the referendum to create a Constituent Assembly. The deal was that Congress would continue to sit while the new body drafted the text of the constitution. Needless to say, the parliamentarians who voted against Correa had the rug pulled from under them by the Electoral Council and would never sit again. Correa's supporters turned up at the parliament building to send them home with a final undignified shove. For the final weeks of its existence, Congress was made up of their substitutes and deputies willing to satisfy Correa's desire for a new assembly. The Electoral Council called the vote for 15 April 2007.

I travelled to Quito for that plebiscite, just three months to the day after Correa had taken office. Outside the polling stations men sold barbequed chorizos and cold sodas for a couple of dollars as the entire country, or so it seemed, turned out to cast their ballot. Lines were long, people were upbeat and the voting stations bustling. The 'Yes' campaign won with a vast 81.7 per cent of the vote. People wanted the process of change to continue at pace. They wanted Rafael Correa. Later that year, elections to choose delegates for the assembly were held, and this time Alianza PAIS put up its candidates. It took 74 of the 130 available seats.[41]

One of them went to his trusted ally, Alberto Acosta, who had initially been made energy and mining minister. As the member with the highest number of votes, he was named president of the Constituent Assembly. It didn't take long for Acosta and Rafael Correa to fall out, barely eighteen months into Correa's first term. Clashes over mineral exploration and mining rights kept escalating and were only going to lead to one outcome. With Acosta increasingly critical of the president's plans and of the rapid timetable of legislation being pushed through by the assembly, the staunch socialist and committed environmentalist walked out on the National Assembly and, by extension, on Rafael Correa. The former mentor would eventually label his disciple's ten years in power as 'the wasted decade'. He was the first of Correa's political contemporaries and allies to split with him. Others would follow, the president's inner circle shrinking over time to only the most trusted and the most proven loyalists. These last-ditch defenders usually had a personal connection to Correa, either from home or the Lasallian school or from their scouting days. In contrast, Alberto Acosta was faithful to his ideas rather than to any individual. Nearly everyone I spoke to about Acosta granted him that grudging respect, even if they didn't necessarily see eye to eye with him politically. The one thing he couldn't be accused of was being fickle or abandoning his principles for the trappings of power.

On 15 February 1967 oil was discovered in Ecuador. Thick crude gushed forth from the Lago Agrio 1, witnessed by a delegation from Texaco-Gulf, which was carrying out exploration in Ecuador at the invitation of the military junta running the country at the time. The discovery, as for so many oil nations, has blessed and cursed Ecuador in equal measure. The president who would most benefit from its heady dividends, the astronomical oil price of the early 2000s, was a toddler at the time. A month shy of the fortieth anniversary of that discovery, he was sworn into power. And President Rafael Correa intended to use that oil wealth for everything he'd written about and taught in university classrooms for years.

To assess what he achieved in government, it's perhaps wisest to look at his time in power in two parts. His first term and part of his second were a period of great optimism in Ecuador. Ecuadorean journalist friends of mine recall being swept up in the sense of possibility in their home nation, a place all too often characterized as a backward banana republic. Scores of social programmes were implemented by the government using the glut of oil money, again leading to the accusation that Correa was merely an Ecuadorean version of Chávez. In fact, his social development concepts were different from those in Venezuela and tailored to the Andean country's specific characteristics and needs.

Correa's social programmes revolved around the same ideology that Evo Morales had championed in Bolivia: *sumak kawsay*, the Quechua term translated into Spanish as '*buen vivir*', or 'wellbeing'. The philosophy, supposedly pertaining to an indigenous ancestral worldview, was laid out in the 2008 constitution. At its heart, dozens of projects were put forward which attempted to tackle the plight of the most invisible and vulnerable sectors of society. They included a programme of labour protections for domestic workers, a new ministry to help returning migrants reintegrate into Ecuador and an aggressive programme of university grants so that the brightest students in public education had the opportunity to travel abroad and study in some of the best universities in the world, as Correa himself had done a decade earlier.

Experts and leading scientists in a range of fields were encouraged to come to Ecuador and set up new programmes or carry out research in its best academic institutions. An ambitious environmental scheme called Yasuní ITT was proposed with the aim of keeping the oil reserves of the Yasuní National Park – estimated at a billion barrels – underneath the ground. The idea was that in exchange for suspending exploration in the Amazonian biosphere reserve, the international community would donate more than $3.5 billion to keep the oil where it was, around half of what Ecuador could have earned for the resource, and help facilitate the transition to a sustainable energy economy.

It was exciting, new and dynamic thinking that seemed to be propelling the country forward, much of it coming from the young people who were getting on board with the Citizens' Revolution, supporting the ministries and providing their initiative and expertise. As a friend involved in publicity for some of these projects put it, 'the country was portrayed like it was a new Switzerland and, thanks to the income from the high oil price, everything was put into action quickly'. It must have felt intoxicating. President Correa would call meetings in which he would listen to the proposals for the brightest, most outlandish ideas and, according to some insiders, would cherry-pick the best ones for himself to announce on air. Irrespective of who took the credit, it seemed as if real change was finally being made after decades of lies, corruption and ineptitude. On my trips to Ecuador during that period, there was undoubtedly an energy about Correa's presidency rivalling that of Chávez. He had come to the party a full eight years after Hugo Chávez had taken office and had a lot of catching up to do.

One of his priorities was creating a new infrastructure for the country. Ecuador had long suffered from poor electricity provision, especially outside the capital. In 2009, drought and low rainfall at one of the country's main hydroelectric dams, the Paute Dam, led to daily hours-long blackouts for an entire three-month period. The government's response was to build eight hydroelectric dams which were intended to bring a definitive end to such energy crises in the country. Built primarily by Chinese state-owned firms, they were supposed to be bigger than Paute and turn Ecuador into an energy exporter while simultaneously reducing the price of domestic electricity consumption. Provincial airports with tiny runways would be turned into new, state-of-the-art terminals, while road links and highways would be built across the country to finally connect the hinterlands to the major urban centres.

But whenever things sound too good to be true, they probably are. Undoubtedly hundreds of thousands benefited from the many social development schemes during those first five or six years. Thousands were employed on big infrastructure projects, students obtained university grants without which they couldn't have otherwise studied, families were plucked from poverty and indigenous communities received the basic support and infrastructure they had been craving for decades. The investment into schools, hospitals and roads was working: the growth rate in 2011 was up to 8 per cent, above the government's own forecast of 6.5 and well above the previous year's growth rate of 3.6 per cent.[42] It was paying huge dividends for Correa himself, too, who achieved after five years in power the highest popularity rates of any leader in Latin America.[43] As Correa said to me: 'We invested $100 billion in ten years, and it transformed the country.'[44]

However, not all of it changed for the better. As Correa moved into his second term in power, the oil price began to tail off. The Ecuadorean bubble began to burst. Before long, the ministry supporting returning migrants shut down, the Yasuní ITT environmental scheme was abandoned and Ecuadorean students abroad found their state grants drying up. The luxurious airports in distant provincial municipalities never received enough passengers to justify their costly construction and the hydroelectric dams were left either half finished or with serious structural issues. To this day, Correa hails one of them, the Coca Codo Sinclair Dam, built by China's state-owned hydro-engineering company, as an example of astute investment and the huge infrastructural strides made on his watch. Yet, by all accounts, it is a disaster. Constructed in the shadow of the active Reventador volcano, a precarious location at best, Coca Codo Sinclair cost around $2.25 billion, most of which was paid for with a loan from a Chinese development bank. Operational from late 2016, it soon began to suffer from thousands of tiny cracks and damage to its turbines and machinery.[45] China had become the principal owner of Ecuador's debt while the watchword for corporate corruption in Latin America, the giant construction company Odebrecht, was increasingly involved in bigger and bolder projects across the country. The margin for corruption was huge.

The true white elephant of Correa's time in office, however, was not Coca Codo Sinclair. The years of extravagance and reckless wastefulness can best be summarised by the word '*yachay*', which means 'knowledge' in Quechua. At the height of the reconstruction of the nation, a plan was launched for 'Yachay, the City of Knowledge'. A vast new town hosting a sprawling university campus, the online video illustrating the architects' vision of the final result is both impressive and depressingly unrealistic. Imposing modern blocks for state-of-the-art laboratories and computer rooms are situated on the top of a perfectly manicured hillside where students freewheel on their bicycles between lecture halls and dormitories. The world's biggest firms, from Microsoft to Intel, would set up new and innovative research labs in the Ecuadorean town, a destination intended to tempt firms away from Frankfurt, South Korea and Silicon Valley.

Fast-forward several years and almost $5 billion, and the site of this scientific hothouse is a town without a mooring. In a questionable setting in the first place, amid dense sugarcane fields and dark-green hills of banana trees, it is cut off from urban hubs by poor transport links, many of the buildings were built to the wrong specifications for a university supposedly specializing in science and technology. Labs and buildings lie unfinished or empty. The billions pumped in haven't yet improved the roads into Yachay. Some students took up their courses at Yachay Tech and are working hard to obtain a decent degree, but it is a long way from becoming the centre of excellence, for Latin America and the rest of the world, that Rafael Correa claimed it would be when he opened it.

At the same time, his relationship with the indigenous population had begun to sour. Both when campaigning and as president, Rafael Correa heralded his time as a fresh-faced graduate in Zumbahua and his fluency in Quechua as evidence of his pro-indigenous credentials. Indeed, when he was eventually sworn in as president, there was a special ceremony in the remote Andean town by Indian elders to bless and protect him, a new leader who appeared to connect with the native peoples of Ecuador more than any previous president in the modern era. 'I will never fail you,' Correa promised them.[46]

Yet, like many close relationships in his life, it wouldn't last. In

2010, conflict was brewing between the main indigenous organization in the country, the Confederation of Indigenous Nationalities of
Ecuador (Conaie) and the president. The Indian organizations were
furious at Correa for several steps which they saw as betrayal. They
included a highly controversial mining law by the government which
would have removed Conaie's right of veto over extractive projects
proposed by transnational mining and energy companies on their
ancestral lands. Conaie also held up passage of a water law through
parliament which would have handed control over irrigation in the
indigenous communities to a state agency.[47]

The threads which tied Conaie and Correa eventually snapped
in June 2010. The president was hosting a summit on indigenous
rights in Otavalo, a picturesque town in the Otavalo Canton, in
Imbabura province, surrounded by three stunning volcanic peaks
and renowned for its extensive handicrafts and textiles market. In a
sign of the growing distrust between Rafael Correa and the country's
main indigenous social movement, he decided not to invite Conaie
to the regional summit. It was a huge snub. In response, the group
organized an event of their own and they marched on Otavalo in the
traditional dress of their communities, of intricate woven headpieces
and ornate wooden spears. The protest was crushed by the police.
Around thirty leaders faced charges of terrorism and sabotage,
prompting one former indigenous member of Correa's government
to criticize him for intensifying 'his repressive attitude towards
the indigenous movement'.[48] In 2011, Conaie pulled its support for
Correa entirely and the relationship slid into open hostility for the
remainder of Correa's time in power, as they pushed back at the
criminalization of their protests against the terrorism charges.[49]

For those who benefited from the days of surplus under Rafael
Correa, the people whose kids unexpectedly went to university or
whose salaries and pensions improved significantly or who found
healthcare easier and cheaper to access – many of those supporters
will never abandon him or drop their adoration of and gratitude for
their leader. Yet as things began to collapse, many started to question what was behind the Citizens' Revolution. Even once-committed

supporters started to ask some tough questions: why did China control so much of the national debt? What was the government's relationship with the state-owned Chinese constructors or Brazil's Odebrecht? What had happened to the billions of dollars generated by the high oil price or that were lent by China? Why was China being repaid in crude oil, accounting for as much as 80 per cent of national production, in order to service the bill? After the first few years of Correa's presidency, of making hay while the sun shone, many wondered if they were really the intended beneficiaries at all. It was becoming hard to avoid far darker issues: murky business deals with China, a surfeit of costly, crowd-pleasing yet hugely ill-advised infrastructure projects and an insatiable desire to hold power against the weakest possible opposition.

The ashes of Eloy Alfaro had been on a circuitous route over the past century. First buried in secret in Quito, in the 1940s they were taken to Guayaquil and now, in late 2007, they were being moved once more, to be finally laid to rest in his birthplace, Montecristi. The remains of 'el Viejo Luchador', 'the Old Warrior', were being transported back to his hometown along a wide asphalt highway on white and chestnut liveried horses ridden by the presidential guard in full ceremonial dress accompanied by military vehicles decked out in flowers.

In the city of Montecristi, a regimental band played outside the Ciudad Alfaro Civic Centre as the cortège drew near. A twenty-one-gun salute was followed by the national anthem as three guardsmen wearing epaulettes and sashes carefully carried the glass-encased urn into the mausoleum. Next to the military men in their pristine uniforms and regalia stood the civilian leaders dressed in Montecristi superfinos, some of the highest-quality Panama hats in the world for which the city is known. Overhead a fighter jet roared past.

Some regional figures had made the trip, among them Colombia's conservative president, Alvaro Uribe, but this was Rafael Correa's occasion. He was the one who had ordered the remains of Ecuador's greatest son be moved from Guayaquil to Montecristi. In the mausoleum, the urn was removed from its glass case and passed to Eloy Alfaro de Alba, a direct descendant of the revolutionary leader, who placed it in its final resting place. Beside him, Rafael Correa – whose own mother claimed a distant family heritage to Alfaro – was flitting around with excited, nervous energy.

Of course, for Correa, any association with Eloy Alfaro was welcome. Leader of the country's Liberal revolution at the end of the nineteenth century, Alfaro was Ecuador's original charismatic strongman. He led a radical movement to overthrow the Catholic president, Gabriel García Moreno, and was forced into exile in Panama when it failed in 1860. The battle between Conservatives and Liberals at that time was a struggle over the separation of church and state, freedom of religion and universal voting rights. In 1875, García Moreno was assassinated and Eloy Alfaro eventually became Ecuador's president in a coup in June 1895.

Once in power, he set about legitimizing his dictatorial rule. He ordered major public works to modernize the country, like the railway between Guayaquil and Quito, a huge feat of engineering in the Andes at the turn of the twentieth century. He forced a permanent wedge between church and state, abolished the death penalty and freed indigenous slaves from indentured labour in the haciendas. Yet Eloy Alfaro was no warm-hearted liberal. He wielded a fearsome control over Ecuador trying to rebuild it in his own image with himself alone as the arbiter of what was best for the nation.

His second term also came at the barrel of a rifle when he forced out a Liberal president in 1905. The move split his traditional support, a division widened by acts of electoral fraud, vote-rigging, corruption and dictatorial control. Despite the completion of the railway and provision of potable water to Quito, Eloy Alfaro was eventually ousted and – as he went back into exile in Panama – his loyalist supporters and soldiers wrought havoc in Ecuador, making the country ungovernable. Recalled to Quito ostensibly to restore calm, Alfaro was arrested on arrival and his supporters defeated. An angry mob broke into Penal García Moreno, the prison where he was being held, and shot Alfaro and his lieutenants. Their bodies were pulled and mutilated over the cobbled streets of Quito until the pulpy remains reached El Ejido, a park in the north of the city. There, the crowd lit several fires and incinerated the bodies in what became known as '*la Hoguera Bárbara*', the Old Warrior burned in 'the barbaric bonfire'.

In Ecuador, time softened the image of Alfaro as a dictator and instead he was seen as a great leader, a brave and bold soldier who took on the excesses of the established conservative elites and the church. The ceremony to move his remains, not even a year after taking office, was a calculated decision by Rafael Correa. Get it wrong and he'd have been accused of disturbing the dead, of meddling with resting spirits, even of grave robbing. Yet such was the height of Correa's popularity at that early point in 2007, it was mainly seen as a respectful act to honour the national hero and rehouse him in more dignified surroundings, to bring him home – a sentiment which played well to the millions of Ecuadoreans watching the event live on national TV. It was only with hindsight that it began to be seen in terms of the cult of personality that would come to typify the Correa presidency.

It is a common populist trope in Latin America to associate oneself and one's political movement with a deceased national hero. Fidel Castro's revolution was dedicated to José Martí long before it was guided by Karl Marx. Hugo Chávez would later carry out a similar act with the remains of the Great Liberator, Simón Bolívar, moving him into a cavernous new mausoleum in Caracas, his own image riding on the coattails of the founding father. Especially in those first months of his time in power, Rafael Correa wanted the public to see a common thread between the Liberal Revolution and his own 'Citizens' Revolution'. And, partly fed by his own maternal link to Alfaro, to draw comparisons between himself and the radical reformer from Montecristi.

As Luis Edgar Devia Silva slept soundly in the depths of Ecuadorean jungle, he had no idea a team had been despatched to kill him. Had he known, it would have come as little surprise. He was on Interpol's 'red' list and there was a $5 million reward on his head. Better known by his *nom de guerre*, Raúl Reyes, he was the second-in-command of the FARC, the Marxist guerrilla army at war with the Colombian state for more than forty years. In that time, he had evaded capture on several occasions. On this night, though, in the early hours of the morning of Saturday 1 March 2008, his enemies would catch up with him.

Around 10.30 on the night before, Friday 29 February, word reached a Colombian military team assembled near the Colombian–Ecuadorean border: they had the co-ordinates for Reyes' encampment and confirmation that he was still in it. For months, it was believed that Reyes was regularly crossing the River Putumayo into Ecuador to escape capture by the Colombian authorities. Rafael Correa's government had denied any suggestion that there was a permanent FARC base on their side of the border, only admitting occasional incursions onto its soil. Now the Colombian military team had the location, N 00°23'10.66", W 076°20'59.88", and a green light from President Alvaro Uribe to launch the attack, code-named Operation Phoenix.[50] Two Embraer Super Tucanos took off and set course for the camp, around two kilometres inside Ecuadorean territory. The Colombian air force reached the rebel base and fired Griffin Laser-Guided Bombs onto their target.

Raúl Reyes awoke to the sound of the approaching aircraft. His comrades were yelling Colombian swear words and calling for everyone to take cover as the attack drew closer. In their underwear and pyjamas, the guerrillas tried to scramble to safety into the undergrowth, grabbing their rifles and wellington boots as they ran. But it was too late. At least twenty fighters were killed as the bombs fell on the site. Raúl Reyes, the group's deputy leader, was among them. Some reports said he stepped on a FARC landmine in the confusion while attempting to escape. After pursuing him for decades, the Colombian government had finally brought down one of its chief targets.

After the bombs had fallen, a group of elite troops were dropped into the area in four Blackhawk helicopters. A video recorded by one of them, taken from a camera strapped to his gun, later emerged. As he scouted around the destroyed site, he discovered the body of

Reyes, his bearded face unmistakable even in the dark. As the soldier continues to probe, he finds a woman wincing with pain from an injury to her leg. Her accent wasn't Colombian or Ecuadorean and she would later tell the authorities she was Mexican, a leftist student from a conference in Quito who had travelled to the camp as a guest of the FARC. Four of her countrymen were also killed in the raid.

The soldiers weren't bothered about the remaining guerrillas or foreign students, however. Yelling at those hidden in the surrounding jungle cover to surrender and not to be killed 'fucking stupidly', the soldier told them 'we got the beardy we came for'.[51] The troops then took the body of their prized target back to Colombia as well as three laptops, two hard drives and around $40,000 in cash found at the scene. A team of forty-four Colombian police agents stayed at the site to wait for the Ecuadorean authorities to arrive.

At around one in the morning, Alvaro Uribe telephoned Rafael Correa to inform him that a clash had taken place in which Raúl Reyes had been killed. President Uribe confessed that it had occurred inside Ecuador but hid the fact that it had been a carefully planned operation. Instead he left his Ecuadorean counterpart with the impression that the Colombian army had been in hot pursuit of Reyes and had crossed the border inadvertently. 'I take responsibility,' Uribe later said, 'but if we had communicated [our plan] ahead of time, I'm sure it would have failed.'[52]

As the truth of an unauthorized military incursion onto a neighbour's soil began to emerge, Correa became more and more worked up. In an address on national television, he railed at the Colombian government and described the attack in detail to the public. He told them how the bodies of the guerrillas had been found wearing 'sleepwear' which immediately knocked down the Colombian government's argument it had been a chase or 'in legitimate self-defence'. As far as he was concerned, it was 'a massacre', the Colombian aircraft had encroached 'at least 10 kilometres into our territory to carry out the attack', and the rebels had been shot in the back.[53] He promptly ordered the expulsion of the Colombian ambassador in Quito. Tension with Colombia lasted for months, stoked in no small part by

Hugo Chávez, who seemed as livid as Correa over what he considered the violation of Ecuador's national sovereignty. Both countries broke off diplomatic relations with Colombia over the incident.

However, Chávez's anger might have had less to do with the integrity of Ecuador's land borders and more to do with the intelligence operation establishing Raúl Reyes' whereabouts. He was located after a satellite telephone call was intercepted between Hugo Chávez and the FARC leader. In 2007, Chávez had been acting as a mediator with the FARC to help facilitate a humanitarian exchange. The FARC's Secretariat trusted Chávez, the kind of socialist leader they wanted in Colombia, and he had negotiated with the guerrilla army's leadership over the hostage releases. Chávez hadn't been part of the process for several months, after Uribe had become angry at the way he bypassed Colombia's diplomatic service. However, on that particular day – 27 February 2008 – the Venezuelan president called the Marxist guerrilla leader to thank him in person following the successful release of four hostages, ex-congressmen who had been held by the FARC for almost seven years.

The two men believed they were speaking on a secure line. However, the FBI and the DEA picked up the call and passed the relevant intelligence on Reyes' location to the Colombians. Two days later, he was killed.

For Correa, the entire episode was the excuse he needed to throw the Americans out of Manta. A large airfield on the Pacific coast, the US had leased a sizeable part of it for ten years, signing an agreement under President Jamil Mahuad in 1999. Under the terms of the deal, the US military could keep almost five hundred personnel at the site, entirely rent-free. American AWACS spy planes stationed at Manta ran anti-drug-trafficking surveillance operations, searched for speed boats and submersibles leaving Colombia and made drug interdictions in the Pacific. They also fed their intelligence to the Joint Interagency Task Force in Key West.

Rafael Correa had repeatedly said during his campaign that having a foreign military base in Ecuador would be a thing of the past if he was elected, promising to let the ten-year lease lapse when it came up for renewal. The Raúl Reyes killing was enough to ensure his threat would be carried out. Air force Lt-Col. Robert Leonard, the commander at the base, denied their involvement in the raid. 'It has nothing to do with our mission and we had nothing to do with what happened then,' he said of the incursion. 'In fact, during that particular date the AWACS that you see,' motioning to the huge aircraft behind him, 'were sitting here on the ground, they weren't even flying on those days.'[54]

It didn't ring true to Correa and it didn't matter anyway. By then, throwing out the Americans from Manta was just good politics. On 19 March, a little over two weeks after Reyes was killed, the Constituent Assembly approved what was a widely popular decision. In fact, a ban on foreign military bases in Ecuador would be written into the new constitution that September. 'It's as if we had a base in New York. This would be incomprehensible for North Americans,' said Correa's security minister, Gustavo Larrea.[55] In July 2008, Quito officially informed the US of their decision over Manta and, a year later, the lease expired.

Correa was prepared to defy the Americans on more than just security or military matters. In December 2008, the Ecuadorean finance minister, María Elsa Viteri, paid a trip to New York and Washington DC. While there, she intended to rub shoulders with political actors and investors who might be influential to the fledgling Citizens' Revolution in Ecuador. What she didn't expect to do was default on $3.2 billion worth of global bonds. In fact, Viteri believed she had an agreement with Correa that he wouldn't enact a default, doing her best to find a more palatable solution for the international markets which wouldn't isolate Ecuador from outside financing. That agreement was shot down by a phone call from Rafael Correa in which he told his minister he'd decided that Ecuador was to become the first Latin American nation since 2001 to default on its debt. Her pleas were futile, his decision final. The plan was to fail to pay around 40 per cent of its £10 billion debt, a 'debt that was obviously immoral and illegitimate' as Correa put it at the time.

Viteri panicked. Unable to face the investment bankers and

politicians to whom she'd already given assurances, she instead went directly to the airport in Washington DC to return to Quito and thrash it out with the president. It fell to the interior minister, Fernando Bustamante, and the foreign minister, Ricardo Patiño, to explain the decision to the infuriated investors. Patiño, an ideologue and vehement critic of the IMF and World Bank, had no such qualms in addressing them. He relished the opportunity to go to the Rockefeller Center and to Wall Street to lecture the capitalists, to tell them to their faces that they deserved it. He had long been fundamentally opposed to the external debt and was firmly of the belief that it was grotesque and unpayable. That chimed with Rafael Correa who had calculated that, with commodity prices in the stratosphere, he could probably afford to have a poor credit rating – despite the insistence of his diplomats that the idea was imprudent.

Like the decision over the Manta military base, it allowed him to take bold and decisive anti-American steps that would play to his base, and also brought him a certain freedom in the face of external pressure. Correa revelled in a reputation as a maverick ready to ignore the prevailing advice from his ministerial colleagues or ambassadors. He was in a strong position, one that few Ecuadorean presidents before him had ever fully enjoyed.

'It was audacious,' admits Fernando Bustamante, 'but it was very successful for a time. At least while the commodities boom lasted.'

'*Señores*, if you want to kill the president, here he is!' Rafael Correa yanked loose his tie to reveal his chest and continued to bait the angry mob with the microphone. 'Kill me if you wish! Kill me if you have the strength! Kill me if you're brave enough instead of cowardly hiding among the crowd.' As moments of presidential theatre went in Latin America, it seemed histrionic. It was hardly Salvador Allende turning his AK-47 on himself in La Moneda Palace in Santiago in 1973 as Pinochet's troops stormed the building, or the suicide live on air on Havana radio of Eduardo Chibas, leader of the Cuban People's Party, in 1951. But Rafael Correa was not actually trying to get himself killed. He was goading the crowd, one that certainly wanted to see him gone at that moment, if not necessarily dead.

Several did die, however, on that strange, mutinous afternoon at the end of September 2010, including a twenty-eight-year-old elite soldier carrying out an order to rescue the president.

The events of 30 September 2010 started with a bad leg. Ten days earlier, President Correa had finally undergone surgery on his worn-out right knee; a metal plate had been inserted into the damaged joint and twenty-five stitches put in place. That Thursday was the first day the doctors allowed him on his feet without a walking frame and to use crutches instead. It was not, it turned out, a good day to be immobile.

As he was convalescing in the presidential palace, reports started to reach him of an uprising by disgruntled police angered by a move to bring their pay and conditions under the Law of Public Service, extending the period between promotions and eliminating the medals and bonuses which accompanied each one. Unfortunately for Correa, most police simply saw it as an austerity law which would drastically cut their well-deserved benefits. Recalling those moments nearly a decade later, Correa unsurprisingly blames the press, his habitual adversary, for 'disinformation' and 'manipulating the news' over the bill in order to sow conflict and topple his government. Manipulated or not, the rebellious police were rapidly taking over the city. The Mariscal Sucre International Airport in Quito, the country's principal airport, was shut down by uniformed police drawn up on the main runway. Motorcycle units of officers arrived at the National Assembly, interrupted the session of parliament as it debated the law and intimidated and clashed with the deputies. Roadblocks were set up with burning tyres and barricades, and Ecuadoreans saw the surreal sight of civilians trying to contain unruly police officers.

As the police took to their barracks and refused to go on duty, some citizens made the most of the absence of authority by sacking some banks and shops in Quito, while the city of Guayaquil was on edge after more looting and violence. Rafael Correa, wobbly of knee but not of conviction, decided the only way to deal with the uprising was to address the rebels in person. It was a page straight from the Fidel Castro playbook – he had employed the same method of personal intervention on the only occasion when the Cuban people marched to the Malecón in fury at the economic situation in 1994. However, try as he might, Rafael Correa was no Fidel Castro.

He arrived at the main regimental police barracks in Quito and forced his way to a balcony to deliver his improvised speech. This was his 'kill me if you dare' moment. He says that he wanted to tell them they'd never had it so good. That he had increased their salaries, improved their holiday allocation, provided them with new bulletproof vests and equipment. His voice was drowned in a sea of abuse:

'They called us "communist son-of-a-whatevers",' remembers Correa. 'They chanted "¡viva Lucio Gutiérrez!" When I gave my speech from that balcony next to their commander and they shouted "No! That's a lie!", that's when I knew this was a trap and that there were political motivations behind it.'[56]

Correa came down from the balcony and attempted to make his way out of the barracks but found his path blocked by the hostile horde. He was trapped inside a courtyard with an ugly mob of angry cops who believed he was taking their overtime and their bonuses away. The moment can be relived on video as Correa, his weakened knee trembling beneath him, is pushed and pulled by the crowd. The rebel officers yelled insults at Correa and threw stones in his direction. Aware of his vulnerable knee, some protesters hit him in the right leg. Others tried to snatch his gas mask as the rioting policemen fired tear gas canisters towards the president's team. Correa's security detail had been blindsided by the rapid escalation of events and was at a loss as to how best to protect their president. With aggrieved and armed police officers everywhere they turned, it was fast turning nasty, and increasingly looking like a serious miscalculation to have gone down to the barracks in the first place. As the throng in the courtyard swayed around him and his security guards struggled to keep him safe, a tear gas canister exploded just inches from his head.

If his life hadn't been in danger before then, it certainly was now. As far as he was concerned, this wasn't just a few disgruntled policemen. This was a *golpe de estado*, a *coup d'état* threatening the life of the incumbent president. Following events from a rooftop in Caracas, as the closest BBC correspondent to the action I went on air mid-afternoon and didn't stop talking until the small hours. Updates were being fed into my ear as I spoke or between interviews I would catch snippets of the continuous coverage of the barracks on local television. At the time it was never clear from the pictures whether Correa was truly at risk of being killed. Yet looking back at online videos of the mob – and having spoken to the man himself about that night – it was clearly a terrifying, volatile few hours. But it would get worse.

'I won't relent,' Correa insisted later in a phone call to CNN. 'If something happens to me, remember my infinite love for my country, and to my family I say that I will love them anywhere I end up.'[57] By that point, Correa had fainted from the pain of his knee and his men had carried him to the nearest safe haven: the police hospital inside the compound. With the chaos growing outside, the dozen or so men who made up his security team barricaded the door to prevent the rioting police officers from charging the room. To the outside world, the confusing pictures of a stand-off taking place inside the headquarters of the national police suggested that Rafael Correa's government teetered on the edge of collapse. In Venezuela Hugo Chávez jumped to his friend's defence. From Caracas he denounced the uprising as a coup and said the right wing in Ecuador was attempting to do the same thing that the Venezuelan opposition had done to him in April 2002.

Inside the police hospital in Quito, Correa was still hemmed in. Unable to leave the clinic, the president took refuge in a ward while nurses and medical staff pleaded with the officers to stand down because they said there were children among the patients at the hospital. Correa agreed to see a delegation of the protesting officers. The policemen who came to speak to him demanded that he exempt the police from the Public Service Law and guarantee there would be no change to their benefits and pensions. Correa refused point blank: '*A mí me sacan como presidente o como cadáver.*' He'd be taken out as president or as a dead body, he told his captors, but he wouldn't give in to blackmail.

A helicopter tried to land in the barracks to evacuate Correa to the presidential palace but was prevented from touching down by the protesters. Unsure of what was happening, some politicians from Correa's party began to discuss reversing the Public Service Law to bring a swift end to the crisis. Correa claims he instructed them via mobile phone to stick to their guns. From inside the clinic he declared a state of emergency to last for ten days.

'It struck me as an unnecessary recklessness,' says Fernando Busta-mante, Correa's former interior minister. Correa's decision to confront the police head on was 'a way of aggravating things', he argues. 'I would have thought there were less risky and more conventional ways to solve the problem. But he had an unlimited confidence in his own charisma. Perhaps he thought that if he went down there, looked them in the eyes, they wouldn't just submit, they would applaud him. He was absolutely convinced that his personal charm was capable of stopping anything.'[58]

As always in such chaotic moments of violent upheaval in Latin America, the military holds the key, and on this occasion they stayed loyal to Rafael Correa. Even the Washington-based Organization of American States echoed Hugo Chávez's concerns about an unconstitutional takeover, calling it 'a *coup d'état* in the making'.[59] If any of the military top brass entertained ideas of joining the police revolt, it was clear from the reaction of both left- and right-wing political forces in the Americas that they wouldn't have been recognized or considered legitimate. After several hectic hours, the head of the armed forces in Ecuador, Ernesto González, made the military's loyalty to Correa clear in a press conference: 'We are in a state of law. We are loyal to the maximum authority, which is the president.'[60] The state of emergency had handed the military new powers to take control and, as it became clear that the face-off inside the police headquarters wasn't about to end amicably, an elite unit of special forces from the *Grupo Intervención y Rescate*, or GIR, was ordered to swoop in to rescue Correa and return him to La Carondelet.

Among the team sent to retrieve the president was a young GIR commando named Froilán Jiménez. In photographs he can be seen wearing his uniform of dark camouflage fatigues and black beret, alongside other members of his unit, toting an M16 automatic rifle. Still in his twenties, his babyface made him an unlikely looking elite soldier. Jiménez was one of the hundreds of troops sent down to secure the streets around the police headquarters, break up any remaining roadblocks and suppress the uprising. It fell to his GIR unit, specialists in hostage recovery, to take back Correa.

They reached the compound in land cruisers and forced their way to the hospital. With their arrival on the scene, the violence quickly ramped up. Night had fallen, and reports were coming in that the smaller revolts elsewhere in the country were failing. The police in Quito were isolated and losing momentum. The GIR unit, some forty to fifty men in some ten vehicles, located Correa inside the hospital and took him towards the door, cocooned protectively by their riot shields. Shots from the policemen outside still rained down on the clinic. The GIR team finally bundled the president out of the hospital and into a waiting SUV. Again, gunfire rang out. As the vehicle pulled away, one of the guards gripping onto the outside of the moving car crumpled to the ground and slid down a small embankment, critically injured. 'Somebody's down injured but the car with the president of the Republic inside has left,' the excited presenter on national television told the audience. That somebody was Froilán Jiménez. The next picture of him would appear a day later, in his coffin, the grim-faced members of his GIR unit as pall-bearers, an Ecuadorean flag draped over the casket.

Jiménez was one of eight dead and almost 300 injured in the uprising, his death the usual tragic and unnecessary footnote that accompanies an attempted putsch. The day might not have started as a coup but, by the time it ended with police gunfire raking the presidential motorcade, it had quite clearly become one. As is so often the case in Latin America, the investigation into who shot Jiménez and from which direction was thoroughly botched. The legal case was halted, then restarted. Froilán Jiménez had been painted as a national hero by Correa's side and, as the embarrassing accusation grew that he might have been killed by friendly fire, the entire investigation stalled. President Correa and several of his ministers were called on to testify but never did, and by 2019 the case had fallen into limbo. The result is that, a decade on, no one is any the clearer as to exactly who fired the shot that killed the young commando, fuelling the conspiracy theory that it was one of his own comrades and that the cause of his death is being covered up.

Back at the presidential palace, Correa was finally surrounded by friends once more, rather than opponents baying for his head. Thousands of Alianza PAIS supporters had spent hours there calling for his safe return. As midnight approached, they stayed out on the street to wave their flags, cheer the president and hear his firebrand speech. He didn't disappoint them:

'There was great infiltration [in the revolt] by those political parties which we know so well,' he yelled into the microphone over the commotion of the crowd, blaming the uprising on the former president, Lucio Gutiérrez. 'They do nothing but conspire, conspire, conspire.'

He had wept, he told them, not through fear but for the 'needlessly spilt' blood of 'Ecuadorean brothers'. As it had been for Hugo Chávez, during his brief ousting in April 2002, the day of anarchy provided the ideal justification for Correa for further authoritarianism. In the years that followed, he would ramp up his attacks on the press considerably. Whenever he singled out individual journalists for criticism on air or clamped down on press freedom, he would point to the events of 30 September 2010 saying the media outlets had perpetuated the violence against him, had even instigated it. The attempted coup by the police was a frightening moment but every strongman needs evidence to back their claim that their enemies are plotting to have them ousted and killed. This was Correa's.

For the time being, however, he just seemed relieved to still be alive. A leader who was constantly aware of his macho image as a brave and capable man, he also used it as evidence that he was made from stern stuff. The narrative of his supporters emphasized that he went down to the barracks to face down his opponents, and only left in a hail of bullets, covered by police shields, once it became clear they wouldn't listen to reason.

'You know I don't scare easily,' he told the adoring crowd.

'Look, President Correa, if you're this sensitive, then Twitter and Facebook might not be for you. And to be honest, being a world leader might not be for you either!'

The British comedian and political commentator John Oliver was part way through an excoriating monologue about Rafael Correa on his late-night satire show *Last Week Tonight* on HBO. Known for skewering the subjects of his comedic attacks to devastating effect, Oliver didn't hold back on the Ecuadorean leader, Correa's left-wing credentials counting for nothing when it came to exposing his antics on his own weekly show, *Enlace Ciudadano*, or 'Citizen Link'.

The programme, known in Ecuador as simply *la Sabatina* – the Saturday show – was Correa's version of Hugo Chávez's *Aló Presidente*. It ran every Saturday for three or four hours over the full ten years of his mandate. Hosted by Correa and simultaneously broadcast on two television channels and numerous radio stations, the programme was eclectic to say the least, as Oliver's mockery showed. He had cut to a moment on one of the *Sabatinas*, from Correa's birthday, where a nationally beloved clown, Tiko Tiko, had appeared on stage to sing to Correa. Correa would sing, crack jokes and generally play the role of charismatic president-presenter.

However, it wasn't the clowns or the music that made John Oliver train his biting sarcasm on Rafael Correa. It was Correa's naming and shaming of individuals on Twitter and Facebook for perceived slights and online abuse. Not only did he call out his critics by name, residence and age, he would encourage his army of pro-Correa trolls to attack them online. 'For each tweet they'll send, we'll reply with ten thousand,' he said.

One opponent had set up a Facebook page called 'Crudo Ecuador' which posted rude memes and photographs of the government. Far from sophisticated satire, the feed of gags and bad jokes garnered around 200,000 followers. Ironically, once Correa drew attention to it in his *Sabatina*, it received thousands more. The person who set up the page chose to stay anonymous so the president asked his supporters to out him. 'Let's see if when we find out who this person is… he'll be so funny.'[61]

These were clearly not the actions of a thick-skinned or impervious individual. Yet as his brother pointed out, they were in keeping with the characteristics which had made him popular in the first place. Correa is 'obstinate, and he never loses,' Fabricio remarked of his brother's seemingly pathological inability to let anything go. The problem was that by then his popularity was waning and what might have once been seen as obdurate strength now appeared unduly sensitive and merely vindictive.

For his part, Correa simply doesn't acknowledge his defensiveness. He has an inbuilt capacity to justify any such actions as being someone else's fault, generally that of his opponents in the press. By early 2012, Correa had launched an all-out war against the media. Traditionally, the model of the media in Ecuador was broadly similar to Venezuela – the main outlets firmly in the hands of conservative private owners who had spent years in league with their favoured leaders and were diametrically opposed to a leftist like Rafael Correa taking power. From day one, his reaction to them was ferocious.

Correa would call critical journalists in Ecuador the 'corrupt press' and 'hired assassins in ink'. He held innumerable *cadenas*, obligatory national addresses, in which he would criticize specific reporters or columnists and refute their stories. In early 2011, he had brought defamation, libel and 'moral injury' cases against two journalists, a columnist, three newspaper directors and the periodical itself after the publication of a book, *El Gran Hermano*, or the Big Brother, about his brother's business dealings and a column entitled 'No More Lies'. The libel case against the two journalists, Christian Zurita and Juan Carlos Calderón, was for a staggering $10 million and the columnist Emilio Palacio eventually fled to the US to request asylum.

In January the following year, Correa's harassment of the press went international with several US newspapers condemning him in their editorials. 'President Rafael Correa of Ecuador is leading a relentless campaign against free speech,' was the verdict of the *New York Times*[62] while the *Washington Post* said he was carrying out 'the most comprehensive and ruthless assault on free media under way in the Western Hemisphere'.[63] At the time, the government's attacks on individual journalists were enough to justify such a response. A year later, though, Correa stepped up his campaign, attempting to regulate the media's 'illegitimate, immoral political power' by creating a new Communications Law.[64] Known as the 'Ley Mordaza', 'the Jaw law', it gave teeth to a government's commission to sanction and fine the media more easily. In the first four years of its existence, the law was used to slap 675 sanctions on different local media outlets and generated $754,000 in fines.[65] Commentators in Ecuador likened the situation to some of the worst places for journalism and free speech in the world:

'A good part of the Communications Law was taken from the reforms of Viktor Orbán in Hungary, from the right,' Mónica Almeida, co-author of an unauthorized biography of Correa, told the Spanish daily *El País*. 'That gives you an idea that he isn't of the Left. These are governments of an authoritarian tendency that want to rise up and hold on to power, irrespective of which side of the political spectrum it's on.'[66]

Whenever challenged over his fractious relationship with the media, Correa complains of what he perceives as a decades-old and concerted effort to bring him and his allies down. 'Lynching by media, co-opting of justice,' he called it, with the aim of 'destroying the reputation of leaders of the left by bringing up uncontextualized and generalized issues of corruption'.

The evils of the press is an issue he warms to immediately, on any given occasion: 'They don't inform, they manipulate,' he insisted when we spoke. 'We have areas in common with media who are the guardians, the watchdogs of democracy. But over the history of Latin America, they have mainly been the watchdog of the dictatorships.'

*

Julian Assange was cornered. All legal avenues were narrowing. His appeal in the UK Supreme Court against extradition to Sweden over a rape and a sexual assault charge had been denied less than a week earlier. He was bailed on a bond of £240,000 put up by wealthy backers such as Jemima Khan, and the Australian investigative journalist Phillip Knightley. He had been staying at Ellingham Hall, a sprawling country pile in Norfolk as a guest of Vaughan Smith, the founder of the Frontline Club, the foreign correspondents' hangout in west London. Yet even with such generous benefactors, the walls were closing in around him.

There was a possibility that he could take his case to the European Court of Human Rights in Strasbourg, but he had been advised that the chances of victory there looked slim at best. As far as Assange was concerned, the sexual assault charges were baseless, trumped up, a very obvious smokescreen. His enemies' plan, he and his backers argued, was to first get him to Sweden and from there he would be extradited to the United States to face charges over WikiLeaks, charges which could include espionage and for which he could potentially face the death penalty. He was already the subject of a grand jury investigation in the US over the WikiLeaks revelations, particularly the 'information dump' in 2010, perhaps the biggest intelligence leak in history. In July 2010 the WikiLeaks website in conjunction with the *Guardian*, *Der Spiegel* and the *New York Times* published thousands of classified military documents and sensitive diplomatic cables from the wars in Afghanistan and Iraq. Earlier that year, WikiLeaks had also published a video of two US helicopters in the Amin district in Baghdad opening fire on civilians as the pilots were urged to 'light 'em all up'. A van that had appeared to attend to the wounded was also fired on. The dead included a Reuters photographer and his assistant. When Assange published the tape, he would title the video 'Collateral Murder'.

Assange's source, US army intelligence analyst Chelsea Manning, had already been in jail for two years for leaking the classified material to WikiLeaks. The Australian hacker and digital publisher had to act or he would be joining her in serving a long sentence in a US prison.

All of it – from the rape allegation in Sweden to the espionage charges brewing in the US – was unjust, he protested; he was being punished and persecuted by a vengeful superpower for telling the truth, for informing the world of war crimes.

There weren't many presidents who would have agreed with Assange's analysis of his circumstances; even if they did, who would have been prepared to risk the wrath of Washington by granting him a safe haven? However, Assange knew one who would take the risk. He had interviewed him just weeks earlier on his TV show, *The World Tomorrow*, for the Russian state-owned channel Russia Today.

Seeing no other choice, Assange travelled to Knightsbridge, walked past Harrods and up the steps of the Ecuadorean Embassy. It was 19 June 2012. Do you wish he'd never darkened your door? I asked Rafael Correa. He shrugged.

'Neither pleased nor sad,' he said. 'It was what we had to do and if the opportunity presented itself again, we'd act in exactly the same way.'

He was referring to his decision to grant Julian Assange asylum. He and his colleagues had spent several weeks considering the request but, ultimately, Assange had found a sympathetic ear.

We gave him asylum because the possibilities of a fair process were nil if he was extradited to the United States. The *gringo* hawks wanted the head of Julian Assange. The life of Julian Assange was at risk. They wanted to judge him on laws that carried the death penalty, for spying, for treason, and that contravened all human rights law – starting with the Inter-American Convention on Human Rights and the constitution of the Republic of Ecuador. That's why we gave him asylum.

At the time, I was one of the journalists who scrambled to Quito. It seemed unlikely in the extreme that the British government would grant him the safe passage he was asking for to reach the airport and travel to Ecuador. However, rumours were rife that he would be smuggled out of the embassy one night, past the officers from Scotland

Yard posted at the door around the clock. Suddenly he'd appear at a victorious rally alongside Rafael Correa high in the Andes. It was a fantasy. Assange would spend the next seven years inside that embassy in London. By the end, he'd driven the staff to distraction with his constant use of a white noise machine to mask his conversations, his allegedly 'very unpleasant' toilet habits, poor personal hygiene, skateboarding inside the embassy corridors and failing to clean up after his cat.[67] The tall, confident platinum-blond figure who walked in would be dragged out in 2019, kicking and screaming, bearded, dishevelled and grey.

In June and August 2012, journalists charged around Ecuador after Rafael Correa for comment, first in Guayaquil and then Quito. He was defiant, surly and refused all requests for interviews. Then, one afternoon, the British government suggested they might storm the Ecuadorean Embassy building in London. The Foreign Office under then foreign secretary William Hague had warned in a note that under its commitment to the 1987 Diplomatic and Consular Premises Act it could revoke the diplomatic status of an embassy on UK soil so that police could enter the building and arrest Assange. For Correa, such intimidation from a colonial power was all he needed. I was called to an odd little television studio somewhere in Quito. The president's office insisted that they themselves would film the interviews rather than let us use our own camera operators – Correa didn't trust the foreign media any more than he did the local press. On a bizarre-looking set of black leather furniture against whitewashed walls and floor, which had the effect of making us look like we were floating, he tore into the British government and supported Assange to the hilt.

'Let's separate two things,' he told me. 'One is the asylum of Julian Assange. The other is the unheard of and explicit threat, made in writing a day before we granted him asylum, telling us that because of a national law from 1987 the United Kingdom could enter our embassy to arrest Assange... this is unprecedented. It would create a terrible precedent for international relations and diplomatic premises around the world.'

He was measured on camera but clearly fuming. How dare Britain? How dare a Conservative government thousands of miles away threaten him and the integrity of his embassy and the wellbeing of his staff? It was one of his favourite themes – the double standards of powerful states and how some countries believe they're superior to others, a refrain he would echo when we spoke again in Belgium at the end of the decade. 'I think Britain has been enormously clumsy,' he said of the Foreign and Commonwealth Office.

On the other side, there was no lack of voices arguing that it was a bit rich for Rafael Correa to be cast in the role of protector of the press and the freedom of expression, especially following his attempt a year earlier to sue two journalists for $10 million for writing a book about his brother. 'You have a journalist, or an activist, seeking political asylum from a government that has – after Cuba – the poorest record of free speech in the region,' said José Miguel Vivanco, director of Human Rights Watch's Americas division, 'and [which carries out] the practice of persecuting local journalists when the government is upset by their opinions or their research.'[68]

When I put that point, or a version of it, to Correa in 2012, it was the only moment the mask slipped a little on his hitherto controlled fury. To compare the two things was specious, he said. The media companies in Ecuador weren't like those in Britain, there was no BBC – a model of public service broadcasting he seemed genuinely to respect. They had been involved in trying to topple his government, he claimed, a reference to what he saw as their deliberate 'misinformation' campaign about the police reforms supposedly intended to provoke the 2010 uprising. What he did for the human rights of Julian Assange, as someone who could go to the lethal injection table for publishing diplomatic cables the world had a right to see, had nothing to do with his own battle with the privately owned opposition media at home.

Ecuador had featured quite prominently in some of the cables that Assange and his team published on WikiLeaks. In 2011, Correa's government requested that the US ambassador, Heather Hodges, leave Ecuador following a WikiLeaks publication of a cable over alleged corruption by the head of the Ecuadorean police force, General Jaime Hurtado Vaca. He spent a little over a year as the police commander before resigning in June 2009. In the classified cable, the US Embassy said that it had 'multiple reports that indicate [Hurtado Vaca] used his positions to extort bribes, facilitate human trafficking, misappropriate public funds, obstruct investigations and prosecutions of corrupt colleagues, and engage in other corrupt acts for personal enrichment'.[69] The cable implied Correa knew of the corruption allegations against Hurtado Vaca before appointing him but did so anyway because he 'may have wanted to have a [police] chief whom he could easily manipulate'.[70]

Rafael Correa angrily denied the US accusation against him – as did General Hurtado Vaca – and Ambassador Hodges was expelled from the country, just one of the high-profile casualties of the WikiLeaks scandal. The opportunity to throw out a US ambassador was an important symbolic gesture for Correa and one he relished. Although Washington called the decision 'unjustified', Hodges was on the plane home. When it came to asking for asylum a year later, Assange knew he was pushing at the open door of a president who had applauded WikiLeaks, and Assange personally, for exposing Washington's classified communications about his country. The two men, both criticized as egocentric and narcissistic, as vainglorious and arrogant, also appeared to have a strong personal rapport, joking together over their critique of the US in the Russia Today interview.

What, then, of the human rights of the two women who claimed they had been sexually assaulted by the Australian activist? Correa had openly said that what Julian Assange was accused of doing to the two women in Sweden wasn't even considered a crime in Latin America. Yet surely, I said, they had the right to have their case heard, too? This was the point in our conversation when he became most dismissive: 'This is irrelevant,' he said with an airy wave of the hand. 'I was answering a question from a Swedish journalist. He asked my opinion and I gave it to him.'

★

In his time as president, Rafael Correa had two very different vice-presidents next to him. One of them would go on to take over the presidency from him after he stepped down in a dignified handover of power. The other would be sentenced to six years in prison for taking millions in bribes in the Ecuadorean chapter of the Odebrecht scandal. Yet of the two it was the former that Rafael Correa would describe as 'a traitor, a corrupt infiltrator'.[71]

The two men were Lenín Moreno and Jorge Glas Espinel.

Lenín Moreno was Correa's first VP, on the ticket as his running mate in the frenetic election campaign in 2006. He was an integral part of a new, more inclusive cabinet which included an indigenous woman, an Afro-Ecuadorean and the first civilian defence minister, all intended to indicate a clean break with past governments. Paralysed from the waist down after he was shot during a robbery in 1998, Lenín Moreno is the only high-profile politician in the entire region who is a wheelchair user. Moreno is an accomplished and astute political operator, but his appointment was also an undoubtedly brilliant PR move by Correa and his early advisers. 'It was a powerful form of virtue signalling,' recalls former colleague Fernando Bustamante. 'It showed the commitment of Correa and his movement to the most undervalued sectors in Ecuador.' Moreno was the kind face of the administration, the one who remained calm, who spoke politely, who made time for the press. He was in sharp contrast to the irascible Correa and the bombast of his persona on live television or his aggression towards journalists. 'Many saw them as a good-cop/bad-cop,' remarks Bustamante. 'It wasn't deliberately designed that way, but that was an unanticipated outcome.'

It wasn't easy for Moreno to adapt to becoming paraplegic. After thieves stole his car and left him for dead in a pool of blood in a Quito parking lot, he was lucky to survive at all. He openly admits to having suffered bouts of deep depression. He turned his life around through humour. A big believer in the therapeutic qualities of laughter, he has written books with titles such as *Theory and Practice of Humour, Being Happy is Easy and Fun* and *The Best Jokes in the World*.

But Correa no longer sees the funny side of his former vice-president. 'The greatest phony of our times,' he called him in a video released to his supporters during violent street protests against Moreno's government in Ecuador in October 2019. '[Rafael Correa] is a neighbourhood thug,' was Lenín Moreno's withering assessment of his predecessor.[72] The breakdown of their relationship is permanent and beyond repair. Despite his selection of Lenín Moreno in 2006, it seems he was never a true confidant or trusted ally. An insider from the early campaign meetings says that he was chosen on the suggestion of Gustavo Larrea, one of the co-founders of Alianza PAIS. Moreno and Larrea were close from their university days. After graduating, Lenín Moreno opted for the world of private business before moving to the public sector and being plucked to join the Citizens' Revolution as a representative of some of the most marginalized citizens in Latin America.

A great deal was achieved in that area by the Correa government, largely under the supervision and pressure of Vice-President Moreno. In 2012, a Disabilities Law was approved in Ecuador that aimed to 'guarantee the prevention, detection and suitable rehabilitation of disabilities' while also 'ensuring the exercise of the rights of disabled people' under the constitution. Once Moreno was the chosen successor of Correa – only after, it should be noted, Correa reluctantly accepted that he couldn't run again himself – the outgoing president campaigned for the Alianza PAIS candidate. 'The Citizens' Revolution will continue,' Correa proclaimed on the campaign stump, 'and we believe that the best Ecuadorean to guide the next stage of this political process is the incredible human being, Lenín Moreno Garcés.'[73] The praise went both ways, as Moreno exalted Correa during the campaign in similarly effusive language: 'Things have been done properly under leadership that has been tenacious, firm, intelligent, hardworking and, above all, carried out in the service of the country's poorest by our comrade, friend and leader, Rafael Correa Delgado.'[74]

The first signs that Moreno had no intention of continuing Correa's political legacy – despite an assurance to the contrary during the campaign – came just weeks after the presidential sash passed between the two. First, Lenín Moreno improved ties with Conaie, the country's main indigenous organization that had distanced itself from Correa over the course of his decade in power in protest at his mining and environmental policies. The successor's snub to Correa was clear. And so it continued: Moreno quickly brought his government closer to NGOs that Correa had detested, to the media, to private business owners Correa accused of being in the pay of Washington, to Washington itself. Before long, the hostilities turned personal.

Moreno removed his vice-president, Jorge Glas Espinel, over charges he was facing in connection to Odebrecht. Jorge Glas had taken over from Moreno as Correa's VP in 2013 when Moreno became the UN's Special Envoy on Disability and Accessibility for a few years. Glas was Correa's man on the inside. A fellow Boy Scout from the same troop in Guayaquil, he was there in part to ensure continuity from one leader to the next and in part to protect Correa from the kinds of 'lies' or 'false testimonies' that had seen his Brazilian counterpart, Lula da Silva, put behind bars. Lenín Moreno permitted two judicial investigations to go ahead, one into Correa and one into Glas. The investigation into Glas was another example of the Odebrecht scandal crossing international borders and claiming a member of a country's top political leadership. After Jorge Glas was suspended, it was found in court that he had accepted around $13.5 million in bribes from the Brazilian constructor, paid out via his uncle, who was also on trial. The vice-president of Ecuador was sentenced to six years, as were his co-defendants. His lawyer said the sentence was 'wicked' and 'barbaric' but there was nothing he could do. After he had been absent from his post and unable to perform the functions of vice-president for ninety days, he was officially stripped of the title.

The Correa charges relate to something entirely different, a bizarre incident called the Balda Case, in which Rafael Correa is accused of ordering the kidnapping of an opposition deputy, Fernando Balda, while the latter was in exile in Bogotá. Balda began his political career in the ranks of Alianza PAIS but soon broke away and joined the opposition. He fled to Colombia in 2010 after publicly criticizing

Correa and members of his government, comments for which he faced libel charges. Amid what he constantly denounced as persecution by Correa, he settled in Bogotá and became close to the inner circle of Colombia's right-wing ex-president, Alvaro Uribe. In 2012, a group of kidnappers on the streets of Bogotá surrounded Balda and forced him into a car. However, the operation to abduct him was bungled as nearby taxi-drivers alerted the police, who stopped the car, arrested the gang and released Balda.

Investigations in Colombia found that the criminal group who'd snatched Balda were working in tandem with three Ecuadorean intelligence agents. Their intention was apparently to take him back to Ecuador to answer the charges against him. They were acting, it was claimed in their statements to the Colombian police, on orders from the Ecuadorean president. Rafael Correa says the idea that he orchestrated an attempted kidnapping of Fernando Balda is absurd, laughable and politically motivated. Nevertheless, his hand-picked successor allowed the case against him to proceed to the point that, were he to return to Ecuador, he would immediately be arrested and face trial. An extradition order for Correa is registered with the Belgian authorities over the Balda Case, one which they have yet to act on.[75]

Over coffee in Louvain-la-Neuve, Correa says he always considered Moreno a potential traitor to him and his movement. Yet he didn't expect the degree nor the speed with which his former running mate would turn on him after he left office. The mud is flying from both sides. Rafael Correa brought a wad of papers to our meeting in Belgium which included the number of a bank account in Panama which he insisted I note down, and claimed that it contains Lenín Moreno's illicit funds.

At the heart of his successor's undoing of Correa's political legacy – whether treason or pragmatism – was an effort to end the high social spending plans based on a high commodities price. Moreno ushered in a new phase of austerity including taking a multibillion-dollar loan from the IMF, the World Bank and the Inter-American Development Bank to balance the public purse, bringing with it a sharp drop in his popularity. In October 2019, a measure to remove a fuel subsidy in place since the 1970s, Decree 883, sparked massive protests against Moreno. Plumes of tear gas engulfed Quito, masked protesters and indigenous demonstrators threw stones at police and were met with baton charges and water cannons. The cabinet moved to Guayaquil for their own safety and for several days it looked like Moreno's time in power might not reach two years. In the end, he relented and rescinded Decree 883 in time to save his presidency. It was another sign of the weakness of Ecuador's institutions and the ease with which a presidency can be derailed by popular protests. He might have become another short-lived name on the wall of *El Pobre Diablo*, the bar that once housed a shrine to Ecuador's presidents.

Throughout it all, from his home and inside TV studios in Belgium, Rafael Correa never stopped stoking the flames. In interviews and via Twitter, he ramped up the pressure on Moreno to step down, roundly criticized the heavy-handed police response to the protests and urged his supporters to keep the faith:

'I was wrong about Moreno,' he admitted in a video message on social media. 'But I wasn't wrong when I said everything was a question of time and that our people, patient but never absent, prudent but never cowardly, would rise up with the force of a hurricane. We will recover the fatherland. The glory days will return.'

Such is Rafael Correa's need for absolute loyalty that many of the names mentioned in this chapter – Alberto Acosta, Lenín Moreno, Fernando Bustamante, Gustavo Larrea, Fabricio Correa – fell out with him and are now considered his adversaries. Some of those involved at the start of his political career or who worked in his first administration, like Alberto Acosta and Fernando Bustamante, found that it was essentially impossible to disagree with the president and still maintain a workable political relationship with him. He required nothing less than complete adherence to his word at all times, something an intellectual of Bustamante's ilk was never likely to comfortably adapt to.

Parting ways with Alberto Acosta was a split with a fraternal political ally, a brother-in-arms. But Correa has also cut ties completely with his biological brother, Fabricio Correa. 'I won't speak about my brother while my mother is alive,' Rafael Correa told me, 'because I know what my brother Fabricio is. That's why I never put him in the government, never let him near the government.' He proceeded, nonetheless, to talk about him quite a bit. There were 'fake companies in Panama, everything that we have always combatted'. In 2006, Rafael Correa claims his brother Fabricio approached him, saying he had established a relationship with an important contact inside Odebrecht and offering to facilitate a link between the Brazilian company and Correa's administration. 'Ah no, that means Odebrecht is a crooked company,' Correa says that he told himself and subsequently never followed it up. 'Today I'm even thankful for him,' jokes Correa of his older brother, 'probably because of him I saved myself from the Odebrecht scandal.'

'It's a fabrication, a lie,' was Fabricio's reaction to the suggestion that he was the Odebrecht point man into his brother's office, saying Rafael Correa first made a connection with the tainted Brazilian construction firm during a visit to Brazil as finance minister. There followed a long and confusing diatribe in which he named all kinds of distant and murky names behind the company's controversial involvement in Ecuador. Whenever I spoke to them about Odebrecht, Fabricio blamed Rafael and Rafael blamed Fabricio.

A few things are clear, however. First, that Rafael Correa's government threw Odebrecht out of Ecuador in September 2008 over a contract dispute and sent troops to seize hundreds of millions of dollars' worth of infrastructure projects being carried out by the firm. Specifically, Odebrecht was accused of carrying out shoddy work on the San Francisco hydroelectric dam, a 230-MW construction on the Pastaza River in the Andean highlands. The work was completed in 2007 but a year later it lay idle, its turbine blades damaged by contaminated sediments from the eruptions of the Tungurahua volcano.[76] Correa didn't just oblige the company to leave, he wanted to put its executives behind bars and came very close to doing so.

It was only significant pressure from Itamaraty – Brazil's Ministry of Foreign Affairs – and the personal intervention of Lula that prevented this from happening. Instead, Correa settled for expelling the company from Ecuador and telling them never to come back.

Had the story ended there, it would have been hard ever to accuse Rafael Correa of an illicit relationship with the corrupt company. He would have simply been able to point out that he was the only regional president to very publicly eject it from his country. However, a few years later he let them back in. The infrastructure projects built by Odebrecht in Ecuador after they were allowed back are the ones that have brought the corruption allegations and charges against the former president. Meanwhile the older brother, Fabricio, took the decision to turn even more furiously on his sibling. The two had fallen out years earlier after the publication of *El Gran Hermano*, which alleged that Fabricio had won multimillion-dollar government contracts and that President Correa was aware of them. Though Correa eventually dropped his defamation suit against the book's authors following a huge outcry in Ecuador and abroad, he simultaneously cancelled all his brother's contracts with the state.

With no love lost between them ever since, Fabricio has given testimony against his younger brother, turning state witness in the prosecutor's case against members of Correa's inner circle. Neither man thinks they will ever patch things up. In fact, the older Correa tells a story of their mother's eightieth birthday. A party was organized by their sister, family members came from across the country and the United States. Rafael arrived but, according to Fabricio, refused to cross the threshold until his older brother vacated the premises. It soured the celebration but made one thing abundantly clear to the estranged sibling: their rift transcended blood and was for life. They will next meet, probably, at their mother's funeral where Fabricio expects a similarly cold shoulder: 'If he acted like this while she's alive, I have no reason to think it will be any different at her burial.'[77]

*

'Away, and mock time with fairest show: False face must hide
what the false heart doth know'

Macbeth, Act I, Scene VII

Fernando Bustamante, Correa's erudite and scholarly former
interior minister, chuckles at the idea that he might have been a more
apt choice, a more balanced figure, to take the role of presidential
candidate in 2006.

'Never, not in my craziest fantasies, could I imagine myself as a
candidate for such a position. I don't think I have the condition for
it nor have I ever. When it comes to being a politician, I'm not sure I
have the skills for that kind of success.'

But Correa had them, in plenty. He was, as one of his economics
students from the early 2000s recalls, 'astute, really quite brilliant'.
Not necessarily brilliant in the academic sense, the student was quick
to clarify, not exceptionally analytical or accomplished or profound.
But 'skilful, quick and incredibly street-smart'. If anyone on the San
Francisco campus in Quito in the early 2000s was going to go on to
have a dazzling political career, it was Rafael Correa.

He drew people into his populist project, he made them believe
in him. From those who turned up penniless to his rallies, to those
who abandoned their lucrative jobs to join his government. Yet the
arc of his career is an almost Shakespearean tale – a tragedy, replete
with treachery, sedition and corruption. Bustamante is reminded of
Macbeth. 'Here we have a knight who is loyal to a cause, who returns
from war and meets three witches who prophesy that he will become
the king of Scotland, something that wasn't within his possibilities
or aspirations.'

Macbeth is urged to conspire against King Duncan by his wife,
Lady Macbeth. 'Taking power in this instance is basically the result
of disloyalty,' Bustamente says, 'of treason and a succession of acts
which bring him to commit crimes each one greater than the last,
climbing at an unstoppable scale to reach power.' The disloyalty and
treason seen in the Rafael Correa presidency by its former players
appear to refer to the idea of abandoning their original ideals and

aims in favour of purely personality-led governance. The movement ultimately became all about him and not about its ideas. Even less about *el pueblo*.

It may be tempting to see Correa as possessed of Macbeth's 'thriftless ambition', to see him as a king with 'a fruitless crown' upon his head and 'a barren sceptre' in his grip. In his case Lady Macbeth was not his Belgian wife, who remained largely uninterested in attaining the summit of Ecuador's political power, but the PR machinery and the cult of personality that ensured he became a certain kind of populist leader.

Yet rather than Elizabethan England, it is perhaps better to look closer to home to understand the kinetic, explosive presidency of Rafael Correa. He was always, and remains to this day a Boy Scout, tied to the values of public service and camaraderie, companionship and self-sufficiency that he fell in love with as a young boy. He thrived inside that organization, especially when he was near the top of it – setting up and then running his own Scout troop in Guayaquil. 'Once a scout, always a scout', as their own slogan testifies.

It seems he always had that instinct, even from a very young age. Fabricio Correa recalls that while other kids would play cops and robbers, his younger brother used to play at being president and ministers with his pals. When some young people enter student politics, it is to test the waters at university, to try out new things and push new boundaries. For Rafael Correa it was the environment in which he could first quench his thirst for political recognition, deference and power.

Yet there is a certain contradiction to Akela Rafael Correa. While one might expect a committed Scout to be obedient and accommodating to leadership, in that regard he most resembles his father in his compulsion to challenge authority. His innate defiance is a thread which runs throughout his life, from the Lasallian Brothers to his university chancellor at USFQ to the established interests and private media owners in Ecuador. Without resorting to cheap psychology, one could argue that it was evident in his decisions to grant asylum to Julian Assange, to refuse to extend the lease on the US military base at Manta, to expel the US ambassador, to default on billions of dollars in foreign debt. The ability to defy the largest and most powerful authority of them all – Washington in all its guises, from the White House and the Pentagon to the State Department and the IMF – was an opportunity too good to pass up. All of it was applauded at home and lauded on the world stage by like-minded men and women. At his height, he was backed by a team – a troop, perhaps – consisting of Hugo Chávez, Evo Morales, Daniel Ortega, Cristina Kirchner in Argentina, Pepe Mujica in Uruguay, Lula in Brazil, and even Fidel Castro, the most adventurous and audacious leader among them.

Correa himself is adamant that he wasn't then and still isn't either a populist or an autocrat: 'If you're popular in Spain or Germany, you're a great politician. If you're popular in Latin America, you're a populist,' he told me with a flourish, one of his oft-repeated arguments. The comparison with European democracies, especially the hypocrisy of those which operate beneath the undemocratic institution of a monarchy, is a theme of which he is particularly fond.

A charge that is often levelled at Correa is that he is *'prepotente'*, 'arrogant'. It is a quality that he has displayed on many occasions, on podiums and in interviews, a smile which is construed as smug and a condescending tone he takes with journalists and political opponents. His superiority complex – that I understand this, but you simply can't – was something some of his former students complained about. Combined with a very short fuse, the impression he gives is of a man with a powerful ego and a supercilious bearing.

Yet in Louvain-la-Neuve, as he sat for several hours in a patisserie over coffee and pastries, he appeared to have shed much of that haughtiness. There was no security detail, no armoured car waiting outside, no cameras or clamouring crowds. His tone remains defiant and any sense that he has softened with age is misplaced. He retains the embers of his youthful passion and charisma. Yet he seemed older, greyer, stuck in what one former ally accurately described as 'a desperate limbo'. Negotiating a return to front-line politics in Ecuador, and overcoming both the judiciary and his political adversaries, will be tough.

In late 2019, tyres were once again burning on the streets of Quito and Rafael Correa was back on the airwaves, talking to the media, his old adversary, via Skype from his apartment in exile, the bit between his teeth, firing invective at his successor with a zeal of a man on the permanent campaign trail.

NICARAGUA /
DANIEL ORTEGA

*'He controlled everything. You felt it was
a crime to be young'*

DANIEL ORTEGA

It was the middle of the night before Christmas Eve. Six-year-old Alina Obando Arce was jerked awake and immediately knew something terrible was happening. Great chunks of dried mud were shaking loose from the ceiling of their adobe house and falling on her and her younger sister, Francy, with whom she shared a bed.

The room was shaking and wouldn't stop. Beneath the girls the ground trembled, above them the roof heaved and groaned. The family's few possessions, their pots and bits of furniture, were scattered around the floor of their meagre home in the San Sebastian neighbour-hood in the centre of Managua, and Alina could hear the next-door neighbours screaming, a haunting sound that was echoing across a city descending into panic.

It was 23 December 1972, and Managua would never be the same again. Nor, for that matter, would Alina.

She began to cry and called for her mother. No answer. She yelled out again, and still nothing. As the eldest child, she tried to take charge, grabbing her sister's hand and dragging her into their parents' room where her two-year-old brother also slept.

'I shouted at her "*mamá, mamá, mamá*" But she didn't say any-thing. All I remember was she made a kind of sigh. And that was it,' Alina recalled fifty years later, bursting into hot, child-like tears at the memory. She still lives in the same *barrio*, running a small store selling candies and banana chips, barely half a dozen blocks from where her childhood abruptly ended one cruel December night.

Alina's mother, Juana Liset, was just twenty-three when her head was crushed by a wooden beam in the massive earthquake that struck Managua that Christmas. She was nine months pregnant.

She had already felt some mild contractions the day before, but the hospital was far from her *barrio*, so she had decided to wait until the child – a little girl as it turned out – arrived of its own accord. Instead, mother and unborn daughter were among the roughly 10,000 people who died that night or over the next few horrific days, trapped beneath the rubble or fatally injured and uncared for.

The scenes that greeted Alina once an uncle pulled her from the wreckage of their home were apocalyptic. The historic centre of

Managua was almost entirely destroyed and in San Sebastian it was impossible to find a family who hadn't lost at least one member. As fears grew over the spread of disease, thousands of cadavers were simply dumped into mass graves or doused in kerosene and set on fire where they lay. Bulldozers cleared rubble and mutilated bodies alike. Funeral rites were ignored as many of the dead were just wrapped in sheets and left on the streets until the army came by to pick them up and bury them.

Juana Liset was lucky – she did receive a proper burial. As the eldest child, Alina was considered mature enough to bid farewell to her mother and was taken to a funeral on the city outskirts by an aunt. Too small to see properly, she had to stand on tiptoes to peer into the open casket, her mother's skull only partially restored, the dead child still in her womb.

It was a personal tragedy for thousands of people, and one of the darkest moments in Nicaragua's modern history.

The man presiding over the chaos was General Anastasio Somoza Debayle, the ex-president who was still commander-in-chief of the armed forces. A graduate of La Salle military academy and West Point, he was the latest incarnation of the powerful Somoza dynasty to control the country, as they had been doing more or less without interruption since 1936.

'Will the capital as we now know it cease to exist?' he was asked by a television journalist.

'That is right,' he answered bluntly in fluent English. Around him, the few buildings that still stood in the city centre were being pulled down or dynamited. 'We're going to live in tents until we make an appreciation of the situation and the government decides what we're going to do.'[1]

What he meant was 'until *I* decide what to do', because Somoza *was* the government. All three branches of it – the judiciary, the parliament and the executive – as well as the National Guard and the police. He was the state in all its guises. With martial law quickly declared, he became the de facto leader of Nicaragua as his father and his brother had been before him.

Somoza alone decided which buildings stayed up and which would be flattened. Flying over the ruined capital in an American helicopter, he pointed his finger at a neighbourhood or a street and before the day was out it was demolished. The view from above also gave him a unique perspective on how to rebuild the city, and how he and his cronies could profit from it.

Somoza had amassed an estimated $500 million business empire. He controlled the main airport, much of the arable land, a shipping line and the country's ports. Thus far, he had stayed away from banking and construction, leaving those particular gems to other rich families.[2] Yet the temptation of millions of dollars in foreign aid and donations to rebuild the destroyed capital was too much for him.

USAID funds were channelled through Somoza Debayle's bank, Banco de Centroamerica, to his construction companies which then carried out expensive rebuilding and infrastructure work. His inner circle got in on the act, buying up cheap plots of land on the outskirts of Managua where the city would be rebuilt and selling them on to the state for obscene profits. The *New York Times* reported that Managua Public Registry documents showed General Somoza's aide-de-camp, Col. Rafael Adonis Porras Largaespada, had paid $71,428 for a piece of land on 4 June 1975, and then sold it to the Somoza government for $3,342,000 in late September of the same year.[3]

That alone would have been bad enough in the wake of the country's worst disaster in living memory. However, a particularly gruesome and egregious example of his corruption would forever characterize Somoza as a leech or vampire – a bloodsucker, feeding off the poorest in Nicaragua.

Among the multiple companies Somoza owned was one called Plasmaferesis. In three large white buildings in Managua, 250 beds could accommodate up to fifteen hundred people, or donors, a day.[4] The company paid poor Nicaraguans a pitiful fee for their plasma. Inside Plasmaferesis, people gave blood which was centrifuged, the plasma separated, frozen and shipped to the United States to treat haemophiliacs. The plasma-less blood was then mixed with saline and reinfused into the donor. For a president's side income, it was a wildly unethical but hugely profitable business.

At a rate of $5 for a unit of plasma, the profit margin for Somoza and his Cuban-American business partner, Pedro Ramos, was 300 per cent. Their annual turnover was in the tens of millions. And volunteers were in no short supply. It was almost painless and the donors received a hot meal and a small fee afterwards. It quickly became a popular way among the city's homeless, destitute and drunks to earn a little cash and many attended the clinics as often as twice a week.

By 1977, the blatant and literal bleeding dry of Nicaragua's poor for profit was creating unwelcome headlines for Anastasio Somoza Debayle. In a series entitled 'The Vampire Chronicles', the editor of La Prensa newspaper, Pedro Joaquín Chamorro, investigated and exposed the president's nefarious business practices. In particular, Pedro Ramos, the Miami-based Cuban partner, was named, identified and vilified. He took swift and brutal revenge.

In January 1978, a car pulled up alongside Chamorro's and forced it onto the curb. Three gunmen got out and shot him eighteen times. The newspaper man, one of the leading voices in Nicaraguan journalism, died in the ambulance on the way to the hospital. As the sirens wailed and the paramedics tried in vain to save him, Chamorro knew who had done this to him, even if he'd never met the men who actually pulled the triggers.

He had written to General Somoza three years earlier and opened his letter by saying 'before receiving the blow of repression which will surely leave me immobilized, I write you this letter to clarify points about the current situation'.[5]

There followed an excoriating list of how Somoza's dynastic rule, which resembled 'that of a king in children's stories', was being discussed in the markets and street corners of Nicaragua. Of the popular hatred of his companies, and their inexorable creep into every facet of daily life. Of how continental public opinion could now see beyond his 'disguises of legitimacy, democracy, popularity and civility'.

It was a declaration of war, and both men knew it. It would have been no surprise to Chamorro that within three years Somoza's goons had ended his life. So much so that he signed off the letter with words that repeated his opening statement with chilling accuracy: 'I await, with a clear conscience and a soul full of peace, the blow that you have destined for me.'

Yet his killing – and that of another journalist a year later – would prove to be decisive self-inflicted blows against Somoza, too.

In the aftermath of the earthquake, a disparate band of rebels who had been fighting against the regime in the mountainous and rural regions of the country since 1961 began to come together under a common goal. The conditions were ripe for rebellion. People who were already hungry and illiterate now had nothing to lose. Around half of Nicaragua's farmers were making do with just 3.4 per cent of the country's arable land, while a select few of Somoza's allies owned almost a third of the country's cultivable area.[6]

The group was named after Augusto César Sandino, the rebel leader who forced out the US troops occupying Nicaragua in 1933, before he was murdered by Anastasio Somoza García, the first patri-arch of the Somoza clan. As his son, Anastasio Somoza Debayle, was blithely siphoning off earthquake relief funds forty years later, the Sandinista Front for National Liberation, or FSLN, had begun to shoulder their rifles and daub their faces with war paint, rallying under a red-and-black flag.

That Somoza Debayle was a bloodthirsty dictator was no coinci-dence. It ran in the family. When his father ordered the killing of Sandino in 1934, he went to macabre lengths to ensure that the rebel's remains could never be found.

Augusto César Sandino had achieved something unique in Latin America – he had forced the Americans to leave his country. When modern leaders in the region complain of the Americans meddling in their nations for more than a century, they aren't wrong. Aside from Cuba, perhaps nowhere was the interference of the USA felt more profoundly than in Nicaragua. A contingent of US marines had been in the country since 1912, as they had in a number of Central

American and Caribbean nations, protecting their economic interests, particularly those of the United Fruit Company and the Standard Fruit Company, through the so-called 'Banana Wars'.[7]

Born in the rebellious and largely indigenous Masaya department of the country, Augusto Sandino had refused to accept the inevitable rise of US imperialism through the 'manifest destiny' of the Monroe Doctrine, which stated that the USA should in effect be the dominant power in the New World, north and south.[8] Nor would Sandino accept any malleable puppet regimes installed by the North Americans. The Constitutionalist War in 1926, which pitted Conservative against Liberal, saw Sandino rise to prominence as an audacious general for the Liberals. The conflict ended through a US-brokered peace treaty in 1927 but Sandino considered the terms unjust and merely a continuation of America's interventionism in Nicaragua. Disobeying the order to lay down arms, instead he mounted a guerrilla campaign against the US marines and the newly formed National Guard, a militia and police force which emerged from the peace agreement. The National Guard was led by Anastasio Somoza García.[9]

Sandino's guerrilla war spanned six years, attacking US-owned mines with a rebel army of *campesinos* and gold miners trained in the mountains of Nicaragua. Yet through sheer tenacity and cunning, combined with the Great Depression which made overseas adventures too costly for Washington, they managed to force out the marines in 1933. A year later, Somoza García betrayed the terms of the peace agreement and double-crossed Sandino by having him kidnapped as he left a meeting at the presidential palace and swiftly murdered. Somoza's men buried him but are rumoured to have later exhumed and possibly dismembered the body, either for trophies or to spread it around Managua to stop Sandino's followers from taking possession of his remains.

It was a cruel end for Nicaragua's national hero.[10] Not that he officially carried that title back then. That honour would be bestowed upon him much later, in 2011, by Daniel Ortega – the man who led the Sandinista movement, but who his opponents say is now more reminiscent of Somoza than Sandino.

★

Daniel Ortega's life, his metamorphosis from rebel to ruler, from *Comandante* to *caudillo*, has been one of the most remarkable in the region's recent history. Perhaps only Fidel Castro has been as controversial and divisive.

It began shortly after the Second World War in a small municipality called, aptly for the birthplace of a guerrilla leader, *La Libertad*. Ortega was born into radicalism. His father and his mother married quite late for those times, when both were well into their thirties, and after two children died in their infancy Daniel was their first to make it past his third birthday. Named after his father, young Daniel was followed by two brothers and a sister over the next five years and seems to have been well loved and cared for. His mother, Lydia Saavedra Rivas, was especially supportive of his later radicalization, regularly visiting him when he ended up in prison and organizing the mothers of other guerrillas in protests and hunger strikes.[11]

Both parents were staunch opponents of Somoza García and his repressive rule. When the family moved to Managua, Daniel Senior was still struggling to move up the social ladder. The family wasn't in abject poverty – Daniel's father had previously been an accountant in a gold mine – but nor were they particularly far above it. While the children went to private Catholic schools in the capital, a sign of either wealth or aspiration, their income wasn't steady and at times the boys had to be pulled out of class until the bills could be paid.[12]

The boys' first incursions into rebellion began while still in their teens, encouraged by their parents' clear approval of the Cuban Revolution and the left-wing rebel groups and early Sandinistas as they started to emerge in the 1960s. Gradually, the haphazard attempts at forming a revolutionary front were being given some coherence by the FSLN, specifically through their co-founder, Carlos Fonseca. Having spent time in Cuba under the auspices of Fidel Castro and Che Guevara, Fonseca engaged more closely with Sandino's political thoughts and strategies of guerrilla warfare in the archives in Havana than he ever could in Managua, where all traces of Sandino were wiped away by Somoza. He turned the group towards Nicaraguan nationalism and moved away from a strict Marxist interpretation of revolution. He tried to imbue the Sandinista movement with the need for education, intellectualism, self-improvement and a rejection, at least in principle, of machismo. Women would hold positions of power and would be seen as equals on the field of combat. Religious belief and practice were also accepted within the Sandinista ideology, another key difference with the atheistic Cuban revolutionary tradition, largely because it would have been difficult to persuade the devoutly Catholic Nicaraguan people to join the cause if it meant they had to abandon their faith.

Daniel Ortega, not yet fifteen, and his brothers joined the Sandinista youth wing and met Fonseca in 1962 at his family home, located in the same working-class *barrio* that became the FSLN's first urban stronghold. As one commentator observed about joining the Sandinistas: 'The only ideological commitment that was an absolute requirement for membership was to revolutionary violence', and the Ortega brothers, especially Daniel and Humberto, had that in abundance.[13]

Daniel Ortega soon had his first encounters with the police and was sent to prison, initially for short periods over acts of general agitation – participating in protests or some act of symbolic vandalism. In the climate of fear under Somoza Debayle and the National Guard, he was lucky he wasn't killed outright. Many of his comrades were murdered, often barely out of high school.

Before long, Ortega had killed, too. It was a significant step for the young man, taking a life in cold blood, but it was one he would never regret. The murder in question was that of Gonzalo Lacayo, a well-known sergeant in the National Guard, a sadist who had already tortured Daniel Ortega in jail. He has retold the story on several occasions of how he and three other Sandinistas gunned Lacayo down one night on a street in Managua, comparing it years later to the way the French Resistance might have killed a member of the Gestapo.[14]

He was never tried over Lacayo's killing, although several others were massacred by the National Guard over it as they sheltered in a clandestine FSLN safe house. As other Sandinistas had already been killed for the murder of Lacayo, Ortega was never formally linked to it by the authorities. Yet they still managed to deliver their retribution in the harsh sentence Daniel Ortega received in 1967 for robbing a branch of the Banco de Londres on Kennedy Boulevard in Managua. He was sentenced to fourteen years in jail.

These bank robberies were not petty thefts. They were intended to raise funds for the FSLN via what they called *recuperaciones*, a way of 'recuperating' the money illegally obtained by the country's oligarchs and using it to return the nation to the people. It was a nimble justification for the cash – 225,100 córdobas, around $32,000, in the case of Ortega's heist – and it certainly provided the San-dinistas with much-needed funds for their coming battle against Somoza Debayle.

Initially, as inmate 198 in La Modelo prison, Ortega had to sit out that fight. There is a theory that he never quite shook prison off afterwards and certainly the stories of the conditions and the torture he endured describe a cruel and painful experience, typical of incar-ceration for political prisoners in so much of Central America.[15] Over the first few months he was subjected to repeated cruelty by the guards, including being hooded and beaten and having electrodes attached to his genitals. His poems from inside jail reveal a man in torment being pushed to his mental limits.

For all that, Ortega would only serve half his sentence. Not because of any benevolence on behalf of Somoza, but through the extra-ordinary daring of his comrades.

Between Christmas and New Year 1974, with Managua barely on its feet after the earthquake, a former agriculture minister, José María 'Chema' Castillo, held a festive soirée at his residence. The lavish reception by the wealthy cotton exporter was in honour of the US ambassador, Turner B. Shelton. As the guests from Managua's elite sipped fine rum and nibbled on canapés, an audacious plan was unfolding in the darkness around them.

Thirteen Sandinistas of the 'Juan José Quezada' Command led by Eduardo Contreras had taken up position in cars surrounding the house. The moment Ambassador Shelton left the compound, the guerrillas struck. As one of them, Germán Pomares, would later explain on camera, 'it didn't suit us to have the Ambassador there given the tradition there is in Nicaragua of gringo interventions in our country. So, we watched until the Ambassador left. We know that as soon as the toast was done, he would be the first to leave.'[16]

When they burst from their cars firing their guns, it was as though the entire Somoza regime was caught off guard. As a former high-ranking security official, Chema Castillo had an arsenal of weapons in his home but he was killed in the initial exchange of shots. The group quickly took the entire party of dignitaries hostage, including some valuable pawns and bargaining chips such as the Nicaraguan ambassador to the United States, Guillermo Sevilla-Sacasa, who happened to be married to Somoza's sister, Lilian. One of Somoza's cousins was also at the event, as was the foreign minister. All were now held captive by the rebels, the cream of Somoza's society suddenly in the hands of the Sandinistas. Considering the regime had been playing down the guerrilla threat for the past few years and insisting to Washington that the group had been crushed, it came as a huge embarrassment to Somoza.

If it had been left to Somoza alone, he would probably have sent in his National Guardsmen, guns blazing. But with his sister's husband in there, she persuaded him to show uncharacteristic restraint. Instead the dictator had to listen to the FSLN's demands: $5 million in cash, the release of fourteen political prisoners, safe passage to Cuba for the freed Sandinistas and the opportunity to broadcast a radio, television and newspaper message nationwide.

He managed to push them down to a million, but the rest of the demands were met. Daniel Ortega found himself hauled out of La Modelo prison and bundled onto a plane to Havana. Several moments in the Nicaraguan conflict have passed into Sandinista folklore. If any marked a genuine turning point, a juncture which established a 'before' and an 'after', this assault on the cocktail party was one of them. From here on, Somoza knew he was facing an existential challenge and that the guerrillas were much more capable than he had hitherto given them credit for. He promptly invoked martial law and put in place a state of siege that would last for thirty-three months.

In Cuba, Ortega forged ties that would last the rest of his life, none more so than with Fidel Castro. The older revolutionary was fully supportive of the Nicaraguan Revolution and a decade later attended Daniel Ortega's inauguration in Managua after the 1985 election – although he rather upstaged the Sandinista president. Castro would also play a crucial role in training, arming and unifying the Sandinistas.[17]

The time Ortega spent in Cuba was formative, instructional and inspirational. The parallels were obvious. Here was an established revolutionary government which had removed Fulgencio Batista, a dictator akin to Somoza, a movement based in the countryside but supported in the urban centres, carried out by young men and women who looked and sounded a lot like the Sandinistas. The Cuban rebels were led by a young, charismatic visionary who had also spent time in jail for political insurrection. Most importantly, it was a revolution which, at the time it took power, was backed by the vast majority of the Cuban people, who were exhausted by the abuse and corruption of the deposed regime.

Though the Sandinista revolution was in its relative infancy and still in the thick of the armed struggle, Cuba's example convinced Ortega – if nothing else – that he could win.

The attack on the 1974 Christmas party held by Somoza's cronies escalated the tempo of the revolution. Four years later, another assault brought the battle to a head.

Again, it was an incredible display of daring and gall, the kind that's only attempted by the young, the foolhardy and those with nothing to lose. All three of those descriptions applied to the guerrillas of the Rigoberto López Pérez Command when they carried out *Operación Chanchera* – Operation Pig Butcher – on 22 August 1978. The porkers in question were, according to popular slang, the country's congressmen, the national parliament their pigsty.

It was essentially a suicide mission. In his account of the attack, the great Colombian novelist Gabriel García Márquez describes it thus: 'The plan seemed simply too much madness. It involved taking the National Palace in Managua in broad daylight, with just twenty-five men, holding the members of the Chamber of Deputies hostage and obtaining as a ransom the release of all political prisoners.'[18]

But that is precisely what they did. Twenty-five FSLN rebels dressed in uniforms of the elite troops of the National Guard bluffed their way past the palace security through sheer bravado, barking orders at the guards and putting the fear of God into them by growling 'look sharp, *el jefe* is coming'. Aged forty-two, the group's leader, Edén Pastora, known as 'Comandante Cero' (Commander Zero), was a little older than most of the other guerrillas. 'Comandante Dos' was Dora Maria Téllez, a brilliant, tactically astute and courageous fighter, and the only woman in the operation, twenty years Pastora's junior. Within just three minutes, they had stormed the main chamber and had taken some 2,000 hostages using a few Uzis, old Second World War-era Garand rifles, some grenades and a Browning pistol.

In some respects the operation was similar to the cocktail party assault at Chema Castillo's home in that it struck at the heart of '*Somocismo*'. Again, its utter flagrance and barefaced audacity lent it an element of surprise which blindsided the dictator and his entire apparatus of repression. Again, their high-stakes approach was incredibly risky but it brought great dividends to the FSLN. And, once again, the Sandinistas left unscathed and with exactly what they wanted. As the entire chamber of deputies was held at gunpoint, including several members of his family, Somoza Debayle had no choice but to negotiate. Following two days of intense pressure and mediation by the archbishop of Managua, Monseñor Miguel Obando y Bravo, scores of political prisoners were released and some funds were paid out, though much less than the $10 million the Sandinistas had initially demanded.[19]

The twenty-five Sandinistas, five negotiators and the four most valuable hostages walked out of the National Palace and were taken to the airport to meet their newly released comrades. There they boarded a Venezuelan Airforce C-130 plane for Panama. From there, they flew onwards to Cuba.

Four decades on from that gripping, reckless operation, Comandante Cero and Comandante Dos provide the clearest illustration of the modern split within the Sandinista movement and the polarization of views over Daniel Ortega.

First, Edén Pastora. Once described as a combination of 'a tropical Rambo and a Central American Che Guevara', even in his eighties he was still an uncompromising man with a wild look in his eyes.[20] Like Daniel Ortega – and indeed Somoza – he was another Nicaraguan whose path was set for him long before adulthood. His father, a *campesino* called Pánfilo Pastora, was killed by Somoza García's thugs for refusing to hand over his farm when the dictator swept through the countryside illegally accruing land. The story goes that his widow, Edén's mother, spent the next decade tracking down each of the men who murdered her husband and contracted hired killers to deliver the vengeance she sought. Edén was seven years old at the time.

Edén ushered me into his den in Managua, past an array of bored-looking cops and his personal security detail sitting on rocking chairs in his front patio. Among his entourage were some of his sons, he said, showing me a photo on the wall of him as a guerrilla leader standing in the verdant mountains of southern Nicaragua flanked by two young men. 'I was the only commander to take his kids to the front line of combat with him. They were sixteen and eighteen years old.'

After those two sons, there followed many more. Pastora was well known for his prodigious family. He has twenty-one children and twenty-seven grandchildren, he proclaimed proudly, like a man who has just found out his wife is pregnant again. Around half are adopted he explained, and, as if to prove the point, he yelled out for one of them to come in.

'Who's your *papá*?' he asked a confused-looking guy in his forties.
'*Usted*,' he answered.
'And how long have you been with your dad?'
'Thirty-two years.'
'And how many of you are there?'
'We're twenty-one in total.'
'Okay, that's all. Thanks, son.' The man nodded respectfully and pulled the door closed.

'He fought alongside me in two guerrilla wars and I adopted him,' Pastora explained once we were alone again. 'He's my son, and I love him like I love them all.' It seemed to matter to him a great deal that I understood this. It was apparently a clumsy attempt to counteract his reputation as a *mujeriego*, or ladies' man, while simultaneously making me aware of it.

His other great love was fishing. On the shelves behind his desk, beside photos of the grandchildren and pictures of Fidel and Chávez, were models of sailing boats and schooners, a fishing rod and tackle propped up against the wall. Pastora saw himself in the macho tradition of Hemingway – fighting, fucking and fishing – and four decades on, his heroism in the National Palace only added to his outsize persona.

'I had three dreams in my life,' he said. 'One was the palace', nodding at the notorious image of him, framed on the wall, holding his rifle aloft in victory in 1978 as he boarded the C-130 at Managua airport. 'Another was to clean the Río San Juan', a reference to a huge environmental controversy over his role in dredging the river in 2010. Although the river belongs to Nicaragua, in 2009 the International Court of Justice in The Hague ruled Costa Rica could navigate it. Environmentalists feared dredging the Río San Juan would stem the flow of freshwater into the Barra del Colorado national reserve on the Costa Rican side of the border. Eventually the operation sparked a border conflict between the neighbours after Pastora was accused of violating Costa Rican sovereignty by allegedly relying on Google Maps to determine the site of the dredging. Interpol received an international arrest warrant from Costa Rica for his capture which, had he stepped out of Ortega's sphere of protection inside Nicaragua's borders, they could have enacted at any time.

'The last is to retire on a boat and sail the world. To feel free in the only place where I feel free, which is at sea. But Daniel won't let me! He says I have to stay here with him.'

Yet 'Daniel' only wanted 'Cero' back by his side after his return to office in 2007. Before then, the two men fell out spectacularly. After *Operación Chanchera*, Edén Pastora was considered, if not exactly a national hero, at least a potent symbol of anti-Somoza sentiment. After the Sandinistas took power, he was appointed vice-minister at the Interior Ministry, under FSLN co-founder Tomás Borge, and head of the armed Sandinista militias. He was not, however, part of the military junta that ran the country.

It didn't take long before he broke with the Sandinistas altogether. By 1981 he had resigned his government positions and went into exile, first in Panama and later Costa Rica. Then came the events which seem so incongruous with his daring feats in the name of the FSLN, but perhaps in keeping with Pastora as a man of inherent contradiction and paradox. From 1982, he formed a splinter group, the Democratic Revolutionary Alliance (ARDE) which fought alongside the right-wing 'Contras' to force out Ortega and the Sandinista government, accusing them of betraying the spirit of the revolution.[21]

Ignoring for a moment the incredible brutality and extraordinary bloodshed of that conflict during the 1980s, Pastora's period as an ally of the Contras brought him into an unholy union with the very forces he'd fought so hard to defeat a decade earlier: former National Guard members with financing and training from the CIA. When I met him, he was dismissive of such Cold War inconsistencies, simply saying 'the cause I have embraced my whole life [is] the revolutionary Sandinista cause in benefit of my people'.

It takes some deft, or deliberately obtuse, ideological reasoning to explain away his time fighting alongside the Contras as an example of the true depth of his Sandinista credentials. Still, Edén Pastora was welcomed back into the Ortega fold in the twenty-first century. And, just as a born-again Christian is often more committed and evangelical than those born into the church, so it is with reformed Sandinistas:

> If Daniel is a dictator, it's because he dictates that we build hospitals, he dictates that we build schools, he dictates that we build roads, ports, airports and social programmes. So, yes, in that sense, he is a dictator, one who's giving orders to pull us from poverty and misery.

★

Comandante Dos, Dora María Téllez, is the diametric opposite of Edén Pastora. As courageous as any in the Sandinista ranks, she was just twenty-two when she played an instrumental role in the assault on the National Palace. Even her estranged former commander grudgingly admitted 'Dora María was a good fighter' before launching into a tirade against her, including the spurious accusation that she is motivated by 'bank accounts and dollars'.

It is hardly a surprise the two former comrades no longer saw eye to eye. Their lives had diverged completely since Téllez fought under Pastora in the Southern Front. She later led the battle for the city of León and was probably the best known of the women Sandinistas. Given Pastora's innate chauvinism and thirst for the limelight, that may well have contributed to their mutual dislike. But it's on their judgements of Daniel Ortega that the two were furthest apart.

I dialled up the Skype address I'd been provided with at the agreed time. As the camera adjusted and the image sharpened, Dora María came into view, sitting, as I imagined she would be, against a nondescript brick background in an undisclosed location. Her cropped hair is now grey and she wears rimless glasses, but otherwise she looks much the same as she does in the photographs of her as a young guerrilla. The green fatigues, black beret and red and black armbands may be gone, but none of the intensity. Her answers are measured and calm, but it is clear she is bristling with anger over the state of Ortega's Nicaragua.

Previously she would give interviews to journalists inside her home in Managua, her piercing, inquisitive eyes no doubt even more searching in person. But she tells me she has decided to return to life in a clandestine safe house for her own protection. Whatever her critics say about her, Téllez is someone who knows how to survive while openly opposing an autocratic ruler, and in late 2018 she deemed it necessary to go into hiding from Daniel Ortega. Violent street protests had erupted in Nicaragua as demonstrations over pension reforms exploded into a nationwide student-led call for Ortega to go. Repression and retribution against the organizers and many participants by pro-government paramilitaries and security forces posed a constant threat. As a high-profile sympathizer of the anti-Ortega protesters, Dora María was a target, too. A friend of hers was taken in and questioned over her whereabouts, then immediately deported. After she went into hiding, the police entered her home and rifled through her possessions, supposedly searching for weapons.

'That gives you an idea of why I can't lead a normal life,' she tells me on the video chat. 'Well, no Nicaraguan can lead a normal life,' she corrects herself.

Dora María left the Sandinistas over Ortega's increasing *caudillismo*. She had served as health minister in the Sandinista government but felt Ortega was not committed to the democratization of Nicaragua and was 'appropriating' the party. In 1995, convinced that there was no changing the FSLN from within, a group broke away to form the Sandinista Renovation Movement, or MRS.

'Unfortunately, we were right,' she says, flatly. 'He created *Orteguismo* and liquidated the Sandinista Front as a party.' There is a 'tyranny' and a cult of personality at the heart of Nicaragua, Téllez argues, and she has no qualms in comparing her former leader to the strongman they deposed: 'Ortega is the successor of the Somoza dynasty. The family of Daniel Ortega and [his wife and vice-president] Rosario Murillo are the successors of the Somoza legacy. The model they have imposed on Nicaragua is exactly the same as the model of the Somoza family in the 1960s and 1970s.'

The result is that the entire country is trapped, she says, looking at me directly down the barrel of the camera. There is 'zero democracy, completely corrupted institutions, a regime which solely remains in place through repression and terror'. She is fearful for the fate of Nicaragua's young people who are being, as she put it, 'sacrificed for the infinite ambition of the Ortega-Murillo family'.

'It's exactly the same as we saw under Somoza and his family.'

Dora María Téllez is an accomplished historian, and in 2005 she was offered a position at Harvard. The Bush administration had recently appointed the Cold War hawk John Negroponte as Director of National Intelligence. The State Department refused to issue her with a visa, choosing still to define her as a terrorist for her role in the National Palace attack. It caused an outcry in the academic community with one renowned sociologist comparing Téllez to the United States' Founding Father: 'Dora Maria is as much a terrorist as George Washington.'[22]

The memory of the assault on the palace in 1978, an operation that bordered on the insane, would stay with these ex-guerrilla leaders for the rest of their lives. Yet the two of them would never be able to sit down together or reminisce as old comrades or sift through fable and fact over a rum, as long as Daniel Ortega remained a Sandinista.

Comandante Cero told me he considered himself 'an old man but still with the spirit of a young one'. Nevertheless, his adventures were at an end. 'Dead, dead, dead, dead,' he said pointing to faces in a framed photograph of the high command of the Southern Front of the FSLN, 'all but two of us are dead.' He didn't know it then but he would be next. His right hand, which once gripped his rifle so firmly, trembled uncontrollably and although he talked a good game, much of his bravado was a façade built up over decades of war and machismo. Instead, he wouldn't fall on the battlefield or die on the open seas. Rather, his was an altogether more mundane exit. In June 2020, after ten days in hospital with 'acute respiratory illness', the indefatigable Edén Pastora breathed his last laboured breath. Given the Sandinistas' tireless defence of Ortega's botched strategy on COVID-19, neither Pastora's family nor the Nicaraguan health authorities were willing to cite coronavirus as the reason for his death but it was widely believed to be the case.

In any case, Pastora knew long before he died that his dream of sailing the ocean in blissful retirement was never going to happen. In theory, at least, he would have been arrested the moment he left Nicaraguan waters. Undiluted loyalty to Daniel Ortega – to the cult worship of *Orteguismo* rather than the Sandinistas' original values – was in his interests. He wasn't about to rock the only boat he had left.

So, over his final years and months, he stayed resolutely on message, particularly about the young men and women protesters killed in the violent street demonstrations in Nicaragua in 2018. They were 'terrorists'. He spat out the word and refused to see any of the same spirit in them which first inspired him to pick up arms against an authoritarian leader. The student protesters had no cause for complaint, he insisted: 'In ten years there has been peace, progress, freedom. A revolution in liberty and democracy. They had no good reason to try to force out the government.'

As I left, he stopped me on the front porch to explain that when one of the demonstrations came past a year earlier people had started throwing stones at his house – 'attacking my cave,' he said with indignation. His wife had to persuade him to stay indoors because he was ready to 'get a machine gun and mow down those *terroristas hijueputas*', the hothead never far from the surface. He laughed as he retold his story but, given the human rights abuses perpetrated by the state and armed pro-Ortega paramilitary gangs, it wasn't very funny. Comandante Cero saw it differently, saying any abuses were just the inevitable result of warfare and revolutionary struggle:

'The violence of war is pain, it's weeping. There's no saints on that side or on this side.'

As Americans settled down in front of their television sets on 20 June 1979, they probably wouldn't have expected Walter Cronkite to warn them to send their children out of the room. The reason, the veteran newscaster of CBS Evening News explained, was that they were going to see shocking video footage of the execution of an American in Nicaragua. The film showed the brutal murder of Bill Stewart, a reporter with ABC News, by one of Somoza's National Guardsmen. His local interpreter, Juan Francisco Espinoza, had also been killed.

CBS had decided to broadcast the film, said Cronkite, 'because it is an important documentation of the savagery of the Nicaraguan war'.[23]

There followed forty seconds of grainy images which would completely alter US public opinion towards Nicaragua and simultaneously end Washington's support for the Somoza regime. Narrated using audio clips of a phone call with Jim Cefalo, the soundman with the ABC team in Managua, Cefalo described what happened and what the American public was now watching over their TV dinners: the grisly killing of his colleague by the Nicaraguan state.

Bill Stewart had arrived in Managua in late May, as the guerrilla army launched its 'final offensive' against Somoza. The crew had filed stories from across the country, most recently in the university city of León, where they had amassed hours of footage with the Sandinistas. As things in Managua reached a crisis, the ABC team were staying at the Hotel Intercontinental, where most foreign news crews were based, and made regular trips around the capital in a van to gather material. These were the days before twenty-four-hour news channels demanded an interminable churn of output, and the ABC crew would film during the day, edit in the late afternoon and file in time for the early evening newscasts. On this particular story, their driver remembers they had no set task beyond gathering images from the government side, as they were well stocked with material on the Sandinistas.[24]

They drove to the poorer slums in eastern Managua and ended up in the neighbourhood of El Riguero, where the streets were closed off by barricades and skirmishes constantly flared up between National Guardsmen and Sandinista units. That particular morning, the conflict in one area had settled down and they had filmed a sequence with a group of good-natured guardsmen who were relaxed and even played guitar for them on camera.

When they reached another checkpoint a little further on, the young Nicaraguan interpreter, Juan Espinosa, got out to approach the guardsmen. The American reporter, Bill Stewart, got out too and joined Espinosa to request permission to film.

The soundman, Jim Cefalo, remained in the crew's van with the driver, Pablo Tiffer López, and the cameraman, Jack Clark.

It isn't hard to imagine how Stewart and Espinoza must have been feeling as they walked up the road to the barricade. They would have certainly been wary – a journalist as experienced in the field as Stewart would have always been careful – but probably not unduly worried. After all, he had his press card in one hand, issued by President Somoza's office, and a white flag in the other. Yet neither the paperwork nor the universally recognized symbol of truce would save them.

Things moved so fast that the journalists' relative calm must have dissolved into pit-churning fear within seconds. First, Juan Espinoza was taken away by the guards to a point out of the line of sight of the crew in the van. Shots rang out. One of the guardsmen had taken the arbitrary decision that he was a Sandinista and, rather than seek any confirmation or grant him any semblance of legal process, simply eliminated him, there and then on the side of the road. At home, unaware of her husband's fate, Espinoza's wife was eight months pregnant with their second child.

In the van, Jack Clark instinctively pressed record on his camera and trained his lens on Bill Stewart. The guardsman returned to Stewart and ordered him to kneel. He did so, while using his limited Spanish to tell the soldier 'no hablo español. Soy periodista. Soy americano'. The guardsman either didn't care or didn't believe him and told him to lie face down on the asphalt and put his hands behind his head. Stewart slowly complied while continuing to insist he was a journalist, holding out his government-issued credentials. A carefully aimed kick to the ribs by the soldier silenced the newsman.

'He's getting nasty,' murmured Jim Cefalo inside the van, the team's growing concern for their colleagues audible on the videotape. The scene in front of them was playing out almost in slow motion, as it would later that night for millions of viewers on all three news networks – CBS, NBC and, of course, ABC themselves – in homes across the United States. They were horrified yet powerless to stop what happened next. The guardsman stood over Bill Stewart and appeared to say something. Then he put his rifle to the back of the journalist's head and pulled the trigger.

Bill Stewart's body convulsed once and collapsed back onto the tarmac. 'They killed him,' Cefalo gasps, in disbelief. Jack Clark's camera pivots up and blurs. But he had captured the moment on tape.[25]

The American public, the news media and the Carter administration were outraged. The killings were 'an act of barbarism that all civilized people condemn,' said President Carter. 'When [journalists] are made innocent victims of violence and war, all people who cherish the truth and believe in free debate pay a terrible price.'[26]

More than just condemnation for Somoza Debayle, though, those words would be his downfall. Within a month he would be gone, ending a dynastic rule which dated back to the 1930s. President Jimmy Carter had been waving the banner of human rights in his foreign policy for almost three years and the abuses taking place in Somoza's Nicaragua were constantly at odds with his administration's rhetoric.

Somoza had briefly reined in some of the worst excesses of his National Guard, earning him a personal letter of praise from Carter. The US State Department opposed the letter, arguing that a pat on the back from the White House was sending the wrong signal at the wrong time.[27] Although he toned down the compliments in a second draft, the letter was sent. Carter's supporters said the presidential praise was intended to encourage more positive steps, but in Nicaragua Somoza wielded the letter for political ends, waving it at any diplomat or journalist who questioned his rule.

Added to that, there had been $150,000 in the US foreign aid budget in 1979 which went to training National Guard troops, the same troops who had now just murdered an American reporter in front of the entire nation. Needless to say, Carter was done with Somoza. It was hard enough to support him after the assassination of *La Prensa*'s editor, Pedro Joaquín Chamorro. Now it was completely impossible.

The secretary of state, Cyrus Vance, pushed the Organization of American States to urge Somoza to step down – a problematic request given the dictatorial and murderous character of many of the member states at that time. Still, they delivered the resolution Washington had requested, demanding the immediate replacement of the Somoza regime and free elections in Nicaragua.

The diplomatic pressure and loss of Washington's support accelerated events on the ground with the Sandinistas' 'final offensive' closing in on an isolated Somoza. At its end, the war had claimed tens of thousands of lives and Somoza was bombing Nicaraguan cities with airstrikes, causing hundreds of civilian casualties. By mid-July, he had nowhere left to turn and, not one to take his own life, took the only other route out: via the airport in a private jet. On 17 July 1979, he left Nicaragua with coffers and coffins, loading onto the plane as much of the country's treasury as he could steal and the caskets of his father and his brother. He flew to Miami but Carter, profoundly aware of what granting asylum to the deposed dictator would look like, refused him the right to stay.

Furious and embittered, Somoza Debayle ended up in the arms of a like-minded despot, General Alfredo Stroessner in Paraguay, who gave him a lavish residence in Asunción. He thought that '*Somocismo sin Somoza*' would be acceptable to Washington and that he would eventually be allowed to return to Managua, once a sympathetic conservative leader took over. Meanwhile, he waited in Paraguay for the imminent uprising of the Nicaraguan people from 'under the yoke of Communism'.[28] When they understand the true nature of international communism, he was quoted as saying, 'they will be on their knees begging me to return'.[29] In fact, he would never go back. A year later, he was assassinated in Asunción by a team of seven Argentinean leftists allied to the Sandinistas who hit his Mercedes-Benz with a bazooka and riddled it with bullets. Their mission was code-named Operation Reptile. Once he was dead, Carter did then allow Somoza to enter Miami, to be buried by his family.

In exile, he had busied himself with writing his memoirs. The resulting autobiography, *Nicaragua Betrayed*, is an angry, self-aggrandizing rant against Jimmy Carter and a vain attempt to justify four decades of his family's repressive rule. Appallingly written, it's only rendered readable by the insight it offers into the mind of a deluded dictator.

Rather, the final word on that sad, violent chapter in Nicaraguan history is probably best summed up by Bill Stewart in his last lines in front of a camera, delivered at a barricade in Managua moments before his murder, a National Guardsman softly strumming on a guitar behind him: 'It is said that in every society it is the young men who fight old men's wars. And that is especially true here in Nicaragua, for those who are fighting and dying on both sides are very young indeed.'

If those young men – and women – of Nicaragua thought they were going to get any respite from the violence once Somoza was gone, they were mistaken. When the FSLN opened the country's bank accounts, they found them bare. Nicaragua had a foreign debt burden of $1.6 billion, as little as $20 million in the Treasury's reserves and a thoroughly bankrupt economy.

The Sandinistas turned to Washington for help. As co-ordinator of the Junta of the Government of National Reconstruction, Daniel Ortega visited President Carter in the White House in September, standing alongside him in the Rose Garden dressed in his guerrilla fatigues and oversized TV-screen glasses. It made for a lasting image, though no aid would be forthcoming. Sending money to a pro-Marxist, anti-American revolutionary government with a guerrilla leadership trained in Cuba wouldn't have flown at the best of times. In an election year like 1980, there was no chance. Carter was facing defeat at the polls, especially with the Iranian hostage crisis dominating the headlines during his campaign, and in November the actor-turned-politician Ronald Reagan returned the Republican Party to the White House in a landslide.

Over the next eight years, President Reagan became obsessed with Nicaragua. In foreign policy terms, it overshadowed all other concerns and was his most controversial legacy, more than the invasion of Grenada in April 1983 or the bombing of Libya in 1986. That a small, impoverished Central American nation played such an all-consuming role in the Reagan administration eventually compelled the *New York Times* to dub the 1980s 'the Nicaragua Decade'.[30]

The president's fixation with Nicaragua began even before taking office, when he claimed in a radio appearance in 1978 that the Somoza regime had 'never been known as a major violator of human rights'.[31] During his campaign, he made his opposition to the Sandinistas equally apparent: 'there is no question that most of the rebels are Cuban-trained, Cuban-armed and dedicated to creating another communist country in this hemisphere.'[32] There was an immediate frostiness in relations following the change in administration and channels of communication established under Carter instantly dried up. 'There was a complete blackout... there was no way of communicating,' recalls the Sandinista ambassador to Washington, Rita Delia Casco. 'We really got into their guts... it was a very irrational feeling.'[33]

Reagan would wage war on Nicaragua on two fronts: militarily, albeit through covert means rather than American boots on the ground, and economically, by asphyxiating the already crippled Nicaraguan economy.

The economic war shared a certain similarity to the US embargo on Cuba, by that stage two decades old and showing little sign of toppling Castro. Nevertheless, Reagan's advisers urged the same approach in Nicaragua, to try to force out the Sandinista-led junta through increasing the poverty of its people. This was the Heritage Foundation's policy recommendation to Reagan in October 1980 while he was still a presidential candidate:

> Nicaraguan workers continue to have an emotional attachment to the revolutionary movement. This attachment can be expected to weaken as the economy deteriorates... There are some indications of growing broad-based support to take arms to overthrow the Sandinista government, and this support could increase as further problems develop... Economic shortcomings

might provoke at least limited civil unrest by the end of the current harvest season.[34]

Reagan listened. Within two days of entering the Oval Office, he froze all economic aid to Nicaragua. Wheat exports to the country were suspended and credit lines from Washington-based international financial institutions cut off.

Within the year, he had signed National Security Decision Directive 17 (NSDD-17) authorizing the covert training and financing of the Contras, the right-wing anti-Sandinista group made up in large part of former members of the National Guard. Initially, the covert operations were justified under the pretext of arms interdiction, ostensibly to cut off the supply of weapons from the Sandinistas to left-wing guerrillas in El Salvador.[35] At the same time, a number of splinter groups peeled away from the Sandinistas, including Comandante Cero's dissident outfit. While these factions were not ideologically aligned with the Contras, they shared a common goal of removing the FSLN from power.

The result was civil war. Just as the country was getting over the violence which brought about the downfall of Anastasio Somoza Debayle, an equally brutal conflict began with Washington's hand easily traceable in the bloodshed. There are plenty of statistics and descriptions which illustrate the extent of the fighting but *Envio* magazine – a left-wing, pro-Liberation Theology publication put out by the Jesuit Central American University (UCA) in Managua – summarized it succinctly, in September 1985:

> The Reagan administration's aggression against Nicaragua has caused the death of more than 12,000 Nicaraguans on both sides, has wounded or disabled many thousands more, and has left 6,000 children orphaned. It has meant destruction and economic losses that are enormous for a small country already devastated by underdevelopment and the ravages of the Somozas, which had barely begun on the road to reconstruction when the aggression started.[36]

By the end of the conflict that number of dead would rise to more than 30,000 and the wounded, disabled and orphaned too numerous to properly quantify. The Contras were guilty of atrocities and war crimes including widespread rape, torture and even public executions, including the throat-slitting of nurses, labour union leaders and provincial Sandinistas. The Associated Press published the contents of a CIA manual distributed to the rebels, called *Psychological Operations in Guerrilla Warfare* which showed the Contras had received instruction in how to 'neutralize carefully selected and planned targets' like judges, police and local officials.[37] It seemed clear that, when carrying out their appalling acts, many Contras did so with a US-penned handbook in their pockets doling out lessons on how to crush the enemy without mercy.[38] This was a war obsessively waged by President Ronald Reagan, who was determined to force the Nicaraguans to 'cry uncle'.[39]

In the middle of it all, Nicaragua tried to hold elections. During its five-year existence, the Junta of the Government of National Reconstruction had carried out social programmes which had boosted the FSLN's popularity in the years before the vote and many Nicaraguans were still thankful for the way they had despatched Somoza. In particular, a literacy programme, the 'National Literacy Crusade', had been enacted which reduced illiteracy rates by around 40 per cent. With echoes of the successful campaign in Cuba, brigades of young people travelled to rural regions to teach people in the villages to read and write. The programme was applauded internationally – except by Washington – and recognized by UNESCO. The Junta was led by Daniel Ortega and dominated by the Sandinistas, whose six members were the most influential, though there were representatives from a range of socialist and opposition parties as well as the autonomous university and the clergy.

In the face of Washington's hostility, Ortega increasingly turned to and was fêted by the Soviet Union and Cuba. The Sandinista Popular Army replaced the National Guard and was trained and supported by their communist allies. The more Reagan pushed for Ortega's removal, the more Moscow and Havana pushed back, turning Nicaragua into the Central American locus of the Cold War.

For his defiance to US hegemony, Daniel Ortega was fast becoming the darling of the international left, who saw him as a modern-day Sandino standing up to Washington's might. President Reagan and his supporters, meanwhile, saw him as the embodiment of the communist threat in the hemisphere, second only to Fidel Castro.

Ortega's oratory was never quite as polished as Fidel's but what it lacked in finesse it more than made up for in grit. He had an earthiness that Nicaraguans responded to, epitomized in the opening speech of his candidacy for president, in front of the Sandinista Assembly in 1984.

In the first free elections in Nicaragua's history, which only the Sandinista Revolution has made possible, [the] people will reiterate on 4th November 1984 the vote for a revolution that they cast every day in the factories, trade unions, cooperatives, neighbourhoods, shops, classrooms, in the building of the new Nicaragua.

The people will vote for their programme, their plan of struggle.

The people will vote for their conquests and gains in the revolution.

The people will vote massively for the Sandinista Front.[40]

He was right. The main conservative opposition candidate, Arturo Cruz Senior – who later admitted to having been on the CIA's payroll – boycotted the vote.[41] It was a strategic error. To expect the electorate to stay away from the polls or agree with Reagan's dim view of Ortega was a huge misreading of his popularity. Rather than being concerned by his authoritarian streak, a majority welcomed his image of strong leadership amid a violent guerrilla war and he was elected by a huge margin. With a turnout of around 75 per cent, Daniel Ortega gained a little over two-thirds of the votes cast.

The people had finally granted him the presidency of Nicaragua. It was the power that, despite his denials, he had always sought – even if Washington didn't recognize his victory. International election observers from the European Union, Canada and the Catholic Church vouched for the validity of the vote, deeming it free and fair. President Reagan called it a 'Soviet-style sham election'.[42] By the time Ortega was sworn in, the White House was losing the propaganda war on Nicaragua, with much of the press and the international community unconvinced by Reagan's characterization of the Sandinistas as the epitome of all evil and the violent Contras as 'the moral equal of our Founding Fathers'.[43]

Running out of democratic options, the Reagan administration started to ramp up the covert and illegal measures. In February 1984, a special CIA unit started to mine Nicaraguan ports at El Bluff, Corinto and Puerto Sandino. Vessels from at least six different nations were damaged in the operations prompting an international outcry. Even close allies like Great Britain, where Margaret Thatcher was prime minister, criticized the mining of Nicaraguan harbours as a 'threat to the principle of freedom of navigation'.[44]

In Washington, too, the House and Senate railed at the move. The CIA had failed to properly alert the Senate Intelligence Committee of its plans and the Oval Office was coming under mounting pressure to stop dragging the United States into an increasingly ugly and intractable war. The mining of the harbours would be held up by Reagan's critics in Congress as a reason to halt CIA funding for the Contras.[45] That year, Congress voted to ban any further funding to the rebels in a huge blow to the Reagan administration's desire to remove the Sandinistas by force.

On 12 September 1985, Nicaragua took the United States to the International Court of Justice at The Hague. By then, Ortega's government estimated the mining of the ports had cost them around $10 million in sunk fishing boats and damage to foreign ships.[46] However, the real damage from the Contra war was to the country's production capacity: 'the total loss over this half decade has been equal to approximately one year's worth of exports, half of that in 1984 alone.'[47] Add to that the loss of loans and development projects blocked by Washington, and Ortega had a strong case at The Hague.

So strong, in fact, that he won. The ICJ found in Nicaragua's favour and concluded that the United States was 'in breach of its obligation under customary international law not to intervene in the affairs of another state' and 'not to use force against another state'. Crucially, by the distribution of a CIA manual to the Contras, the US had encouraged 'acts contrary to general principles of humanitarian law' although the court didn't find the United States culpable for the acts themselves.

The US defence was to simply not recognize the court's jurisdiction and it has refused to pay the reparations due to Nicaragua ever since. In the United Nations, it has successfully vetoed any subsequent efforts to make it comply with the findings.

Ordered to cease funding the Contras at home, humiliated at The Hague, Ronald Reagan probably should have left it there. But his obsession with the Sandinistas was not spent, and he was about to enter the most controversial and illegal phase of his conflict with Ortega: the Iran-Contra affair.

It would almost undo his presidency.

The report of the congressional committees investigating the Iran-Contra affair in November 1987 defined it as follows: 'Iran and Nicaragua – twin thorns of US foreign policy in the 1980s – were linked in a credibility crisis that raised serious questions about the adherence of the Administration to the Constitutional processes of Government.'[48]

With more than thirty years' hindsight, it does now seem almost unbelievable that President Reagan would risk everything by circumventing Congress. He had been told by the House in the clearest terms that he must stop the CIA backing for the Contras and that no further funds would be made available for the right-wing paramilitary groups he tried so hard to paint as 'freedom fighters' and 'Christian guerrillas'.[49] To then tie the fate of that conflict – and his own legacy – to the other complex and entrenched issue of his presidency, the holding of American hostages in Iran, was rash in the extreme. Some argued it was nothing short of criminal.

In the words of the committee's investigation:

> The United States had sold arms to Iran and had hoped thereby to gain the release of American hostages in Lebanon. However, even though the Iranians received the arms, just as many Americans remained hostage as before. Three had been freed, but three more had been taken during the period of the sales.[50]

That the administration even had dealings with the government of Ayatollah Khomeini over the hostages was already at odds with the president's supposedly most firmly held beliefs, let alone the fact that he had sold them weapons in breach of an arms embargo. Yet it was the next revelation, the link to the conflict in Nicaragua, that took away the breath of many in Washington at the time. The attorney general confirmed that the funds from those sales had been 'diverted' to the Contras, in flagrant disregard of the congressional decision to end military aid to the group.

The scandal went to the top of the administration with President Reagan implicated but ultimately never proven to have had full knowledge of the plan. Both the congressional committee and the Tower Commission, ordered by him, absolved him but the congressional report contained this damning assessment: 'The ultimate responsibility for the events in the Iran-Contra Affair must rest with the President. If the President did not know what his National Security Advisers were doing, he should have.'[51]

Still, the scandal went high enough, even without the president's head rolling. Among those convicted were the secretary of defense, Casper Weinberger, for perjury and obstruction and the national security adviser, Robert McFarlane, for withholding evidence. He later attempted suicide over the affair. Both were later pardoned by

George H. W. Bush in the final days of his presidency, as was then assistant secretary of state, Elliott Abrams, who subsequently had his career resurrected by the Trump administration when he was given responsibility for its policy towards Venezuela.

Lastly, there was the man who was seen as the Reagan administration's fall guy, Lt-Col. Oliver North. His televised testimony provided the iconic image of the scandal as he stood before the joint-congressional committee, dressed in a pristine uniform, his right hand raised as he was sworn in for the hearings. But North was no lamb to the slaughter. He was unrepentant, openly admitting to having misled Congress and describing the plan to funnel Iranian funds to Nicaraguan paramilitaries as 'a neat idea'.[52] Conservatives loved him for it and saw him as an American hero. Critics of the conflict, though, considered North to be the shining example of all that was wrong with Reagan's policy on Nicaragua. He was indicted on sixteen felony counts for, among other things, shredding huge numbers of documents. His jail time was suspended and all his convictions were gradually dropped or reversed in the early 1990s. He went on to make a comfortable living, first as a commentator on Fox News and later as president of the National Rifle Association.

What of Daniel Ortega in all this? In November 1987, he made his second trip to Washington for a meeting of the Organization of American States.

'I have always been willing to have a dialogue with the President of the United States,' he told the National Press Club, remarking on the difference in the reception he received on his first visit, when Carter hosted him in the White House, and the hostility of the second under Reagan. 'But the President of the United States is not willing to have a dialogue with me.'[53] Ortega's pitch of inherent reasonableness, dressed in jacket and tie rather than olive-green fatigues, to the assembled editors of the most important US media outlets was very canny.

'I'm appealing for the President to keep his word [in favour of negotiation] and to be responsible, to follow through on his word. This is a good opportunity for us to meet here in Washington. I imagine he's here and not at his ranch in California,' he joked.[54] The Sandinistas are not allied to the Kremlin, he insisted, our only ideological commitment is to the people of Nicaragua and to the Non-Aligned Movement. The Soviet Union respected the Nicaraguan position and Moscow's support for the peace process, recently brokered by Costa Rica, wasn't contingent on anything. We would hope the United States gives the same unconditional support, he said.

At that stage, following earlier failed attempts at a lasting peace plan, a deal had been signed in August 1987, overseen by the Costa Rican president Oscar Arias. Ortega felt Reagan gave lip service to wanting the plan to succeed but little more. In the end, the Esquipulas peace plan did provide enough of a basis for other more solid peace agreements in the region, as the years of violent civil war in Central America finally drew to a close. Hundreds of thousands had lost their lives in Central America – an estimated 200,000 dead in Guatemala's conflict alone. The turn of the decade brought the fall of the Berlin Wall, perestroika and the collapse of the Soviet Union, and there was little public appetite in the United States for any further involvement in regional dirty wars. The American public was tired of the presidential obsession that led to 'Iran-Contragate' and, at the dawn of the tech-driven, consumerist 1990s, there seemed little need for more Cold War fighting. The Soviet threat was evaporating. America had won. Even McDonald's had opened a franchise in Moscow's Pushkin Square.

Ronald Reagan had been replaced in the Oval Office by his vice-president, George H. W. Bush. It may have been galling for the outgoing President Reagan to leave Washington for retirement in California with Daniel Ortega still in power in Managua. Before long, though, even the most bitter memory of Daniel Ortega would fade for Reagan, dissolved by the ravages of Alzheimer's disease, the first signs of which some believed were apparent long before he left office. His doctors and his inner circle refuted the suggestion, saying symptoms of the disease did not appear until the early 1990s.

In Managua, Daniel Ortega had held onto power despite the best efforts of the Contra rebels, but he had perhaps underestimated how much damage years of civil war and conflict with Washington had done to his people. Nicaraguans wanted to usher in a new era, too. And what the Reagan administration and the Contras couldn't do with the bullet was about to be achieved by the ballot instead.

Ortega hadn't expected to lose the elections in 1990. Nor had most pollsters, for months ahead of the vote confidently predicting a Sandinista win. Even Jimmy Carter, in town as the chief election observer and at the FSLN's headquarters during the vote count, fully anticipated being the first to congratulate Nicaragua's *enfant terrible* on securing another five-year term. Instead, Ortega's challenger, Violeta Chamorro, widow of the slain journalist Pedro Joaquín Chamorro, became the first elected woman president in the Americas.

The factors which led to Daniel Ortega's unforeseen loss were at once intricate and simple. The simple answer was exhaustion. Nicaraguans were worn out after so many years of continuous war. In the tireless battle against Somoza's regime and later against those trying to bring down the Sandinistas, countryman had been killing countryman, sister murdering sister, for nigh on twenty years without respite.

The world was changing. The Cold War was over. So why, some people asked, did they need a Cold Warrior at the helm? Between 30,000 and 40,000 people had died in the conflict with the Contras and the nation longed for a sustained period of peace.

Violeta Chamorro seemed to personify that promise of a new start. Representing fourteen opposition parties under an umbrella grouping called UNO – the National Opposition Union – she was a powerful symbol of national unity. As a widow, she knew what it was to lose a loved one to Nicaragua's political violence. The Chamorro family was split: one of her sons had joined the Contras while two more of her children were active Sandinistas, including the editor of *Barricada*, the official FSLN newspaper.

As a candidate who was against Ortega but also had a personal history of opposition to Somoza, who had supported the revolution but criticized its excesses, Chamorro seemed to encapsulate the sense of unity that voters wanted. Video footage of her on the campaign trail shows her arriving at rallies in a wheelchair, the result of a broken knee. She hobbled to the podium on crutches, dressed in a white blouse or white linen skirt, even her wardrobe aiming to convey peace.

'She is a symbol, and that is enough,' one UNO official told the *New York Times*. 'Not of the past, or the present, or even the future. She is a symbol of what might have been.'[55] Her speeches implored Nicaraguans to seize the moment, to see their plight as part of a wider struggle in which long-downtrodden peoples were rising up, whether against the Soviets or against Augusto Pinochet. The hour, she told them, had arrived:

> Nicaragua must win its freedom once again. All across the world people like you are burying Communism and proclaiming democracy. So set your watches! Set them to the same hour as Poland, as Bulgaria, as Czechoslovakia, as Chile! Because this is the hour of democracy and freedom – this is the hour of the people![56]

Daniel Ortega's slogan, meanwhile, was to promise '*Todo será mejor*', 'Everything will be better'. Rather than inspiring people or instilling them with optimism, for many Nicaraguans it felt like a lament that things could hardly get any worse. As well as the legions of dead brothers, aunts, uncles, sisters and children, the economy had suffered terribly under the strain of sanctions and the high cost of war, and was now among the poorest in Latin America. On a key issue to many voters, military conscription to the army, Ortega had tied himself in knots and refused to rule out the draft. One theory goes that at the last minute, once alone inside the polling stations, plenty of mothers voted against the man who would continue to send their sons to fight, to die or be maimed.

Beyond the collective frustration at living in a perpetual state of war, the more intricate and complex reasons behind Ortega's loss, as always, involved the United States. In his comprehensive work on Daniel Ortega, Kenneth E. Morris argues that there was a link to the fact that the US had invaded Panama in the weeks ahead of the vote in Nicaragua in February 1990, ostensibly to arrest President Manuel Noriega on drug-trafficking charges. He believes the inference to the electorate was clear: vote for the US-backed candidate or Nicaragua could be next. At the very least, he says, they were voting in an atmosphere of intimidation and fear: 'They therefore voted for the presidential candidate who promised reconciliation over the one who was a magnet for more Yankee aggression.'[57]

On 25 February 1990, Violeta Chamorro defeated Daniel Ortega, taking almost 55 per cent of the vote to Ortega's 40 per cent. In the National Assembly non-Sandinista parties took 51 seats to the 39 for the FSLN. After a tense night, when Chamorro didn't claim outright victory but, rather, waited for Ortega to concede, the Sandinista leader finally came in front of the cameras at after six in the morning and accepted that 'a majority' had voted for the UNO.

At Chamorro's inauguration in a baseball stadium in central Managua, Daniel Ortega handed over the presidential sash, and the two briefly embraced. It was the first peaceful transition of power from one elected president to another in Nicaragua's history. In her first act, Chamorro immediately cancelled the unpopular military draft but had made an important concession to the Sandinistas, agreeing to keep on Daniel Ortega's brother, General Humberto Ortega, as the head of the army – much to Washington's chagrin. As her motorcade left the stadium her open-top car was pelted with water bombs by a Sandinista section of the crowd, the dousing a reminder that the road ahead was going to be fraught with difficulty.

US vice-president Dan Quayle was in the audience and later met Chamorro to inform her that President Bush was signing a formal determination that Nicaragua was no longer a Marxist-Leninist country, immediately removing sanctions and restoring its sugar export quota. They would also start to send aid payments, long denied to the Sandinistas, in the form of $2.5 million in medical relief.[58] She would need that and much more from Washington as she inherited a broken economy, hyperinflation and a guerrilla army dragging its heels over laying down its arms. To cushion their electoral loss, a number of top Sandinista *comandantes* took over cattle farms, land, luxurious homes and vehicles that had belonged to the state in an ugly kind of corrupt fire sale before leaving office, known as 'the *piñata*'.

Politically, Daniel Ortega took a moment to lick his wounds. When push came to shove in 1990, he had arguably demonstrated his democratic credentials by handing over power, if not exactly willingly, at least reasonably graciously. He did, though, strike an ambiguous note about now 'governing from below'.[59] On the face of it, it could have been a reference to returning to grassroots politics but others saw a more ominous meaning: the threat of constant meddling in the fragile peace and of making Nicaragua as ungovernable as possible for Chamorro.[60] Of his successor, he merely said: 'She has shown her will and her strength. Now that will and strength will be put to the test.'[61]

Still, the moment had marked him. Some believe the 'devastating loss has shaped Ortega's political and electoral strategies ever since'.[62] Certainly, it would inform his future plans and profoundly influence his thinking from then on. Ortega learned plenty by being kicked out of office – especially on how to avoid it happening again.

Zoilamerica couldn't sleep. She had developed a peculiar way of holding herself in bed, her hands thrust between her legs, cupping her genitals. Even four decades later, when she was in her fifties, she would awaken to find her body had assumed that unnatural position, to protect itself. It had been ingrained into her over the years starting, she says, a little before her tenth birthday. She was protecting herself from her stepfather, Daniel Ortega.

Ortega had entered her life in a safe house in Costa Rica sometime around 1977. By that stage, Zoilamerica Narvaez Murillo had already lived an itinerant existence. Her mother, Rosario Murillo – a poet and maternal grand-niece of Augusto Sandino – had been a secretary for Pedro Joaquín Chamorro at *La Prensa*. A radical, fiercely intelligent and unconventional woman who had lost a son in the earthquake of '72, she had spent time in prison for her pro-guerrilla political activities in 1976. On her release, she opted to abandon Nicaragua altogether as the war entered its final phase and moved her young family from Panama to Venezuela and finally Costa Rica.

When Daniel Ortega met them following his months in Cuba, Zoilamerica was unimpressed and dismissive of him.[63] She remembers him as just 'another boyfriend in my mother's life', saying she and her two brothers didn't grasp the full significance of what their mother's new man would mean for them, especially for her.[64]

Initially, it meant more months in hiding. Ortega, Murillo and the children moved to a safe house for the family only. It was there, in the quiet of that secret location, that Zoilamerica says Daniel Ortega began to molest her. The abuse allegedly began when he slipped into her bedroom one night, and began to touch his stepdaughter, who was not yet ten years old. Their isolation meant that no one saw him, and no one stopped him. Crucially, it also meant no one could independently verify her claims.

She says the 'stealth' in which they lived, using false identities and invented back stories, was advantageous to Ortega. A little girl who already told people she was Guatemalan to protect her mother and stepfather and hide their whereabouts from their enemies was predisposed to keeping secrets. Or, as she puts it, she was living 'in a world of silence, absolutely enclosed... [with] the owner of my life, a slavery that went on for a long time'.[65]

She says it got worse when they moved back to Nicaragua and, once Zoilamerica reached puberty, the abuse went from touching and molestation to rape. It was accompanied by psychological manipulation from her adoptive father, imbuing her with a paralysing sense of guilt and shame which she says prevented her from ever telling her mother.[66] Yet Zoilamerica remembers one night when she heard Murillo confronting Ortega furiously, suggesting her mother was aware that something was happening.

Today Zoilamerica lives in exile in Costa Rica once more, banished from Ortega's Nicaragua after publicly accusing him of rape. In her modest apartment, she delivers her memories of that time in a clear voice, with no hint of equivocation or hesitation on the tougher questions or the more uncomfortable descriptions. It isn't an easy testimony to listen to. A friend of mine, as a young paralegal, processed dozens and dozens of pages of her original statement when she first raised the allegations against Daniel Ortega in March 1998. He has never forgotten many of the details and was left in no doubt as to their authenticity.

Daniel Ortega, on the other hand, expressed his 'indignation'[67] and accused Zoilamerica of lying and manufacturing 'a real conspiracy' against him.[68] He rarely spoke in public of the allegations, except to deny them outright, then leaving it to his proxies and supporters to protest his innocence throughout the very damaging scandal. Ultimately the case against him never went forward, not because he managed to successfully disprove it but because he enjoyed parliamentary immunity. Ever since, his supporters have never held back on Zoilamerica, accusing her of everything from being a CIA agent to a nymphomaniac.

That was to be expected, perhaps. What hurt and surprised Zoilamerica most was the reaction of her mother. Not once did Rosario Murillo come to her daughter's defence. In fact, she essentially disowned her. Murillo added her own voice to those besmirching Zoilamerica's reputation by describing her as 'brainwashed'[69] and an 'ungrateful child'.[70] The rest of the family, including her younger brothers, turned against her, too, and formed a ring of steel around Daniel Ortega. But the number of trusted individuals within that inner circle was much reduced following the sexual abuse scandal. It would shrink even further in the years to come.

In late 2005, Rosario Murillo and Daniel Ortega married, having been together for three decades. By then, he had spent sixteen years in opposition and unsuccessfully stood for the presidency at each election since he'd been voted out of power in 1990. He was comprehensively beaten in 1996 and 2001.

However, in 2006 there was a different wind blowing through Latin America, one being fanned by Hugo Chávez in Venezuela. It would help relegitimize the FSLN leader following his stepdaughter's allegations of abuse. The accusations had caught him off guard and arguably still cost him the election in 2001. Yet they wouldn't harm his political career in the long term and once that wind from Caracas was in his sails, nothing would stop Daniel Ortega and Rosario Murillo from governing Nicaragua in their own image for many years.

Sandor Dolmus knew from a very young age that he wanted to be a priest. He found peace in the ritual and reverence of the church that he couldn't find anywhere else in his life. He admired his diocesan priest, Monseñor César Bosco Vivas, a focal point for the community in León, the city in northwestern Nicaragua where he lived.

Even in as Catholic a nation as Nicaragua, Sandor stood out for his religiosity. Unlike his friends, his heroes weren't Ronaldo or Messi but Pope Francis, the first Latin American pontiff, or Monseñor Oscar Romero, the martyred Archbishop of El Salvador canonized in 2018.

Still just fifteen, he was then too young to join the seminary, although he had the backing of the church to enter the priesthood in a few years. For the time being, he made do with being an altar boy at the cathedral.

He would never wear the priest's cassock, however. The sun was barely up when he was killed. At six in the morning on 14 June 2018, Sandor was standing at a barricade set up just metres from his house with a group of neighbours and other young people.

Suddenly, the air filled with the crack of gunfire and the protesters at the barricades scattered, diving for shelter. Sandor was hit in the chest and slumped to the ground. He had been shot by a high-velocity rifle fired by someone in a group of pro-Ortega paramilitaries who had that morning spread out from the FSLN headquarters in the town. He was dead within seconds. His last Facebook post, written that morning, read: 'Lord Jesus I put in your hands your country, Nicaragua, especially León, do not abandon us. Send us peace. I have never heard of you abandoning anyone, help your León, help us to overcome evil.'

The funeral the following day was harrowing in the extreme. The other altar boys at the cathedral, tears streaming down their cheeks, carried his casket out of the church and loaded it into the hearse.

At the graveside his mother, Ivania Dolmus, was overwhelmed with grief, letting out low, guttural heaves and almost throwing herself into the grave with her only child.

A year later, I met Ivania near the spot her son was killed. Now more composed but in no less pain, she recounted how he died in an even, enraged voice. She was still amazed at how easily he could be murdered with no one on the government's side having to answer for opening fire on unarmed teenagers. 'It's been a year and we have never seen any justice. Nor are we getting our hopes up because as it was the police themselves who killed him, they will never investigate who did it,' she says.

He may have been an only child, but Sandor didn't lack company at home. The tumbledown house was split between different branches of the family. One aunt and her kids in one bedroom, another relative and their children in the next and so on. Out back, in a cramped patio, a dog chained to a wall barked at anyone who walked past, and scrawny chickens clawed at their wire cages. Sandor's grandmother was cooking tortillas over firewood, the smoke filling the open space and coating soot an inch thick on the walls and ceiling of the only shared bathroom.

As I sat and chatted to Ivania, it was clear she had channelled her grief into activism. Hundreds were killed in that violent summer of 2018 and she held one man responsible: 'President Ortega. If not with him, then who? The police and paramilitaries just follow orders from above. He is the only one responsible – him and his wife.'

Gradually more women arrived, other members of the 'Mothers of April Association', a group set up by Ivania and named after the month in which the government's repression began. The association works alongside the Organization of American States with mothers whose children were killed at the barricades. The women show me photos of their dead sons, one mother keeping on her phone the picture of him face down in the street in a pool of blood as a reminder of what they did to him. Should she ever find herself tiring or letting up in her search for justice, she would look at the shocking image to remind herself to keep fighting.

On the first anniversary of Sandor's killing, a mass was held in the cathedral in León where he had served as an altar boy and where Nicaragua's beloved national poet, Rubén Darío, is buried beneath the chapel. During the service, a group of pro-Sandinista militants turned up in the plaza outside, playing pro-Ortega anthems on loudspeakers to drown out the mass inside. It was an act of real ugliness, a moment in which the country's radical politics meant that even a fifteen-year-old boy couldn't be remembered in dignity and peace.

How had Daniel Ortega reached this point? Not two decades on from his humiliating defeat at the hands of Violeta Chamorro, here he was, in his third consecutive term as president – his fourth overall – with his men prepared to open fire on schoolkids and then intimidate their families at the funerals and memorial masses to maintain his grip on power. The answer as to how he became responsible for such repression involves his metamorphosis from guerrilla to politician, from wearing military fatigues to white collarless shirts. And, ironically enough, his supposed conversion to the church.

During his time in opposition, Ortega underwent a certain degree of soul-searching, as did the Sandinistas as a political movement. After 1990, schisms started to appear in the FSLN, and before long Dora María Téllez left to form her 'Sandinista Renovation Movement'. Others followed her lead.

'He had managed to gain complete control over the party's machinery,' Téllez explained, speaking to me from her hiding place. 'Even though some of us were part of the leadership, we decided to leave in 1995. The Sandinista Front had taken a path of no return, one which had the footprint of *caudillismo* left by Ortega.'

Ortega made three attempts at the presidency before taking it back in 2006. In each case, his portion of the vote stayed broadly the same, securing around 40 per cent. He was the second-placed candidate in the 1990, 1996 and 2001 presidential elections, losing by between 13 and 14 per cent on every occasion.[71] Things had to change for 2006 and he – and Rosario Murillo – made sure they did.

First came his new outfits. He quickly shed the military apparel, and even the thick-rimmed glasses, to convince the people he was a changed man. In the 1996 election, his opponent, Arnoldo Alemán, used archive footage of him dressed in full combat gear in his campaign ads, with no additional commentary, to imply that the same unreformed radical lurked beneath the new clothes. The tagline at the end of each commercial just read: 'Remember the past.'[72] Ortega's choice of white collarless shirts was supposed to evoke a kind of Pentecostal evangelist, asking the people for forgiveness, especially in the more remote communities.[73]

His makeover extended to more than just his wardrobe. His transformation over that time saw him jettison the hard-edged anti-imperialist rhetoric and adopt a softer, more business-friendly tone. The signature red and black of the Sandinista flag was replaced with campaign posters in soothing pastel shades of pink, yellow and sky blue. Even the campaign song was a Spanish-language version of John Lennon's 'Give Peace a Chance'.

Still, his success in 2006 was not down to the clothes he wore, or which song played when he walked on stage, but, rather, thanks to a cynical political pact and to apparently finding God.

Ortega had been an avowed enemy of the man who beat him in 1996, President Arnoldo Alemán. When he lost, Ortega cried fraud and refused to accept the result, and the insults the two men had thrown at each other during the campaign bordered on the violent.

Alemán accused Ortega of being a 'bloodthirsty Communist tyrant guilty of genocide' while Ortega said that Alemán 'was worse than Somoza and should be dealt with only by force'.[74] Yet within a couple of years, they changed their tune entirely. Ortega was calling the Alemán administration 'very democratic' and Alemán praised Ortega as a great leader.[75]

The two men had realized a non-aggression agreement was in their mutual interest. From the middle of 1998, they began to hold a 'political dialogue' to put together what they called a 'governability accord', a plan to redraft the constitution and amend electoral law.

It was a stitch-up, an agreement intended to carve up power between them – the ruling Liberal Constitutional Party (PLC), under Arnoldo Alemán, and the FSLN, the main opposition party in Congress, under Daniel Ortega.

Under the 'Alemán–Ortega Pact', or simply 'The Pact' as it became known in Nicaragua, both men achieved what they were looking for. Alemán wanted former presidents to be automatically made deputies in the National Assembly, thereby granting himself the opportunity to become head of that institution. In return, Ortega got the election rules changed, specifically regarding what it takes to win a presidential election. The bar for victory was lowered from 45 per cent of the popular vote to 40 but with the crucial caveat that 35 per cent would be enough provided the candidate had a 5 per cent lead over their nearest challenger. For a man whose share of the vote had hovered between 38 and 42 per cent, it was a vital step towards securing the presidency.

Other moves included creating new positions on the Supreme Court to which they could appoint their allies. Between the two parties, they controlled 90 per cent of the popular vote, so few voices with any real weight were able to prevent the grubby backroom deal from becoming reality.[76] It is no exaggeration to say that, since it was reached in 2000, 'The Pact' has been the determining factor in Nicaragua's twenty-first-century politics and set out a path to authoritarianism that Daniel Ortega gleefully embarked upon.

Yet the plan didn't initially work for either man. Perhaps still tainted by his radical past and by Zoilamerica's accusations of sexual assault, Ortega lost in November 2001 to Enrique Bolaños, who had been Alemán's vice-president. The outgoing president was facing a slew of corruption charges, his administration tainted by widespread graft and self-enrichment.[77] His successor wasn't going to be tarred with the same brush so Bolaños gave the green light for the corruption cases against his former boss to go ahead. Alemán was sentenced to twenty years for embezzlement and money laundering, and served a few years mainly under house arrest, before Ortega took power and the Supreme Court overturned the decision.

It wasn't until the 2006 election, then, before Daniel Ortega finally had all his ducks in a row. Not only did he need to win by a smaller margin, but the PLC's divisions over corruption in the Alemán administration split their vote. It was also in this campaign that Ortega fully embraced the church and adopted the role of the devout and repentant sinner.

'Jesus Christ is my hero now,' he said, courting Nicaragua's faithful. He honed a persona of televangelist rather than leftist guerrilla, taking his lead from Hugo Chávez's astute ability to marry socialism and Christianity in the same package.[78] He and Rosario Murillo married in a church ceremony in late 2005, lest their common law arrangement alienate the Catholic vote. After a ceremony officiated by Cardinal Obando y Bravo, the former archbishop of Managua and previously Ortega's 'arch-enemy', now they could claim the Ortega–Murillo union was duly blessed in the eyes of the God and respectful of the holy institution of marriage.

His devotion and that of Rosario Murillo is dubious at best. The Nicaraguan poet, writer and former Sandinista Gioconda Belli believes it's all a cynical act, indicative of his obsession with power: 'The FSLN in its desire to win once again insults religion. If before it denied God, now it abuses Him for political ends. Both approaches are equally profane, equally manipulative.'[79]

Their conversion began with traditional religion, she says, by befriending Cardinal Obano y Bravo and garnering the vital Catholic vote in Nicaragua. As the years passed, they have increasingly nurtured the non-traditional Protestant churches – Evangelicals, Pentecostals, Baptists and Seventh-day Adventists – to keep pace with their recruitment boom in the region.[80]

If it is an act, it's one they have kept up now for some years. Amid the violence of 2018, Ortega and Murillo received a bible dedicated and signed by a once-notorious US Pentecostal televangelist Jimmy Swaggart, and hand-delivered by another, Dan Burritt, of Dan Burritt Ministries. In the video of the moment, Ortega speaks to the camera of the book being 'a divine gift, a gift of salvation' and of making 'a promise of transformation in Christ'. Murillo looks over his shoulder, murmuring and nodding her approval, her eyes wide and credulous with devotion. It is the earnest look of having been 'saved' worn in church by millions of born-again believers in the Americas. 'They are experts at wearing masks,' retorts Gioconda Belli.

Fictitious or otherwise, his conversion worked. Ortega won in 2006 with no larger percentage of the vote than he had in the past. But under the new rules, he was again the president of Nicaragua. A last-minute intervention, more strategic than divine, undoubtedly helped him. Cardinal Obando y Bravo gave a sermon days before the vote on 'the prodigal son', which was interpreted as the influential priest's blessing of Ortega's return to power.[81]

As always in Nicaragua's politics, there was a quid pro quo. The Cardinal got something for his timely sermon, namely the backing of President Daniel Ortega and the FSLN in parliament for a draconian new abortion law which banned it in all cases, even where the mother's life is at risk. For a supposed Sandinista, the group who had championed women's rights, especially their reproductive rights, to be backing a ban on therapeutic abortion showed how far Ortega had moved ideologically in pursuit of power. His running mate was Jaime Morales Carazo, a former Contra.

Between 1995 and 1998 the FSLN and Daniel Ortega faced their darkest moments. Splintered and divided into factions, only two of the original FSLN leadership had stayed inside the party. One of them was Ortega, who had lost an election in 1996 and was facing public disgust, possibly jail time, over his stepdaughter's accusations of sexual abuse. Yet within just eight years, displaying a chameleon-like ability to change his colours, he had clawed his way back to being president. Though he had discarded crucial Sandinista ideas and twisted his ideologies to get there, he arrived in office just in time to coincide with the high point of the Latin America left's Pink Tide. And he has stayed there ever since – either by force of will or just by force.

The smoke was toxic and asphyxiating. The rooms were filling up with thick, black plumes, choking Cinthia Velásquez López and forcing her to crawl on her knees towards the door. All around her, the sound of breaking glass and screams from inside the house combined with the noise of gunfire and commotion from outside. She was disorientated and terrified. As best she could with the acrid smoke constricting her throat, she yelled for her father but couldn't find him in the worsening blaze. It had all happened so fast, the family home in flames in minutes.

At a little after six in the morning on 16 June 2018, the Velásquez family was woken by the noise of automatic gunfire. As they peered out of the windows, they could see armed police and radical pro-government paramilitaries in pick-up trucks surrounding their home and shooting at it. The family lived above a small mattress factory they owned in Managua's Carlos Marx neighbourhood. Days earlier, Cinthia's father, a pastor named Oscar Velásquez, was said to have refused to let the pro-Ortega forces place snipers on his roof, a strategic point in their battle against anti-government protesters. This attack was apparently their revenge.

As the assault went on, Oscar huddled his family together in one room and told them to pray, insisting that God would show them a way out. But as they implored Him to save them, the home caught alight and now everything was on fire. The building was filled with flammable materials – cheap sponge mattresses and polyester covers – as well as the fuel tanks of the two cars parked inside. They couldn't reach the front door as bullets and firebombs were still raining down on their home, as Cinthia recounted to me a few months later, her face soaked in tears as she gulped out the words:

When the bombs exploded, the house shook. I counted at least thirty firebombs. The house was shaking, the tiles were falling from the walls. Then, when the whole house was on fire, and there was no way out for anybody, my father hugged us and said 'I'm sorry, I can't get you out. They've attacked us, but may God forgive those who did this to us.'

The family tried to make it upstairs. That's when they lost each other in the heat and confusion.

Cinthia's father, her mother, her brother and his wife and their two children – a girl aged just three and a five-month-old baby boy – never made it out. Cinthia only just managed to escape, following her cousin towards the balcony, locked shut with a padlock, and imploring her teenage sister, Maribel, to do the same. The cousin forced the door open enough for them to squeeze through, the skin on Maribel's arms and shoulders now severely peeled, blistered and cracked.

But their ordeal still wasn't over. As they called out for help from below, they were met with mockery by the masked gunmen, goading them. 'All we could hear were my parents' cries and the children crying. The flames were engulfing them,' Cinthia recalled. The fire brigade arrived, and their neighbours began to appear from their homes, bringing hoses and water in buckets. Cinthia, Maribel and their cousin, Francisco Javier Pavón, managed to jump from the balcony and scramble to safety in a neighbour's home.

There, as neighbours live-streamed on their mobile phones as her home was razed and the children's charred bodies were brought out by the firemen, Cinthia turned to the Internet, too, to decry those who had burned her family alive.

'My family is dead,' she wailed between heaving sobs, almost collapsing with grief. 'The children, my brother, my dad, my mum, they killed them all. I curse Daniel Ortega and all his family and all his people.' The Facebook Live video went viral and, as she had publicly identified the perpetrators, Cinthia went into hiding just hours after the funeral.

When I made contact with her some weeks later, Cinthia agreed to meet me in a safe house where she was being protected by human rights activists. Softly spoken and still raw with grief, it was the first time she had spoken to a journalist about the horrific fire since the day it happened. Over the weeks in hiding, she had remained just as adamant about who was to blame:

'They were paramilitaries. It was the paramilitaries. I saw them. You can see them in the video, in front of the church, the patrols of civilian pick-up trucks and the police. It was the police, too. We saw them.'

The video Cinthia was referring to is CCTV footage from a shop over the road. It shows armed and masked civilian gunmen, supported by the police in patrol vehicles, surrounding the building. Neighbours I spoke to and the testimony of the cousin who also survived the inferno, Francisco Javier, confirmed Cinthia's version of events, that the culprits were pro-government paramilitaries and the police. During the months of repression, in a stunning display of nepotism and self-preservation, Ortega had promoted his son's father-in-law, Francisco Díaz, to chief of the National Police. Shortly after the arson attack, the US State Department brought sanctions against Díaz, as well as the head of the Sandinista Youth wing and the treasurer of the FSLN.

Even for war-hardened Nicaraguans, growing accustomed to tales of heavy-handed repression that summer, the killing of Pastor Velásquez and his family was particularly shocking. A photograph circulated online and in the newspapers of the two children, toddler and baby, dressed in miniature replica Barcelona football kits, their deaths as inexplicable to a dismayed nation as those of their parents and grandparents.

Except to the staunchest Sandinista, or, rather, *Orteguista*. I spoke to plenty, from inside the highest offices of government to the police to the informal armed units accused of carrying out attacks in the name of the Sandinistas. All of them said the same thing: the fire at the mattress shop was caused by the protesters – '*los terroristas*' – and the paramilitaries weren't paramilitaries at all. Rather, they were 'voluntary police', an acceptable part of the state security apparatus.

Official euphemisms aside, I tracked down a group of paramilitaries and managed to persuade them to sit down and be interviewed on camera. In a secret location several hours drive from Managua, I met an armed group of masked men in a dimly lit room on a building site. They ranged in age from the commanders, who were old enough to remember the war against the Contras, to the foot soldiers, some of whom weren't even born when Ortega lost the vote in 1990.

Those who were authorized to speak on camera tore into my description of them as paramilitaries: 'Calling us paramilitaries isn't right – we've never been military. We're volunteer police who acted to clear the streets, but we never shot to kill,' one said through his balaclava. 'We're simply a support force,' added his friend. 'The balaclavas are to hide our identity, to protect our families, our children. If we didn't use them, our families run the risk of being killed.'

Videos showing the informal forces fighting alongside the police in Nicaragua's streets in 2018 included some serious thugs. Yet this group insisted that wasn't a fair description of them at all. 'I come from a peasant family, a family of farmers and agricultural workers. I had no previous knowledge of guns,' one of them claimed.

One thing the gunmen shared with the official security forces was an unflinching belief in Daniel Ortega and his legitimacy as president. Ortega was re-elected in 2011 and then again in 2016 after term limits were scrapped, a move which was widely criticized by the opposition and the church. By then, the Sandinistas' control of the Supreme Court, the National Assembly and the Electoral Council was complete. International observers had been blocked from attending the elections and in 2016 even the main opposition candidate was forced out. The vote was little more than a formality. Ortega garnered more than 70 per cent at the ballot box with the first lady Rosario Murillo as his running mate. His lifelong companion and confidante, his wife and soulmate, was now his vice-president, too.

None of that made the Sandinista militiamen sitting in front of me uncomfortable. They didn't believe for a moment they were defending a *caudillo*, much less a dictatorship. Rather, they saw themselves as defending Nicaraguan democracy:

A dictatorship isn't formed in democracy. All Nicaraguans voted and it was our will that the president be elected. I don't see that because a group of people say 'the President must go' that the president should step down, when he's been elected under the constitution.

When the students first took to the streets and set up barricades, it was ostensibly over social security and pensions reform, but quickly grew into a wider protest over Ortega–Murillo's stranglehold over all aspects of Nicaraguan politics and the economy. There were armed radicals in both camps and at least twenty-two police officers were killed between April and September that year – a figure backed up by the findings of international bodies like the UN's Office of the High Commissioner for Human Rights (OHCHR). But in the vast majority of cases, from the unarmed altar boy, Sandor Dolmus, to the Velásquez family inside their mattress factory, the blame lay with a violent pro-government element working in tandem with the police: formal and informal forces joined by an obdurate loyalty to Ortega.

Before I left the group of hooded paramilitaries, I put it to them that some of their comrades in Managua had carried out the arson attack on Cinthia's family. Unwittingly echoing the words of Comandante Cero, they said the victims should be chalked up as mere casualties of war.

'There was a clash in the street and a Molotov cocktail landed on the house,' said a young voice from behind his facemask. 'No one was sent to attack it, especially not with children inside.'

'It's very nice, that example you use, of the children dying in the mattress factory,' replied his buddy, his voice dripping with sarcasm at this foreign journalist besmirching the good name of the 'volunteer police'. 'But what about our friends, policemen, who were gunned down, who were set alight at the barricades? We have suffered a lot, too, as a party and as human beings.'

When I met Cinthia she was already showing clear signs of post-traumatic stress under the strain of clandestine life. She wasn't like Dora María Téllez or former Sandinista commander Monica Baltodano or any of the other FSLN guerrilla women who'd spent years living on their wits, hiding from the police and evading capture. Rather, she was a pastor's daughter, a worker in a family-run mattress shop, who had lost almost everyone she held dear over a political crisis she never participated in or wanted any part of.

And her younger sister was still alive. Fifteen-year-old Maribel had spent thirty-seven days in a coma and had severe burns all over her shoulders and long angry scars snaking down her arms. Cinthia told me she longed to be with her, but their only remaining family had shunned her for speaking out against Ortega, fearful of what it could mean for them, too. Cinthia was still trapped, suffocating on the black smoke, its foul smell lingering in her nostrils, unable to hold back the tears every time she spoke of her ordeal and unable to ease her torment no matter how often she returned to her father's beloved bible. For her, there was only one way out.

A few months after I spoke to her, Cinthia retracted her statement, first in front of a judge and then in a ghoulish documentary by a pro-Sandinista TV show. The producers took her back to the burned-out shell of the family home and filmed her as she wept bitterly over the children's blackened toys and cribs, all set to mournful music. Beyond distasteful, it was harrowing to watch her say that, no, she had misspoken in her grief and, in fact, the arson attack wasn't carried out by pro-Sandinista gunmen and the police after all. The police weren't even there that day, Cinthia now stated, wringing her hands under the stress. They were 'several blocks away'. Rather, the culprits were a few people from the local neighbourhood, with generic nicknames like 'Skinny' and 'Cat-Face' who had been manning the barricades and had apparently decided to kill her entire family that morning.

Two individuals were swiftly arrested, sentenced and then released a couple of months later as part of an amnesty deal authorized by Ortega. No one is currently being investigated or serving any jail time for the deaths at the mattress shop. From the judiciary to the police to the balaclava-wearing radicals, the fire was perhaps the clearest example of just how far Ortega's supporters were prepared to sink to keep him in power.

The only chink of light in this darkest of episodes in Managua's modern violence was that at least Cinthia had been reunited with her younger sister, seen together in the government's propaganda film, holding hands in the ruins of their gutted family home.

In the moments after retaking the presidency in 2006, Ortega immediately struck a conciliatory tone in front of the cameras, appearing with the second-placed candidate to shake hands in a dignified declaration of victory. Peace was in the interests of the country and the economy:

'Conditions in our country are being built to launch a practical new culture of politics,' he said. 'A culture of politics that will move Nicaraguans to work beyond our diversity and our differences with a constructive will.' It was a utopic picture of Nicaragua in keeping with his new-found Christianity and spiritualism. He also spoke of marrying investment in the financial industry with investment in the social sector, to 'attack poverty and create the jobs Nicaraguans demand'.

The *Pax Nicaragua* worked. In the decade after 2007, Nicaragua grew at one of the highest rates in the region, surpassed only by the shipping and tax-haven economy of Panama. Mining, tourism, financial services and construction were all recipients of a doubling of Foreign Direct Investment from $381 million in 2007 to $835 million in 2015.[82] Between 2010 and 2013, Nicaragua had almost 5 per cent annual growth, higher than in Costa Rica, a far more established and less volatile democracy. GDP per capita also went up from US $1,350 in 2007 to $2,090 in 2015.[83]

Part of this progress was down to timing, his return to office coming on the crest of a wave of high commodity prices being ridden by Hugo Chávez. By 2011, Central Bank figures showed that Chávez had bankrolled his leftist ally to the tune of $1.6 billion over four years – the equivalent of a year's annual budget for the Central American nation.[84] The economy Ortega inherited was still recovering from having been one of the poorest in the Americas for years, its poverty only surpassed by Haiti and Honduras. Now, helped by Chávez's oil-based largesse, the Nicaraguan economy showed some strong signs of recovery under Ortega.

The country's relative stability was important, too. Unlike other Central American nations, especially Honduras and El Salvador, gang crime was not as widespread or as severe. Ortega had buried the hatchet with the business elites and the church in Nicaragua, and the country had become markedly more attractive to foreign investors. Reliable poverty figures are always hard to find in Nicaragua but

Daniel Ortega was able to make an impact there, too, as he had promised on election night in 2006. Hundreds of millions in petro-dollars from Venezuela were earmarked for Sandinista social pro-grammes and, even allowing for corruption and seepage, this made a big impact within a handful of years: life expectancy rose three years to almost seventy-six, enrolment in primary education increased to 94 per cent and unemployment was halved.[85]

Daniel Ortega was in his element, too. Following the sexual abuse scandal involving his own stepdaughter, he might have expected to be shunned at home and abroad for the rest of his political life. But now the 'left-wing swing' in the region was helping him to be reintegrated, even reinvented on the world stage. It certainly boosted his international profile to be part of the Chávez–Lula–Evo nexus. He was closer in age to Hugo Chávez but closer in revolutionary history and anti-imperialist credentials to Fidel Castro. His own story, in defeating Somoza and defying Washington, lent him an aura of notoriety within the Latin American left. He lacked the wisdom to be considered an elder statesman perhaps, but he was certainly a man whose name carried real historical resonance.

The relationship with President Barack Obama was a case in point. At the Summit of the Americas in Trinidad and Tobago in April 2009, President Obama had been in office for a matter of weeks. The summit was his first meeting with regional leaders and the entire spectrum was there, from Chávez and Ortega to less complex rela-tionships like Lula and Michelle Bachelet of Chile. The world's press descended on the Caribbean meeting, excited to see how the more outspoken anti-American leaders would greet him. Chávez, ever the performer, couldn't resist a little sideshow by presenting Obama with a book – *Open Veins of Latin America: Five Centuries of the Pillage of a Continent* by the Uruguayan writer Eduardo Galeano. Published in 1971, *Open Veins* is a classic left-wing work, still very popular on university campuses, which lays out the continent's history through its brutal and exploitative colonial past.[86]

Ortega's approach at that first encounter lacked all of Chávez's humour and charisma. Instead, he embarked on a long, rambling diatribe – a kind of abridged version of *Open Veins* – in which he brought up nineteenth-century grievances, referred to Obama as the 'president of the empire' and cited a long list of Washington's 'terrorist policies' against Nicaragua.[87] Asked later what he thought of Ortega's speech, Obama quipped: 'It was fifty minutes long, that's what I thought.'

Still, as part of his more softly-softly approach to Latin America, President Obama had little reason to pick a fight with Daniel Ortega. There were noises of discontent and 'concern' from the State Department in 2011 when he changed the constitution to allow indefinite re-election, but they were half-hearted at best. By then, it had already happened in Venezuela and was under discussion in Colombia, Bolivia and Ecuador. The White House didn't much like Daniel Ortega but was focused on a bigger regional prize in the latter half of Obama's presidency: re-establishing diplomatic ties with Cuba.

Added to which, the country's economy was doing well. Tourism was growing, foreign investors were prepared to put in their cash and the street-gang problem was being kept at bay. So, too, was illegal immigration to the north, less common by Nicaraguans at that time than their Central American neighbours. A bit of political huffing and puffing from a Cold War blowhard was a small price to pay. Washington was not, it is fair to say, overly concerned about Ronald Reagan's nemesis in the decade before April 2018.

The three defendants were dressed in their navy-blue prison uniforms, which resembled hospital scrubs more than jail outfits. As they listened to the testimony against them, words that could condemn them to decades in prison, they rolled their eyes and whispered to each other, giggling in disbelief. It's not that they weren't taking the proceedings seriously. It's that the proceedings themselves weren't serious.

The young men, Kevin, Marlon and Hansell, were accused of burning down a radio station and were facing terrorism charges for allegedly masterminding the attack. The guards stood around them in a semi-circle, fingering their shotguns and automatic weapons with nonchalant boredom as they listened to the state's witnesses place them at the scene. 'He was carrying a Molotov, judge. I remember that one in the middle', and other such broad, incriminating evidence.

Their lawyer, in a pressed white shirt, blue striped tie and horn-rimmed glasses, was officious in his questioning but appeared incompetent or impotent, or both. There would be nothing that amounted to much of a defence for the three student friends. As the court clerks ushered the press out, one of the three, the supposed leader, Hansell, briefly acknowledged the presence of the international media in the room with a resigned shrug to our television camera. There would be no getting out of this, no legal recourse or meaningful process of appeal. This was Ortega's courtroom, Ortega's judge and Ortega's justice. After several more days of the show trial, they were each sentenced to seventeen and a half years in jail for terrorism and related offences.

Outside the courtroom, their mothers were gathered waiting for word from inside. Family members weren't allowed to enter terrorism trials, they told me. They crowded around my cell phone to see the photos of their children in court, buoyed by the glimpse of their sons' defiant smiles. More than just prohibited from watching proceedings, though, they were banned from giving vital evidence, despite the fact that one of them, Hansell's mother, Liliam Ruiz, swore on all that was good and holy that the boys had been at her place when the radio station was torched.

No matter, the system had them now, another family member said. As we spoke, a dilapidated taxi pulled up and a blind couple got out, led to the courthouse gates by an eleven-year-old boy. Maritza Castellón had represented Nicaragua in blind chess and her husband, Juan Pablo García, was a Paralympic marathon runner. The night before, Maritza explained, armed pro-Ortega paramilitaries had kicked in the back door of their home and dragged off their seventeen-year-old boy, Engel. The hooded men never identified themselves or produced an arrest warrant. In the darkness, they pleaded with the men to leave their son alone until one of them stuck a gun into Maritza's chest and told her to either get out of the way or he'd shoot.

Such stories were shocking. Nicaragua was fast descending into thuggery and the parallels with the military dictatorships in Latin America of the 1970s were obvious: state forces turning up in the dead of night to detain students, no warrant, no due process, no habeas corpus. Human rights violations reminiscent of Somoza himself. Speaking to *Playboy* in November 1987, Daniel Ortega recalled his own political awakening in the face of the abuses of his youth:

> There were so many injustices in our society, and one felt an urgency to do something. The elections were rigged. Somoza controlled the political process; he controlled the economy; he repressed with his National Guard. He controlled everything. You felt it was a crime to be young.[88]

Thirty years later, the irony is lost on no one in Nicaragua. Especially not the congregation at the Church of the Divine Mercy. On 13 July 2019, students squeezed onto the pews alongside well-known opposition figures, jeans and sneakers next to freshly pressed *guayaberas* and airy summer dresses. Most wore white for peace or black for mourning, some held flowers, Nicaraguan flags and placards which read: '*Free the political prisoners!*' and '*Act before they kill them!*'

At the front, two large photographs were held aloft of Gerald Vásquez and Francisco Flores, the two men who a year ago that day had been killed in a hours-long onslaught on the church. At the height of the protests, the state forces and the paramilitaries had cornered dozens of demonstrators inside the church building and were firing on them with automatic weapons. All night, the police refused to budge and the injured young men, unable to receive treatment, bled out in the chaplain's house. It was only the mediation of the Vatican and foreign diplomats at the highest level which brought the violence and the tense stand-off to an end.

A year later, the outer walls of the Church of the Divine Mercy were still pockmarked from that night and, even as people came to celebrate a mass for the dead, a ring of heavily armed police in riot gear formed around the chapel. Among those in the congregation was Juan

Sebastián Chamorro – a leading opposition voice and the nephew of slain newspaper editor Pedro Joaquín Chamorro and of the former president, Violeta Chamorro. I chatted to him in the grounds after the mass had ended. 'Ortega was an autocratic person from the very beginning, so I'm not really surprised to see the consolidation of this regime,' he said, nodding towards the lines of riot cops on the road opposite us. Yet the lengths to which Daniel Ortega had been prepared to go to hold onto power had still shocked him: 'A year ago this church, for twenty hours, was attacked with live ammunition with kids inside here. It's really, really surprising to see Ortega committing this kind of violence. We expected almost anything from him but not the killing of more than four hundred people.'

His uncle, of course, had helped to seal Anastasio Somoza Debayle's fate, such was the demand for change when he was gunned down in 1978. In the letter he'd penned to Somoza which had set the chain of events of his murder into motion, the fearless newspaper man had written the following condemnation:

You, General – no more or any less than other men who have reached the cusp of power – are caught in a stratosphere of poses, pride, bombast, fulminant and disproportionate threats which has no future but that of its inevitable descent.

Naturally, if you are still reading this letter at this point, you will be asking 'and this gentleman, my irreconcilable adversary, why is he telling me these things? Is it to help me?' Such a reason is far from my motivation, let me be frank, but rather another:

To make everyone else see the truth of this unsustainable situation and the urgent need to save a country, by asking you peacefully and calmly to remember that Nicaragua also belongs to us; for which, if there is any remnant of patriotism left in you, you owe it to us to leave us in peace, to let others understand us, organize us and try to rescue Nicaragua, even if only for the future generations.[89]

*

It is tempting to picture Daniel Ortega, holed up in his lavish compound in Managua, rereading that letter today and contemplating its words. It is tempting to imagine that he can still recognize the resonance of that reasoning, can still see that the logic of Chamorro's writing applied not just to Somoza Debayle but to all men at 'the cusp of power'.

And not just men. Rosario Murillo, often painted as a ruinous combination of Lady Macbeth and Dick Cheney, is by all accounts now just as powerful as Daniel Ortega. And just as hated. In 2013, dozens of twenty-metre-tall metallic monuments in the shape of trees had sprouted up across Managua. Brightly painted and covered in lights, they were called '*Arboles de la Vida*', 'Trees of Life', and cost around $3.5 million to construct and erect.

The brainchild of Rosario Murillo, for her they were important symbols for the city, icons of regeneration and a visual representation of her belief in the healing influence of Eastern mysticism. For the protesters, they were gaudy baubles, a mockery of the real needs of the people. They were an obvious target for the demonstrators, who began to cut them down during the protests in 2018.

The cry went up: 'Pull! Pull!' Everyone heaved on the chains lashed around the towering steel structure. A man with a hacksaw cut furiously into the main column as onlookers shouted encouragement and chanted 'The people, united, will never be defeated!' Suddenly it began creaking and, with a loud crack, the metal sculpture buckled and gave way, arcing to the ground with a great clang, its collapse greeted by more whooping and applause. They were sending a message to the Ortega–Murillo government that it would be the next to fall.

Ortega doesn't work with the same intensity as Murillo. She is the one who gets up at four in the morning to start work. Without her, Gioconda Belli insists, Ortega wouldn't have achieved the power he has or been able to ride out the moments when protesters were pulling down their monuments.

'He brings the power, she organizes it,' says Belli, quoting an observation by Murillo's daughter, Zoilamerica. 'Rosario Murillo has traditionally been the organizer of all this power they have accumulated, the one who meets with the mayors and the politicians.' She organizes the militants and the propaganda machine, her Orwellian insistence on the party line leading to her being referred to in Nicaragua as '*la Gran Hermana*', 'the Big Sister'. Her intense work rate is fuelled by an almost messianic belief in their right to control power.

Daniel Ortega was once the Sandinista star that shone most brightly, who captured the imagination of left-wing students on university campuses from Manchester to Montevideo. Yet this is now a shared project. Murillo has as much of a stake in it as he does and has helped the dynasty stay ahead of its opponents. Like any family business, as Nicaragua was for the Somozas, too, the question of succession is important. Ortega is now in his mid-seventies. If anything should happen to him or if there is any truth in the rumours of his ill health, she is perfectly poised to take over.

On the fortieth anniversary of the Sandinista Revolution, Ortega and Murillo – husband and wife, president and vice-president – appeared in front of an organized rally in Managua. He was in a white shirt with a blue baseball cap, she in a luminous yellow visor, matching scarf and a multicoloured blouse. He looked grey and pallid, his voice tired and lacking bite. This was supposedly their victory lap, a celebration of having doggedly held onto power through the uprising of 2018.

Yet it felt strangely hollow. The crowd dutifully cheered when Ortega spoke of elections in 2021. They were already preparing to win them, he told them, and there would be 'reforms to the electoral law so no one can say afterwards that we stole the election'. The opposition denounced what they said would be 'cosmetic' changes, mere tweaks to allow him to perpetuate his time in power or, if he finally chose to step aside, pass the baton to his wife.

In 2018, when that same annual celebration had taken place in the middle of a year of violence and repression, Daniel Ortega was joined on stage by Bruno Rodríguez, the Cuban foreign minister.

It was a clear display of brotherhood amid a worsening human rights situation. On that night, Ortega had been more exercised, seemingly relishing the battle against the protesters. It is as though he finds life with his back against the wall easier or, perhaps, it is what comes more naturally to him.

He was being isolated regionally again, as he had been in the past. Thirteen Latin American countries, ranging from Argentina, Brazil, Chile and Uruguay in the South to Central American neighbours like Costa Rica, Guatemala, Honduras and Panama had criticized his violence against civil society. For Ortega, however, the demonstrators weren't reasonable pacifists politely asking him to stand down or to bring the elections forward. They were a 'murderous, coup-mongering satanic sect' that Nicaragua's archbishops needed to 'exorcise'.[90]

At one time, Ronald Reagan took delight in describing Ortega as a 'dictator in designer glasses'. Ortega retorted that for the US president, Nicaragua was 'his hobby, a dark hobby'.[91] Today the glasses are long gone. And so is Reagan.

What remains is, in no small part, a creation of Washington's. The reasons for Ortega's despotic authoritarian rule don't lie solely in Havana or even in the much-publicized visits to Moscow at the height of the Cold War. He was and still is a thoroughly Nicaraguan phenomenon. Washington – through successive governments and residents of the White House – played a pivotal role in creating the current conditions in this small Central American nation. For any progress to be made, say Nicaraguan academics and thinkers, there must be a clear-eyed acceptance of how Nicaragua was first subjugated as 'Washington's backyard'; of how a murderous, corrupt ruling family received unequivocal support from the US for decades, until the very end when the murder of an American journalist made it too politically sensitive back home; of how an obsessed administration sponsored a brutal guerrilla war against the elected government, using illegal funds and covert training.

If an unaccountable populist autocrat is in power in Managua, the US State Department knows exactly how he got there and how he became attractive to the electorate along the way. So does Congress, the Pentagon and USAID. Ironically, Daniel Ortega displays many of the features that the current US president Donald Trump admires in his counterparts around the world. Trump is drawn to populist *caudillos* and in many regards Ortega, if he espoused the conservative politics of the right, would have been a natural fit.

It's said that Franklin Delano Roosevelt uttered about Anastasio Somoza García: 'he may be a son of a bitch, but he's our son of a bitch.' Whether or not that is true, it's clear that Washington sees Daniel Ortega as an SOB all right – just not one of theirs. Instead, the Trump administration's then national security adviser, John Bolton, a man who served Ronald Reagan as assistant attorney general during the Iran-Contra affair, coined a different term: the 'troika of tyranny', a three-pronged trident he sees as comprising communist-run Cuba, Maduro's Venezuela and Nicaragua under Daniel Ortega.

None of which is to absolve the Ortega–Murillo government of a single moment of its violence or one small act of its repression. Their control in Managua now is total. Protest is essentially banned. Dissent is crushed. Four hundred or more were killed in a matter of months. It isn't hard to see why former Sandinistas feel deceived by Daniel Ortega and compare him to the dynasty they forced out in 1979. There is barely a state institution left that displays anything resembling independence: 'There is no separation of the powers of the state,' Gioconda Belli, Nicaragua's celebrated poet told me, her voice a combination of fury and despair. She added that Cuba's influence and inspiration in Ortega's Nicaragua was most evident 'at the *barrio* level, organizationally'. Entire neighbourhoods are controlled by pro-Ortega groups called *Consejos del Poder Ciudadano* or *Consejos del Liderazgo Sandinista*. Broadly fashioned on Cuba's 'Committees for the Defence of the Revolution', they are community vigilance structures in which members watch out for and report any anti-government behaviour. All branches of government, especially the judiciary and the legislature, have become mere instruments of the executive, bending as required to his rule. That only leaves the fourth estate. However, freedom of speech has been under attack in ways truly reminiscent of Somoza.

The Chamorros remain an influential journalistic family in Nicaragua. One of Pedro Joaquín's brothers, Jaime, has continued to edit *La Prensa* in his mid-eighties and one of his sons, Carlos Fernando Chamorro, was driven into exile in Costa Rica after government agents raided the offices of *Confidencial*, an online magazine he runs. For four hours one night in December 2018, they turned the place upside down. They destroyed the office and took laptops, equipment, files, company documents and personal papers. 'This wasn't a personal attack, this was an attack against the press,' Carlos Fernando told me down the line from Costa Rica. 'It was another example of more than seven hundred aggressions on the independent press in Nicaragua,' he said, referring to scores of cases of journalists being physically attacked, even killed, having their equipment stolen and being silenced or exiled. Television channels, radio stations, newspapers – even people posting material on YouTube – have been targeted if they have criticized Ortega.

La Prensa has been especially squeezed. The editors say the government has held up their supplies of newsprint and ink in customs and forced the publication to cut back to a slim pamphlet of three or four pages. Its staff have been decimated and the newspaper can no longer afford the luxury of investigative reporters at a time when it needs them most.[92] That Rosario Murillo once worked as a secretary at the newspaper, helping its editors to publish their condemnation of a tyrannical ruler, is part of Nicaragua's inherent absurdity.

On 18 January 2019, the anniversary of Pedro Joaquín Chamorro's letter to Somoza Debayle, *La Prensa* published a special edition making their own protest at the continued harassment under the Ortega–Murillo government.

The front page was blank. Inside, the editorial simply read: 'Have you imagined living without information?'

CUBA /
FIDEL CASTRO

'Rights are to be taken, not requested;
seized, not begged for'

JOSÉ MARTÍ

Around nine in the evening on 15 February 1898, C. H. Newton, the bugler on the USS *Maine*, blew Taps. Soft and clear, the unmistakable refrain – the American equivalent of the Last Post – echoed across Havana's harbour on the warm Thursday night. Taps was used by the US military at dusk for flag-lowering ceremonies, though by 1891 it had become the officially recognized bugle call for the funerals of fallen soldiers. As Newton played the melancholy air from the battleship's deck, it must have sounded hauntingly beautiful as it reverberated across the water and briefly silenced the drunken chatter in the quayside bars. But on this particular muggy Havana evening at the turn of the twentieth century, the melody was a portent of death.

The USS *Maine* had docked in the Cuban capital three weeks earlier. A hundred metres long from stern to bow, she was originally designed as the latest in 'ironclad' armoured battleships: coal-fired with two echeloned gun turrets and a hull made from thick American steel. But long delays in her construction and launch meant that by the time the *Maine* was commissioned in 1895 she was already obsolete. With the United States ever more concerned about its interests in Cuba as the island fought for independence from Spain, the US warship was sent over the Florida Straits from Key West on an ostensible courtesy visit with the remit to protect American lives and property.[1]

Spain maintained its grip over Cuba long after it had lost its other colonies in the Americas, but the War of Independence marked the last moments of the European power's hold in the Caribbean. The struggle had already claimed the life of the poet, revolutionary leader and 'Apostle of Cuban Independence', José Martí, killed on the battlefield in May 1895. Martí had unified the movement and organized the campaign for his homeland like no other leader. His valour in battle and his patriotic poetry inspired his followers into war long after his death and he became a martyr to the cause, the national symbol of liberty and freedom from tyranny.

Cuba was under the control of its governor general, the reviled General Valeriano Weyler. His '*reconcentrado*' policy forced the peasantry from their land, destroyed their crops and burned their livestock in order to flush the insurgents from the countryside. The repression had worked; the independence fighters, led by Máximo Gómez and Antonio Maceo, were set back years in their effort to retake their nation from the colonizers. The human cost was astronomical. With the rural poor confined to internment camps, disease was rife and at least 150,000 died from starvation and illness. It earned General Weyler the name 'the Butcher' in the US newspapers, many of them keen to emphasize Spain's cruelty in Cuba.

While America wasn't actively involved in the conflict, it was clearly on the side of the insurgents and applauded their effort to secure a *Cuba Libre*. But Washington's support didn't stem from an altruistic desire to see Cuba, or indeed other countries in the Americas, achieve full independence. The US was keen on forcing Spain out to exert its own control over the island, in particular its lucrative sugar industry. Sending the USS *Maine* the ninety miles from Florida to Havana was a thinly veiled act of sabre-rattling dressed up as good neighbourliness.

Around forty minutes after C. H. Newton blew Taps, an explosion was heard across Old Havana, so loud that windows shattered several streets away from the port. The sailors and longshoremen came running from their bars into the street to find the *Maine* listing badly, her hull split in two, flames shooting high into the darkness. The air filled with urgent shouting, desperate orders and the screams of the sailors being crushed and burned alive below deck. Detonations echoed into the night as the ship's munitions ignited, spreading further confusion and panic. Men threw themselves from the deck into the sea but were pulled under by the sinking battleship and drowned in the harbour. Horse-drawn fire engines arrived at the port but with the *Maine* moored out in the bay and rapidly going down, there was little they could do from the shore. On board, Captain Charles D. Sigsbee ordered the surviving seamen to abandon ship. He was the last to leave the *Maine* as it lurched and shuddered, then slid beneath the black waters. 266 of the 350 men on board died, among them the young bugler Newton.

Once safely on board an American steamer docked nearby, Captain Sigsbee sent a telegram to Washington DC: '*Maine* blown up in Havana harbor at nine-forty tonight and destroyed. Many wounded and doubtless more killed or drowned.' Then, conscious of how this disaster would seem amid the growing tensions with Spain, he added: 'Public opinion should be suspended until further report... Many Spanish officers including representatives of [General Weyler's successor] General Blanco now with me to express sympathy.'[2]

Suspending public judgement wouldn't be easy. Havana-based correspondents dashed to the scene and filed the first reports of what would become a huge news story in the United States. Caution be damned, the newspapers of Randolph Hearst and Joseph Pulitzer exercised little restraint in laying full responsibility at the feet of the Spanish. Their reports on the explosion would later be held up as classic examples of 'yellow journalism' – sensationalism in which the facts were twisted, even invented outright, to whip up the public clamour for revenge. Eye-catching headlines fuelled the narrative of a supposedly blatant Spanish attack: '*Maine* explosion caused by bomb or torpedo?' asked Pulitzer's *The World* two days later. The paper sent a team of divers to Havana to establish the answer. 'Destruction of the War Ship was the Work of an Enemy,' Hearst's *New York Journal* proclaimed unequivocally and offered a $50,000 reward for 'the detection of the perpetrator of the *Maine* outrage'. The facts weren't getting in the way of a good story, and the slogan 'Remember the *Maine*' was quickly adopted by the press.

While it was far from the sole reason – the US had been eyeing Cuba for decades and relations with Spain were fast deteriorating – the *Maine*'s destruction lit the blue touch paper to war. On 20 April 1898, President William McKinley received authorization from Congress for the use of military force. The US issued an ultimatum to Madrid to withdraw from the island and the following day Spain severed diplomatic relations with Washington. War had begun between two world powers, one rising in strength by the year, the other desperately clinging to the final remnants of an empire that had once spanned the globe.

The war quickly reflected those relative strengths. The US blockaded the port of Santiago in the east of Cuba and its far more modern and superior navy sunk a Spanish fleet when it attempted to force its way through. The ten-week conflict would cost Spain dearly. In the Treaty of Paris which ended the Spanish-American War, Spain had to relinquish control over not just Cuba but Puerto Rico, Guam and the Philippines. The era of Spanish dominance of the seas, which had begun in 1492, was over.

Cuba, meanwhile, became a US protectorate. Its independence was relative, a settlement negotiated between a victorious foreign superpower and the vanquished European colonialists. The United States stayed in Cuba until 1903, but even when its troops left, the island – the largest in the Caribbean – remained firmly within the Americans' sphere of influence. The economy had been rebuilt with US capital and American firms had taken control of entire industries from the sugarcane and tobacco fields to the factories. The controversial Platt Amendment then codified America's dominion over Cuba. The Amendment was part of the Army Appropriations Bill of 1901 and included seven conditions under which the US would withdraw from Cuba, the eighth condition specifying that the Cubans accepted the previous seven.

Cuba had little choice but to insert the seven clauses into its constitution, thereby giving the Americans the right to intervene in their internal affairs for 'the maintenance of a government adequate for the protection of life, property and individual liberties'.[3] The United States also had huge sway over the island's foreign policy and retained a vast coaling station and naval base in Guantánamo Bay, on the strategically advantageous southeastern tip of Cuba. The Platt Amendment contained all the key ingredients – political, military and economic – that were needed to establish complete US authority over the island for the next three decades. Cuban anger at America's interference in its affairs would last far longer.

The sinking of the *Maine* became the source of endless conspiracy theories. In the immediate aftermath, beyond Randolph Hearst's inflammatory headlines, both the Spanish and the Americans launched investigations into the incident. The US inquiry was led by Captain William T. Sampson. His findings, published within a month, were that the explosion had been caused by a mine although there was no clear evidence to support the claim. In essence, Sampson's investigation was just another cog in the unstoppable machinery of war.

In 1911, the *Maine*'s gnarled metal hull, which had been protruding above the waters of the harbour as a constant, grisly reminder of the men who had drowned there, was raised by a team of US navy engineers. They built a cofferdam around the ship's husk and drained the water from around her. The remains of sixty sailors were recovered from the wreckage and returned to the United States for burial at Arlington National Cemetery. They were laid to rest alongside dozens more who had initially been buried in Havana's Colón Cemetery and were later disinterred. The destroyed hulk of the *Maine* was towed out into the Atlantic and scuttled, where it lies at 600 fathoms. Even with the opportunity to inspect the fractured hull before they consigned it to the bottom of the sea, the Americans still concluded it had been destroyed by a mine placed by a hostile power.

It wasn't until as late as 1976 that a clear-eyed and dispassionate US investigation into the event was carried out, albeit in a private capacity, by navy Admiral Hyman Rickover. Exhaustive research by a team of naval historians and engineers reached the far more credible conclusion that the *Maine*'s sinking was both accidental and self-inflicted. A fire in the coal bunker, placed dangerously close to the ship's magazine, was the most likely cause, Rickover concluded. With the benefit of hindsight, that finding certainly seems more probable than the idea that the Spanish were mining their own ports.

Yet the theories about the battleship's demise persist, fuelled in large part by the Cuban government. Such were the benefits to the United States of the Spanish-American War that the prevailing belief on the island – one pushed for years in schools and official publications – was that the sinking was a false flag operation: Washington allegedly murdered 266 of its own sailors in a bid to spark a war with Spain. The Cuban Communist Party newspaper *Granma* once wrote that the men were 'immolated to serve as a pretext for American intervention that in 1898 prevented the island from gaining true independence'.[4]

In 1925, a memorial to the victims was erected on Havana's waterfront promenade, the Malecón. A twelve-metre-tall structure of two marble pillars, it was adorned with two cannons from the *Maine* and part of the ship's weighty anchor chain. At the top sat an open-winged bronze American eagle. A year after its construction, a hurricane barrelled through Havana and ripped the eagle from its moorings. Another bronze bird was built, this time with sleeker, more aerodynamic wings. But it, too, would come down from its perch.

In 1961 it was prised off with a crane on the orders of Fidel Castro, following a defeated invasion of the island by CIA-backed Cuban exiles at the Bay of Pigs. The eagle was torn down and split into three pieces on impact. The head was spirited away in the mêlée of cheering anti-US protesters but eventually made its way back to the Americans. The Cubans still have the two other pieces, the body kept and preserved under the custodianship of the official historian of Havana awaiting the day that bilateral relations improve sufficiently to allow them to be fused together. After the symbol of American strength was pulled down, a new plaque went up on the eagleless monument: 'To the victims of the *Maine* who were sacrificed by the imperialist's voracity in their desire to take control of the island of Cuba.'

The Platt Amendment wouldn't be annulled in Cuba until 1934. In that time, the Americans interfered in the island's affairs on numerous occasions, in particular following election results of which they disapproved. Between 1906 and 1909, the island was under direct rule by US consular and military officials and between 1909 and 1921, US troops entered the country on four separate missions.[5]

It was a period of dizzying sugar highs and lows. At its height in 1920, a pound of Cuban sugar fetched around 22.5 cents on the world market but following the Wall Street Crash in 1929 the same amount barely fetched a single cent.[6] The fluctuating economy and the growing agitation over US meddling made the island a breeding ground for fervent nationalism. A series of populist *caudillos* delivered handouts to their clientele while simultaneously lining their own pockets. Gangsterism and political assassinations were rife. Some middle-class students and intellectuals formed an urban guerrilla organization called ABC for its strictly hierarchical and alphabetical system of cells. The group carried out acts of sabotage and terrorism in an effort to oust President Gerardo Machado who had taken office in 1924. By August 1933, discontent at Machado's repressive rule coalesced into a general strike led by students and left-wing organizations, including a fledgling Communist Party. With pressure being exerted by Washington, which was loath to send its troops into the political maelstrom once more given popular animosity against the Platt Amendment, Machado stepped down and went into exile.

In the weeks that followed, the US-installed government couldn't cope with the wave of revolutionary action sweeping the island. Factories and university campuses were occupied, scores were settled amid scenes of mob violence and stones were thrown at police on the streets of Havana and Santiago. The authorities responded in their typically repressive way but in September, a month after Machado had been ousted, a group of sergeants and enlisted men decided to take matters into their hands. They removed the docile US-friendly president in a putsch that would become known as the Sergeants' Revolt, or the Cuban Revolution of 1933.

One of the rebel officers was Fulgencio Batista Zaldívar, a mestizo sergeant who was born into abject rural poverty in Oriente province. A former labourer and sugarcane cutter, he was not part of the officer class or, for that matter, its usual race. Photographs of him at that time show a short soldier in a freshly pressed khaki uniform and knee-high leather boots, his thick, dark hair slicked back behind protruding ears. Batista had moved to the capital as a teenager after the death of his mother and, having worked the railways for the United Fruit Company for a time, he eventually found his way into the army. By 1933, he had gained the rank of sergeant and was the stenographer for the group that forced out Machado. It was a daring move by all the non-commissioned officers who had participated, but Batista would profit the most from the uprising.

The mutinous military officers created a five-man junta – the Pentarchy of 1933 – selected in alliance with the anti-Machado student body in Havana, the *Directorio Estudiantil Universitario*. After just five days in power, the group chose one of their number, Dr Ramón Grau San Martín, to take over the presidency. Sergeant Batista was promoted to the rank of colonel and was made the army's chief of staff, the kind of extraordinarily rapid leap up the military hierarchy only possible in a *coup d'état*.

Not satisfied with becoming head of the army, Batista had designs on the presidency. Grau was in office for just a hundred days before Batista, in cahoots with the US State Department's representative in Cuba, Sumner Welles, forced him out. The mixed-race general from an impoverished rural town became the island's right-wing *caudillo*, initially screened by a series of puppet leaders before he eventually secured power for himself in a carefully managed popular ballot in 1940. Over the next two decades, the public's initial embrace of Batista for having overthrown Machado turned into such widespread popular rejection of his iron-fisted, corrupt rule that it would bring a second, far more profound revolution to Cuba, one that would alter the country irrevocably.

The man who led that revolutionary movement, who would become Cuba's most important leader since José Martí, came from the same part of the island as Batista. Fidel Castro Ruz was born in Birán, a soporifically humid rural outpost in the sugar-growing province of Oriente. As a young child Fidel unknowingly trod a fine line between respectable landed gentry and illegitimacy. His father was Ángel Castro Argiz, a penniless Galician immigrant who had become a wealthy landowner. Ángel had an extramarital affair with his maid, Lina Ruz, and eventually left his wife to settle down with her. But he took his time in recognizing the young Fidel and having him baptized, a paternal slight that left its mark on the boy.

Birán was the town that Castro built. Ángel first came to Cuba in the 1890s from Galicia as a conscript to defend colonial rule during the War of Independence. When he returned to the island shortly after the fighting ended, he began working in the mines and later the sugarcane plantations for the United Fruit Company. By the early 1910s, he had discovered a path to wealth. He bought a little land on the side of the Camino Real, a muddy route between Santiago de Cuba and Nipe Bay on the northern coast, where he could sell his wares to the horse-drawn traffic traversing the island. Little by little, that farm – Finca Las Manacas – grew into a fiefdom typical of the era: a school, a general store, a lumberyard, a bar, a blacksmith, a post office and rustic huts for the Haitian sugarcane and timber workers.

Fidel was the third of Ángel's seven children with Lina Ruz, although he already had several with his first wife, María Argota. Of the siblings, Fidel was closest to Ramón and Raúl and his half-sister Lidia. Another sister, Juana, would later fall out with him spectacularly having once been her brother's faithful devotee. Finca Las Manacas is today, of course, a museum to Fidel Castro. Most of the original furniture was destroyed in a fire when Ángel fell asleep one night with a cigar still burning, but everything from its wooden school desks to its enamel bathtubs has been painstakingly recreated and protected from the damp tropical air and the encroachment of the jungle. I was shown around the estate by the official historian of Birán, Antonio López, a friendly, efficient man in his sixties. His tour consisted of a hagiography, as expected in a town where besmirching the Castro name is nothing short of blasphemy. He showed me the tiny schoolroom where Fidel first sat in on classes before being sent to study under the Jesuit priests in Santiago and Havana.

'Fidel once said he was glad to be the son and not the grandson of a landowner,' said Antonio, wiping the sweat off his brow with his polo shirt, 'as there still wasn't a family culture of privilege or entitlement.' Ángel Castro wouldn't live to see his sons, Fidel and Raúl, become the two most powerful men on the island. He died in 1956 and is buried alongside their mother on the family farm.

For at least one other Castro son, though, life did not really change much from those early days of rural tranquillity. Mártin Castro, the half-brother of Fidel and Raúl, never left Birán, living in a neat but boxy concrete home on the edge of the town. When his revolutionary siblings took the island by storm in 1959, Mártin was offered the chance to move to Havana and join them at the heart of government. He turned it down. He was a *'guajiro'* through and through, a country boy, and was happier where he was, among his animals and the open pastures of their province, content with rural anonymity.

Mártin had a different mother from Fidel and Raúl but the Castro family resemblance was striking, especially in his nose and brow, Ángel's strong Galician bloodline shining through decades after his death. He recalled his half-brothers as vigorous, exuberant and rebellious, particularly Fidel: 'He had a little horse called Careto and would go hunting with a small rifle, that's what he enjoyed most,' he said, rocking gently in a chair on his narrow porch.

Fidel was apparently fascinated by the Haitian and Afro-Cuban sugarcane workers, who were essentially indentured labourers on his father's farm. Still with slave names like Negrito and Mongo, they lived a miserable existence on the Castro estate. Like almost all sugarcane cutters across Cuba, their deal with the master was deeply exploitative. Ángel would pay them in credit at his stores and deduct a fee for providing them with flimsy huts. 'Fidel would steal vouchers for credit from our father's store,' Martin Castro remembers with a cackle, 'and then go over to the Haitians' homes and give them out!'

Embellished memories aside, Fidel's awakening to poverty at Finca Las Manacas was something he acknowledged years later: 'I wasn't born political. But from very young I observed things that stuck in my mind, helped me understand the realities of the world.'[7] Today, beyond the coachloads of sandal-shod visitors to the museum, Birán retains its sleepy village atmosphere. Men gather in the tiny plaza around the state-run shop, sharing a little rum after a morning in the fields or buying cheap sodas and luncheon-meat sandwiches in the subsidized cafeteria.

Mártin Castro's rudimentary concrete house was one of the products of a 1960s plan enacted by Fidel to build 400 homes for the townsfolk, though only 218 were ever completed. Mártin worked the land until his body gave out. When tending to the fields and his animals finally became too much for him, he eased into his rocking chair and watched village life go by. In September 2017, he died of an aneurysm, aged eighty-seven, only a stone's throw from where he was born. 'I often wonder what would have happened if Dad had joined with Fidel,' his tearful daughter, Josefa Beatriz, told me a few months later, her grief still raw.

One might equally ask what would have happened if Fidel had stayed with her father in their hometown. It is not an exaggeration to say that after he moved away from the sugarcane plantations and cattle fields of Birán, Fidel Castro would alter the course of Cuban, and world, history.

At his height, Fidel Castro was infinitely more charismatic than Hugo Chávez, and a far more sophisticated guerrilla leader than Daniel Ortega. He easily outweighed the popular appeal of Evo Morales and had a sharper intellect than Rafael Correa. He was more determined and iron-willed than Lula, and possessed more daring, political astuteness and audacity than all those leaders combined. He was also crueller and more ruthless towards his critics. His enemies in Washington and Florida grudgingly respected his combination of resolve, cunning and undying commitment to his beliefs. He was the kind of leader Cubans admiringly refer to as 'a man of action'.

Yet his most notable actions – which ranged from the brave to the foolhardy, from the brilliant to the brutal – were carried out in the twentieth century. When he died in 2016, he was described as the last warrior of the Cold War, an icon of a bygone bipolar world, who had challenged US hegemony from just ninety miles away. His inclusion in a list of twenty-first-century populists might initially seem odd. Fidel belonged to a generation well before Chávez and Lula and Evo Morales, but he is undoubtedly the most important of them all.

It isn't possible to write about contemporary populism and the Left in Latin America without reference to Fidel Castro, and, to a lesser extent, his younger brother and hand-picked heir, Raúl.

Castro had a huge influence on all the left-wing populists in Latin America who came after him. Each of them visited Cuba, sat at the feet of Fidel and kissed the ring of the communist elder statesman. Most received instruction or training on the island, honed their thinking in Havana or were inspired by what they saw and heard. None more so than Hugo Chávez.

He became at once Fidel's disciple and his salvation. He became so important to Cuba that in 2005 the Cuban vice-president, Carlos Lage, declared that 'Cuba has two presidents: Fidel and Chávez'. The Venezuelan leader's emergence as a major political figure in 1999 coincided with Cuba's lowest point, the euphemistically titled 'Special Period', a time of biting austerity and rolling blackouts following the collapse of the Soviet Union, which had subsidized and bankrolled the regime for decades. His radical new socialist energy and Venezuela's copious oil wealth were gifts that Fidel could scarcely have dared to hope for a few years earlier, when the Berlin Wall was being torn down by cheering hordes with chisels and pickaxes and state socialism seemed to become obsolete.

And Fidel was very present in the new century. He spent nine years in office after Chávez took power in Venezuela and they frequently travelled between Caracas and Havana for high-profile summits and secret meetings. Even as Fidel's health was failing, the two men formed a bond over those years that set the tone for the rest of the region. Latin American governments were defined by whether they staunchly opposed the Castro–Chávez nexus and aligned themselves with Washington, or thoroughly approved of it and took part gleefully in baiting the 'imperialists'. Fidel was more than just a presence in the Pink Tide in Latin America; he was that movement's very touchstone and political compass.

Fidel's effect can be detected all over contemporary Latin America, in small ways and large, and over many decades. So many moments reveal that influence: his urgent phone call to Chávez, his political protégé, to impar his instrumental advice in the middle of the coup attempt in Venezuela in April 2002; Fidel helping the feuding Sandinistas to bury their differences for long enough to mount a sustained final push against Somoza in 1979. His influence also took the form of long-term bilateral policies, vital to Cuba's economy, such as the posting of thousands of Cuban medics and intelligence agents to Venezuela, Bolivia and Nicaragua. He fostered regional integration under the ALBA group of nations, a Spanish acronym for the 'Bolivarian Alliance for the Peoples of Our America'.

A brainchild of Chávez and Castro in 2004, ALBA was an exclusively left-wing Latin American club inspired by Simón Bolívar's vision of a United America. Or so went the official rhetoric. In large part, it was created to obstruct the Bush administration's plans for a Free Trade Area of the Americas (FTAA) and counteract the strength of the Washington-based Organization of American States. Its members – some larger allies like Ecuador, Bolivia and Honduras but otherwise mainly Caribbean island nations keen on the favourable terms the alliance offered for Venezuelan oil imports – met frequently in Caracas or Havana to agree joint co-operation on everything from hurricane preparedness to a common currency. Bolivia and Ecuador were ALBA members until Morales and Correa left office, when their successors speedily quit the group.

In Cuba, even after he was forced to pass the reins to Raúl in early 2008, Fidel Castro remained a crucial power behind the scenes. While he relinquished his previous degree of minute control over decision-making, no major steps were taken – from relaxing the restrictions on private business to re-establishing ties with the USA – without his prior approval.

Fidel Castro was born some twenty years before Daniel Ortega and Lula, and almost forty before Rafael Correa. In his usual indiscreet fashion, when Castro was gravely ill with peritonitis in January 2007, Hugo Chávez told the world's press in poetic language that Fidel was 'back in the Sierra Maestra again', a reference to the lush green mountain range from which he launched his guerrilla war, 'and locked in a battle for his life'.[8] Cuban officials were aghast at their Venezuelan ally's imprudence – the *Comandante*'s health was a state secret in Cuba – and immediately went into damage limitation mode. Chávez was called to Havana for a series of photographs at the recuperating Fidel's bedside.[9]

Apart from the fact that he was older than them, Fidel Castro also differed from the younger generation of Latin American leftists because he wasn't a popularly elected leader who used his overwhelming support at the ballot box to alter the constitution and perpetuate his time in power. Castro was a genuine revolutionary strongman who seized power and held onto it. He was also a nationalist long before he was a Marxist-Leninist and he saw his struggle in the tradition of the great Cuban poet and revolutionary José Martí, wherein 'rights are to be taken, not requested; seized, not begged for'. An autocrat from the start, Fidel smashed his way into power on the back of a commandeered tank, riding a tidal wave of rebellious fervour. He emerged from the same *caudillo* tradition that had forced Spain to relinquish control of the continent in the nineteenth century, although, caught up as he was in the geo-politics of the Cold War, his enemy wasn't colonial Europe but the United States. The sheer intensity of the crises he lived through in his six decades-long conflict with Washington have no parallel anywhere else in the world. Every obstacle the other left-wing leaders in the region encountered as they implemented their populist agendas, from healthcare reform to the nationalization of US energy firms, from land redistribution to censorship of the press, Fidel had faced long before and usually involving far greater consequences. Hugo Chávez took Venezuela to the brink of an armed conflict with its neighbour Colombia over a diplomatic spat – which was quickly defused with no real likelihood of a weapon being fired. Fidel Castro took the world to the brink of thermonuclear war in 1962 and was prepared if necessary to let Cubans 'immolate' themselves for his cause.

His supporters say that the main similarity between the Pink Tide leaders and Fidel Castro was that they were all 'revolutionaries', that the younger generation walked a path first cleared by Castro decades earlier. He was the pioneer, the vanguard, they argue, of 'twenty-first-century socialism'. But it's not quite as simple as that. As I hope I have illustrated, the left-wing movements in the Americas differed radically from each other according to their context. The striking steelworkers in São Paulo led by Lula had relatively little in common with the Andean coca growers' movement, which in turn scarcely resembled the militaristic leftist radicalism of Hugo Chávez or the Sandinistas' guerrilla war or the economist-led Citizens' Revolution in Ecuador. The Cuban Revolution was more profound and lasting than any of them.

Admittedly, their commonalities as political projects – and their similarities to Cuba – echo Castro's socialist priorities. Under Fidel, the impoverished island achieved huge advances in healthcare and education. From the moment it took power, the revolutionary government took great steps to improve the lives of the island's poorest. 1961 was designated the 'Year of Education' and around a million Cubans were mobilized in the campaign to abolish illiteracy. Hundreds of thousands of *campesinos* were taught to read and write by brigades of teachers and student volunteers who travelled from the cities to live and teach in the villages. It brought genuine results within a year: school enrolment rates soared, illiteracy rates plummeted and Cuba became known for its well-educated, well-qualified population. The Cuban literacy campaign remains one of Fidel Castro's greatest achievements – and it cemented the support of the rural poor for decades.

There were programmes to treat preventable diseases, to train children in music and ballet and sport, to lift the wellbeing of the nation and the family. Anyone who fails to recognize the Cuban Revolution's positive achievements between 1959 and 1990 is simply blinded by ideological conviction. It is churlish to ignore them. The results were real and were often (although not always) verified by international bodies and had a positive impact on vast numbers of Cubans. Furthermore, it is true that they carried all this off in the face of a perpetual and harsh economic embargo imposed by Washington, though the Cuban government's overreliance on this excuse for the country's continuing economic malaise eventually wore very thin. The current underfunded and crumbling condition of the island's healthcare system and its schools should not detract from the fact that Fidel Castro prioritized these issues at home and attained real results, especially during the Cold War.

But it would be just as blind to ignore the ugly and cruel sides of the Castro regime, a ruthlessness refined over decades of control. Expressions of dissent are not tolerated, protests are virtually non-existent and repression for voicing opposition of any kind is swift and merciless. Various groups and individuals have pushed back against the Castros over the years, from the early days of the revolution to the dawn of the Internet generation on the island, and none have fared well. Most were condemned to prison, forced out into exile or silenced, but there has been no meaningful attempt to engage with their demands or tolerate their criticism. Today, the island's human rights record remains shameful.

There were five areas in which Fidel acted as an example and a benchmark to other left-wing populist and autocratic leaders in the Americas. Firstly, in his sheer audacity. His bravado continually wrong-footed his enemies, from the battlefield to the diplomatic arena, as he took the least likely and most provocative steps again and again. Also in his radicalism. Half-measures or pragmatism rarely featured in Castro's strategies, either domestically or internationally. In his 'anti-imperialism' and by maintaining a constant state of conflict with the United States, the great external enemy against which his revolution was defined. Apart from the short-lived thaw in relations between President Obama and Raúl Castro, fewer and fewer Cubans can recall a time when the country wasn't at loggerheads with Washington. Fidel was a master of divide and rule in that regard. It was reportedly Fidel who first coined the term '*gusanos*', meaning 'worms', for Miami Cubans, a hate-filled word intended to deepen the sense of us and them between Cubans who left the island and those who stayed, even within the same family.

Fidel Castro was also profoundly influential in his creation and use of the island's extensive espionage apparatus, intelligence services and police, themselves modelled on Stalinist and Soviet examples. Without his spies, state security agents and neighbourhood-level eyes and ears, staying in power in Cuba for sixty years would have been almost impossible. Lastly, one has to mention Castro's repression of dissent and his control of the media. No prisoners have been put against the *paredón*, the firing squad's wall, for years and the last recorded use of the death penalty on the island was in 2003. But everyone in Cuba, from members of the Council of State to the workers in the tobacco fields, knows full well the consequences of speaking out. Arbitrary arrests of dissidents are common, the loss of a steady state job remains a constant threat, family members can be intimidated and harassed. As a journalist in Cuba, even after the death of Fidel Castro, I found it harder than anywhere else to find people who were prepared to deviate – on the record – from the government's clearly prepared script.

Castro's lessons were learned and employed to differing degrees by the five men whose careers are described in this book. Some, like Daniel Ortega and Hugo Chávez, employed most of them. Others, like Lula, were perhaps most influenced by Fidel's towering personality and his bravado. The story of Fidel Castro is one of incredible obstinacy, grit and good fortune, the like of which will not be replicated in the Americas for many lifetimes. The estimated 638 assassination plots against him are evidence of a life spent in conflict with Washington and the CIA. Yet of equal importance is Castro's legacy in modern Cuba itself, an island today floundering through its worst economic crisis since the Special Period and struggling to carve out a role for itself in contemporary Latin America.

Fidel Castro stepped off the flight and onto the tarmac in Bogotá with his travelling companion, Rafael del Pino Siero, and couldn't help but betray his excitement, briefly cracking his normally composed demeanour. He was eager to visit Colombia, a country on the brink of great things, full of youthful promise and political opportunity. The thin Andean air fairly crackled with the prospect of social revolution and they were exhilarating times for an enterprising, idealistic law student with leadership aspirations. Castro and del Pino were already experienced in the gangsterism of Havana's student politics. Fidel frequently walked around campus with a revolver. His name was beginning to appear more often in the press as a radical student leader and he had briefly been arrested in connection with two politically motivated murders, but released for a lack of evidence.[10] He had even participated in a foiled expedition to the Dominican Republic to overthrow the dictator Rafael Trujillo. That rash escapade aside, this was his first taste of politics outside the island.

He and del Pino were in the Colombian capital to participate in the 1948 Pan-American Students Conference, organized at the behest of Argentina's president Juan Perón in protest against the Washington-led Ninth International Conference of American States. There was a plan to hold a vote at the summit to enlarge the Conference into a pan-continental body called the Organization of American States – which Castro and other young Latin Americans saw as another example of Yankee imperialism. Students from across Latin America arrived in Bogotá that April to raise their voices against Washington's expansionism in the region. But what the two Cuban students didn't realize as they waited at the carousel for their luggage was that they were about to witness a moment that would tear Colombia apart.

Rafael del Pino might not have been a blood relative but, with Raúl still coming of political age, there was no one Fidel Castro trusted more at that time. Trust was a vital commodity in Havana's cutthroat politics. The two had been inseparable during their first year at university, and in the battle for control of the student government they had gravitated towards one political faction, the UIR – the Insurrectional Revolutionary Union. They had already survived their first clash with their adversaries on campus, the Socialist Revolutionary Movement led by Castro's clearest rival, Rolando Masferrer.

Both Rafael del Pino and Fidel could have been killed in an armed stand-off a year earlier, such was the volatility of Havana's trigger-happy student gangs. However, facing down the violence and intimidation of their rivals had brought them closer and united them in the belief that they would one day run Cuba under a more just system. In national, rather than the factional student politics,

Fidel was a member of the Orthodox Party under its charismatic founder, Eduardo 'Eddy' Chibás, who used his popular Sunday radio programme to denounce corruption by the ruling *Auténtico* Party. It has often been asked whether Fidel's membership of the *Ortodoxos* was just a ruse and he was already a Marxist by the time he took his student trip to Colombia. As Castro explained it in 1981:

> I had already entered into contact with Marxist literature... I felt attracted by the fundamental ideas of Marxism, and I was acquiring a socialist conscience... At that time there were some Communist students at the University of Havana and I had friendly relations with them, but I was not in the Socialist Youth, I was not a militant in the Communist party... I was acquiring a revolutionary conscience, I was active, I struggled, but let us say I was an independent fighter.[11]

In truth, it appears that Castro and del Pino arrived in the Colombian capital armed with little more than revolutionary zeal and a stack of pamphlets they'd printed in Cuba. They showered their crudely produced propaganda on the audience at the Colón Theatre one night, at an event attended by Colombia's president, Mariano Ospina Pérez. For that stunt, which Castro would later describe as a 'bit immature', they were arrested but released within the day.[12] They were also shaken down by Colombian intelligence officers, though all the authorities found when they turned over their boarding house were a few books and left-wing papers. And, of course, a photo of Jorge Eliécer Gaitán.

That was hardly surprising. Jorge Gaitán was a hero to young leftists and liberal-minded students across Latin America. He was the Liberal Party's candidate for president of Colombia and was hugely popular among the poor. As a lawyer, he had defended the rights of striking banana workers and brought a case against the United Fruit Company and the Colombian army for shooting workers on the picket lines, resulting in several deaths. A virtuoso orator, Dr Gaitán railed against the Colombian oligarchy and called for land reform to address the stark inequalities in the countryside. Fidel was so struck by the man who was expected to become Colombia's next president that he requested a meeting with him, and was granted one at two o'clock in the afternoon of 9 April 1948.

Jorge Gaitán would never attend the meeting with Castro. As Fidel finished his lunch and began to make his way towards Gaitán's office, a delusional and mentally unwell son of a stonemason, Juan Roa, was running his fingers over the grip of a revolver. Unemployed and possibly schizophrenic, Roa had fallen under the spell of a German astrologist named Johan Umland Gert. Under Umland's teachings, he became obsessed with the esoteric spiritual movement, Rosicrucianism, and convinced that he was the incarnation of Colombia's greatest independence hero, Francisco de Paula Santander. Decades on, it is still hard to know if Roa wanted his name to echo down the generations, like Santander – known as '*el Hombre de las Leyes*', or 'the Man of the Laws' – or if he was an unwitting patsy in a bigger conspiracy.

Juan Roa tucked the gun into his jacket and stepped out into the bustling streets of Bogotá.

Juan Roa was the second person to die that day. No one actually saw him fire the weapon but Jorge Gaitán received a single bullet to the back of the head and two in his back outside the entrance to his office building. Roa was stopped by a police corporal at the scene and ushered into a pharmacy in a vain effort to protect him from the angry mob. Roa pleaded with the policeman to save him: '*No me mates, mi cabo*', 'don't kill me, corporal,' he implored. Fearing for their own safety, the officer and the drugstore owner opened the shutters and left Juan Roa to his fate at the hands of the furious Gaitán supporters.

When they had finished kicking and beating him, they dragged his bloodied body to the Plaza Bolívar and dumped it outside the presidential palace. Someone had bludgeoned his head with a brick and he had been repeatedly stabbed in the frenzied attack. Juan Roa's pulpy, misshapen corpse was virtually unrecognizable, such was the violence of the mob's retribution.

His death was swallowed up by the wave of violence in the capital known as the *Bogotazo*. In the looting and burning that followed the murder of the popular politician, hundreds, perhaps thousands, of people were killed. The first that Fidel Castro knew something was wrong was when he saw people running in all directions as he made his way to Gaitán's office. 'They've killed Gaitán, they've killed Gaitán,' they yelled. Soon both he and Rafael del Pino became embroiled in the rapidly escalating uprising. They roamed the streets of Bogotá with pro-Gaitán gangs carrying rifles 'liberated' from a ransacked police station. Some historians with a specific political bias have tried to place Castro closer to the action, as an instigator or a communist agitator. But the evidence suggests that he and del Pino were just swept up in the anarchy like thousands of others on that infamous April day.

Still, the *Bogotazo* left a lasting impression on Fidel Castro. Not because it was successful, but because it wasn't. The protest had been chaotic, disorganized and lacked clear leadership. 'I saw great disorder, great indiscipline, no organisation,' he later recalled.[13] However, he also found it intoxicating: 'Bogotá was a hellish storm centre, but it was exciting. It was fun,' Castro admitted. 'I was a student in revolt at the old generation. I fought against the status quo, I was for democracy and real liberty for all Latin America. I felt important.'[14]

The two men made it back to Havana alive with help from the then Cuban ambassador to Bogotá who got them onto a cargo plane and out of the country fast. The disarray in Colombia, however, would not be resolved so quickly. There followed a decade of civil war called *La Violencia* in which as many as 200,000 died. Losses were heaviest in the countryside, where peasant armies of Liberals and Conservatives fought each other, with the armed forces and the Colombian Communist Party also involved in the warfare. It was from the vestiges of that conflict that the Marxist rebel group, the FARC was born.

Fidel and Rafael's brotherhood would not last. Within a few years, del Pino fell out with Castro over the increasingly communist direction of the revolutionary movement. After the revolution triumphed in January 1959, Rafael del Pino – who was a US citizen – started

running small planes into Cuba to smuggle out anti-Castro activists.[15]
A little over six months later, he was apprehended trying to help a
Cuban friend flee to Miami. Their shared experience of the *Bogotazo*
was not enough to spare him from Castro's ire. Del Pino spent the
next eighteen years in jail and died in his cell, aged fifty-one.

Haydée Santamaría lay back on the prison bunk and closed her
eyes. This day hadn't gone well. Later some would say that the entire
enterprise was doomed from the start, but Haydée hadn't seen it that
way. Neither had her brother or her fiancée. The three of them were
committed to this youthful underground movement, even if it cost
them their lives.

For some of them, it already had. Reflecting on the day's catastrophic events, she felt a cold, hard knot of fury tighten in her
stomach. Fidel's plan had seemed sound. They were to launch the
attack on the Moncada military barracks in the eastern city of
Santiago de Cuba on 26 July 1953, the day after carnival. The soldiers
would be in their bunks, they reasoned, hungover and asleep.

A year earlier, Cuba had experienced another coup that had reinstalled the military strongman Fulgencio Batista to the presidency.
Batista had left power in 1944 and spent his time in New York and
Miami but returned to Cuba ostensibly to stand in the 1952 election.
However, just twelve weeks before the vote, with the army's backing,
he seized power. Inexorably his rule had become harsher and more
repressive, especially against students, unionists and the labour movement. Disaffected members of the Orthodox youth wing, angry at
what they saw as inaction and procrastination by the party leadership, argued for direct action against Batista. Many *Ortodoxos* were
also deeply disillusioned after the loss of their leader, Eduardo Chibás.
As the island's most popular radio commentator, his exit was always
likely to be somewhat theatrical. However, few could have imagined
he would go out the way he did.

On Sunday 5 August 1951 he strode into the studio of the CMQ
radio station to broadcast his weekly show. Rather than launch into

his usual diatribe about the corrupt state of public life under President Carlos Prío Socarrás, who had defeated him at the polls in 1948, he spoke instead of Cuba's unfulfilled potential for greatness: 'Because of her geographical position, the richness of her land and the natural intelligence of her inhabitants, Cuba has reserved in history a great destiny, but she must realise it.'[16] In his broadcast, Chibás continued to warn his devoted audience of an impending coup by Batista and urged them to rise up against a broken and rotten state: 'Comrades of the Orthodoxy, forward! To economic independence, to political liberty, to social justice! People of Cuba, rise up and move! People of Cuba, awaken!'[17]

As his oration reached its crescendo, Eddy Chibás was cut off for the commercial break, so his audience didn't hear his final point – of his show and his life. 'This is my last call to awaken the Cuban people,' he said as he pulled out a revolver and fired a bullet into his belly. Unfortunately for Chibás, as he made the ultimate sacrifice for his cause, listeners at home were being treated to an advertisement for Café Pilón – 'the coffee that is tasty to the last drop'.

It's possible that Chibás never intended to commit suicide, but only to injure himself to make an impact. If so, he badly miscalculated. The bullet perforated his stomach and he was taken from the radio studio, bleeding profusely, by a number of his supporters, among them Fidel Castro. Despite a concerted effort to save him on the operating table, he would survive for eleven more days before slipping into Cuban political folklore. Months later, as he had predicted, Batista staged a *coup d'état*.

Many of the young Orthodox Party members who had experienced violence and torture at the hands of Batista's thuggish police made their way into Castro's orbit. Haydée Santamaría was among them, led to Fidel by her younger brother, Abel. It had been a dangerous and heady time. Twenty-nine years old and unmarried, she had won a reputation among the band of miscreants for her outspoken nature and quick wit. From their first meetings in the small apartment in the Vedado district of Havana, Castro treated her as an ally. He had made her feel valued despite her rural education and lack of a university diploma.

She had seen a change in Abel, too. He arrived in the capital at nineteen looking for a way to pay for his studies and was now working as a bookkeeper for a Pontiac dealership. In their home province of Las Villas, his pent-up frustration at their dire economic circumstances had sometimes boiled over into fistfights and bar brawls. But Abel had discovered a new energy under Fidel Castro, engaging in a worthy cause and finding someone to believe in. Almost immediately he had thrown his lot in with the inspirational young lawyer, more than a little seduced by the image of a political outlaw.

Using a mimeograph machine, they had begun to print and distribute an underground newspaper called 'Son Los Mismos', They Are the Same, out of her apartment. Later renamed by Fidel 'El Acusador' or The Accuser, the pamphlet mocked Batista with political cartoons and urged readers to engage in acts of sabotage and rebellion against his regime. Abel had been given the role of training the cells of like-minded militants which had begun to crop up across Havana and around the country. Masquerading as hunting enthusiasts, they carried out target practice in a shooting club on the outskirts of Havana.

Haydée – or Yeyé as she was often called – was just as committed as her brother, though perhaps a little warier. She, too, considered Fidel a visionary and was prepared to do whatever it took to wrest the country from the grip of the *caudillo*. But whereas Abel's support for Castro was blindly unconditional, she retained a sense of independence. She was protective of her younger brother and feared that he was already on the path to imprisonment or, more likely, a death by firing squad.

Plus now, of course, she had a new reason to stay alive. Clandestine work had led her to Boris. A tall, strong-featured twenty-four-year-old with thick, dark hair, Boris Luis Santa Coloma had been introduced to Haydée through another activist and she had immediately fallen for him. Six years older than him, she knew that he had a reputation for being both a playboy and coldblooded. Despite the warnings, she wanted to get to know him better and was elated to see him turn up at her door as an avowed fellow plotter. It had been a short but urgent romance, intensified by the dangers they were running.

Now, sweating in the fetid humidity of her prison cell, she didn't know if this morning had been their last moment together. Yet she hadn't hesitated to volunteer. When the moment came to join Fidel's reckless uprising in Santiago, Haydée Santamaría was one of the first to step forward. Castro had given her the unenviable and crucial task of transporting weapons to the eastern city. She was cool and brazen, even daring to ask a soldier to lift her luggage, weighed down with ammunition, off the train.

'What do you have in here?' asked the soldier, struggling with the suitcase. 'Books,' she answered without a flicker of anxiety.

As the water dripped into her dank cell in Moncada, she thought of that moment. If she had been brave then, she would have to be doubly so now, in the hands of the army, captured and imprisoned by the same men she had tried to kill hours earlier.

The attack had gone as badly as they could have feared. From the outset, misunderstandings had compounded mistakes – cars full of firearms got lost in the winding streets of Santiago, fighters were left without their weapons and orders went unheeded. As confusion reigned, the rebels tried to storm the compound, now robbed of the element of surprise. They were outnumbered and outgunned, 131 of them against a regiment of Batista's soldiers. As the dead and wounded piled up, it became painfully obvious that there was little chance of sparking the nationwide coup that he had hoped for. Fidel ordered a hasty retreat. While he and Raúl were among those who got away, nine of their comrades were killed and another eighteen were captured and immediately executed, their bodies strewn around the barracks to give the impression that they had died in combat.

The attempted coup was an abject failure and one that would not be without consequences for the plotters. The troops had lost friends at the sentry posts – fifteen soldiers and three policemen died in the attack – and they were in no mood for tolerance towards the culprits. As Haydée contemplated her chances, she heard footsteps approaching. She stood up from her bed in the cell she shared with Melba Hernández, her fearless comrade and the only other woman involved in the attack. Melba stood by her side and slipped her hand into Haydée's, the two of them bracing themselves for retribution.

A sergeant came into their cell followed by three other men, a savage grin on his face. In his hand, he carried a moist and bloodied globule. He took Haydée's hand and placed the warm object onto her palm.

'*Es de tu hermano*,' he told her.

Horrified, she looked down at Abel's eyeball, freshly gouged from his face.

Fidel Castro possessed something unique. It is hard to define the exact combination of characteristics in his personality which inspired such devotion and fear in equal measure. I lived in Venezuela under Hugo Chávez and saw first hand his deification by his supporters and the depth of feeling in the pseudo-religious cult of *Chavismo*. Lula supporters have wept in front of me on numerous occasions as they struggled to put into words their gratitude to their president.

Still, they had nothing on the devotion aroused by Fidel Castro. Hundreds of thousands – probably millions – of Cubans over successive generations were prepared to go just as far as Abel Santamaría for Fidel and his revolution. Abel was tortured and killed by Batista's men, hour after agonizing hour until death may well have come as blessed relief. Yet he didn't confess or tell the army the hiding places of his comrades. Haydée lost more than her brother in the aftermath of the Moncada attack. Boris was also killed. In various official versions of the story, she was shown his mangled genitalia and, on being told by the soldiers that he was dead, she apparently retorted: 'To die for the fatherland is to live.' For that and her unwavering support of the revolution's urban network, Fidel described her as the personification of 'heroism and dignity in the Cuban woman'. But she never fully recovered from the loss of the two men she loved most during Moncada. In 1980, she took her own life, a detail largely glossed over by the official historians in Cuba. Suicide is considered an abandonment of duty by the revolution. So, despite her sacrifice and years of service, Fidel Castro did not attend Haydée Santamaría's funeral or deliver her eulogy.

Batista is said to have ordered ten rebels killed for each dead soldier. By the end of the spree of violent revenge, some fifty-five young insurgents had been murdered by the regime. In another example of Castro's extraordinary good fortune, when he was eventually picked up, the truck driver transporting them to the barracks – where the group would surely have been beaten and executed – took pity on the captives and handed them in to the local police station instead. Fidel and Raúl were among the few survivors of the Moncada attack to serve prison time over the ill-equipped, misjudged revolt. Choosing to represent himself in court, Castro delivered a blistering defence of their actions against the Batista government on national-ist grounds. 'History will absolve me', he defiantly proclaimed to the judges, the text of his speech still printed and sold in government-run bookshops almost seventy years after the event.

Fidel was sentenced to fifteen years in the Presidio Modelo jail on the Isla de Pinos. Other rebels received between ten years, in the case of Raúl, to just a few months where irrefutable evidence of guilt was lacking. Jail time has long been a rite of passage for the populist leader, a spell behind bars underlining to *el pueblo* the courage of their would-be saviours' convictions. Both Hugo Chávez and Daniel Ortega spent months in prison for their early attempts to seize power. Evo Morales only spent a few nights in jail, albeit with the threat of terrorism charges hanging over him. Incarceration, as long as it was for honourable or 'revolutionary' reasons, has often proved a perfectly acceptable route to the presidential palace in the Americas.

The Castro brothers served less than two years before Batista issued an amnesty for political prisoners. It was a grave tactical error to free them, one he would soon come to regret. Fidel and Raúl learned from the leniency they were shown and, once in power, would display no such benevolence to any conspirators against them.[18] They went into exile in Mexico where they began to formulate plans for a true revo-lution in Cuba, one that Batista would not survive.

In Mexico City, they plotted day and night, Fidel holding court at Café La Habana on the corner of Calles Bucareli and Morelos. At a table strewn with used coffee cups and ashtrays overflowing with blackened cigarette ends, Raúl had introduced him to a young Argentinean doctor. Good-looking and self-confident, the twenty-seven-year-old physician, Ernesto Guevara, had already seen a great deal more of the Americas than his new Cuban comrades. Guevara had immediately clicked with Raúl. So well, in fact, that he had asked the younger Castro to be the best man at his wedding to Hilda Gadea, a left-wing Peruvian economist. But Ernesto also had much in common with Fidel.

Both had witnessed violent upheavals in Latin America first-hand. Castro had been in the *Bogotazo* in 1948 while Guevara had been in Guatemala in 1954 when the Yankees had ousted the leftist president, Jacobo Arbenz. Both were educated professionals, one a lawyer, the other a doctor. Most importantly, they seemed to agree perfectly on questions of international politics from the moment they met. Fidel would later describe the young Ernesto as 'already an educated revolutionary'. Guevara accepted their offer of the post of chief medical officer on their yet to be defined mission and submitted himself completely to Fidel's leadership. They would become the three prongs of the same socialist trident: Fidel, Raúl and, as he would become, 'Che' Guevara.

They found about eighty other rebels willing to join them on their incredibly risky plan, and now their main difficulty was funds. Eventually, the money would come from the United States. A tour by Fidel around several Latin American cities in search of wealthy benefactors produced a paltry $1,000 donated by Cuban immigrants. But after wading across the Rio Grande and entering the United States illegally, Castro met the deposed president of Cuba, Carlos Prío, at a motel in McAllen, Texas. Prío gave Castro the cash he and his band needed to launch a revolution.

Within a few months, the three men at the cafeteria table – the two siblings and their brother-in-arms – would sail back to Cuba clandestinely on a barely seaworthy yacht, *Granma*, that had been purchased for them by a Mexican sympathizer, Antonio '*El Cuate*' del Conde. It remains one of the great mysteries of modern Latin American history that with just eighty-two men, they managed to disembark in Cuba and successfully execute the insurrection they had planned over coffee and cigarettes in a Mexican café. But their revolution had an inauspicious start.

Fidel lay silent, perfectly still, hardly daring to breathe. All around him in this cane field were the sounds of soldiers searching for him, parting the thick stalks and rustling the leaves of the plants. Across his chest lay a Belgian-made rifle, its butt nestled beneath his chin, his finger poised over the trigger. By day, the heat and humidity in the rain-soaked field had been oppressive. Now the darkness had descended and with it a chill that cut to the bone. On either side of him he could feel the shivering of other men, their bodies providing little warmth in the mud, the contagion of their fear almost outweighing the comfort of their companionship. Above their three prone bodies, the night sky was crisp and cold and cloudless. Their only protection from another aerial assault was the sugarcane stalks that covered them.

The nocturnal noises of the jungle around the cane fields were incessant. Moving from their hiding place was impossible but staying put was suicide. As his two companions tried to drift into a fitful sleep, Fidel began to reflect on the catastrophic circumstances of their landing and wondered if his brother was still alive. When the *Granma* had set off from the port of Tuxpan in the Mexican state of Veracruz, it was heavily overloaded with men and equipment. For seven days and nights, as the vessel let in water, the crew had attempted to navigate the treacherous seas as they sailed for almost 2,000 kilometres to Cuba. Almost all of them were either seasick or weak with hunger and thirst. At one point, a man went over the side and was fortunate to be dragged back on board.

Two days later than planned and miles from their original rendezvous on the beaches between Niquero and Pilón, the yacht arrived on Cuba's southeastern coast and immediately ran aground in thick mud. As Che Guevara later observed, the revolutionaries' supposedly triumphant return to Cuban soil 'wasn't a landing, it was a shipwreck'.

It soon got much worse. Their late arrival meant that the 26 July guerrilla network had launched an urban offensive too early which was easily crushed. All it succeeded in doing was to alert Batista to the rebels' imminent landing somewhere in Cuba. As the men waded ashore, bedraggled and dispirited, and climbed into the foothills of the Sierra Maestra mountains, they left signs of their presence at every turn, making it easy for Batista's men to track them. Once they reached a clearing called Alegría de Pío, meaning the Rejoicing of the Pious, the revolutionary force was ambushed by the Cuban army. It was a massacre. The vast majority of the guerrillas were killed or captured in this opening skirmish. As the army opened fire, a few fighters managed to escape into the surrounding sugarcane plantations including Fidel, Che Guevara, Raúl, Camilo Cienfuegos and Juan Almeida.

It was 5 December 1956. Five days and nights later, when Fidel and his two comrades, Universo Sánchez and Faustino Pérez, finally crawled out of the sugarcane field, and set about trying to locate the other revolutionaries who had been scattered in the ambush. It was no small relief to emerge from their hiding place. They had survived on morning dew and sucking the syrup from broken sugarcane stalks. Batista's men had tried to flush them out by setting fire to an adjacent field, forcing them to inhale mouthfuls of acrid smoke and try as best they could to stifle their coughing. Although he didn't show it outwardly, even Fidel had begun to wonder if they would come out alive. Yet Castro's almost supernatural good fortune, later described by one of his comrades as 'mysterious destiny, or providence', would become not only a feature of his continued survival but of the revolution's.[19]

Once they reached the tiny hamlet of Cinco Palmas and the home of a *campesino* sympathetic to the revolutionary cause, the mountain rendezvous point they had sacrificed so much to reach since disembarking the *Granma*, all sense of despair immediately drained from Fidel. The first good news was that his brother was there to greet him. Raúl and four men with him had survived and they had rifles and ammunition. Their group would swell to fifteen when the indefatigable

Guevara turned up a few days later. To the others inside the hut, their struggle looked hopeless. Yet Fidel was inexplicably elated, convinced that now they would go on to victory, buoyed by his abnormal levels of self-belief and determination.

The fact that the band of rebels did eventually overthrow the Batista regime remains one of the greatest achievements in the history of guerrilla warfare. Shortly after the Alegría de Pío massacre, Batista's government announced that 'Dr Fidel Castro' had been killed. In Washington, few if any in the Eisenhower administration had ever heard of a rebel army in the Cuban mountains or its bearded leader. Certainly no one in DC could have anticipated that he would bring down a US-backed military dictatorship in Cuba within two years, install a Marxist government and become Washington's *bête noire* for decades.

The guests and staff on the eighteenth floor of the Shamrock Hilton hotel in Houston, Texas, couldn't make out the details of the foul-mouthed row going on in Spanish inside suite 18-C. But it was obvious that the two men yelling at each other behind the closed doors weren't far from coming to blows.[20]

For those who knew them well, this argument had been brewing, not just for the eleven days in late April 1959 during which Fidel had been travelling around the United States, but over the past two years. Raúl Castro, thus far an unflinchingly loyal servant of his older brother's vision – and the other voice inside that Houston hotel suite – was probably the only person in Cuba capable of standing up to his domineering sibling.

While the precise words or insults hurled at each other weren't recorded, indeed both men would deny that a falling-out had even taken place, the subject of their discussion was no secret. Fidel had spent two weeks in the US wooing the Americans, trying to assuage their fears that the communists had just landed on their doorstep.

He had dutifully smiled as the American journalists asked him time and again about his younger brother's communist leanings and desire to encourage revolutionary movements in Latin America. Fidel, just thirty-two years old, had spoken in English to the assembled newspaper editors at the National Press Club in Washington and told them he had come to America with 'the sincerest feeling of friendship'. His offer of amicable relations hadn't been reciprocated. He had met Vice-President Richard Nixon, but President Eisenhower had snubbed him, electing to play golf that day instead.

While it was uncomfortable to have to endure the incessant questions about Cuba's intentions towards US-owned companies in Cuba, the charm offensive was going well as far as Fidel was concerned. And such pragmatism was vital: there was no point in getting on the wrong side of Washington just yet.

Raúl didn't see things that way. As far as he was concerned, he hadn't risked his life in the Sierra Maestra 'for a few reforms' and, in one of their increasingly heated phone calls, he told Fidel that people in Cuba were saying he'd sold out to the Yankees.[21] The twenty-seven-year-old Raúl Castro was already a committed Marxist. He might have held back from showing it too publicly as they fought for control of the island, but now they had taken Havana. Batista was gone. This was the moment for sweeping political change, to rip up the old model and build a communist society, as he and the other Marxist guerrillas had always hoped.

Yet here was his brother, joking with the press in Washington DC, back-slapping in Princeton, eating hot dogs and ice cream in New York, cuddling children at the Bronx Zoo. He seemed more a politician than a revolutionary. And if that wasn't enough, it had just been revealed that a group of Cubans had been behind a failed incursion on the eastern coast of Panama intended to overthrow the ruling oligarchy. Rather than praising their mission, Fidel used his US trip to distance himself from their valiant efforts.

The atmosphere between the brothers was toxic well before Raúl disembarked an Air Cubana flight in Houston. By the time they met in the luxurious suite in the Shamrock Hotel, both were incandescent. Whether Fidel was genuinely impressed with the Americans he'd met or if he was playing them for fools is the subject of much academic debate. Initially, he may have simply been trying to find a modus vivendi with the imperial power before choosing the moment to reveal his hand. But Raúl couldn't be sure and nor could Che, equally as committed as the younger Castro to a Marxist-Leninist revolution. In fact, Raúl had taken a key step of his own, one that at that moment, fuming in an ostentatious Hilton hotel room, Fidel didn't know about. He had already made contact with the Kremlin.

The question as to whether Fidel fell willingly into the arms of the Soviets or was pushed into them by the hostility of the US government is difficult to answer with any real certainty. I tend to believe that he had already planned to align his revolutionary government with Moscow even as he was shaking Nixon's hand. The two men met in Nixon's private office, Castro bearded and dressed in his crumpled jungle fatigues, as though he had just stepped out of the bush, Nixon in a sharp grey suit. He regarded Castro 'with his roguish, scrutinizing look', as Fidel later described it: 'I wasn't a clandestine member of the Communist Party as Nixon had come to believe,' recalled Castro.

> I discovered at university that I was first a utopian communist and later a radical socialist. My only fault in speaking with Nixon was to have the repugnance to explain with frankness my thoughts to a vice-president and probable future president of the United States, an expert in economic concepts and imperialist methods of government which I had not believed in for some time.[22]

Between the years when Fidel Castro came to power and his death, 1959 to 2016, he went through eleven US presidents: Eisenhower, Kennedy, Johnson, Nixon, Ford, Carter, Reagan, George H. W. Bush, Clinton, George W. Bush and Obama. In terms of 'twenty-first-century socialism', his relationships with those last three occupants of the White House are the most pertinent. But the Cold War years turned Fidel into a global figure and his audacity, radicalism and anti-Americanism made him an icon for the left around the world.

At their brief meeting, Nixon was singularly unimpressed by

Castro. But he was sufficiently concerned to recommend to his boss that the hirsute revolutionary be removed from power as quickly as possible. Plans were soon drawn up for an invasion by Cuban exiles to overthrow Castro and his new regime. At that stage, its modalities were still undecided. It would take two years from Castro's failed charm offensive in the USA to put the plans into effect, and by then a new president, John F. Kennedy, would be in office.

Dolores Fis Hernández was exhausted. Her baby boy was teething, and she had barely slept for days. For two nights, the young mother had lain awake as much through her own anxiety as through the child's crying. It was the night of 16 April 1961. Despite their isolation, in a wooden shack on Cuba's southern coast, Dolores and her husband, Armando, knew that the tension with the United States was coming to a head.

Before bed each evening they huddled around their small short-wave radio and listened to the broadcasts on Radio Rebelde. Diplomatic ties with the United States had been broken a few months earlier and, since then, Fidel Castro had warned the Cuban people that an invasion was imminent. Two nights earlier, piston-engined B-26 Invader bombers with false flag markings had launched airstrikes on three airfields in Santiago, San Antonio de los Baños and Ciudad Libertad. Some Cubans had already lost their lives, including a young, idealistic artilleryman called Eduardo García Delgado. The twenty-five-year-old revolutionary would be posthumously celebrated for his zeal after he smeared the letters 'F-I-D-E-L' in blood onto a wooden door as he lay dying from his wounds.

Such moments of heroism felt remote to Dolores, an uneducated Afro-Cuban woman trapped in the crossfire of world affairs. She was born and raised in this sodden backwater and her family survived by producing charcoal. Backbreaking, arduous work, she lugged huge bundles of firewood for miles to turn into the cheap fuel. Since Fidel and his revolutionaries had taken power, though, she felt more hopeful about the prospects of the poor.

Suddenly, a boom jolted Dolores from her slumber. It was a little after midnight. She shook her husband awake:

'Wake up. Listen! They're firing on the beach,' she whispered.

'No, no. That's a boat, they're unloading materials,' Armando answered, rolling over.

'They're bombing Playa Girón,' Dolores hissed insistently.

Her husband forced himself to his feet and into his shoes. He woke up his father and his brother in the adjoining plot of land and the three men went to investigate while Dolores waited at home with her sister-in-law and their children. When they returned, they confirmed Dolores' worst fears: Cuba was under attack and it was happening barely a mile from her home, at a stretch of beach on the Bahía de Cochinos, the Bay of Pigs, in the province of Las Villas.

'You should start building a trench,' one of the men helpfully suggested. 'With what?' retorted Dolores, 'A dog's tooth?' In the end, the two women decided that it was too risky to stay in the village, makeshift trenches or not. Before they fled for the countryside, they ransacked a neighbour's empty home for food. They grabbed sugar and coffee and biscuits for what would be an arduous journey deep into the countryside with tired and hungry children under their arms.

At eighty-three, Dolores' dark skin is cracking, and she has lost her sight in one eye. But, even now, she recalls in fine detail the days when her village was invaded and tells the story with great colour and a sense of drama. Committed revolutionary that she was, she says that had the invasion happened a year earlier, she might well have dug that trench and stayed in it armed with nothing more than a dog's tooth. Burdened now with a baby, though, she knew she had to get away from the impending battle. As she and her sister-in-law ran, their tiny village was about to become the focus of world attention. Eventually, it would become shorthand for covert CIA operations in Latin America.

Today, as you drive into the town, there is a billboard that triumphantly proclaims: 'Girón: the first defeat of Yankee imperialism in Latin America'. The Cuban state's jingoism aside, it's not factually wrong. Until that point, the US had largely been able to do as it pleased in the region – overthrow elected governments and install friendly ones the length and breadth of the Americas. But the anti-Castro forces were roundly defeated on the shores of Girón and the mangrove swamps of the Zapata Peninsula. When Fidel Castro forced back and then captured more than 1,200 CIA-trained Cuban exiles, Washington was humiliated and left in no doubt as to his abilities as a military strategist. Castro arrived in the Bay of Pigs on the afternoon of 17 April to take charge of the operation. By that time, the 'mercenaries', as they would henceforth be known in Cuba, had managed to make some headway onto the mainland. Still, the CIA's entire endeavour was beset with problems from the start.

First, it was woefully underplanned. In March 1960, President Eisenhower took the decision to approve $13 million for an operation overseen by the CIA director, Allen Dulles, and Richard Bissell, the agency's deputy director for plans. Given the relative ease with which the CIA had brushed aside the left-wing presidency of Jacobo Arbenz in Guatemala six years earlier, they were confident of a reprise in Cuba without exposing Washington's role. In Miami, the agency enlisted 1,400 men, many of whom had left the island when Castro took power, to form the 2506 Brigade. They took them to Useppa Island off the Florida coast and trained them for the amphibious assault.

By the time John F. Kennedy entered the White House in January 1961, the plan, code-named JMATE was almost ready. He just had to give it the green light. Despite his residual doubts, he did so on 4 April 1961.

The CIA's own description of one of the most ignominious events in its chequered history is refreshingly frank: 'As the number of days till the invasion shortened, Kennedy's concern that the operation would not remain covert grew. He was adamant the hand of the US Government remain hidden at all costs. Kennedy thought changing the invasion site from Trinidad would make future deniability of US involvement more plausible, so he gave the CIA four days to come up with a new one. And so, a month before the operation was set to get underway, the landing location changed from Trinidad to the Bay of Pigs.'[23] The site was moved, and Kennedy approved the renamed Operation Zapata.

That decision, the report continues, presented an 'array of problems', not least that Fidel regularly went fishing and diving in that part of Cuba and knew it 'like the back of his hand'. What the CIA report fails to mention is that if the exiles were expecting to be greeted as liberating counter-revolutionaries in that region, they were very much mistaken. The rural poor of the Las Villas province, people like Dolores Fis and her family, loved Fidel and after just two years of his rule were highly unlikely to take up arms against him for a group of unknown men storming the beach in the dead of night.

It was also a terrible location for an invasion. Only one road in and out, approximately fifty miles from the rendezvous point in the Escambray mountains, dense, mosquito-infested swamps lay between the beachhead and the mountain range. The invading force ran aground on the reef around Girón. Clearly visible from the shore, the element of surprise was lost as were a great many weapons which slipped into the sea around the foundering launches.

However poorly executed the *Granma* landing was in 1956 or badly bungled the Moncada attack in 1953, this was worse. Yet a battle was soon underway for control of the island and, as Fidel knew better than anyone, given the right conditions, victory could be achieved against the slimmest of odds. Castro had no intention of underestimating the Cuban exiles in the same way that Batista had underestimated him. So he came at them with everything he had.

The FAR, the Revolutionary Armed Forces of Cuba, easily outnumbered and outgunned the invaders. With Kennedy desperate to maintain some semblance of plausible deniability, he called off further airstrikes after the initial attacks on 15 April. The men of 2506 Brigade were on their own. Once he had routed the attackers, Castro rubbed the Americans' noses in their defeat, offering to return the captured survivors in exchange for 500 tractors worth almost $30 million. More than a year and a half later, on Christmas Eve 1962, most of the captured exiles (including Félix Rodríguez, who would eventually hunt down Che Guevara in Bolivia) were sent back to Florida in exchange for food and medicine worth almost double that amount.

Some fifty-five years later, the CIA's account still betrays the agency's resentment at President Kennedy's decision to call off the aerial assaults and not back up the invasion with further military support:

The salvaged and undamaged Cuban planes that had survived the 15 April strikes, the very planes that should have been destroyed that morning had Kennedy not cancelled the planned strike, were now flying overhead wreaking mayhem on the [2506] Brigade.[24]

In an interview in 1975, Raúl Castro put it more succinctly: 'Kennedy vacillated.'[25] It was a hesitation for which the anti-Castro Cubans in Florida never forgave him.

Three weeks after the revolutionaries took Havana and Fulgencio Batista fled to the Dominican Republic with millions of dollars from the state coffers, Fidel Castro embarked on his first foreign visit as Cuba's leader. When choosing a destination for his victory lap, one Latin American ally stood out above all others: Venezuela. A year earlier its people had also seized their moment against a dictatorial ruler, Marcos Pérez Jiménez. On 23 January 1959, Castro and his entourage landed at Maiquetía airport near Caracas in an American Super Constellation airliner operated by the Venezuelan airline, Aeropostal.

The moment was captured in black-and-white newsreel footage. As Fidel shielded his eyes from the blinding Caribbean sun, the first face he saw bounding up the steps to greet him was the interim Venezuelan leader, Rear Admiral Wolfgang Larrazábal. Behind him, a swaying crowd of overjoyed well-wishers, hoping to catch a glimpse of the victorious revolutionary, waved Venezuelan and Cuban flags and the red-and-black banner of Castro's 26th July Movement. Touched by the outpouring of support, he made an impromptu speech in the airport: 'The peoples of the Americas know that their internal strength comes from their unity and that the continent's strength also comes from its union.'

The theme of unity – albeit solely among parties of the left – was one he would raise often on that first trip to Venezuela, and would repeat decades later on his subsequent visits to the country under Hugo Chávez. The January 1959 trip was an unqualified success for Fidel. He delivered important speeches at a joint session of Congress and at the Central University of Caracas. His public address at the Plaza del Silencio had been attended by many thousands of applauding Venezuelans, keen to hear the famous Cuban rebel in person.

He told them that 'for me, arriving in Caracas was even more emotional than the arrival in Havana because here I have received everything from those who have received nothing from me'. He called the crowd to embrace continental unity and urged those listening and watching across Latin America to snap out of their complacency: 'If only the destiny of our peoples could be a single destiny! How much longer are we going to be in lethargy?'

Castro was fêted as a Latin American hero in Venezuela. He took a ride up the Ávila mountain on the impressive cable-car system built by Marcos Pérez Jiménez. At the summit, he gazed at the spectacular view across the Valley of Caracas from the Hotel Humboldt. He had a poem dedicated and read aloud to him by the Chilean poet Pablo Neruda and enjoyed lavish dinners and drinks receptions in his honour at the Cuban ambassador's residence. After the hardships of the jungle, they were moments that the guerrilla leader savoured.

However, a polarizing character such as Fidel Castro wasn't universally well received. In particular, he met the cerebral president-elect, Rómulo Betancourt, at his home and it was immediately clear that they were on an inevitable collision course. Betancourt was a staunch defender of democratic principles and created the self-titled 'Betancourt Doctrine' intended to deny diplomatic recognition to any *caudillo*, whether of the left or the right. Betancourt would later be known as 'the Father of Venezuelan Democracy'.

Their relationship deteriorated from the moment Betancourt took power. Fidel willingly provided arms, training, even some key advisers to leftist guerrilla groups in Venezuela to try to overthrow his counterpart. It prompted Rómulo Betancourt into a curt and lasting riposte: 'Tell Fidel Castro that when Venezuela needed liberators, it didn't import them; it bore them.' Perhaps the lowest bilateral ebb between the two nations came during the Cuban missile crisis in 1962, when Betancourt was President Kennedy's main point man in Latin America. That consolidation and reinforcement of Venezuela's relationship with Washington would last until Hugo Chávez took office in 1999.

It wasn't until that point, exactly forty years after his first visit, that Fidel had his man in Caracas. If Venezuela was Castro's earliest ally, it would be his last friend, too, as the bilateral bond he formed with Chávez outlasted the two men.[26] The close ties between Chávez and Castro began the moment the former soldier emerged from Yare prison in 1994 after serving his sentence for leading a failed coup. By December, he travelled to Havana and was greeted at the airport by Fidel, the elder statesman of Latin American socialism. Over the next few years, their relationship blossomed, marking the start of an unbreakable tie. Cuba began to ramp up its intelligence presence in Venezuela. After Chávez narrowly survived his April 2002 coup attempt, thanks in part to counsel implored down the telephone by Fidel, Cuban advisers began to multiply in Venezuela. They quickly played a prominent role in Venezuela's political life and inside its military, acting with the full knowledge and approval of the host nation's commander-in-chief.

In August 2019, the Reuters news agency in Caracas published an in-depth investigation based on two leaked military agreements which claimed to reveal the full extent of Cuba's role in Venezuela's internal affairs.[27] The Reuters report identified a crucial moment as late 2007, after Hugo Chávez's only loss at the polls when he was denied the right to stand for indefinite re-election. As Chávez licked his wounds, Castro shared with his disciple the key to remaining in power for decades: ensure absolute control of the military.[28]

On 26 May 2008, at a meeting in Caracas, Venezuela's defence minister, Gustavo Rangel, and Cuba's vice-minister of defence,

General Álvaro López, signed a bilateral agreement. Reuters reported that under the accord Cuba's armed forces were given free rein to train soldiers in Venezuela and review – even restructure – parts of the Venezuelan military. Furthermore, their investigation said that the pact authorized Cuba to bring Venezuelan intelligence agents to Havana for instruction and to pivot the entire mission of Venezuela's intelligence service away from international espionage and towards spying on its own soldiers.[29]

The aim was to prevent another insurrection from taking root within the military, once a regular occurrence in Venezuela – as Chávez could testify – but one which Cuba had successfully avoided for decades. They would create, in effect, the 'Bolivarian Armed Forces' in which the essential task of protecting the constitution was supplanted by the new job of upholding *Chavismo*. In the Cuban case, the military under Raúl Castro controls key economic sectors on the island, from seaports and import duties to tourism and hotel chains. In time, the Venezuelan armed forces would extend that business model further. They became responsible for oil wells, natural gas plants, hydroelectric dams, water supply, gold mining, diamond mines, border security, airports, and the subsidised food supply to name just a few of the main activities. In return, they provided resolute and steadfast support first to Chávez and latterly to Maduro. Meanwhile Cuba's counter-intelligence services weeded out any hint of dissent in their ranks.

Venezuela's Directorate of Military Intelligence, or DIM, was the main focus of Cuba's influence. The Cuban Defence Ministry restructured the organization and created specialist new units inside the DIM containing officers who had received months of espionage training in Havana.[30] In 2011, Chávez changed the DIM's title to better reflect its new duties and it became the Directorate General of Military Counterintelligence, or DGCIM. It grew to an estimated 1,500 officers and it was accused in a United Nations report of torture 'including electric shocks, suffocation with plastic bags, water boarding, beatings, sexual violence, water and food deprivation, stress positions and exposure to extreme temperatures'.[31] Inside the

Venezuelan military they became known as 'the Men in Black' for their black uniforms, though some agents were infiltrated into the ranks while dressed as ordinary guardsmen. Military arrests shot up and former soldiers spoke of a culture of deep paranoia and crippling fear inside the Venezuelan armed forces. The Cubans were present in every barracks, influential at the highest levels.

In a dingy, dimly lit apartment in the Parque Central district of Caracas, I met Pedro Galindo, a lieutenant on active duty in the army. Over glasses of sickly sweet malt soda, he felt sufficiently emboldened to talk to me as he planned to flee the country with his pregnant girlfriend in the near future. He told me of how the soldiers' morale was on the floor but no one dared speak out or complain. 'The army is living under the slogan "¡Viva Chávez!",' he told me. 'They do not permit the freedom of thought or expression inside the Venezuelan army.' Subversive conversations, let alone planning any kind of insurrection, were impossible under the conditions imposed by the DGCIM, the lieutenant explained. Every morning, the salute to the flag now included the call 'Chávez lives!' to which the entire unit was expected to respond 'and the struggle continues'. Any trooper seen not answering that pledge with sufficient gusto would be quickly identified and reprimanded. A socialist army wasn't what Pedro had signed up for and he saw exile as his only solution. He firmly blamed Cuba for a politicization of the armed forces which began under Chávez but was deepened by Maduro.

It wasn't only a disillusioned lieutenant who told me of Cuba's influence over the Venezuelan military but also a former member of Chávez's inner circle. As a general, Clíver Alcalá was credited as the man who first declared Venezuela's armed forces 'Bolivarian' and 'revolutionary'. A few years after he retired from the army, we met in a rooftop bar in a Caracas hotel, his general's uniform jettisoned for the grey suit and pink tie of a politician. He told me the Bolivarian project he had spent years defending was a sham and had descended into 'anarchy' under Maduro. Such outspoken comments would eventually see him exiled, too.[32] In military terms, though, the former *Chavista* general applauded the efficient way Cuba had achieved its aim by preventing exactly the kind of internal revolt he had participated in with Hugo Chávez in 1992: 'I don't think there'll be [another] military coup. In fact, I'm convinced there won't be. The armed forces have now been so divorced from such actions that any adventures would be stopped before they even began.'

Cuban security aid wasn't purely altruistic, however. Fidel Castro needed the 'Bolivarian Revolution' to endure in Venezuela to guarantee the survival of his own revolutionary project. Cuba's subsidized energy arrangement with Venezuela is more important to the island than any other. At its height, more than 100,000 barrels of Venezuelan crude a day were sent to Cuba. Although that figure has fallen off significantly, as the Venezuelan oil industry is on its knees, Caracas will always try to ensure Cuba's domestic consumption is covered. And Cuba pays for the oil using human capital rather than hard currency in the form of thousands of doctors, nurses and intelligence personnel.

Nowhere has been more important to Castro's Cuba than Venezuela. For as long as the two revolutions persist, they will maintain a binding, entwined and co-dependent relationship, irrespective of the pressure from Washington. Following the death of his most important follower, of his favourite son in March 2013, Fidel Castro described Hugo Chávez as quite simply 'the best friend the Cuban people had in their entire history'.

Aleksandr Ivanovich Alekseev was appointed Soviet ambassador to Cuba partly against his will. He had protested that he wasn't up to the task and 'didn't know enough economics'. Nikita Khrushchev dismissed that argument. He had the trust of Fidel Castro and that was all that mattered in Cuba. 'So as far as economics is concerned, we'll give twenty advisors if you need them,' retorted Khrushchev. The discussion was over.[33]

Almost as soon as he was given the job, in May 1962, Alekseev was called to the Kremlin for a briefing. The Soviet premier wanted to know whether he thought Castro might be willing to accept the deployment of medium-range missiles with nuclear warheads in Cuba. As a calm diplomat, Alekseev tried to show no outward reaction to a question that, as he put it, 'knocked him off his feet'.[34] Despite the churning in his stomach, Alekseev kept his eyes fixed on the men of the Politburo and, without wavering, he gave them his considered opinion: Fidel Castro would not agree.

Surely, he wouldn't, Alekseev reasoned. Castro's revolution had garnered support and guarantees of aid from other Latin American countries since the Americans' reckless misadventure at the Bay of Pigs. CIA-backed invaders storming a small Caribbean island was too much for even traditional US allies in the region and they openly backed Cuba's calls for its independence to be respected. In part, they were taking the opportunity to tell Washington to stay out of their affairs, too. But that new-found solidarity with Cuba would disappear overnight should Castro accept Soviet nuclear warheads just ninety miles off the coast of Florida. It would be an act of incredible foolhardiness.

Still, the Soviets had made their decision and Alekseev was to broach the matter with Castro. On the Sunday evening before he left for Havana, he was summoned again, this time to Khrushchev's dacha in Zhukovka. Once more, the members of the Politburo were gathered, and they ordered Alekseev to finesse their message.

'Comrade Alekseev said that Fidel would not accept our proposal for the deployment of the missiles. So, I think that we need to talk with Fidel not as if such a decision has already been made,' said Khrushchev, 'but as if we could consider these questions if, say, Fidel came to such a conclusion that would oppose American attack plans.'[35]

So that's how it went. Once back in Cuba, Alekseev contacted Raúl Castro and told him that one of the members of the Soviet delegation who had entered the country wasn't 'Engineer Petrov' at all. In fact, he was marshal of the missile forces, Sergey Biryuzov. Raúl understood the implications immediately and within three hours they were seated in a room with Fidel. On the Cuban side, only the Castro brothers were present, with Raúl taking meticulous notes.

Aleksandr Alekseev and his comrades began the pitch to Fidel, but as he was speaking it dawned on the Soviet ambassador that the wily Cuban revolutionary had already decided that such an esca-lation was necessary. Still, they went through the delicate dance of putting the nuclear deterrent on the table. The Soviets relayed the message from Comrade Khrushchev that Cuba's independence was important to Moscow. Fidel nodded sagely.

'Tell us, *Comandante*, what do you need to help Cuba preserve its independence?'

'We are prepared to do an awful lot,' Biryuzov interjected en-couragingly. 'Even, as Comrade Khrushchev mentioned, we could consider the possibility of deploying nuclear weapons in Cuba.'

Castro didn't flinch but stroked his beard a moment. 'Yes, that's an interesting idea,' he replied slowly. 'If it would help the socialist bloc, we in Cuba are prepared to take this risk.'

Alekseev wasn't convinced the plan had anything to do with the socialist bloc at all. Nevertheless, he had the answer Moscow wanted, and that would do for now. That the Cuban leader was prepared to take the extraordinarily risky step showed he was unlike anyone either Washington or Moscow had ever dealt with in Latin America. His supporters still maintain it was a sign of his fearlessness and profound commitment to the revolutionary cause. His detractors say he was unhinged, engaging in a foolish game of chicken between the superpowers that not only jeopardized the lives of the Cuban people but put the population of the entire planet at risk.

'That story is badly understood,' says Fabian Escalante, rocking back in his chair, six decades later. At the time, Escalante was a twenty-one-year-old counter-intelligence agent. He showed an uncommon talent in the field and would later rise to become the head of Cuba's state intelligence agency, commonly known as G2. As I arrived at his home thoroughly soaked from a torrential Caribbean downpour, a blackout struck his neighbourhood of Havana and the lights went out. Sitting in the dark with the rain lashing the roof and the thunder rumbling outside only added to the ominous sense of secrecy and intrigue as Cuba's ex-spymaster began to reminisce.

'In 1962, I was the head of a small counter-intelligence unit,' he recalled in a deliberate voice, 'which was dedicated to discovering

and preventing actions by the CIA and counter-revolutionary organizations.' He first became aware of the plans to install Soviet missile
bases in Cuba in August of that year. Escalante believes that, rather
than being seen as a failure, the missile crisis should be regarded as
a testament to the Cuban people's ability to keep a secret. Lampposts
were uprooted at the dead of night, he said, to make way for vast
weapons that couldn't fit down the main streets. People in Pinar del
Rio, at the western end of the island, knew something was up much
earlier than most and the operation had become an open secret in
Cuba within days. More than forty medium-range nuclear missiles
were installed in Cuba in a manoeuvre which involved much of the
Soviet cargo fleet, eighty-five ships, docking in the port of Mariel
right under the Americans' noses. Yet still, the former intelligence
chief remarked with a satisfied smile, Washington didn't know
anything until a U2 spy plane took photos of the missile sites in
mid-October.

Those thirteen days in October 1962 took the world closer to nuclear
destruction than it has ever come before or since. As Ambassador
Alekseev's memories bring to life in fascinating detail, Fidel Castro
was central to the whole affair. He could have easily answered to the
Soviets that such a move was a provocation too far, that he didn't
want to turn the rest of the region against him or insisted on some
other way of sending the White House a message. However, using the
parlance of his brother, when faced with the ultimate choice he didn't
vacillate. Whether that makes Castro a brilliant and bold strategist or
the victim of his own towering ego is a debate that Latin Americanists
have had for decades.

As the Cuban missile crisis, or 'the October Crisis' as it's known in
Cuba, unfolded before the eyes of a horrified world, Castro was bru-
tally overruled by the Soviets in their negotiations with Washington.
The final decision – to remove the warheads from Cuba in exchange
for the removal of obsolete nuclear-tipped 'Jupiter' missiles from
Turkey, plus a guarantee not to invade the island – was taken without
Fidel's input. He was apoplectic. Being portrayed as a pawn in a wider
battle wasn't something his vanity welcomed. In the days immediately

after the eyeball-to-eyeball confrontation, before the dust had fully settled, Castro made his displeasure abundantly clear in a letter to Khrushchev: 'What we [the Cuban people] did in the face of the events, Comrade Khrushchev, was prepare ourselves and make ourselves ready to fight. In Cuba there was but one type of alarm: the alarm of combat.'

He went on to say that 'the eyes of many men, Cubans and Soviets who were ready to die with supreme dignity, shed tears on hearing of the surprising, unexpected and practically unconditional decision to withdraw the arms'. It was in this letter that he said 'our generous people were ready to immolate themselves'. If history is to truly 'absolve' Castro as he once claimed, it must first take into consideration that particular sentence. His critics say people should harbour no illusions about him when it comes to the Cuban missile crisis. As others sought to de-escalate the crisis, he remained absolute in his assertion that millions of his people were prepared to go up in a storm of nuclear dust for his intransigence. Even most Castro supporters agree he wouldn't have hesitated to order the annihilation of the island if he'd felt it was necessary to uphold its freedom.

The lighting was too harsh for television. The quality of the audio was poor, the images grainy and often out of focus. The resulting footage was overexposed and flickered, lending a dream-like ethereality to the proceedings. Yet the nightly broadcasts held all of Cuba rapt.

Stripped of his grey dress uniform, General Arnaldo Ochoa stood before the tribunal in a black-and-white-checked shirt and flared jeans. 'Ochoa Sánchez, the law permits you the right to speak. Do you wish to?' Over the days of the trial – 'Causa No. 1' of 1989 – he had heard his name denigrated, been accused of theft, drug trafficking and, worst of all, treason. He had listened in silence as they had outlined his relationship with the vilest forces of capitalism and how he collaborated with a Colombian drug cartel, besmirching the uniform he wore until recently with pride. He certainly did have something to say.

'Yes,' he replied in a firm, clear voice. Looking at the military tribunal before him through his thick-rimmed square glasses, General Ochoa – revolutionary hero and supreme commander of Cuba's campaigns in Africa, where he had defeated a South African invasion of Angola – delivered his devastating testimony.

A moment arrived in my military life that I felt tired. Very tired. At times in Angola, I found myself in very difficult situations, for me, very complex. I think that this combined with so many years of acting alone, I took the wrong path. There have been more than enough words and there are many facts. I prefer that the facts speak for themselves.

He would continue to deliver an extraordinary confession for a revolutionary of his standing: 'While our [communist] party was declaring that it had nothing to do with drug trafficking, I was involved in it,' Ochoa testified. 'I want to tell my comrades-at-arms that I believe I betrayed my country, and I say in all honesty, one pays for treason with one's life.'[36]

'Ochoa's words of self-accusation before the cameras were stunningly direct,' wrote Julia Preston at the time in the aptly titled *The Trial that Shook Cuba*, 'although his demeanour was remote and reflective.'[37] 'Are you the same Ochoa from Ethiopia?' one of the tribunal members asked him in feigned disbelief. 'Possibly not,' answered Ochoa, resigned to a fate that, even if he still had the fight left in him, he couldn't have avoided. He insisted that the events for which he was on trial were his sole responsibility calling them 'the artifice of my mind' and swore that neither Fidel nor Raúl Castro had been involved. Nothing he would say before the tribunal nor a single moment from his glorious revolutionary past would bring him any mercy from Fidel. The island's ultimate power had long since decided his fate.

Two days later, a deftly edited version of Ochoa's testimony was televised to a disbelieving nation. All of Cuba watched as the decorated hero was plunged into ignominy and public disgrace. In the clear-eyed knowledge of the price for treason, Arnaldo Ochoa openly recognized that his words could bring him before the firing squad. Yet he didn't flinch: 'I promise you all that, at that moment, my last thought would be of Fidel, and of the great revolution he has given our people.'

Before General Ochoa was put on a show trial, he had been one of the most decorated and celebrated members of the Castro inner circle. His spectacular fall from grace marked a pivotal moment for many revolutionaries in Cuba, a tipping point in which they finally accepted that the revolution wasn't an even-handed or just system but a totalitarian one in which every decision hung on the orders of one man. If ever evidence was needed of Castro's demand for total loyalty, don't look at his imprisonment of Rafael del Pino, his friend from the *Bogotazo*, don't look at his absence from Haydée Santamaría's funeral or his harsh treatment of even his most harmless critics. Look at the trial of Arnaldo Ochoa.

Like the Castros, Arnaldo Ochoa came from Oriente province and was also the son of Spanish immigrants. It hadn't taken much to convince him to join the 26th July Movement. He had been disgusted by what he'd seen growing up – the rural poverty, the exploitation of the workers and the slave-like indenture to which they were subjected. The parallels with the experiences of the Castro brothers were clear.

Once he'd become part of their effort to overthrow Batista, Ochoa joined the rebel army at the first chance he got. In 1957, he reached the guerrillas in the Sierra Maestra and tied his future to theirs. It would take him to the highest echelons of the new Cuba. He played a vital role in the battle for Santa Clara in December 1958, a turning point in the revolution that led to the fall of Havana, and fought at Fidel's side against the CIA-trained exiles at the Bay of Pigs. He also travelled to Venezuela to support the leftist guerrillas there against President Rómulo Betancourt. By 1965 he was a member of the Central Committee of the Cuban Communist Party and one of the most influential men on the island.

However, it was in Africa where he excelled. In the 1970s he fought in Congo, Ethiopia and Angola as Cuba tried to influence their civil wars. He trained local troops, advised on military strategy and even directed them in battle. Even after those conflicts ended badly, he emerged with great credit and garnered the praise of his Soviet comrades. By 1985, his stock had risen to such a point he was awarded the country's top honour: Hero of the Republic of Cuba.

Throughout it all, he had remained loyal and steadfast. His close relationship with Raúl Castro was key. The two men were close allies in the internal power struggles of the revolution and good friends in their private lives. Their children played together at weekends and they enjoyed being family men, unlike the more aloof Fidel. With the revolution entering its thirtieth year, their staunch commitment to Marxist-Leninism and to Fidel as a leader had served Ochoa and Raúl well. Neither had particularly expected to make it this far in life. But now their youthful adventures had evolved into something much more complex as they struggled to keep the island economically afloat amid the imminent collapse of the socialist bloc.

The USSR looked increasingly precarious under Mikael Gorbachev and Raúl was acutely aware that, without the estimated $5 billion dollars a year in Soviet economic aid, the Cuban Revolution would be in serious jeopardy. Combined with the sustained pressure from the US embargo, the hardships for most Cubans would be long and painful. The situation had the potential to bring the Americans their long-awaited victory in Cuba without firing a shot.

That had to be avoided at all costs. As the summer of 1989 approached, General Ochoa's star was reaching its zenith. He had given three extraordinary decades of service and was about to be rewarded further. He was due to be designated the head of the Western Army, which would officially make him Raúl's number two, the third most powerful man on the island after the Castro brothers, with responsibility for protecting the capital.

Before the announcement could be made, standard background checks had to be carried out. They were common and weren't expected to cause any ripples. After all, no one was more loyal than General Ochoa. Almost immediately, though, rumours began to swirl.

Accusations were made against him by some of his comrades, insisting that he had been involved in the export of illegal ivory from Angola. The stories soon began to widen to include diamond smuggling and the illicit sale of weapons to Nicaragua, all of it allegedly taking place on his watch.

Then came the knockout blow, the supposed link with a name so tarnished that no one closely associated with it ever emerged completely clean: Pablo Escobar. General Ochoa was accused of conceiving of a plan involving "really big business, not just kilos" with the infamous Colombian drug lord to facilitate the Medellín cartel's drug routes into the United States via Panama. As the 1980s drew to a close, Havana was increasingly worried that Washington only needed the smallest pretext to invade the island. Indeed, the US did exactly that in Panama a year later using drug-trafficking charges against President Manuel Noriega as their justification. The revolutionary leadership confronted the general with the evidence.

Ochoa didn't deny involvement with the Colombian drug traffickers; in fact, he never contested the link to Pablo Escobar or the Medellín cartel. Yet, while he confessed to having done some 'atrocious things', he offered no specifics about what those things were.[38] Rather, he simply insisted that he had always acted in the revolution's best interests. The accusation from Castro's opponents is that Arnaldo Ochoa was merely carrying out orders and was a scapegoat for Raúl who, as the defence minister and head of the armed forces, must have known very well what his men were doing.

Raúl exhorted his friend to admit his guilt, to beg for forgiveness and throw himself at the mercy of Fidel. General Ochoa, hero of the wars in Africa and Cuba's finest internationalist, refused to cave and wouldn't budge from his position. He was arrested on 12 June 1989. Although it gripped the nation, the televised trial was a sham. Just eight days after it began, he was found guilty of 'high treason against the fatherland'.[39] The military tribunal recommended that the man who had been days away from becoming the most influential non-Castro in Cuba bear 'the full weight of the law', shorthand for death by firing squad. Ochoa himself had made the decision easy for them by saying 'I deserve to die' during his testimony.[40] To compound his humiliation, he was stripped of the military honours and medals he'd acquired through a lifetime of dedication and service as well as the title of Hero of the Republic.

Sentenced alongside him were his aide-de-camp, Jorge Martínez Valdés, and two top intelligence officers, Antonio de la Guardia and Amado Padrón Trujillo.[41] Antonio de la Guardia's daughter, Ileana de la Guardia, barely out of her teens, remembers how she held back the tears at her father's sentencing to try to transmit some of her strength to him from across the courtroom. Now living in France, she is in no doubt as to why her father ended up in such a predicament:

> From about 1985, we started to feel the influence in Cuba of the reforms in the Soviet Union, perestroika. These were issues which were being openly talked about. My friends and I used to sit in the garden with my father and talk about how if things were changing in eastern Europe, then Cuba should change too. I didn't imagine that expressing those opinions could mean being arrested or executed.[42]

As the firing squad lifted their rifles, ex-General Arnaldo Ochoa Sanchez may well have thought of Luanda. Its seafront promenade, the Marginal, had always reminded him of the Malecón in his beloved Havana, where his final dawn was now breaking. He knew intimately the Soviet-made weapons whose barrels he was staring down: an SKS semi-automatic carbine had been in his hands throughout his deployment in Africa, and was a fitting rifle with which to end his life.

Ochoa was under no illusions. There would be no last-minute clemency from Fidel. His end was decided from the very moment the accusation was made, from the instant he showed the slightest defiance of Castro. A firing squad was an honourable death for a revolutionary. Honourable, but not just.

Furthermore, it shouldn't be an underling who gave the order to bring the curtain down on such a distinguished revolutionary life. It was not right that his men, loyal to the last, be forced to extinguish their leader. So Ochoa made a final request of his executioner as the Special Troops filed in, hoping that a soldier of his standing would be granted a dying wish.

'Remove my blindfold,' he asked of their superior, 'and let me give the order to fire myself.' After a moment's conference, they acquiesced to his desire to die on his own command. Most of the men in the firing squad had once hero-worshipped General Ochoa, and just weeks ago would have followed his every word. If this was to be his final order, they would faithfully carry it out.

Flanked by the other three men, General Ochoa steeled himself.

¡Preparen!

His voice rang out clear and true. The firing squad lifted their weapons. He had given this order before and found them to be the three hardest words an officer could utter. This time, however, they must have come almost with a sense of relief, at last a degree of control over events and an end to the Kafkaesque nightmare that had seen him recast from hero to traitor in the space of a month.

¡Apunten!

The men pulled back their safety catches and their rifles clicked in near unison. Ochoa may have noted the date to himself: 13 July 1989. He was fifty-seven. The morning breeze wafted across the back of his neck as he let the macabre and solemn scene hang for a few short seconds.

¡Fuego!

It was nearly 4 p.m. when the number 79 bus came down Quinta Avenida. It didn't slow down to let passengers on between 72nd and 74th Streets as usual, but instead picked up speed. The Cuban guards standing outside the Peruvian Embassy had been on high alert over the past two weeks amid sporadic and increasingly drastic attempts to make it onto Peruvian soil in search of asylum. Even though they were posted to prevent exactly this type of kamikaze action, the guards hadn't seen the *guagua* coming towards them.

The bus crashed through the embassy gates. Shots were fired by the Cuban guardsmen and ricocheted around the compound. One of the guards crumpled, shot in the stomach. The six people on board – three men, one woman and two children, led by the driver, Héctor Sanyústiz – fell out and scrambled over the line onto Peruvian territory. As well as killing the guard, the gunshot might as well have been a starting pistol for a mass exodus to begin. It was 1 August 1980.

Cuba immediately demanded that Peru hand over the six people from the bus. Lima refused and their diplomatic ties collapsed instantly. Furious at the insubordination and the embarrassingly public method of fleeing the island, Fidel said anyone who wanted to go could do so. The news was like an explosion, its sonic boom emanating from the Peruvian Embassy in Miramar to every corner of Cuba. Thousands who had been patiently plotting or waiting for an opportunity to leave suddenly saw a door to the United States open a crack and ran to shove their foot in before it closed for good.

Within days, the embassy courtyard teemed with people, some 10,000 by most estimates, a sweltering, writhing mass of humanity, eating whatever came their way, defecating wherever they could find a spot. As the sanitary conditions worsened in the oppressive heat, they grew more desperate with each passing hour, yet were stuck in legal limbo until someone in officialdom – whether from Washington, Lima or Havana, or some combination of all three – told them where to go and what to do. One thing was clear, though: no one was leaving their hallowed spot inside Peru's jurisdiction, whether sitting on the roof or perched in the branches of the trees, until their safe passage out was granted. Eventually, diplomacy prevailed and Cuba granted the asylum seekers the necessary papers to leave. In the United States, President Jimmy Carter agreed to accept around 4,000 migrants.

By the end of 1980, 125,000 had reached the US on boats that came for them from Florida. Cuban Americans crossed the stretch of ocean that separated them from their loved ones in Havana and picked people up from the port at Mariel in anything that floated. Fishing vessels, small yachts and recreational boats were all dangerously overloaded with men, women and children, from eighty-year-olds to newborns, seeking a life away from communist rule.

Among the children huddled onto the boats was a thirteen-year-old boy from Holguin, Juan Carlos Zaldívar. A committed young communist, Juan Carlos had participated in pro-government demonstrations whenever ordered to do so, including some where effigies of 'deserters' were burned. The government would also organize 'actos de repudio', or 'acts of repudiation', vitriolic demonstrations outside the homes of people leaving the island in which neighbour would turn against neighbour, yell slogans and spit at them, call them traitors and tell them to fuck off to the Yankees and never come back. Thanks to these odious displays of nationalism, many Cubans left their homeland not only stripped of their homes and possessions but also with the sound of their countrymen's hateful chants ringing in their ears.

Now, suddenly, the adolescent Juan Carlos found himself one of the same 'deserters' he'd been taught to despise. Undue pressure had been placed on the young boy's narrow shoulders. In a heartfelt gesture, not necessarily intended to abrogate his parental responsibilities, his father, Pachuco, let the children take the final decision. Between them, Juan Carlos and his sister had to decide whether to uproot the family and join their uncles and aunts and cousins in Miami. After agonizing for two days, the teenagers agreed they should give their family the chance to go to America.[43]

To the outside world, the Mariel boatlift, as it became known, looked like a humiliation for the Cuban Revolution. The images of ordinary people abandoning the island in their droves the moment they got the chance were seized upon by the anti-Castroite community as confirmation of the harsh realities of life under communism. Plus, it made for great television. American news channels filed report after report from Havana, from the high seas and the immigration shelters in Miami. Camera crews recorded tearful families reuniting after decades apart or heard from young Cuban parents grabbing this rare opportunity with both hands to build an American life for their children.

Even in the emotionally charged evacuation, though, Fidel made sure he came out on top. He emptied the country's jails and mental institutions and had the inmates and patients placed on the boats heading for Miami. It was a diabolical masterstroke. In one swoop he cleared the island of a significant part of its 'undesirables' and simultaneously dumped the problem on his greatest enemies. It precipitated a huge spike in violent crime in south Florida and a drug wave that would take years to get under control. As a result, there was a stigma attached to being a '*marielito*' which would be eternally tough to shift.

Fidel sent the migrants on their way with a vitriol-laden speech from the Plaza de la Revolución, his words an *acto de repudio* in themselves:

> Those who don't have revolutionary genes, who don't have revolutionary blood, who don't have a mind that can adapt to the idea of a revolution, who don't have a heart that can adapt to the effort and heroism of a revolution, we don't want them. We don't need them.[44]

*

In truth, almost every time there was an exodus from Cuba, Fidel Castro ended up winning by purging the island of his critics and opponents. The first wave of outward migration came immediately after the revolution. His victory on New Year's Day 1959 was confirmed when the deposed president fled in the dead of night, accompanied only by his loot, his family and a few of his most trusted men. Subsequently, between January 1959 and April 1961, there followed an estimated 125,000 exiles to the United States, most of them settling in Miami.[45] Former government officials and wealthy business owners were spurred to the exit by the show trials and summary executions of Batista's henchmen and police officers carried out in La Cabaña, an eighteenth-century fort in the Bay of Havana.

Many thought they would only be going for a few months. Domestic workers were told to look after the homes, their absentee owners confident they'd be back home by Christmas once this bothersome radical was gone. However, most would never set foot on Cuban soil again, refusing to do so while Fidel Castro was alive. Between December 1965 and April 1973, a further 261,000 Cubans were air-lifted from the island to the United States, reaching a total of 800,000 exiles by late 1980.[46]

In the process, Miami became a thriving economic powerhouse. The pull of life in the US remains as strong to many Cubans as when Héctor Sanyústiz rammed a bus into the Peruvian Embassy gates. In the mid-1990s at the height of the Special Period, tens of thousands, exhausted by the economic ruin of the socialist regime, arrived in Florida on rickety boats and makeshift rafts. Determined either to float to a better country than post-Soviet Cuba on inflatable inner tubes or be eaten by sharks, countless died in the attempt each month. The 'Rafters Crisis' became so critical that the US had to house the ones they picked up at sea at the naval base in Guantánamo Bay until the Clinton administration reached an agreement with Fidel Castro about flying them to the US.

At that time of heightened tension, an anti-Castro exile group from Miami called 'Hermanos al Rescate', or 'Brothers to the Rescue', would fly over the Florida Straits trying to spot Cuban rafters and help them safely reach the US. By early 1996, the organization was taking a different tack, dropping anti-government leaflets over the island from light aeroplanes to urge a civil disobedience campaign. On 23 February 1996, one of their number, Juan Pablo Roque – a double agent working for the CIA and the Cuban government – abruptly left Miami and returned to Havana. The following day, two of the group's twin-engine Cessna planes on a leafleting mission were shot down by Cuban air force MiG fighters. Four pilots were killed. A third Cessna, flown by the Hermanos' founder, José Basulto, made it back to the US unscathed. Arguments still rage over exactly how many nautical miles the planes were from the Cuban coastline and whether they had officially violated Cuban airspace when the MiGs engaged.

For Miami-based Cuban Americans, though, such details were immaterial. As far as they were concerned, the incident was an act of war. Fidel Castro had shot down two privately owned US aeroplanes and killed US civilians, they argued. President Bill Clinton, who had been leaning towards improving ties with Cuba, was suddenly prompted to sign the Helms–Burton Act, a bill which tightened the economic embargo and specified that it could only be lifted by Congress. The shoot-down would keep Cuba and the US on a hostile footing for another twenty years.

In response to the Rafters Crisis, Bill Clinton also introduced a new policy called 'wet foot, dry foot' under which anyone coming from Cuba who managed to put one foot on US soil would be granted the right to residency within the year. It essentially fast-tracked Cubans to becoming US citizens. Meanwhile, those picked up on the high seas, i.e. with two 'wet feet', were returned to Cuba. The policy was Washington's carrot, the embargo its stick. It had the dual effect of enticing and incentivizing people to leave with the lure of US citizenship while simultaneously making their lives on the island economically unbearable.

Towards the end of the Clinton presidency, a seventeen-foot boat carrying fourteen immigrants set off from Cardenas on Cuba's northern coast. The rudimentary vessel was built of aluminium pipes and a defective fifty-horsepower engine and was towing three inner tubes from a Russian-made truck.[47]

A storm in the Gulf Stream battered the tiny craft and it capsized. Floating in the rough seas at night, the group gripped onto the tyre tubes for hours, but several couldn't swim and little by little they succumbed to delirium and exhaustion. On Thanksgiving weekend of 1999, fishermen found five-year-old Elián González floating on an inflatable tube around three miles from Fort Lauderdale. His mother, Elisa Brotón, her boyfriend, Rafael Lázaro Munero, and almost everyone else on board had slipped beneath the waves and drowned. The coastguard took charge of the boy and carried him back to the US for medical checks. As Elián's father was in Cuba and calling for his return, against the will of his Florida-based relatives, an epic custody battle began between Havana and Miami. It would last for months and would test the 'wet foot, dry foot' policy to its limit. It also became a proxy battle between Fidel Castro and Washington. On 6 December,

Elián's sixth birthday, Fidel warned the US to return the child to Cuba 'within 72 hours'.[48]

It wouldn't happen within that deadline, but the law was clear, and favoured Cuba: Elián's legal guardian was alive and capable of caring for him. Furthermore, he had been picked up at sea. Under normal circumstances, he would have been returned to the island post-haste. However, the episode unfolded during the 2000 election campaign and quickly became a complex issue for the presidential candidates, George W. Bush and Al Gore. Despite the findings of a lower family court in Florida which granted custody of the boy to his great-uncle in the US – and the constant demonstrations in Miami's Little Havana calling for the child to receive US citizenship – Attorney General Janet Reno ruled that Elián had to return to Cuba. In a pre-dawn raid, heavily armed Immigration and Naturalization Service officers stormed the family home and tore Elián González from the arms of his guardian. An Associated Press photograph of the moment – of a masked INS agent charging into the bedroom pointing an automatic weapon at the terrified boy and his uncle as they cowered in a closet – was syndicated in newspapers around the world. It later won the photographer, Alan Diaz, a Pulitzer Prize. In the 2000 presidential election, the vote in Florida, influenced by the Clinton administration's handling of the case, swung the election. In a fiercely disputed recount, George W. Bush beat Vice-President Gore by just 537 ballots out of six million cast.

Elián's safe return to Cuba was the victory Fidel Castro sought. Protests had been held daily outside the US Interests Section in Havana and, once he came home, Elián González was celebrated like no other boy on the island. Castro would attend his birthday parties and he would sit by Fidel's side at major events. It would be several years before he could fade into the anonymity of military service. Invariably sections of the US media run 'where is he now' features about Elián González, the boy who floated through a tropical storm on an inner tube only to emerge into a bigger one on the other side. These days, though, he is rarely put in the spotlight by the Cuban authorities.

Eventually the Castro government was forced into a degree of flexibility on immigration. Most people who can get their hands on a visa for another country are allowed to leave without prior authorization, although doctors are among those denied such permission. Since 2000, the island has experienced a new exodus, different to the Mariel boatlift or the Rafters Crisis. Rather than trying to cross to the United States by sea, now many try by land. They cross on a tourist visa to wherever they can in South America, often Colombia or Panama, and then head north on a dangerous, ill-advised journey which often involves traversing the Darien Gap. An unknown number of Cubans have lost their lives in the dense rainforest, tangled in the thick jungle vines. Thousands attempt the arduous trip from South American nations to the US–Mexico border on foot or put themselves in the hands of *coyotes*, or people smugglers.

Once there, getting into the US is far harder than it used to be. First, the Obama administration lifted the 'wet foot, dry foot' policy at the request of Raúl Castro and then the Trump administration further ramped up the legal obstacles for all Central American and Caribbean asylum seekers, including Cubans. Meanwhile, Cuba is left with a population of millions of young people keen to leave. The island's dire economy and its effect on hastening outward migration remains the Communist Party's biggest headache in a post-Castro era.

If it had been intentional, the arc of his fall would have been perfectly timed. Like a Buster Keaton pratfall, it began with a missed step, a short stumble and then a face-first collapse onto the concrete. But it wasn't a comedic slip. It happened so quickly, the desperate courtiers barely had time to realize what was happening before their *Comandante* was lying prone at the bottom of a short set of steps.

The cameras present for a graduation speech in Santa Clara in October 2004 caught the entire unseemly moment. Despite the attempts of the Cuban state to suppress the images, they quickly went around the world. Equally rapidly, Fidel appeared on state television to reassure the Cuban people that he 'was in one piece'. Still, it wasn't his first moment of weakness. There had been an incident in the town of El Cotorro three years earlier. Wearing thick fatigues, Castro was delivering one of his trademark three-hour speeches in 30° heat. Sweating profusely, he began rocking slightly under the sun and slurring his words. State television cameras immediately cut to the crowd, but only succeeded in capturing some in tears and others clutching their mouths in shock as Castro was ushered from the stage in evident distress. He was then given oxygen in the back of a nearby ambulance.

On that occasion, too, he would address the people soon after recovering, and even apologized for being the cause of concern. However, after the fall and suspected broken knee in Santa Clara, Cubans began to openly discuss the mortality of their leader. Besides injuring his leg, the increasingly frail seventy-eight-year-old's stumble had also hurt his aura of invincibility, and prompted much glee in Miami and analysis around the world about what Castro's ailing health might mean for the island.

The answer was simple: Raúl. If Fidel was the architect of modern Cuba, Raúl was his draughtsman. As Fidel Castro's health deteriorated, it was clear he would have to enact a decision he had reached years earlier and hand the reins to Raúl. Fidel had always indicated that his brother was his most likely successor, famously saying 'behind me come others more radical than me', in an apparent reference to his sibling. Now, he began to refer to Raúl in public as his *relevo*, a baseball reference for 'relief pitcher': 'He is the comrade who has the most authority after me,' Fidel said of his brother, 'and the most experience. Therefore I think he has the capacity to succeed me.'[49]

A few years after those comments, Castro's health condition turned critical. Despite the official information blackout, his life was in the balance as he struggled to overcome the intestinal disease diverticulitis. On 27 July 2006, a day after marking the anniversary of his attempted overthrow of Batista in 1953, Fidel had an operation to try to stem the problems in his digestive tract. As he slipped under the general anaesthetic, power formally – albeit temporarily – passed to Raúl. However, the operation failed, and the infection leaked into his peritoneal cavity, causing peritonitis.[50] Combined with severe blood poisoning, he flickered between life and death. Anti-Castroite Cubans in Miami were already chilling the champagne for an official announcement that their nemesis was gone. Yet having successfully dodged more than 600 attempts on his life, he wasn't about to fold just yet. He survived once more but he was physically much weakened and his younger brother's temporary control became permanent.

Few except the most committed '*Raulistas*' expected he would be up to the task of filling his brother's enormous boots. However, Raúl had been by Fidel's side from the very start, since the fields and dusty tracks of Birán. The siblings had vastly different characters, with Fidel compulsively drawn to and driven by the limelight, his brother almost allergic to it. Yet though he may have lacked the charisma and braggadocio of his older brother, it is a mischaracterization to see Raúl as solely living in Fidel's shadow or a victim of his overbearing personality. When it fell to him to take over, Raúl Castro would prove himself an equal in many respects. Crucially, he shared the older Castro's traits of brute obstinacy, audacity and radicalism.

Raúl brought real influence to bear on the direction of Cuba. Early on, he was pivotal in the decision to embrace Marxism, evident in the speed with which he spoke to the Soviets. There are theories that Raúl was even in the pay of the KGB before the revolutionaries overthrew Batista. While that remains hard to verify, it seems highly likely that he was in discussion with the Soviets during the Cubans' exile in Mexico after their release from prison.

Five decades later, now formally Cuba's president, he showed a pragmatism which few knew he possessed and which Cuba urgently needed. Raúl was acutely aware that the island's stagnant economy could not go on as it was. The Cuban Revolution would surely go under if its great post-Soviet benefactor, Venezuela, hit hard times. So he took the plunge that Fidel had not been prepared to take. First, he eased the rules on private business and private ownership. Around 500,000 workers were released from state jobs, shedding some of the pressure on the government's coffers. Private enterprise was allowed to grow, if not necessarily flourish, for the first time since 1959.

When it became clear that Hugo Chávez was dying, there was an even greater sense of urgency in Cuba. The 'Bolivarian Revolution' had to survive in order to ensure that the Cuban Revolution would also continue. Quid pro quo: the Cubans would supply healthcare and intelligence services to Venezuela while the South American oil giant would supply the energy and financing Cuba needed. Chávez also picked a mutually acceptable successor in his foreign minister, Nicolás Maduro, who had trained in Cuba as a transport workers' unionist.

Still, once Maduro took over in Caracas, it was clear he was no Chávez. He scraped into power with barely 200,000 votes and Raúl was rumoured to be unimpressed with him. 'He saw him as a bad bet his brother made', a well-placed diplomat told me. The prospect of the Maduro government being ousted at the polls or through some other means hastened Raúl Castro into seeking viable alternatives to Venezuela's oil.

Just weeks after Hugo Chávez, supposedly Cuba's 'best friend' in its history, had been laid to rest, Raúl Castro approved a step as audacious as any carried out by his domineering brother. Through the Vatican and Canada, secret contact was made with Washington for an unlikely thaw with the island's bitterest foe.

The noise began to swell. Applause, whistles and cheers filled the stadium. Even the players, the supposed stars of this exhibition baseball game, put down their bats and gloves for a moment to clap and admire the scene from their unique vantage point on the diamond.

First the two girls stepped out before the crowd in fashionable summer dresses, accustomed to attention but still perhaps a little nervous. Right behind them, the First Lady emerged, the path to her seat blocked by burly Cuban bodyguards and US security personnel with buzzcuts and earpieces, who quickly parted the waves to let her through. Then, as the din reached its crescendo, the two presidents appeared.

Barack Obama's crisp grey suit and black tie of the morning were gone, replaced by more informal attire. The sleeves of his white shirt were rolled up, and his beige khakis and aviator sunglasses lent him an air of nonchalant preppy chic. As he glided through the entourage, waving to the crowd in front of the field, he was far from the archetypal image of the enemy that Cubans had been fed for so long. This wasn't the devil incarnate, it was the President of Cool.

Beside him, the eighty-five-year-old Raúl Castro couldn't have been more of a contrast. In a thick blue blazer, black shirt, grey slacks, a widower for five years he had no First Lady by his side. The two leaders had always played down their age difference but standing next to each other in the bleachers, it suddenly stood out. Castro had already attempted a coup, been to prison, fought a civil war and overthrown a government by the time Barack Hussein Obama was born in a hospital in Honolulu.

The applause for the odd couple was thunderous and sustained. Then, uniformly, as though a collective sense of duty, or an instruction, had taken hold, the home crowd began to chant Raúl's name. The two men didn't quite interlock arms or hug – there had been more than enough awkward body language for one trip. Yet having been fortuitously bundled in with the White House pool of photographers for that moment and given access to the field, I could see that the image of camaraderie they were projecting would endure well beyond a symbolic game of baseball.

The two men had come to the decrepit sports stadium directly from the ornate and painstakingly restored Alicia Alonso Grand Theatre in Old Havana. Home of the Cuban National Ballet, on stage President Obama delivered a virtuoso performance of his own. His speech was televised live on state television, a rare privilege for any visitor, let alone for the first sitting US president to step foot on Cuban soil since Calvin Coolidge in 1928. Cubans recognize history in the making when they see it and almost the entire nation paused to watch the address or listen to it on the radio. An accomplished, witty and warm orator in normal circumstances, Obama didn't disappoint.

'Cultivo una rosa blanca,' he began in Spanish. In two years of thaw that had been heavy on symbolism, it was an extraordinary moment: the US president, in Cuba, quoting José Martí. The BBC's cameraman was inside the home of a Cuban family to film their reactions to the speech and captured the moment the mother simply burst into tears on hearing those words. 'In his most famous poem, José Martí made this offering of friendship and peace to both his friend and his enemy,' continued Obama. 'Today, as the President of the United States of America, I offer the Cuban people *el saludo de paz*.'

Sitting in the VIP box, Raúl Castro watched in mute concentration as the American president, the embodiment of US imperialism, charmed his audience inside the auditorium and in millions of homes across the island. The author of the speech, White House adviser Ben Rhodes, later told me it was the 'sum total of everything [he had] ever learned about Cuba'. If so, he had learned plenty and learned well. The writing was by turns poetic and practical, a lasting eulogy to the tensions of the past while simultaneously extolling the virtues of friendship.

And it was hitting home exactly as the American delegation had hoped. Obama said that despite the short distance from the United States, they had overcome 'barriers of history and ideology, barriers of pain and separation' to reach Cuba. He acknowledged the decades of US aggression towards Cuba and didn't attempt to sugarcoat it in diplomatic language: 'The blue waters beneath Air Force One,' he said, 'once carried American battleships to this island to liberate but also to exert control over Cuba.' He spoke of exiles leaving 'on planes and makeshift rafts... in pursuit of freedom and opportunity' in his nation. He tried to differentiate himself from previous occupants of the White House by mentioning his familial links to Kenya and pointing out the Bay of Pigs invasion happened the year he was born.

Then he reached his key point, just five minutes into his speech: 'I have come here to bury the last remnant of the Cold War in the Americas.' It took people a moment to process. Was he saying it was finally over? That while Cuba hadn't necessarily 'won' its decades-long conflict with the US, neither had it lost? In essence, Washington was publicly acknowledging it would no longer concern itself with trying to overturn communism in Cuba as had been official policy towards the island for sixty years. Rather, Obama was saying that the White

House and State Department would work with them as it did with other regimes with less than palatable human rights records, from Saudi Arabia to Sudan. And he clearly hoped the next US president would honour his approach.

Given the creaking, inefficient Cuban economy, it suddenly became even clearer why Raúl Castro had authorized this détente. His relationship with Maduro in Venezuela was poor, especially compared to his brother's with Chávez. They might not get another chance quite like this for years. With Obama in his second term, these were the final months of a progressive, black Democratic president who was not only amenable to a thaw with Cuba but saw it as a key part of his legacy. Such a prospect would not come around again in a hurry and Raúl Castro knew he had to seize the moment while it presented itself. Moreover, people in Cuba wanted it. They were exhausted after so many decades of hostility towards the United States under Fidel and were emotionally ready to bury the hatchet.

However, it came at a price. As the speech progressed, there was a dawning realization among the assembled members of the Cuban Communist Party that it was probably a bad idea to let a politician as erudite, reasonable and relatable as Barack Obama have the floor without previously editing his comments before broadcasting them. He mentioned human rights, the arbitrary detention of dissidents, even tackled Cuba's torrid relationship with its own people. He spoke of the division created between Cubans on opposite sides of the water and of the conflict between family members of different political hues, painful issues exacerbated by years of revolution. And he praised Cuban Americans in Florida: 'In the United States we have a clear monument to what the Cuban people can build: it's called Miami,' Obama said to audible gasps and nervous titters in the auditorium.

You simply don't speak well of Miami in Havana. It's officially considered a bad and evil place, shorthand for the excesses of capitalism, where the 'gusanos' built their gaudy temples to consumerism, and where malls rather than schools and hospitals dot the landscape. To have the US president come to Havana and say the exact opposite, to praise the place live on national television was more than some hardliners could stomach. As one government source confided in me later, the Cubans internally acknowledged that they 'got it wrong' in allowing their esteemed guest the full freedom of an address on state media.

The bilateral thaw was a gradual process of negotiation, kept on track by a series of key events every few months: from the joint announcement in December 2014 to the subsequent meeting of Obama and Castro on the fringes of the Summit of the Americas in Panama, and the reopening the US Embassy in Havana in August 2015. It all led towards President Obama's historic visit to Cuba in March 2016. They were heady times for Cubans who struggled to believe it was real after so many false dawns. And they were completely uncharted waters for the Cuban government. We saw fastidious officials repeatedly caught off guard during the high-profile moments of rapprochement as press liaison officers to state security agents frantically improvised a process for which they had no precedent. Many were evidently far more comfortable on a hostile footing with the US than a friendly one. Yet they had to obey orders – the decision for a reconciliation with Washington had come from the very top.

Fidel remained uncharacteristically silent during the thaw but when he did finally speak, it was a devastating critique of a process he neither trusted nor had wanted to see during his lifetime. He referred to Obama's trip shortly after the US president left the island in an article in the state-run newspaper *Granma*, entitled 'Brother Obama'. He accused the US leader of using 'honeyed' words to seduce Cuban revolutionaries who, naturally, should see through him.

Even for Cubans who respected Fidel those comments insulted their natural sense of hospitality. 'You don't invite someone to your house and then talk shit about them the moment they've walked out the door,' a pro-government friend said to me later that week. Still, another of Fidel's vitriolic editorials contained perhaps the most prophetic line on the entire détente process. In a letter to the Student Federation published days after the policy was announced, Castro wrote: 'I don't trust the Americans and I personally haven't exchanged a single word with them.'

He would go to his grave clutching onto that single, undiluted thought.

He shuffled into the conference hall, hunched over and stooped, supporting himself on his brother's arm. Long gone the trademark olive-green fatigues, in their place the now familiar Adidas tracksuit and a checked shirt, which hung loosely over his thin frame. The noise that greeted his arrival on the podium, though, was the same as ever.

'Fidel! Fidel! Fidel!' the delegates chanted in unison. The deputies at the closing session of the Seventh Cuban Communist Party Congress rose as one and applauded their *Comandante* vigorously, no one wanting to be seen to lack enthusiasm for such a moment. When he motioned for silence, Fidel Castro once again held his audience rapt. His speech jumped around from theme to theme, moving from domestic agricultural policy to the world's nuclear arsenal. But it gradually became clear that this wasn't the rallying cry of old. It was goodbye.

'I'll soon be ninety years old,' Castro remarked, his voice frail and trembling slightly. Cuban state television cut to images of delegates wiping the tears from their eyes. 'I'd never imagined such a thing! It comes not from any great plan but is simply the caprice of fate.'

'Soon I'll be like all the others,' he continued, in the clearest reference to his mortality that anyone inside the hall could remember. The man Cubans called '*el Caballo*', 'the Horse', was nearing the end of his race. Still, he would bow out – as ever – on his own terms and with a call to arms, convinced of his personal set of moral absolutes and still demanding total dedication to his cause:

'The time must come for all of us,' he acknowledged, 'but the ideas of the Cuban Communists will remain as proof on this planet that if they are worked at with fervour and dignity, they can produce the material and cultural goods that human beings need, and we must fight without truce to obtain them.'

Just seven months later, Fidel Castro was dead.

Unlike the instant dissemination of information in the rest of the world, news travels differently in Cuba. When Fidel Castro died, you had to happen to be watching state television at midnight on Friday 25 November 2016 or you'd have missed it. There was no forewarning of a major announcement that night, no rolling news channels speculating about his health, no inkling that he was gravely ill in the hours beforehand. Most of the foreign press corps in Havana weren't watching state television at that exact moment. A lot of us had been at a wedding the night before and were looking forward to a quiet weekend. But there would be no sleep that night. Very little rest for the next ten days, in fact.

In my case, a Cuban friend was watching TV at that late hour and rang me immediately. His voice constricted and strange, he simply said: 'President Raúl Castro has just come on television and announced that Fidel Castro has died.' Raúl had appeared on screen sitting at his desk, ashen and grave, beneath an image of José Martí and a framed photograph of Che on horseback. Reading from a sheet of paper and looking down the barrel of the camera, as he began to say '*Querido pueblo de Cuba*', his voice faltered slightly. But he quickly steeled himself to inform the nation that Fidel Castro was dead and would be cremated at first light on Saturday morning. There would then follow several days of national mourning, he added. Before the broadcast ended, there was a fleeting sign of how tough it was for Raúl to contain his grief for long enough to deliver the short message. With the TV cameras still rolling, he dropped the paper onto his desk, collapsed exhausted back into his chair and released a huge sigh.

It was the news that so many in Cuba had feared for decades, the loss of their supreme leader and the founder of their revolution. It was simultaneously an announcement that so many in Miami had craved, that some had spent a lifetime trying in vain to achieve. As the mourning began on the island, the information winged its way across the Straits of Florida and in Miami the party got underway. Cars honked their horns and revellers drank into the small hours on Calle Ocho, the infamous epicentre of anti-Castro sentiment. But the celebrations lacked conviction. They were dancing on the grave of a ninety-year-old man and his quiet slip into death – following a peaceful transfer of power in Havana – wasn't how radical Cuban American conservatives had envisaged it. Had Fidel Castro died a decade or two earlier, there would have been fervent talk of a flotilla of boats departing from the US to pick up loved ones from Cuba's shores or an attempted overthrow by extremist exiles. In previous years, that fanatical element had carried out a series of terrorist attacks on Cuba. They include the bombing of a Cuban passenger jet in 1976 by the late CIA agent and most odious of Cuban exiles, Luis Posada Carriles, in which seventy-three people were killed – among them the entire Cuban fencing team. By 2016 the majority of that generation had died or simply lost the fire in their bellies. In the final analysis, all that Miami Cubans did on the news of Fidel Castro's death was raise a rum and say they hoped he'd rot in hell.

Still, that didn't stop the Cuban government's carefully laid plans from grinding into action. In 2007, when Fidel had handed power to his brother, a nationwide mobilization called 'Operación Caguairán' was activated. Thousands of troops, civilian militias and reservists were assembled to maintain order and prepare for any attack on Cuba in the event of Fidel's death.

When that death came almost a decade later, the state's machinery was on a similar state of alert. From the moment of the announcement, bars pulled down their shutters and music was turned off. The lights went on at one of the main clubs in Havana and partygoers were unceremoniously sent home. From our office in Old Havana, we went out to film in the streets and found them deserted and eerily silent. Officers were posted every few hundred metres along all the main avenues and the extent to which Cuba is a police state was once again clear.

Within hours, doctors, nurses, teachers, schoolchildren, firemen, bus drivers, state employees of every kind flocked – or were ferried – to the José Martí monument in the Plaza de la Revolución to pay their respects. They trooped past a wooden altar in their thousands. Some wept as they filed past, others bellowed loud revolutionary slogans, others remained stoic and silent. In keeping with the island's surreal-ism, they weren't filing past Fidel's ashes at all – those were kept inside a safe in the Ministry of Defence. Instead, they bowed their heads in deference to a large black-and-white photograph of a youthful Fidel festooned with a floral wreath. Still, such details mattered little to those who had queued in the midday Havana sun. Despite the careful stage management, this was no North Korean show of exaggerated wailing. Rather, it was a moment of genuine popular grief combined with the cult of the island's largest personality.

The ashes were taken cross-country in a reverse of the 'Caravan of Freedom', the name given to the victorious journey Fidel had taken across the island in 1959. The funeral cortège passed through the same villages, towns and cities where Castro had addressed the crowds shortly after defeating Batista, assuring people the guerrillas would build a different kind of Cuba and that things would change for the better under the revolution. At times, I was reminded of Hugo Chávez's death, still fresh in the memory. Whereas in Venezuela, the faithful had descended on Caracas to view Chávez lying in state, Cuba was taking the opposite approach: taking Fidel back past the people to his final resting place in Santiago.

Along the way, I met people shedding genuine tears and others crying crocodile tears; some there to grieve, others there to be seen to be grieving. For Leandra, the mourning was raw, visceral and real. I met her in Santa Clara in the hours before the ashes of her beloved Fidel reached the town. Her front door was open, and she was staring blankly at the television watching the live coverage of the procession, barely taking it in. In her mid-seventies, her eyes were raw and rubbed, her face sweaty and tear-streaked.

'Come in, *mijo*,' she motioned as I poked an inquisitive head around the door. She was wearing a washed-out yellow dress and sat in the rocking chair of her cluttered home. 'I've cried everything out. I've got nothing left,' she said, and then promptly began to cry a little more. Like so many women of her generation who I spoke to on the sombre journey across Cuba, Leandra told me that she had barely known her father so she felt Fidel's loss as keenly as if he were blood.

'The world doesn't know what it's lost,' she sobbed before taking a few gulps of water to calm down. In such a rarefied environment, few on the island were prepared to voice any kind of pleasure at seeing him gone. It was simply too risky. One dissident posted a video of himself dancing in his bedroom and was subsequently detained by state security. A couple of musicians and an artist furtively told me they were overjoyed to see the end of Fidel but wisely wouldn't go on camera and asked that I change their names if I used any quotes. I had never witnessed such a sensitive moment anywhere, not even for Chávez in Venezuela. The normal operation of the entire island was suspended for ten days in honour of one man. Meanwhile, the police and security forces watched everyone more closely than ever.

None of that much bothered the then US president-elect, Donald Trump. Hours after Castro's death, he took to his favoured means of communication, Twitter, to exclaim: 'Fidel Castro is dead!' He went on to describe him as a 'brutal dictator' whose 'legacy is one of firing squads, theft, unimaginable suffering, poverty and the denial of fundamental human rights'. The Cuban government, officially in mourning, didn't respond but the language and the timing of Trump's comments immediately set the tone for the post-Obama relationship with Washington.

As for Raúl Castro, his epic journey at his older brother's side had finally come to an end. The man who had inspired him from infancy into old age, with whom he had stared down death and defied the most unlikely of odds, was gone. Fidel Castro had once said that what happened to his remains was a 'matter of complete indifference' to him.[51] It wasn't true, of course. Everywhere from the family *finca* in Birán to the mountains of the Sierra Maestra had been considered as a possible resting place over the years. Eventually, it was decided that Castro's ashes would be placed in a tomb in Santa Ifigenia cemetery in the shadow of José Martí's crypt. Castro supporters felt it was befitting to elevate Fidel to the same plane as Martí, the two men who most shaped modern Cuba laying side by side.

Inside the cemetery, the breeze stirred a little but offered no relief from the stifling Santiago heat. The immediate Castro family was there, a smattering of the revolutionary elite and the Venezuelan leader, Nicolás Maduro. But almost no one else: a private ceremony for this most public of figures. The presidential guard gave Raúl Castro the urn. It was heavier than he anticipated and he wobbled momentarily under its weight before regaining his balance. He lifted the hefty oak box and placed it gently inside the stone tomb. Austere to the end, the grave was simple but imposing. The ashes were encased inside a huge granite boulder adorned with a plaque, its bronze letters spelling a single word: FIDEL. Immovable, resolute, obdurate, it was an apt metaphor for the man himself.

Raúl paused and rested his hands on the lid of the box, and held them there in a moment of tenderness amid the pomp and funereal music. He stepped back and the honour guards took a pace forward to screw the plaque into place. As he saluted his older brother, Raúl was briefly on his own in every sense. His wife, Vilma, was gone, Fidel had died, and his closest revolutionary comrades had long since passed away. In little more than a year, he would leave the presidential office and Cuba would officially be governed by someone other than a Castro for the first time in almost six decades.

An astute reader of Cuban politics once pointed out to me that the island's national game isn't necessarily baseball, as everyone believes, but dominoes. Although *pelota*, as baseball is called, remains firmly the country's favourite sport despite an astronomical rise in the popularity of football in recent years, he argues it is more accurate to consider dominoes as the national pastime.

Certainly after sundown, the game is ubiquitous on Cuba's street corners, sidewalks and porches. Men and women sit out, drink rum and smoke and play round after round of *dominó*. The air fills with the unmistakable sound of the *fichas* being tapped on the table top to mark a missed turn and with the frustrated yelling and laughter of the players. Eventually someone will prevail and the players will mix up the pieces face down on the table to begin a new round.

A key objective in Cuban high-speed games of dominoes, points out my friend, is not only to win but to nullify your opponent from taking a turn. It is a blocking form of dominoes. The aim is to create '*tranques*', or blocks, to the point of impasse, knowing you have bettered your opponents' score. Then, the *fichas* are turned over and everything is reset. Fidel Castro, my friend argues, was a master at it. As a political tactician, Castro was generally referred to as a brilliant chess player but in the Cuban context he was more likely engaged in a game of dominoes.

Both in the international arena and in his personal political battles, he would identify the most opportune and strategic moment to create a *tranque*, to trap his opponent and force him into submission. Not only did he win, he managed to entirely quash and cancel out his opponents. The strategy can arguably be seen in key moments of Castro's reign, from the trial and execution of Arnaldo Ochoa to the downing of the Brothers to the Rescue aircraft by Cuban fighter jets. From the Mariel boatlift to the Bay of Pigs. It might even have been true of the Cuban missile crisis, had he not been elbowed out by the Soviets.

In 1965, Fidel Castro pronounced on his all-encompassing power in Cuba during an interview with the renowned American journalist and photographer Lee Lockwood: 'My authority to make decisions is really less than that of the President of the United States,' he insisted. 'If we are going to speak about personal power, in no other country in the world, not even under absolute monarchies, has there ever been such a high degree of power concentrated in one person as is concentrated in the President of the United States. That office-holder whom you call president can even take the country into a thermonuclear war without having to consult the Congress. There is no case like it in history.'[52]

Fidel Castro outlasted US presidents from Eisenhower to Obama. It doesn't take a fawning revolutionary to conclude that on many occasions he outsmarted them, too. From that early meeting with Nixon onwards, Washington wanted nothing more than to remove this turbulent communist from their hemisphere. Whether meddling with Nicaragua, influencing events in Venezuela or simply bucking the post-Cold War trend of the Washington Consensus, he was a thorn in their side. Try as they might, he proved so deeply embedded that they couldn't pull him out, lodged in their flesh for six decades, irritating and provoking them from just ninety miles away. Such longevity alone was an impressive feat, one for which he was duly fêted by the Pink Tide leaders, especially Chávez.

Shortly after Fidel Castro died, the United States entered the era of Donald Trump. Had Castro been at the height of his powers and not at the end of them when the property tycoon and reality TV star was elected to the White House, confrontation would have been inevitable. From entirely different worlds, the two men shared little in common except perhaps stubbornness and self-belief. With Fidel barely six months dead, President Trump set about undoing all Obama's overtures to Cuba, motivated as much by a hatred of anything achieved by his predecessor as by any coherent political strategy towards Latin America.

Under President Trump, the US economic embargo tightened rather than loosened with each passing month. In April 2019, Trump's then national security adviser, John Bolton, addressed the Bay of Pigs veterans' group in Miami on the anniversary of their bungled attack. Announcing harsh new restrictions on Cuba, Bolton told the gathered anti-Castroite crowd: 'we proudly proclaim for all to hear: the Monroe Doctrine is alive and well.' Watching Bolton's speech from Havana, I could scarcely believe that Washington's stated policy towards Latin America in the twenty-first century was simply to echo its position in 1823 on European colonialism, and to proclaim its own hemispheric dominance. One can only imagine what Fidel Castro would have made of such a statement.

In her compelling book on Castro and Cuba, *Without Fidel: A Death Foretold in Miami, Havana and Washington*, Ann Louise Bardach makes a perspicacious observation:

Fidel Castro was a pyrrhic warrior with an epic commitment to battle, regardless of the cost. His legacy is a complex one: a tattered country but a proud people. While one can snipe at the eroded state of the Revolution's declared triumphs of health care, education, and sports, Castro's undisputed gift to his country was nationalism. His credo was simple: Cuba would bow to no one.

It is an astute and insightful description. Having lived on the island for six years, including over Castro's final days, I agree that his nationalist legacy is certainly complex. The word which perhaps best encapsulates modern Cuba is exhaustion. When it finally came, the end of the Castros left millions of Cubans indifferent and under-whelmed. They knew it wouldn't bring any more products to the supermarket shelves. The much-vaunted détente with Obama lay in ruins and there had been no discernible improvement to their pitiful salaries and pensions.

The socialist project on which so many had pinned their hopes as young men and women, for which 'so much blood had been spilt' as Raúl Castro put it, was looking as old and tired as its leading proponents. Once Raúl stepped down from the presidency in 2018, he handed the torch to his vice-president, Miguel Díaz-Canel. A technocrat who had reached that heady position by being the grey man, he never wavered from the established revolutionary script. Any liberal tendencies he had shown as party leader in his province of Santa Clara were now in the distant past and he had been groomed as the next president for some time. To an extent he did represent an effort to inject some fresh blood into the revolution. Miguel Díaz-Canel was born two years after the revolutionaries rolled into Havana on top of Batista's tanks and never saw military action. A smattering of new names and faces were promoted to the Council of State, too, bringing their average age down to fifty-three.

Nevertheless, Raúl Castro didn't leave entirely, remaining in the crucial role of First Secretary of the Cuban Communist Party. His former son-in-law, General Luís Alberto Rodríguez, is the head of the military's commercial wing, GAESA, which includes some fifty-seven companies owned and controlled by the Revolutionary Armed Forces.[53] A little-seen and shadowy figure, he is one of the most powerful men in Cuba.

Fidel Castro wasn't a lavish man by the standards of most Latin American presidents. He enjoyed the finer things in terms of food and cigars, for years wore a Rolex on each wrist and allegedly boasted an exquisite personal library with first editions from Hemingway and Gabriel García Márquez. Yet it would be patently false to paint him as financially corrupt. While his assertion in 2006 that he only earned a salary of thirty dollars a month was clearly misleading, it is also wrong to portray him in the vein of some Latin American kleptocrats.[54] There is no evidence of multimillion-dollar offshore accounts or riches squirreled away in Switzerland. *Forbes* magazine once stated that he was one of the wealthiest leaders in the world with a fortune in the hundreds of millions, prompting an angry backlash from Castro on Cuban state TV's *Mesa Redonda*. The financial magazine's assertion that the state's wealth was Castro's personal piggybank was tenuous at best.

No, Fidel Castro's weakness was not money but power. For five decades his dominion over Cuba was total, his control over the revolution absolute. He combined his masterful use of intelligence services with the complete repression of dissent. And before moving on from power, he shared his core ideals with his two closest disciples, Raúl Castro and Hugo Chávez, to ensure the socialist revolution would outlive its original leadership.

While that strategy worked, as Fidel's tactics generally did, the revolution is sapped and weary. Certainly, as Castro intended, the Cuban government is no longer in thrall to Washington or US business interests or the mafia and there still isn't a casino to be seen on the island. Yet after sixty years of relentless revolution the people of Cuba are drained. When they ask themselves what they have got out of a lifetime of commitment – willing or otherwise – to Fidel and Raúl Castro, the answer is increasingly forlorn. Revolutionaries and pro-Castro supporters will quickly point to the free healthcare and education. Certainly both of those 'pillars of the revolution' remain in place decades after Fidel first prioritized them when reshaping the nation after Fulgencio Batista.

However, today the hospitals are ailing. Doctors don't have the drugs or equipment they need while ambulance drivers and porters may need to be paid under the table to transport your dying loved ones from one ward to another. In education, there is a chronic teacher shortage which receives little official recognition. With many no longer prepared to work for the dismal state wages, every year there are thousands fewer teaching professionals in the classrooms and trainees, assistants, even the school librarians are carrying out classes instead. These are issues which are tough to blame on the Americans' decades-long economic embargo, thoroughly unjust though it is.

The state provides subsidized utilities and food, the revolutionaries also point out. Again, that's true. However, it is struggling to do so. The state simply can't afford to keep 'subsidizing everyone', as Raúl Castro told the April 2018 session of parliament. Meanwhile, the prices of imported goods on the supermarket shelves are beyond the reach of most Cubans. As a result, virtually the entire island is forced to hustle for alternative sources of income to make ends meet. In 2010, even Fidel acknowledged that economically speaking the revolution was reaching an endgame: 'The Cuban model doesn't even work for us anymore,' he said in an uncharacteristically unguarded moment of self-reflection.

Yet Cubans look at other countries and don't always feel jealous. The island is dysfunctional in the extreme but doesn't suffer from the violence or extreme poverty seen elsewhere in Latin America, a point constantly underlined by state media. Furthermore, improved human rights or a shift to multiparty politics simply aren't subjects which occupy most Cubans' minds on a day-to-day basis. Instead they concern themselves with more immediate needs: filling the larder, locating and being able to pay for eggs, chicken, a kilo of tomatoes or a packet of powdered milk.

The youth are acutely aware that they have little or no say in the future direction of their country, so many have simply opted not to engage, an apolitical generation on the most political island in the world. Many simply aspire for the same things as their wealthier cousins in Miami or Madrid, from sneakers to watches to motorbikes, the very trappings of capitalism Fidel encouraged them to reject.

'A revolution is not a bed of roses. A revolution is a struggle to the death between the future and the past,' Fidel said in 1961. If so, the Castros won't feature in Cuba's next battles in anything except name. The island's struggle between its 'future and the past' will finally be led by other, younger women and men, many of whom are increasingly frustrated with the status quo and impatient for change.

Fidel Castro, meanwhile, remains the model for every populist leader in Latin America, on both sides of the political divide, from Chávez to Bolsonaro. A Cold War titan, Cuba's supreme ruler and commander-in-chief, he secured decade after decade in power in the face of the most vehement opposition imaginable, ruthless, implacable and unbending to the end.

Yet how his people wept as his funeral cortège passed by carrying him to his grave.

Epilogue

'¡¿Por qué no te callas?!'

The gathered heads of state and government at the 2007 Ibero-American summit in Santiago were already tetchy. It had been a long three days in the Chilean capital and tempers were fraying. The Spanish prime minister, José Luis Rodríguez Zapatero, was attempting to talk, but Hugo Chávez wouldn't let him. Whenever Zapatero mentioned his predecessor, the conservative José María Aznar, Chávez drowned him out. Aznar was a fascist, said the Venezuelan leader, plain and simple, for having supported a coup attempt against him a few years earlier.

Zapatero came to Aznar's defence saying that although he also wasn't ideologically aligned with the man, a modicum of respect and decorum at such a summit was to be expected. 'Respect?' Chávez asked, incredulous. 'Tell him to respect us. Tell Aznar to show some respect.' Back and forth the unedifying exchange continued until suddenly the Spanish monarch, King Juan Carlos I, snapped. Sitting behind Zapatero, he leaned forward and barked: *'¡¿Por qué no te callas?!'* at the Venezuelan socialist, best translated as 'Why don't you just shut up?!'

It was extraordinary. As far as anyone could remember it was the first time the Spanish king had lost his cool so publicly. It was a source of great amusement in Spain and Latin America to see Rey Juan Carlos I brought to his wits' end by the famously verbose and candid

Chávez. However, beyond the mirth, the royal outburst summed up something key about that moment in recent political history. All the men in this book except Fidel Castro, by then handing over power to his brother, attended the summit as their nation's leader. It took place at the very height of the Pink Tide.

And here was a direct heir of the Bourbons, the Spanish crown that had caused so much destruction in the Americas, telling one of its new leaders, one of the co-founders of twenty-first-century socialism, to 'shut up'? As far as they were concerned, they, too, were descendants of noblemen, the latest defenders of a rich tradition of defiance towards the empires of the Old World. They were the descendants of Simón Bolívar, of Túpac Katari and José Martí. Shut up? No, sir. Not anymore.

If the men and women of the turn to the left in Latin America achieved anything over that period, it was to ensure that the region would not meekly march to Washington or Madrid's drumbeat. Armed with their boundless oil and gas riches, they most certainly would not shut up. Yet the question of how democratic populists become autocracies and dictatorships is a difficult one. It seems to me that it can partly be gauged by how they treat their opponents. Perhaps the tipping point occurs once there is a blatant disregard for the opinions, the supporters or, at its worst, the very lives of their critics. Once that threshold has been passed, the populist appears to morph from the outlandish to the profoundly dangerous.

The Argentine author and journalist Uki Goñi has written and spoken at length about this phenomenon, when the social fabric, '*el tejido social*' in Spanish, that binds a nation together starts to unravel. It is the point where violence, especially when perpetrated by the state, becomes rationalized, normalized and, ultimately, accepted by a populace who have themselves been split into homogenic sets of 'them' and 'us'. The role of the manipulative leader is always strengthened by a complicit press. Or, rather, by propagandists masquerading as the press.

Naturally, reaching such a condition isn't a 'moment' at all. It is a process. It is the gradual, insidious creep of the populist's hand into the lives of every citizen in the nation while simultaneously taking a stranglehold over the institutions of the state. Although this book has primarily focused on the swing to the left, as the key feature of Latin American politics after 1999, this is not a solely left- or right-wing phenomenon. The tricks and deceit, the wool-pulling and co-opting of nationalist symbols to justify an autocratic rule, entirely predates the arrival of Hugo Chávez to office. Indeed, as I hope I have shown, they also predate the arrival of Fidel Castro to power, forty years earlier. As the Pink Tide came crashing down, the same disconnection from reality, misinformation and dressing up of lies as fact has been equally evident in those governments and populists who succeeded it. Former army captain and avowed sympathizer of the military dictatorship in Brazil Jair Bolsonaro is probably the starkest and most egregious example.

There is a common thread between all the governments in this book. For whatever success they achieved in poverty reduction, especially Lula, Evo Morales, Chávez and Correa, they were also object lessons in the dangers of a government, indeed an entire political movement, built on the shoulders of one man.

In that vein, one must also look at Washington DC. Throughout Hugo Chávez's time in power, I can recall a smug sense of superiority towards Venezuela emanating from Western diplomats. Nothing like this crazy guy could possibly happen to us, they implied. Indeed, some even openly stated as much. Our institutions are too robust. Our electorates are too canny and wise to fall for the populist's smoke and mirrors. Since the billionaire reality TV star Donald Trump took over the White House, much of that condescension has been noticeably absent. There has been a sheepish and embarrassed recognition among many of the envoys of Foggy Bottom that I have met that perhaps US politics and its politicians weren't so far removed from or morally superior to the rest of the Americas after all.

Some of the parallels are all too familiar. Talented diplomats and staffers and administrators left, unable to faithfully execute their roles under the climate of the new president. Among them was the US ambassador to Panama, John D. Feeley, whose resignation was accompanied by a blistering op-ed in the *Washington Post*. 'America is undoubtedly less welcome in the world today,' he wrote, lamenting the president's 'unilateral and isolationist path.' But it wasn't just Trump's isolationism which has seen America's sway in the world wane. From governing via social media to neutering the legislature, from accusations of flagrant nepotism and of filling the Supreme Court with sympathizers, from unedifying presidential rhetoric and constant insults to a political party increasingly beholden to one man and his whims – these are things that Washington used to berate leaders in Latin America for.

Although Trump might disagree, Venezuelans, Bolivians, Nicaraguans and many others say they have seen this movie before. They, too, thought their institutions were too robust to buckle. Until suddenly, they weren't and had been irreparably politicized by the actions of a divisive and deeply controversial leader.

At one point, Donald Trump tweeted a video in which, to the tune of Edvard Greig's 'In the Hall of the Mountain King', he appeared next to a series of campaign posters for 'Trump 2020', 'Trump 2024', 'Trump 2028' and so on, until 'Trump 2048'. Then, as the Peer Gynt orchestral piece reached its familiar crescendo, the counter on the sign clicked forward faster and faster: 'Trump 2100, 2200, 2300...' 'Trump 5000', 'Trump 10000' 'Trump 50000' until finally ending on 'Trump 4EVA'. A bit of fun, his supporters hooted, something to bait the humourless 'liberal snowflakes' with. Maybe. But during the election campaign in 2020, Donald Trump then followed it up by first remaining deliberately ambiguous about whether he would even accept the result and then baselessly alleging fraud in key swing states which went against him. As I say, Latin Americans say they've already seen this movie.

In 1994, Carlos de la Torre wrote:

It is no surprise that such leaders act as if they are the embodiments of the national will: they *are* the people. Since they embody the people they are not accountable to any political platform, they instinctively know what is the common good, and whoever is against their plans or policies is an enemy not only of the political leader but of the entire nation.[1]

It was a feature of all the men considered here. They, much like Donald Trump, also thrived on the 'permanent campaign'. Whenever you travelled to any of the countries run by these men, you would invariably find them in campaign for something. Hugo Chávez in particular kept Venezuela on a constant electoral footing, coming out of one referendum and straight into the local or parliamentary elections, then a campaign to amend the constitution, another presidential vote and so on. It was dizzying. But it was also a call for their people to take to the streets, to organize rallies, to be seen and be heard, louder and more colourful and more numerous than their opponents. '¡Jamás volverán!' the jubilant Chavistas would cry of their opponents: 'They'll never be back!' The perpetual campaign was a galvanizing force.

In that extraordinary, unprecedented line-up of left-wing leaders at the start of the twenty-first century, the urgent needs of *el pueblo* were fulfilled for a time. In some countries it worked more than in others, and in some places there were more lasting results. And, especially at the start, the leaders undoubtedly lifted the spirits of their supporters, destigmatized what it was to be poor and marginalized and indigenous. But, by and large, the costs – economic and social – were astronomical, too.

It has been strange for those of us who lived through it, based in the countries in question to witness the project's rapid decline and eventual downfall. To see how after all the excitement and potential for lasting change, after all the bluster both towards Washington and from it, all of the ambitious infrastructure projects and social programmes, the pan-continental vision of unity under a socialist banner ended not with a bang but a whimper.

Instead, when the region combs through the remnants left by the Pink Tide, they will find a legacy which encompasses everything from *Bolsa Familia* to Bolsonaro, Hugo Chávez's charisma to Daniel Ortega's religious conversion, from real GDP growth in Bolivia to a mass exodus from Venezuela.

In his inaugural speech in 1999, the presidential sash resting across his puffed-out chest, Hugo Chávez recalled when he had received the command of lieutenant in 1975 from the then president, Carlos Andrés Pérez. 'From that point, something started to smell rotten to me in Venezuela,' he said, with Pérez sitting in the audience in front of him, an ethical crisis at the heart of government. 'It's time to recognize it,' Chávez continued. 'I think it's time to recognize our guilt. We're all guilty, myself included. Who will throw the first stone? I make a call, my first as president of Venezuela, that we all recognize our guilt. As we do at church, *"por mi culpa, por mi culpa, por mi gran culpa"*,' he said, tapping his heart with his fist, echoing part of the weekly Catholic mass in Latin America.

If so, the rot has now set in far further in Venezuela and in the region since Hugo Chávez spoke those words. Just don't expect his successors to heed his call and recognize their guilt any time soon.

Acknowledgements

In some ways, this book has taken a fair while to write. It's two-and-a-half decades since I first started to gravitate towards Latin American affairs as a student. After four successive BBC deployments in the Americas, myriad reporting trips and countless conversations with people the length and breadth of the region, I finally found myself in a position to tie together some of the strands of the experiences I'd lived through, watched and written about in that time.

In doing so, I have been helped by a great many people, far more than I can name here. Perhaps the best part of being a reporter in Latin America is the close relationships and network of friends one builds up and comes to rely on from the Southern Cone to the Rio Grande. Researching and writing this book has underlined to me just how lucky I am in that regard. I have been able to count on the support of many friends and compañeros across the continent and I am eternally grateful to all of them for their time, advice and encouragement.

But first, I had great support at home: my deepest thanks to my editor, Neil Belton, who was patient and reassuring, his experience and clarity was invaluable and his encyclopaedic knowledge of so many topics lifted the writing throughout. My particular thanks go to Clare Gordon who did more than anyone to make this book possible. I am hugely indebted to her for setting us on the right course from the very start through our shared passion for Latin America and who then held my hand at every step. Thanks, too, to Kate Appleton and the entire team at Head of Zeus.

My agent, Chris Wellbelove, at Aitken Alexander for his unfailing support and for helping me to map out a route using some rudderless early drafts.

My editors at the BBC, Andrew Roy in London and Paul Danahar in Washington DC for their consistent confidence in my journalism and who gave me the freedom to write a book in the first place. To the entire BBC Newsgathering team for their steadfast support from everyday despatches to complex deployments. To Malcolm Balen for his invaluable input, to my colleagues in the Spanish American Service, BBCMundo, and to Tara Neill and all of the staff at the BBC's bureau in Washington DC.

In Venezuela, I am hugely indebted to my friend Vanessa Silva, for her indefatigable energy and relentless support in the research for this chapter. To Héctor Navarro and Fernando Ochoa Antich for their time. To the many who spoke to me, whether named or anonymous, about their adoration for or opposition to Hugo Chávez and Nicolás Maduro.

In Brazil, my sincere thanks to President Lula for agreeing to be interviewed while in prison in Curitaba, José Crispiniano for helping to organise it and to Frei Chico for his time and insight. My deepest gratitude to Luciani Gomes and Moises Zeferino for all their support and companionship on our reporting trips in Brazil and Bolivia. And my thanks to Sergio Roxo, Mariana Timoteo and Tom Phillips for their insight.

In Bolivia, to Boris Miranda for fielding my unending questions about Bolivian history and the life of Evo Morales. Also, many thanks to Cindy Jiménez Becerra, Noah Friedman-Rudovsky and José Baig for all their help.

In Ecuador, I am very grateful to Rafael Correa for his generosity with his time and his openness to discuss even the most painful moments of his life. And to his older brother, Fabricio Correa, for his vivid recollections and memories. Similarly, to former minister, Fernando Bustamante, for giving up his time. I am very thankful for the support I received from Tomás Ciuffardi, María Pessina and Andrés Vergara in Quito and Bruno Boelpaep in Brussels. And to Alan Hernández for his transcription work.

In Nicaragua, my profound thanks to Ismael López for helping me to unpick Nicaragua's tangled past as best I could and for putting me in touch with people at both ends of the country's volatile political spectrum. To John Landy for his unfailingly good company and flawless camerawork. My thanks to Arturo Wallace, Mike Lanchin, Gioconda Belli, Zoilamerica Narváez, Mónica Baltodano, Sebastián Chamorro, Carlos Fernando Chamorro, Dora María Téllez and the late Edén Pastora.

In Cuba, I am eternally grateful to my Cuban family, especially my parents-in-law, Carlos Galiano and Susana Rios-Moore, for their unequivocal support and profound insight into the complexities of their island. To the late William Rakip, Alberto 'Nanito' Moreno and Alberto Lahens for their unrelenting good humour and help over the past six years. To Ben Rhodes for the view from inside the Obama era-thaw, Juan Carlos Zaldívar on the Mariel Boatlift and Fabian Escalante on the Cuban Missile Crisis. To Renata Arens for her memories and the late Elizabeth Frey for her photograph of Fidel Castro. And my particular thanks to Jon Lee Anderson for his constant encouragement and invaluable words of advice.

To my family, especially my parents, Michael and Theresa, for their love and unconditional support from the moment I chose to specialise in a continent so far from where I'm from. To my sisters and my brother, Rachel, Ursula, Helen and Leo and their respective families. This book and the experiences I've had in writing it would simply have been impossible without their help. And my cousin, Jenny Lord, for helping me to navigate the publishing world.

My deepest thanks to everyone who spoke to me in Latin America for this book, especially to the victims of violence and abuse, whether staunch believers in or committed campaigners against the leaders contained in these pages. I have been humbled by the wealth of people who have opened their door to me over the years, sometimes in their darkest moments, and shared their lives and experiences with me. Some appear in this book, many others don't. I am grateful to them all for their generosity in helping me to better comprehend this complex, chaotic, beguiling and beautiful part of the world.

Lastly to my partner, Julia Galiano-Rios, for instilling our travels with a sense of adventure and humour, whose clarity, journalistic nous and deep understanding of her region has kept me on course throughout this endeavour and whose love, patience and infectious laughter have anchored me well beyond writing about political ebbs and tides. This book is for you.

And for our daughter, Isla, whose arrival earlier this year was the greatest deadline I've ever known. No matter where you travel, may your maternal continent always occupy a uniquely special place in your heart.

Havana, September 2020

Notes

Introduction

1   Ernesto Laclau, *On Populist Reason*, Verso, 2005, p. 177.
2   Carlos de la Torre, 'Velasco Ibarra and "La Revolución Gloriosa": The Social Production of a Populist Leader in Ecuador in the 1940s', *Journal of Latin American Studies* 26, no. 3, 1994, p. 703.
3   Agustín Cueva, *El proceso de dominación política*, Editorial Planeta, 1988. As quoted in de la Torre, 1994, p. 710.
4   In fact, Enlai was referring to France's student uprising of 1968 and not the events of 1789. But Richard Nixon's translator, Chas Freeman, who was there at the time, said the misunderstanding was 'too delicious to invite correction'.

Venezuela/Hugo Chávez

1   Inter-American Court of Human Rights: 'El Caracazo Case, Judgement of November 11, 1999'.
2   Ibid.
3   In fact, at his most megalomaniacal, Chávez also changed the national flag, the coat of arms and moved the time zone by half an hour.
4   Cristina Marcano and Alberto Barrera Tyszka, *Hugo Chávez Sin Uniforme*, Random House Mondadori, 2007, p. 35.
5   Ibid., p. 69.
6   Rosa Miriam Elizalde and Luis Báez, Chávez Nuestro, Casa Editora Abril, 2013, p. 341.

7   Author interview with Fernando Ochoa Antich, March 2019 / Ochoa Antich, Fernando, 'Así se rindió Chávez: la otra historia del 4 de febrero'.

8   Marcano and Barrera Tyszka, 2007, p. 101.

9   Agustín Blanco Muñoz, 'Habla el Comandante' as quoted in Marcano and Barrera Tyszka, 2007.

10 Marcano and Barrera Tyszka, 2007, p. 145, footnote 14.

11 Jaime Bayly, 'Entrevista con Hugo Chávez – En Directo con Jaime Bayly', CBS-Telenoticias, 1998.

12 Ibid.

13 Jorge Ramos, 'Entrevista con Hugo Chávez', Univision, 1998.

14 Venevision, 'Respuestas para los Venezolanos', 1 December 1998.

15 Rafael Caldera served two separate terms in office more than twenty years apart.

16 ¿Fallecieron 50.000 personas en la tragedia de Vargas? TalCual, 13 December 2019.

17 Christopher Toothaker, 'Venezuela Rebuilding From Floods', *Washington Post*, 24 December 2000.

18 Carlos Texeira of the Vargas-based 'Red de Ciudadanos Activos Nelson Mandela' as quoted in Laura De Stefano, 'En el limbo quedó la construcción de 12.518 viviendas', La Verdad – Diario de Vargas, 12 December 2016.

19 Few are as detailed or minutely researched as Sandra La Fuente and Alfredo Meza's book *El Acertijo de Abril* (*The April Riddle*) or Brian Nelson's excellent account of those chaotic and confused forty-eight hours, *The Silence and the Scorpion*. Two years after the event, the Venezuelan blogger Francisco Toro also wrote about April 2002 on the 'Caracas Chronicles' blog combining his own day on the streets of Caracas with a thorough analysis: 'The Untold Story of Venezuela's 2002 April Crisis'.

20 For greater detail, Brian Nelson in *The Silence and the Scorpion* goes through the events at Llaguno and Baralt hour by hour, examining the deaths on both sides.

21 'En 2019 no habrá familia venezolana sin vivienda propia', PSUV.org, 28 November 2011.

22 Carola Solé, 'Chávez: 'Ni me acuerdo' del cancer', EFE, 4 October 2012.

23 Author's interview with Hector Navarro, March 2019.

24 Figures for January 2019 distributed by the EU delegation to Venezuela, 24/2/19.

25 '#MonitorDeVíctimas | FAES, el grupo de exterminio de la PNB', Runrun.es, 16 January 2018.

26   Sarah Kinosian and Angus Berwick, 'Convicted criminals are among the special police force terrorising Venezuela', Reuters Special Report, 19 February 2020.

27   Karenina Velandia and Charlie Newland, 'El Helicoide: From an icon to an infamous Venezuelan jail', BBC News, 24 January 2019.

28   Jennifer L. McCoy and David J. Myers, *The Unraveling of Representative Democracy in Venezuela*, Johns Hopkins University Press, 2005.

29   'Venezuela Oil Price Tumbles Further Below $40', *Latin American Herald Tribune*, November 2015.

30   'Economic Survey of Latin America and the Caribbean 2008–2009', CEPAL / ECLAC, p. 107.

31   'Venezuela Key Indicators', *Guardian*, 7 March 2013.

32   Ruth Mayer (director), *Revolution in Ruins: The Hugo Chávez Story*, BBC 'This World', January 2019.

33   Ibid.

34   Patricia Laya and Andrew Rosati, 'Venezuela's 2018 Inflation to Hit 1.37 Million Percent, IMF Says', Bloomberg, 8 October 2018.

35   Stefanie Eschenbacher, 'Rapid Decline', Reuters Graphics, 15 January 2020.

36   Patricia Laya and Alex Vasquez, 'Venezuela Cash Hoard Sinks Below $1 Billion With Gold Locked Up', Bloomberg, 17 January 2020.

37   Richard Gott, 'Chávez leads the way', *Guardian*, 30 May 2005.

38   Defenestration is particularly apt given what later happened to opposition lawmaker Fernando Alban. Around two months after the drone attack, Alban was arrested as he returned to the country after addressing the United Nations in New York over human rights in Venezuela. Held at the headquarters of the state intelligence agency, SEBIN, in Caracas, the government says the deputy took his life by jumping from a tenth-floor window. His family and supporters dispute that, saying he was thrown from the window, possibly after being killed – either intentionally or accidentally during torture. The government gave two conflicting versions of what happened to Alban and the United Nations called for an investigation into the circumstances of his suspicious death.

Brazil/Luiz Inácio Lula da Silva

1   Mike Collett, 'Brazil's 1970 winning team voted best of all time', Reuters, 9 July 2007.

2   Luiz Inácio was called Lula from a young age, a common nickname for Luiz

in his part of Brazil, but he didn't officially change his name to include the sobriquet until 1981.

3 Author's interview with José Ferreira da Silva, Lula's older brother, known as Frei Chico, August 2019.

4 Author's interview with Frei Chico, August 2019.

5 Under the First Republic, when only literate men were able to vote, the electorate was restricted to just 3 per cent of the population.

6 Richard Bourne, *Lula of Brazil: The Story So Far*, Zed Books, 2008, p. 11.

7 'Interview with Luiz Inácio da Silva ('Lula'), president of the Sindicato dos Metalurgicos de São Bernardo do Campo', *Cara a Cara* journal, July–December 1978, translated by Mauri Garcia and Timothy Harding, in *Latin American Perspectives*, Vol. 6, No. 4, *Brazil: Capitalist Crisis and Workers' Challenge*, Sage Publications, Autumn, 1979.

8 Author's interviews with Luiz Inácio Lula da Silva and Frei Chico, August 2019.

9 Alcohol would be the end of Aristides. He died in 1978, penniless and alone.

10 Bourne, 2008, p. 7.

11 Fontes and Correa, International Labor and Working-Class History, Spring 2018: 'The authoritarian regime sought to maintain a façade of democracy and was very concerned with its legal institutionalization. The idea that the "Revolution" (as the coup was called by the military and their conservative supporters) had saved "democracy" from the communists was a central component of the military's official rhetoric. American support helped to consolidate this image.'

12 One of the leading experts on the military dictatorship in Brazil, Marcos Napolitano, sets out the full extent of the control exercised by the Institutional Acts and their 'Complementary Acts' in his work 'The Brazil Military Regime 1964–1985' in the *Oxford Research Encyclopedia of Latin American History*, Oxford University Press USA, April 2018. By ruling that any new party formed had to have at least 120 deputies and 20 senators, the military created a biparty system: 'By the end of 1965, deputies were grouped into two parties – the National Renovating Alliance (ARENA), the official party of the regime, and the "moderate" Brazilian Democratic Movement (MDB) – both officially registered in 1966… The two-party system eventually turned legislative elections into plebiscites indicating who favored and who opposed the military government.'

13 Elena Shtromberg, *Art Systems: Brazil and the 1970s*, University of Texas Press, 2016, Fig. 12, p. 43.

14   Jewell Fenzi, 'Interview with Elvira "Elfie" Elbrick', The Association for Diplomatic Studies and Training Foreign Affairs Oral History Project – Spouse Oral History Series, 24 October 1986.

15   Michael Newton, *The Encyclopedia of Kidnappings*, Facts on File Inc., 2002, p. 96.

16   Julia Carneiro, 'Kidnap of US Ambassador in Brazil: Interview with Fernando Gabeira', BBC Witness, broadcast 29 September 2011.

17   Newton, p. 96.

18   Carneiro, 'Kidnap of US Ambassador in Brazil: Interview with Fernando Gabeira', BBC Witness, broadcast 29 September 2011.

19   Ibid.

20   Bourne, 2008, p. 20.

21   Denise Paraná, *Lula, o Filho do Brasil*, Fundação Perseu Abramo, 2009.

22   Bourne, 2008, p. 30.

23   Ibid., p. 34.

24   Gay W. Seidman, *Manufacturing Militance: Workers' Movements in Brazil and South Africa, 1970–1985*, University of California Press, 1994, pp. 150–51.

25   'Interview with Luiz Inácio da Silva ('Lula'), president of the Sindicato dos Metalúrgicos de São Bernardo do Campo', *Cara a Cara* journal, July–December 1978, translated by Garcia and Harding, in *Latin American Perspectives*, Vol. 6, No. 4, *Brazil: Capitalist Crisis and Workers' Challenge*, Sage Publications, Autumn 1979, p. 93.

26   Ibid.

27   Ibid., p. 94.

28   Anthony Pahnke, *Brazil's Long Revolution: Radical Achievements of the Landless Workers Movement*, University of Arizona Press, 2018, p. 99.

29   As the Brazilian historian Marcos Napolitano points out, the '*abertura*' was essentially to ensure greater control for the military, not less. Just in a different manner: 'The Geisel government represented the return to power of a military faction that favored a more institutionalized authoritarian regime, one that would not rely so heavily on force and direct police repression. According to this political project, power should be gradually handed over to moderate civilian sectors so that the regime's principles of 'security and development' could be consolidated without necessitating direct military control of the state.' Marcos Napolitano, 'The Brazil Military Regime 1964–1985', *Oxford Research Encyclopedia of Latin American History*, Oxford University Press USA, April 2018.

30   GloboNews, rushes, 30 April 1981.

31   Ibid.

32   'Quem explodiu estas bombas no Rio? Veja os fatos e julgue', *Jornal da Tarde*, 2 May 1981.

33   Ibid.

34   Author's interview with Lula, August 2019.

35   Dalva Ramaldes and José Luiz Aidar Prado, 'The Body of the Power: A semiotic study of Lula's figure in the 1989 presidential campaign as portrayed in the Brazilian weekly newsmagazines *Veja* and *Istoé*' –*Brazilian Journalism Research*, Vol. 4, 2008, pp. 169–70.

36   *Veja* magazine, 'Pedro Collar Contra Tudo', May 1992.

37   Larry Rohter, 'A Leftist Takes Over in Brazil and Pledges a "New Path"', *New York Times*, 2 January 2003.

38   Ibid.

39   The government would later describe the plan as 'the main governmental strategy guiding economic and social policies in Brazil'. José Graziano da Silva, Mauro Eduardo Del Grossi and Caio Galvão de França, 'The Fome Zero (Zero Hunger) Program – The Brazilian Experience', Ministry of Agrarian Development (MDA), *NEAD Special Series* 13, Brasilia, 2011, p. 10.

40   A. J. Stein (2014), 'Addressing hunger has high returns on investment', in Global Food Policy report 2013, International Food Policy Institute, Washington DC, as quoted in Katharine S. E. Cresswell Riol, *The Right to Food Guidelines, Democracy and Citizen Participation: Country Case Guidelines*, Routledge, 2017, p. 54.

41   E. Sidaner, D. Balaban and L. Burlandy, 'The Brazilian school feeding programme: an example of an integrated programme in support of food and nutrition security', *Public Health Nutrition*, December 2012, p. 990.

42   Author's interview with Lula da Silva, Curitiba, 28 August 2019.

43   In August 2016, years after Lula had left power, the United Nations Development Programme (UNDP) found the programme was still playing a vital role in the wellbeing and economic income of the nation's poorest: 'The *Bolsa Família* programme (PBF) currently reaches approximately 13.8 million households, corresponding to 25 per cent of the poorest population of Brazil.' The International Policy Centre for Inclusive Growth, Research Brief 55, August 2016.

44   Marta Nogueira and Jose Roberto Gomes, 'Brazil's Petrobras fires up new platform in offshore Lula field', Reuters, 24 October 2018.

45   Paulo Cabral, 'Brazil – Lula's Legacy: A country under construction', BBC World Service, The Documentary, 10 January 2011.

46 As quoted in Duncan Green, 'Tackling inequality, the Brazilian experience' – Beyondbrics, *Financial Times*, 18 March 2013.

47 Bourne, 2008, p. 109.

48 Gibby Zobel, 'Brazil in crisis over corruption claims', *Guardian*, 11 July 2005.

49 'Jean Charles de Menezes inquest timeline', *The Telegraph*, 22 September 2008.

50 'Lula pidió 'justicia' para el caso de Menezes', La Red 21, 10 March 2006.

51 John Campbell, 'Brazil is in Africa' blog post, Council of Foreign Relations, 15 August 2011.

52 In the end, the hosts were dumped out of the competition in the most ignominious fashion, losing 7–1 to Germany in the semi-final, a match and a scoreline which haunts millions of Brazilian football fans to this day.

53 Much to his frustration, Uribe would eventually be prevented from holding a referendum on the matter by the country's constitutional court.

54 Angus MacSwan, 'Brazilian President Lula rules out third term', Reuters, 26 August 2007.

55 Jonathan Watts, 'Operation Car Wash: Is this the biggest corruption scandal in history?', *Guardian*, 1 June 2017.

56 Ibid.

57 Andrew Fishman, Rafael Moro Martins, Leandro Demori, Alexandre de Santi and Glenn Greenwald, 'Breach of Ethics. Exclusive: Leaked Chats Between Brazilian Judge and Prosecutor Who Imprisoned Lula Reveal Prohibited Collaboration and Doubts over Evidence', *The Intercept*, 9 June 2019,

58 Andrew Fishman, Rafael Moro Martins, Leandro Demori, Glenn Greenwald and Amanda Audi: '"Their Little Show": Exclusive: Brazilian Judge in Car Wash Corruption Case Mocked Lula's Defense and Secretly Director Prosecutors' Media Strategy During Trial', *The Intercept*, 17 June 2019.

59 Marisa Letícia was included in the long *Lava Jato* corruption charge sheet alongside Lula but died before the investigating task force could bring a formal case against her. Lula still blames Sérgio Moro and Deltan Dallagnol for her death, suggesting her sudden stroke could have been brought on by the additional stress they placed on her.

60 Dom Phillips, 'Brazilian court bars Lula from presidential election', *Guardian*, 1 September 2018.

61 Leda Nagle, 'Com a palavra o Presidente Jair Bolsonaro', 5 August 2019.

62 Tom Phillips, '"He wants to destroy us": Bolsonaro poses gravest threat in decades, Amazon tribes say', *Guardian*, 26 July 2019.

63 Letícia Duarte, 'Meet the Intellectual Founder of Brazil's Far Right', *The Atlantic*, 28 December 2019.

64 J. Leahy and A. Schipani, 'Lula's legacy of working-class gains at risk in Brazil's election', *Financial Times*, 22 May 2018.

65 Julia Carneiro, 'Brazil's universities take affirmative action', BBC News, 28 August 2013.

Bolivia/Evo Morales

1 Edwin Williamson, *The Penguin History of Latin America*, Penguin Books, 1992, p. 198.

2 Defined as 'Spaniard born in America, and descendants' in Williamson, 1992, p. 683.

3 Eduardo Galeano, *Las Venas Abiertas de América Latina*, Siglo XXI Editores SA, 2000 (1st edn), 1971.

4 Catharina Moh, 'The mountain that eats men in Bolivia', BBC News, 2 October 2014.

5 Perhaps fittingly, Bolivia was the country where the outlaws Butch Cassidy and the Sundance Kid were finally tracked down and killed in 1908.

6 Jon Lee Anderson, 'Burial Lessons: From Che to bin Laden', *New Yorker*, 3 May 2011.

7 Author's interview with Felix Rodríguez, Miami, October 2007.

8 At the end of the interview with Rodríguez, he gave me an unsolicited gift, one he apparently bestowed on many journalists and visitors to his home: a signed copy of that chilling photograph with Che, with the grim and presumptuous caption 'in memory of that day on 9th October 1967 when history was changed a little in our favour'.

9 Jon Lee Anderson, *Che Guevara: A Revolutionary Life*, Grove Press, 2010 (revised edn; 1st edn, 1997), p. 709–10.

10 Ibid., pp. xii, xiii and 728.

11 Sven Harten, *The Rise of Evo Morales and the MAS*, Zed Books, 2011.

12 Ibid.

13 Boris Miranda, 'Evo Morales en Argentina', BBC News Mundo, 13 December 2019.

14 Ibid.

15 Harten, 2011.

16 Christian Burgos Gallardo, 'El Lujoso Museo Construido en un Pueblo con Casa de Adobe y Calles de Tierra', *Los Tiempos*, February 2017.

17 David Mercado and Santiago Limach, 'Bolivia opens $7 million museum honoring President Morales', Reuters, 2 February 2017.

18 Carlos Valdez, 'Bolivia opens $7m museum honouring President Morales', Associated Press, 3 February 2017.

19 Christian Burgos Gallardo, 'El Lujoso Museo Construido en un Pueblo con Casa de Adobe y Calles de Tierra', *Los Tiempos*, February 2017.

20 Bolivia's seat of power was set ablaze in an unsuccessful uprising in 1875 against the then president, Tomás Frías. Even after the building was rebuilt, the name Palacio Quemado stuck.

21 JJ Torres was later killed by a right-wing death squad in Argentina in 1976 as part of Operation Condor, a CIA-backed programme of repression and murder agreed between military dictators in the Southern Cone.

22 Chantelle Bacigalupo, 'In Bolivia, the National Flag and the Indigenous Wiphala Become Symbols of Division', *Remezcla*, 19 November 2019.

23 Harten, 2011.

24 In most Latin American nations, if no one has the requisite percentage of votes, the two leading candidates return to the ballot box for a second-round run-off. In Bolivia at that time, the final decision passed directly to a deciding vote in Congress. The system was rife with horse trading and corruption and wouldn't be changed until 2009.

25 In the first conviction of a former de facto military leader in the Americas, Luis García Meza was convicted in absentia for human rights violations. In 1995, he was extradited back to Bolivia from exile in Brazil to serve a thirty-year prison sentence. Among his crimes, he had illegally sold the original copies of Che Guevara's personal diaries from his doomed revolutionary expedition in Bolivia. He would eventually die in a military prison in 2018.

26 Alex Contreras Baspineiro, 'Evo, una historia de dignidad', UPS Editorial, La Paz, Bolivia, October 2005, p. 10.

27 United Nations Single Convention on Narcotic Drugs, 1961.

28 As quoted in Harten, 2011, p. 69.

29 The concept of *mandar obedeciendo* was also present in other grassroots indigenous movements, particularly the Zapatista rebels in southern Mexico.

30 Harten, 2011, p. 54.

31 As quoted in Eduardo Córdova Eguívar, 'Movimientos campesinos y dilemas de la democracia. El movimiento cocalero y el MAS-IPSP en los niveles local y nacional de la política boliviana, 1996–2004', CLACSO, 2005.

32 Harten, 2011.

33 James Painter, 'Bolivia and Coca: A Study in Dependency', United Nations University and the United Nations Research Institute for Social Development, 1994

34 Ibid.

35 Ibid.

36 Linda Farthing, 'Antidrug Law 1008' in Madeline Barbara Léons and Harry Sanabria (eds), *Coca, Cocaine, and the Bolivian Reality*, State University of New York Press, 1997, p. 264.

37 In particular, the Chapare coca growers bitterly resented the Quechua-speaking then US chargé d'affaires in Bolivia, David Nicol Greenlee.

38 Interview with Evo Morales on 'Historias a Quemarropa' on state-run Bolivia TV, 27 June 2016.

39 Ursula Durand Ochoa, *The Political Empowerment of the Cocaleros of Bolivia and Peru*, Palgrave Macmillan, 2014.

40 Martín Sivak, *Evo Morales: The Extraordinary Rise of the First Indigenous President of Bolivia*, Palgrave Macmillan, 2010.

41 This story appeared in a BBC News Mundo article by Boris Miranda, 'Bolivia: 4 anécdotas personales para entender cómo Evo Morales se convirtió en el presidente que más tiempo ha gobernado en la historia de ese país', 14 August 2018.

42 Córdova Eguívar, 2005.

43 Ibid. Evo went on to recall an occasion when the UMOPAR police took the wedding ring from a dead *compañera*, because 'they couldn't find anything else to steal'.

44 The original 'March for Life' in 1986 by mining union workers was over economic shock therapy measures, intended to combat hyperinflation, which were destroying their livelihoods and incomes. The severe salary caps and job cuts in the state sector were implemented by Sánchez de Lozada as planning minister.

45 Rafael Archondo, 'Breve biografía política de Evo Morales', Umbrales, 19, Universidad Mayor de San Andrés (CIDES-UMSA), 2009, p. 110.

46 Patrick Heenan and Monique Lamontagne, *The South America Handbook*, Routledge, 2013 (first published Fitzroy Dearborn Publishers, 2002), p. 275.

47 Juan Carlos Barrientos and Walter Schug, 'The decision of farmers from the tropical region of Cochabamba in Bolivia to cultivate coca instead of state-recommended alternative products', *Agronomía Colombiana*, Vol. 24, No. 1, January–June 2006.

48 Archondo, 2009, p. 110.

49 Ibid., p. 105.

50 James Dunkerley, 'Evo Morales, the "Two Bolivias" and the Third Bolivian Revolution', *Journal of Latin American Studies*, February 2007, p. 141.

51 Córdova Eguívar, 2005, p. 90 (Translation: author's own.)

52 Raul L. Madrid, 'Obstacles to Ethnic Parties in Latin America', in Steven Levitsky, James Loxton, Brandon Van Dyck and Jorge I. Domínguez (eds), *Challenges of Party-Building in Latin America*, Cambridge University Press, 2016, p. 317.

53 Evo Morales entered the chamber with the additional honour of being the deputy who garnered the highest percentage of votes in his constituency at 71 per cent (Archondo, 2009, p. 118).

54 Marta Harnecker and Federico Fuentes, 'MAS-IPSP de Bolivia – Instrumento Político que Surge de los Movimientos Sociales', Centro Internacional Miranda, 2008, p. 71.

55 In fact, it would ultimately be the undoing of the ASP, with much of the grassroots, non-coca-growing rural poor and indigenous members also turning to Evo by the 2002 election, leaving Alejo Véliz isolated and without a significant base.

56 Harnecker and Fuentes, 'MAS-IPSP de Bolivia – Instrumento Político que Surge de los Movimientos Sociales', Centro Internacional Miranda, 2008, p. 72.

57 Though less than half the population in Bolivia speaks Aymara, Quechua or Guarani, in a 2001 census, 62 per cent of respondents identified themselves as 'indigenous', a figure which rose to 75 per cent in El Alto (Dunkerley, 2007, p. 135.)

58 The case of Marlene's death would be the subject of a civil trial against Gonzalo Sánchez de Lozada in Fort Lauderdale in 2018, the first time that a former head of state of a foreign country faced trial in a US civil court for human rights abuses. While a jury trial found Sánchez de Lozada liable for the civilian deaths and awarded the plaintiffs $10 million in damages, a federal judge overturned the verdict a month later.

59 'Bolivia gas pipeline protest continues', Al Jazeera, October 2003.

60 For a running mate, he decided against the Trotskyite ex-mining union leader Filemón Escóbar and opted instead for the scholarly Álvaro García Linera. As an ex-member of the Túpac Katari Guerrilla Army (EGTK) who had gone to prison for an attempted armed rebellion, García Linera's radical left-wing credentials were unimpeachable. However, Evo also understood that having a silver-haired intellectual with a mathematics degree from a Mexican university as his candidate for vice-president was potentially more palatable to the wealthier classes.

61　Sarah Bush, 'Ceremony Precedes Bolivian President's Inauguration', NPR, 22 January 2006.

62　Sivak, 2010.

63　Juan Forero, 'Bolivia Indians Hail the Swearing In of One of Their Own as President', *New York Times*, 23 January 2006.

64　*Miami Herald* as quoted in Aaron Luoma, 'Reactions to Gas and Oil "Nationalization"', The Democracy Center, April 2010.

65　Gretchen Gordon, 'Gas and Oil Nationalization', The Democracy Center, April 2010.

66　La Razon, 6 May 2006, as quoted in Aaron Luoma, 'Reactions to Gas and Oil "Nationalization"', The Democracy Center, April 2010.

67　Paulo Prada, 'Bolivian Nationalizes the Oil and Gas Sector', *New York Times*, 2 May 2006.

68　EFE, 'Bolivia pagó 828,3 millones de dólares por 12 nacionalizaciones', 17 January 2017.

69　Jair Antunes, 'Evo Morales and the fraud of "nationalization" in Bolivia', World Socialist Web Site, 22 May 2007.

70　Antunes, 2007 / Gretchen, 2010.

71　EFE, 'YPFB: Bolivia's oil and gas nationalization generated $31.5 bn over a decade', 16 April 2016.

72　'Bolivian President Morales tells MEPs: "nationalisation is not expropriation"', European Parliament press release, 16 May 2006.

73　Diego Ore and Eduardo García, 'Bolivia nationalizes four power companies', Reuters, 1 May 2010.

74　María Clemencia Ramírez, 'Coca leaf and the war against cocaine', in Linda J. Seligmann and Kathleen S. Fine-Dare (eds), *The Andean World*, Routledge, 2019, p. 659.

75　Sivak, 2010.

76　'Paupérrima imagen deja Miss Bolivia en el Miss Universo', Bolivia.com, 26 May 2004.

77　'Breakaway Bolivian State Eyes Freedom', NPR, 6 May 2008.

78　He would eject a third major US institution, USAID, in 2013 for allegedly meddling in Bolivia's internal affairs, sending them the way of the DEA and the US ambassador back to Washington.

79　'GDP growth (annual %) – Bolivia', World Bank National Accounts Data (1961–2018).

80　'Bolivia entre los países de la región que más redujo la pobreza', Instituto Nacional de Estadística.

81 Ellie Mae O'Hagan, 'Evo Morales has proved that socialism doesn't damage economies', *Guardian*, 14 October 2014 / Anthony Faiola, 'Socialism doesn't work? An emerging middle class of Bolivians would beg to differ', *Washington Post*, 16 October 2019.

82 Rafael Archondo, 'País teleférico', *Página Siete*, 30 May 2019.

83 'Bolivia launches world's highest cable railway', AFP, 31 May 2014.

84 Rafael Archondo, 'País teleférico', *Página Siete*, 30 May 2019.

85 Mabel Sarmiento, 'De cinco estaciones del Metrocable de San Agustín solo funcionan tres', *Crónica Uno*, 20 April 2019.

86 Boris Miranda, 'TIPNIS, la controversial carretera que puede partir en dos una selva de Bolivia y que Evo Morales "insiste en construir"', BBC News Mundo, 17 August 2017.

87 Mattia Cabitza, 'Evo Morales plays a double game on Bolivia's environment', *Guardian*, 4 July 2011.

88 'Bolivia minister quits over road protest row', Al Jazeera, 27 September 2011.

89 Ramy Wurgaft, 'Evo Morales, en su peor momento tras la repression de la marcha indígena', *El Mundo*, 29 September 2011.

90 Ibid.

91 Miranda, 2017.

92 Emily Achtenberg, 'Bolivia Votes: Can Evo Morales Run Again?', Rebel Currents, NACLA, 9 February 2016.

93 Rafael Puente, 'El confuso debate sobre el referendo constitucional', *Página Siete*, 27 November 2015.

94 Shortly after the referendum, Zapata's aunt confirmed the boy was alive and well, prompting Evo to say he hoped to meet him. After increasingly lurid revelations involving DNA tests, claim and counter-claim, all of which kept Bolivians rapt for months, a judge eventually ruled there was no evidence of a child at all.

95 'Comunicado del Secretario General sobre Informe Preliminar Auditores Proceso Electoral en Bolivia' OAS, 10 November 2019.

96 Iván Paredes Tamayo, 'Encerrado y sin dormir: Así fueron las últimas 28 horas de Evo en el poder', *El Deber*, 4 December 2019.

97 A few months later, a statistical study funded by a leftist think-tank in Washington, the Center for Economic and Policy Research, was published in a politics blog in the *Washington Post*. The researchers refuted the position of the OAS and claimed there was no evidence of foul play in the vote count or the apparent computer switch-off. A second study by independent researchers from Tulane University and the University of Pennsylvania,

and using data from the Bolivia Electoral authorities obtained by the *New York Times*, echoed a similar view about the OAS statistical conclusions, that they were flawed and unduly hasty. 'We can explain the change in trend without invoking electoral malpractice', the authors wrote, albeit with the caveat that they 'do not establish the absence of fraud; we did not observe the election and make no claim of comprehensive evaluation'. Still, for Evo supporters around the world, it was ample evidence that the Washington-based body was institutionally biased against Morales and that its statements about the veracity of the 2019 Bolivian presidential election were designed to sow unrest. They insist that Evo Morales was, in fact, correct on election night to say that the remote rural regions were about to hand him victory.

98 The frustration was combined with existing anger in the region over a severe drought at Lake Poopó, near Evo's birthplace, which many blamed on poor water management by his government. By 2015, Bolivia's second largest water resource had dried up completely with little realistic chance of recovery.

99 Glenn Greenwald, 'Glenn Greenwald's Exclusive Interview With Bolivia's Evo Morales, Who Was Deposed in a Coup', *The Intercept*, 16 December 2019.

100 'Bolivian wildfires destroy two million hectares of forest', BBC News, 10 September 2019.

101 Ibid.

102 Michael Stott and Andres Schipani, 'Evo Morales's legacy: a polarised Bolivia', *Financial Times*, 11 November 2019.

103 Jorge Quispe, 'Entre el arado y el retorno', *La Razón*, 10 June 2012.

104 Thomas Grisaffi, *Coca Yes, Cocaine No: How Bolivia's Coca Growers Reshaped Democracy*, Duke University Press, 2019, p. 8.

105 Jon Lee Anderson, 'Bolivia's Evo Morales Wants to Stay in the Game', *New Yorker*, 20 November 2019.

106 Linda C. Farthing, and Benjamin H. Kohl, *Evo's Bolivia: Continuity and Change*, University of Texas Press, 2014, p. 7.

107 'Informe de la Sociedad Civil Boliviana al Comité para la Eliminación de la Discriminación Racial de Naciones Unidas' – Committee on the Elimination of Racial Discrimination (CERD) report for the Office of the United Nations High Commissioner for Human Rights, Bolivia, August 2010.

108 Álvaro García Linera, 'El odio al indio', Centro Estratégico Latinoamericano de Geopolítica (CELAG), 16 November 2019.

109 James Dunkerley, 'Evo Morales, the "Two Bolivias" and the Third Bolivian Revolution', *Journal of Latin American Studies*, February 2007, p. 137.

NOTES

Ecuador/Rafael Correa

1   The translation of *Tawantinsuyu* from Quechua is 'the Land of Four Quarters', a reflection of the four quarters of an empire which joined together in Cuzco, Gordon Francis McEwan, *The Incas: New Perspectives*, ABC-Clio, 2006, p. 44.
2   Edwin Williamson, *The Penguin History of Latin America*, Penguin Books; revised edn, February 2010, p. 23.
3   Both spellings – 'Atahualpa' and 'Atahuallpa' – are the accepted Hispanized versions of his name in the literature with 'Atawallpa' the most common spelling in Quechua.
4   Mark Honigsbaum, *Valverde's Gold: A True Tale of Greed, Obsession and Grit*, Pan Macmillan, 2004, p. 78.
5   Williamson, 2010, p. 24.
6   Francisco de Xerez, 'True account of the conquest of Peru', an account by Pizarro's loyal secretary, as quoted in Sabine MacCormack, 'Atahualpa and the Book', *Dispositio*, Vol. 14, No. 36/38, Colonial Discourse, Centre for Latin American and Caribbean Studies, University of Michigan, Ann Arbor, 1989, p. 143.
7   MacCormack, 'Atahualpa and the Book', p. 143 / Honigsbaum, 2004, p. 82.
8   Overall, Velasco Ibarra was in office for longer than Rafael Correa but Correa spent longer in a continuous sitting as president with an unbroken decade in power.
9   Carlos de la Torre, 'Velasco Ibarra and "La Revolución Gloriosa": The Social Production of a Populist Leader in Ecuador in the 1940s', *Journal of Latin American Studies*, 26, No. 3, 1994, p. 690.
10 Joseph B. Treaster, 'Velasco, ex-leader of Ecuador, 86, dies', New York Times, 31 March 1979.
11 De la Torre, Carlos: 'Velasco Ibarra and "La Revolución Gloriosa": The Social Production of a Populist Leader in Ecuador in the 1940s', *Journal of Latin American Studies*, 26, No. 3, 1994, p. 699.
12 Ibid., p. 685.
13 Ibid., p. 706.
14 Mónica Almeida and Ana Karina López, 'El Séptimo Rafael: La Biografía no autorizada de Rafael Correa Delgado, expresidente del Ecuador', *Aperimus*, 2017.
15 Author's interview with Rafael Correa Delgado, Louvain-la-Neuve, Belgium, 29 April 2019.

16   Author's interview with Fabricio Correa Delgado, October 2019.

17   Author's interview with Rafael Correa, April 2019.

18   Author's interview with Rafael Correa, April 2019 and Fabricio Correa, March 2020.

19   Author's interview with Fabricio Correa, October 2019.

20   According to a cable from the then US ambassador to Ecuador, Linda Jewell, published by the WikiLeaks website, the US Embassy had also confirmed the rumour for themselves six months earlier, in October 2006.

21   'La prensa fue cauta en caso del papá de Correa', *El Comercio*, 29 April 2011.

22   'El padre Rafael Correa estuvo en la cárcel por narcotráfico', *La Voz de Galicia*, 14 April 2007, quoting EFE.

23   Author's interview with Rafael Correa, April 2019.

24   Almeida and López, 'El Séptimo Rafael', *Aperimus*, 2017 / Author's interview with Fabricio Correa, October 2019.

25   Ibid.

26   Author's interview with Rafael Correa, April 2019.

27   Ambar De Perez, interview with Anne Malherbe, Gamavisión, November 2006.

28   Almeida and López, 'El Séptimo Rafael', *Aperimus*, 2017.

29   'The El Niño Effect': FOSFA International / 'El Niño', BBC Weather.

30   Andres Vergara, 'Dollarization in Ecuador', Willamette University, 2002.

31   Almeida and López, 'El Séptimo Rafael', *Aperimus*, 2017.

32   Vergara, 'Dollarization in Ecuador', Willamette University, 2002.

33   Leading the military side of the protest, effectively turning the moment into a coup, was Colonel Lucio Gutiérrez, the start of his appearance on the public consciousness and subsequent political career.

34   Ibid.

35   'Rafael Correa renunció al ministerio de Economía', *El Universo*, 5 August 2005.

36   Almeida and López, 'El Séptimo Rafael', *Aperimus*, 2017.

37   Carlos Vera, interview with Anne Malherbe, *Ecuavisa*, November 2006.

38   Ibid.

39   'Ecuadorian president Correa calls March national referendum', MercoPress, 15 January 2007.

40   Latinobarómetro opinion poll of 18 regional nations as quoted in Almeida and López, 'El Séptimo Rafael', *Aperimus*, 2017.

41   Once the Constituent Assembly members were sitting, they formally dissolved parliament. They drew up the text of the new constitution, again approved by a huge majority and a National Assembly replaced the old Congress as the country's unicameral legislative body.

42 Marc Becker, 'The Stormy Relations between Rafael Correa and Social Movements in Ecuador', *Latin American Perspectives*, Vol. 40, No. 3, May 2013, p. 43.

43 Ibid.

44 Author's interview with Rafael Correa, April 2019.

45 Nicholas Casey and Clifford Krauss, 'It Doesn't Matter if Ecuador Can Afford This Dam. China Still Gets Paid', *New York Times*, 24 December 2018.

46 Irene Caselli, 'Ecuador President Rafael Correa loses indigenous allies', BBC News, 20 April 2011.

47 Ibid.

48 Ibid.

49 Marc Becker, 'The Stormy Relations between Rafael Correa and Social Movements in Ecuador', *Latin American Perspectives*, Vol. 40, No. 3, May 2013, p. 44.

50 Maite Rico, 'Así fue la Operción Fénix', *El País*, 9 March 2008.

51 Diego Guauque, 'Operción Fénix abatio Raúl Reyes', RCN, 5 March 2008.

52 Maite Rico, 'Así fue la Operción Fénix', *El País*, 9 March 2008.

53 EFE, 'Correa: "No permitiremos que este hecho quede en la impunidad"', 3 March 2008.

54 Mariana Sanchez, 'Ecuador to shut US military base in Manta', Al Jazeera, 17 May 2008.

55 Joshua Partlow, 'Ecuador Giving U.S. Air Base the Boot', *Washington Post*, 4 September 2008.

56 Author's interview with Rafael Correa, April 2019.

57 Rory Carroll, 'Ecuador's President attacked by police', *Guardian*, 1 October 2010.

58 Author's interview with Fernando Bustamante, December 2019.

59 'Ecuador declares state of emergency amid "coup attempt"', BBC News, 1 October 2010.

60 Rory Carroll, 'Ecuador declares state of emergency as country thrown into chaos', *Guardian*, 30 September 2010.

61 Gabriela Torres, 'Ecuador President Rafael Correa's troll warfare', BBC Trending, 30 January 2015.

62 'An Assault on Democracy', *New York Times* editorial. As quoted in Irene Caselli, 'Ecuador's Rafael Correa under fire for media laws', BBC News, 2 February 2012.

63 'Ahmedinejad trip to Ecuador: A meeting of international pariahs', *Washington Post* Editorial Board. As quoted in Caselli: 'Ecuador's Rafael Correa under fire for media laws', BBC News, 2 February 2012.

64   Ibid.

65   EFE, 'Ley de Comunicación en Ecuador cumple 4 años entre la polémica y la necesidad', 25 June 2017.

66   Alejandra Torres Reyes, 'Rafael Correa ha editado su vida y ha acomodado la verdad', *El País*, 28 May 2008.

67   Dan Collyns, 'Why Assange and Ecuador Fell Out', *New York Review of Books*, 1 May 2019.

68   Brian Braiker, 'Ecuador's free speech record at odds with Julian Assange's bid for openness', *Guardian*, 19 June 2012.

69   'Ecuador expels US ambassador over Wikileaks cable', BBC News, 5 April 2011.

70   Jim Wyss, 'WikiLeaks claims second U.S. ambassador, in Ecuador', *Miami Herald*, 5 April 2011.

71   Author's interview with Rafael Correa, April 2019.

72   Freddy Paredes, 'Lenín Moreno tilda de "matón de barrio" a Correa', Teleamazonas, 27 July 2018.

73   'Crisis en Ecuador: Lenín Moreno vs. Rafael Correa, los antiguos aliados cuya enemistad divide al país', BBC News Mundo, 10 October 2019.

74   In December, Rafael Correa posted a video of this portion of Moreno's speech on his Twitter account as an example of how the new president was a 'professional imposter'.

75   In April 2020, in an unrelated corruption case, Rafael Correa was sentenced *in absentia* to eight years in prison for allegedly accepting campaign funds in return for state contracts. As part of the sentence, the court banned him from 'political participation' for twenty-five years. He dismissed the judgement as having been based on lies and 'pure false testimony without evidence'.

76   'Brazil's Odebrecht accepts Ecuador's terms', *Hydro Review*, 3 October 2008.

77   Author's interview with Fabricio Correa, October 2019.

Nicaragua/Daniel Ortega

1   CBS Evening News, 26 December 1972.

2   Alan Riding, 'National Mutiny in Nicaragua', *New York Times*, 30 July 1978.

3   Ibid.

4   Peter David, *Where Is Nicaragua?*, Simon & Schuster, 1987, p. 22.

5   Pedro Joaquín Chamorro, Letter to Anastasio Somoza Debayle, dated 18 January 1975, replicated in *Confidencial*, 10 January 2019. (Translation: author's own.)

6   Alan Riding, 'National Mutiny in Nicaragua', *New York Times*, 30 July 1978: 'Around 0.6 percent of farmers had 30.5 percent of cultivable land.'

7   The definitive work on this period is by Lester D. Langley, who is largely credited with coining the term, in particular his 1983 book *The Banana Wars: United States Intervention in the Caribbean, 1898–1934*.

8   In December 1823, President James Monroe told Congress 'the American continents, by the free and independent condition which they have assumed and maintained, are henceforth not to be considered as subjects for colonization by any European powers'. In essence, that a threat to any one of them from a nation outside the hemisphere was considered a matter for the US to intervene. It became known as the Monroe Doctrine.

9   The apparently apocryphal story is that Franklin D. Roosevelt said of him 'Somoza is a son of a bitch but he's our son of a bitch'. It has equally been cited as a description of General Trujillo in the Dominican Republic and, with no formal record of the comment, it may have either been spread by Somoza himself or never have been uttered at all. Still, it remains a fair description of the position of successive administrations in White House towards Somoza García and his sons.

10   Anastasio Somoza García – or 'Tacho' – did eventually get his comeuppance but it would take time. He forced his wife's uncle from the presidency two years after murdering Sandino and remained either directly in power or behind proxies and puppets until 1955. In that time, he amassed an ill-gotten fortune, particularly during the Second World War, to become the largest landowner in Nicaragua. He was shot by the poet Rigoberto López Pérez in 1956, shortly after amending the constitution to be allowed to remain in office. López Pérez was killed in the moment in a hail of bullets by Somoza's bodyguards. Somoza was airlifted to hospital in the Panama Canal Zone, but died shortly after.

11   Kenneth E. Morris, *Unfinished Revolution: Daniel Ortega and Nicaragua's Struggle for Liberation*, Laurence Hill Books, 2010, p. 18.

12   Ibid.

13   Ibid., p. 31.

14   Claudia Dreifus, 'Playboy Interview: Daniel Ortega', *Playboy* magazine, November 1987.

15   Fabián Medina, El Preso 198: Un perfil de Daniel Ortega, independent publication, 2018.

16   Canal 4 Nicaragua, 'Reportaje Especial: El Asalto a la Casa Chema Castillo', 21 December 2012.

17   Tad Szulc, *Fidel: A Critical Portrait*, HarperCollins, 1986.

18   Gabriel García Márquez, 'Asalto al Palacio', 1978. (Translation: author's own.)

19   The political prisoners included the FSLN's co-founder, Comandante Tomás Borge Martínez, a towering presence in the movement and an important figure for the Sandinistas to have free and involved in planning and operations rather than languishing in one of Somoza's jails.

20   José Adán Silva, 'Edén Pastora, "No regreso con el rabo entre las piernas"', 26 November 2000.

21   His defection from the Sandinistas almost saw him killed. Pastora's legs were twisted and scarred from the shrapnel of a bomb attack in May 1984. While holding a press conference in La Penca, a base camp in Nicaragua, a man posing as a Danish cameraman placed a camera bag containing a bomb near Pastora. It was a miracle his legs weren't amputated. Seven people were killed including three journalists, one of them an American, Linda Frazier, working for the Costa Rican newspaper *Tico Times*.

22   Professor Andres Perez Baltodano as quoted in Duncan Campbell, 'US bars Nicaragua heroine as "terrorist"', *Guardian*, 4 March 2005.

23   CBS Evening News, 20 June 1979.

24   Eduardo Cruz, 'El nica traductor de Bill Stewart', *La Prensa*, 19 June 2011.

25   The quick-thinking driver, Tiffer López, managed to get the rest of the team to safety by persuading the National Guard that they worked for Channel 6, the pro-Somoza channel, and were even allowed to take Stewart's body away as long as they reported that he had been shot by Sandinista snipers. There was no such luck for the translator Juan Francisco Espinoza. It took his mother fully eight days to locate his body, half buried near where he was shot. It wouldn't be until October of that year, several months after the Sandinistas took power, that she obtained permission to disinter him and give him a proper burial. (Ibid.)

26   Linda Charlton, 'ABC Reporter and Aide Killed By Soldier in Nicaraguan Capital', *New York Times*, 21 June 1979.

27   John Goshko, 'Carter Letter to Somoza Stirs Human-Rights Row', *Washington Post*, 1 August 1978.

28   Anastasio Somoza Debayle / Jack Cox, *Nicaragua Betrayed*, Western Islands Publishing, August 1980.

29   Amalia del Cid, 'El Exilio de Anastasio Somoza Debayle', 12 September 2018 quoting July 1979 interview in *La Tercera* newspaper.

30   *New York Times* Editorial Board, 25 February 1990.

31   Holly Sklar, *Washington's War on Nicaragua*, South End Press, 1988, p. 57.

32 Ibid., p. 57.

33 Ibid., p. 65.

34 Cleto DiGiovanni, 'US Policy and the Marxist Threat to Central America', Heritage Foundation Backgrounder 128, 15 October 1980, as quoted in *Envio* magazine, 'The Economic Costs of the Contra War: Nicaragua's Case Before the World Court', September 1985.

35 Sklar, 1988, p. 71.

36 *Envio* magazine, Central American University (UCA), September 1985.

37 Eliot Brenner, United Press International despatch, 1 November 1984.

38 The US distanced itself from the manual, claiming it was the work of an overzealous contractor at the Agency and argued that, if anything, it had tempered the murderous tendencies of the Contras.

39 Steven V. Roberts, 'Reagan Presses Case for Aid to Nicaragua Rebels', *New York Times*, 31 January 1988.

40 Daniel Ortega, 'Speech to Sandinista Assembly, 17 July 1984', published in *Barricada*, 18 July 1984, reproduced in Bruce Marcus, *Nicaragua: The Sandinista People's Revolution. Speeches by Sandinista Leaders*, Pathfinder Press, 1985, p. 445.

41 Stephen Kinzer, 'Ex-Contra Looks Back, Finding Much to Regret', *New York Times*, 8 January 1988.

42 Steven R. Weisman, 'Reagan predicts Nicaragua vote will be a "sham"', *New York Times*, 20 July 1984.

43 Gerald M. Boyd, 'Reagan terms Nicaraguan rebels "Moral equal of our Founding Fathers"', *New York Times*, 2 March 1985.

44 Hendrick Smith, 'Britain Criticizes Mining of Harbors around Nicaragua', *New York Times*, 7 April 1984.

45 Ibid.

46 Daniel Ortega, 'Speech 4th May 1984', reproduced in Marcus, 1985, p. 418.

47 *Envio* magazine, Central American University (UCA), September 1985.

48 Lee H. Hamilton and Daniel K. Inouye et al., 'Report of the Congressional Committees Investigating the Iran-Contra Affair', 13 November 1987, Preface.

49 Betsy Cohn and Patricia Hynds, 'The Manipulation of the Religion Issue' in Thomas W. Walker (ed.), *Reagan Versus the Sandinistas: The Undeclared War on Nicaragua*, Westview Press, 1987.

50 Hamilton and Inouye et al., 'Report of the Congressional Committees Investigating the Iran-Contra Affair', 13 November 1987.

51 Ibid., p. 21.

52 C-SPAN, Iran-Contra Investigation Day 24, 8 July 1987.

53   C-SPAN, Daniel Ortega, President of Nicaragua at the National Press Club, 12 November 1987.

54   Ibid.

55   Mark A. Uhlig, 'Opposing Ortega', *New York Times Magazine*, 11 February 1990.

56   Ibid.

57   Kenneth E. Morris, *Unfinished Revolution: Daniel Ortega and Nicaragua's Struggle for Liberation*, Laurence Hill Books, 2010, p. 163.

58   Associated Press, 'Bush Restores Sugar Quota', 25 April 1990.

59   Morris, 2010, p. 166.

60   Gioconda Belli, interview with author August 2019.

61   Peter Collins, ABC News, 25 April 1990.

62   Eline van Ommen, 'Daniel Ortega's latest election win in Nicaragua is rooted in his traumatic defeat three decades ago', LSE Blogs, 13 February 2017.

63   Or, rather, re-met Rosario Murillo as the two knew one another from before and had been in contact while Ortega was in jail.

64   Michael Lanchin, interview with Zoilamerica Narvaez Murillo, BBC Witness, January 2019.

65   Ibid.

66   Daniel Ortega adopted Zoilamerica Narvaez Murillo in 1986 and she became Zoilamerica Ortega Murillo. Although she has tried to officially drop his surname since making the accusations, she has been unable to in Nicaragua's tangled legal system, so instead simply goes by her biological father's name.

67   Francisco Goldman, 'The Autumn of the Revolutionary', *New York Times*, 23 August 1998.

68   BBC News Mundo, 'Para mí, Daniel Ortega se quedó como el abusador y Rosario Murillo como la madre que fue su cómplice', 6 March 2019.

69   Goldman, 'The Autumn of the Revolutionary', *New York Times*, 23 August 1998.

70   BBC News Mundo, 6 March 2019.

71   Henri Gooren, 'Ortega for President: The Religious Rebirth of Sandinismo in Nicaragua', *European Review of Latin American and Caribbean Studies*, 89, October 2010, p. 49.

72   Douglas Farah, 'Rightist claims victory in Nicaragua', *Washington Post*, 22 October 1996.

73   Ibid., p. 50.

74   Alejandro Bendana, 'Strange Bedfellows: The Aleman-Ortega Pact', North American Congress on Latin America (NACLA) 25 September 2007.

75   Ibid.

76   Ibid.

77 In 2004, the anti-corruption NGO, Transparency International, listed Alemán in the top ten of the world's most corrupt governments, accusing him of taking $100 million from the state coffers: BBC News online, 25 March 2004.

78 Rosario Murillo, then acting as spokeswoman, began speaking in terms of 'Christianity, socialism and solidarity' in interviews.

79 Gioconda Belli, '¿Con quién es Dios?', *El Nuevo Diario*, 18 October 1996 as cited in Gooren (2010).

80 Gioconda Belli, interview with the author, August 2019.

81 Gooren, 2010, p. 50. The sermon was in stark contrast to Obando y Bravo's previous intervention on the eve of a presidential vote in Nicaragua. Gioconda Belli recalls that shortly before the 1996 election the cardinal delivered a devastating sermon containing a parable about the dangers of trusting the serpent – the 'parábola del viborazo' – a not so subtle warning about believing Daniel Ortega which may well have cost him the vote.

82 Manuel Avendaño Arce, 'Nicaragua antes y después de Daniel Ortega: Mejora económica con preocupación politica', *El Financiero*, 21 August 2016.

83 Ibid.

84 Tim Rodgers, 'Venezuela's Chávez bankrolled Nicaragua with $1.6 billion since 2007', *Christian Science Monitor*, 7 April 2011.

85 Manuel Avendaño Arce, 'Economia de Nicaragua se derrumba mientras Ortega se aferra a una nueva reforma fiscal', *El Financiero*, 28 February 2019.

86 After Chávez pressed the book into Obama's hands on their first meeting it briefly returned to the top of the bestseller lists.

87 Tim Rogers, 'Ortega Fails to Impress at Summit', *Tico Times*, 24 April 2009.

88 Claudia Dreifus, 'Playboy Interview: Daniel Ortega', *Playboy* magazine, November 1987.

89 Pedro Joaquín Chamorro, Letter to Anastasio Somoza Debayle, dated 18 January 1975, replicated in *Confidencial*, 10 January 2019. (Translation: author's own.)

90 Tom Phillips, 'Nicaragua: Ortega blames 'satanic sect' for uprising against his rule', *Guardian*, 20 July 2018.

91 Dreifus, 'Playboy Interview: Daniel Ortega', *Playboy* magazine, November 1987.

92 Mary Beth Sheridan, 'Nicaragua's Ortega is strangling La Prensa, one of Latin America's most storied newspapers', *Washington Post*, 4 August 2019.

Cuba/Fidel Castro

1   Tom Miller, 'Remember the Maine', *Smithsonian*, February 1998.
2   Ibid.
3   Edwin Williamson, *The Penguin History of Latin America*, Penguin Books, 1992, p. 439.
4   Peter Orsi, 'Havana restores monument to victims of USS *Maine*', Associated Press, 16 February 2013.
5   Williamson, 1992, p. 440.
6   Ibid.
7   Fidel Castro Ruz, *La victoria estratégica. La contraofensiva estratégica*, Ediciones Akal S.A., 2012, p. 10.
8   Paradoxically, when it came to ill health, it was Chávez who fell on that particular battlefield first.
9   Ann Louise Bardach, *Without Fidel: A Death Foretold in Miami, Havana and Washington*, Scribner, 2009, p. 28.
10 Thomas M. Leonard, *Fidel Castro: A Biography*, Greenwood Press, 2004, p. 12.
11 As quoted in Tad Szulc, Fidel, *A Critical Portrait*, Avon Books, 1986, p. 172.
12 Arturo Alape, *Bogotazo: memorias del olvido*, Casa de las Américas, 1983.
13 Ibid., as quoted in Eugenio Suárez Pérez and Acela A. Caner Román, *Fidel Castro: Birán to Cinco Palmas*, Editorial José Martí, 2002, p. 68.
14 As quoted in Antonio Rafael de la Cova, *The Moncada Attack: Birth of the Cuban Revolution*, University of South Carolina Press, 2007, p. 25.
15 Alfonso Chardy and Jay Weaver, 'Castro victim's kids win record verdict', *Miami Herald*, 5 April 2008.
16 Georgie Anne Geyer, *Guerrilla Prince: The Untold Story of Fidel Castro*, Little, Brown, 1991, p. 84.
17 Ibid.
18 This was a lesson learned by many leaders in Latin America but particularly true of the Chávez and Maduro governments in Venezuela. After his own bungled coup attempt, Hugo Chávez walked out of Yare prison unscathed in March 1994 and straight onto the ballot for the 1998 election. Their critics would not be granted the same luxury with a series of high-profile opposition figures arrested or forced into exile over the thinnest allegations of coup plotting.
19 Servando Gonzalez, *The Secret Fidel Castro: Deconstructing the Symbol*, Spooks Books, 2001, p. 50.
20 Brian Latell, *After Fidel: The Inside Story of Castro's Regime and Cuba's Next Leader*, Palgrave Macmillan, 2005, p. 14.

21 Teresa Gurza, 'Cuba: Past, Present and Future of Socialist Revolution', *El Día*, 19 September 1975, as quoted in Latell, 2005, pp. 8–9.

22 Fidel Castro, *Reflexiones de Fidel*, Oficina de Publicaciones del Consejo de Estado, 2007, p. 83.

23 'The Bay of Pigs Invasion: Featured Story Archive', Central Intelligence Agency, 18 April 2016.

24 Ibid.

25 Teresa Gurza, 'Cuba: Past, Present and Future of Socialist Revolution', *El Día*, 19 September 1975. The full quote is: 'If at that moment he had decided to invade us, he could have suffocated the island in a sea of blood, but he would have destroyed the revolution. Lucky for us, he vacillated.'

26 As late as January 2020, with the Trump administration punishing Cuba for its tight-knit relationship with the South American nation, their successors continued to echo the concept of being a single socialist entity divided by mere geographical distance. 'Cubazuela' is an idea which horrifies the Venezuelan opposition, but Nicolás Maduro called Raúl Castro 'our big brother and protector' and made the unprecedented proposal that their respective ambassadors participate in each other's cabinet meetings.

27 Angus Berwick, 'The Cuba Connection: Imported repression: How Cuba taught Venezuela to quash military dissent', Reuters, 22 August 2019.

28 Ibid.

29 Ibid.

30 Ibid.

31 'Human rights in the Bolivarian Republic of Venezuela: Report of the United Nations High Commissioner for Human Rights on the situation of Human rights in the Bolivarian Republic of Venezuela', 5 July 2019.

32 By March 2020, incurring the wrath of the Maduro government was the least of Alcalá's worries. Already facing charges over arms supplies to the FARC, the US Department of Justice put up a $10 million reward for information leading to his capture on drug-trafficking charges for his alleged role in transporting Colombian cocaine through Venezuela. He subsequently handed himself in. The US also put up $15 million for the capture of Maduro himself, a measure not seen against a sitting president since Manuel Noriega in Panama.

33 'Interview with Alexander Alekseyev [Soviet ambassador to Cuba]', National Security Archive, George Washington University.

34 Ibid.

35 Ibid.

36 As quoted in Julia Preston, 'The Trial that Shook Cuba', *New York Review of Books*, 7 December 1989.

37 Preston, 1989.

38 Ibid.

39 Mark A. Uhlig, 'Cuban General Fully Confesses And Declares, "I Deserve to Die"', *New York Times*, 28 June 1989.

40 Ibid.

41 Antonio de la Guardia's twin brother, Patricio de la Guardia, also a Ministry of Interior intelligence officer, faced charges, too, but had his death sentence commuted to thirty years' imprisonment. He currently lives in Havana.

42 Mike Lanchin, 'The trial of top brass military that rocked Cuba', BBC Witness, 29 July 2019.

43 From the committed socialist boy who chose the US, Juan Carlos Zaldívar, became an award-winning filmmaker whose very personal documentary, *90 Miles*, detailed his family's struggle in adapting to US life after leaving Cuba and his own evolution from a narrow-minded communist youth to an openly gay capitalist exile.

44 In a postscript to the Mariel exodus, the bus driver who started it all, Héctor Sanyústiz, was granted the paperwork to leave Cuba after much diplomacy by the Peruvians. On arriving in the US, he was advised by the FBI to keep quiet about his role as 'the Father of Mariel' – advice he heeded for years until he revealed his identity to the *Miami Herald* in late 1998 (Fabiola Santiago, '"Padre del Mariel" vino a Miami en 1980', *El Nuevo Herald*, 6 September 1998). After his arrival in south Florida, he held a few jobs including cleaning stairways in a hotel. But the injury he sustained in the shooting at the Peruvian Embassy hampered his movement and he lost his job. At one point, Sanyústiz was reduced to collecting tin cans on Miami Beach to sell in Hialeah. Eventually he found steady work driving a construction truck and bought a home near Orlando with his wife. Even as his health was failing following a heart attack, he remained proud of helping 125,000 Cubans flee the island: 'In our glorious exile, we'll support [the families left back in Cuba]. And I will be thankful over all the years of life that I have left.' (Jorge Ferrer, 'Entrevista al "Padre del Mariel", Héctor Sanyústiz', *El Tono de la Voz*, 7 October 2008.)

45 John Scanlan and Gilburt Loescher, 'U. S. Foreign Policy, 1959–80: Impact on Refugee Flow from Cuba', *Annals of the American Academy of Political and Social Science*, Vol. 467, *The Global Refugee Problem: U.S. and World Response*, May, 1983, pp. 117–18.

46 Ibid., pp. 117–18.
47 Antonio de la Cova, 'The Elian Gonzalez Case: The World's Most Watched and Politically-Charged Custody Battle that Reached the U.S. Supreme Court and Determined a Presidential Election', *Harvard Law Review*, 18, Spring 2015, p. 152.
48 Ibid., p. 154.
49 Bardach, 2009, p. 24.
50 Ibid., p. 4.
51 Ibid., p. 25.
52 Lee Lockwood, *Castro's Cuba, Cuba's Fidel*, revised edn, Westview, 1990, as quoted in Hugh M. Hamill (ed.), *Caudillos: Dictators in Spanish America*, University of Oklahoma Press, 1992, p. 295.
53 Michael Smith, 'Want to Do Business in Cuba? Prepare to Partner with the General', Bloomberg, 30 September 2015.
54 Fidel Castro and Ignacio Ramonet: *My Life: A Spoken Autobiography*, Penguin Books, 2008, p. 608.

Epilogue

1 Carlos De La Torre, 'Velasco Ibarra and 'La Revolución Gloriosa': The Social Production of a Populist Leader in Ecuador in the 1940s'. *Journal of Latin American Studies* 26, no. 3, 1994, p. 711.

Image credits

1. Prensa Presidencial – Government of Venezuela, Wiki Commons
2. Pedro Ruiz / Getty Images
3. Jorge Silva / Reuters
4. Carolina Cabral / Stringer / Getty Images
5. AFP / Stringer / Getty Images
6. Win McNamee / Getty Images
7. Bloomberg / Getty Images
8. Gonzalo Espinoza / Getty Images
9. Getty Images / Stringer
10. Guillermo Granja / Reuters
11. NurPhoto / Getty Images
12. Bettmann / Getty Images
13. Inti Ocon / Getty Images
14. Elizabeth Frey / Stringer / Getty Images
15. Eddie Adams / AP / Shutterstock
16. AFP / Stringer / Getty Images
17. Mauricio Lima / Getty Images

Index

INDEX